Praise for *Traveling Music*

Traveling Music is "part autobiography, part travel book, and part an enthusiast's guide to music that's moved him, music that's helped him, and music he's played. . . . It all adds up to some inspiring journeys."
— Richard Flohil, *Applaud!*

"Peart's fluidity and immense analytical perception certainly remind me of some other writers whose capable hands can effortlessly mix narrative and description without losing rhythm. In Neil Peart's case he can perform miracles in both realms."
— last.fm.com

"Peart's lyrical language . . . and juxtaposition of musical interests (Sinatra to Madonna, Linkin Park to the Beach Boys) keep you entertained and maintain the momentum."
— *Now Toronto*

"This is Neil Peart's 3rd and, in my opinion, best book to date . . . [an] autobiography set to music. . . . He reflects on his life, where he's been and where he's going. All of this done through the use of music as a memory recollection tool. . . . A great book."
— estenger.com

"*Traveling Music* is a superb memoir. . . . The book travels in unexpected directions, which makes for a good read. . . . Can't wait till the next one."
— andrewolson.com

Praise for *Ghost Rider*

Ghost Rider is a Drainie-Taylor Biography Prize Finalist

Chosen by The Writers' Trust of Canada
because of its "exceptional merit" as one of
the five best autobiographies of 2002.

"Peart's writing is lyrical and his tale poignant, fully capturing an extraordinary journey, both as a travel adventure and as memoir."
— *Library Journal*

Praise for *Ghost Rider* con't.

"From Toronto to Alaska to Belize, this is a heart-wrenching piece of work that ends with Peart healthy, living, loving and rocking again."
— *Chart*

"This crisply written book is part travelogue and part therapeutic catharsis. It resonates with humour and grief and ultimately personal triumph."
— *Exclaim!*

"A powerful, graceful book."
— *The Buffalo News*

"This is a triumphant book. Sometimes sad, often funny, never dull, and always engrossing."
— *Green Man Review*

Praise for *ROADSHOW*

"In this unique travelogue, Peart leverages his considerable literary penmanship to describe the joys and rigors of a rock tour as well as his impressions of the politics, social mores, and cultural heterogeneity he encounters across states and nations. As Peart travels for his art, he perfectly describes the art of travel."
— *Christian Science Monitor*

"Peart has by now created his own genre — the existentialist travel guide. . . . His intellectual and, dare I say it, spiritual wanderlust elevate his prose writing toward the sublime. . . . Peart has a reporter's eye and a poet's heart, and in *Roadshow*, the twain have met to eloquent effect."
— *The Buffalo News*

"[Peart] narrates clearly with a mix of passion and critical detachment that serves his subjects well. . . . His unique commute . . . offers insights into the land, the people that inhabit it and, not least, himself. It's a hell of a journey."
— *The Hartford Courant*

"Peart uses spare, dynamic prose to explore human relationships in work and friendship, love and grief."
— *Pittsburgh City Paper*

"*Roadshow* is Peart's strongest literary contribution yet. . . . Inspirational and entertaining . . . a must read for all who value adventure, relationships, and humor. . . . The memorable and real events are exciting, thrilling, scary, happy, and sad — retold with captivating and vivid description. . . . As a transmission of life philosophy and values . . . the author tells his story powerfully, yet subtly."
— BMW *Owners News*

"A thoughtful, fascinating and at times hilarious read, for Neil Peart is a true man of letters . . . [with] extraordinary gifts as a story teller. . . . It is his unabashed enthusiasm for life and his thirst for knowledge — all knowledge — that touched me the most."
— Jim Ladd, KLOS Los Angeles

"A real great read not only for rock fans, but for anyone who wants a tour of the American landscape in the words of one of music's greatest drummers and lyricists. Neil takes the reader on a great ride that is not to be missed."
— Eddie Trunk, VH1 VJ, and host of the syndicated radio show *Eddie Trunk Rocks*

"Neil Peart straps us in the sidecar for a thrilling travelogue that takes us from behind the music and out on a Roadshow you'll never forget!"
— *Music Connection*

"Consistently funny . . . *Roadshow* has many light-hearted moments."
— *Cleveland Free Times*

"Neil rides a motorcycle to Rush concert events and writes about his en-route experiences on two wheels with the same heart that defines his drumming."
— *Motorcycle Mojo*

Books by Neil Peart

The Masked Rider: Cycling in West Africa

Ghost Rider: Travels on the Healing Road

Traveling Music: The Soundtrack to My Life and Times

Roadshow: Landscape with Drums, A Concert Tour by Motorcycle

Far and Away: A Prize Every Time

TRAVELING MUSIC

The Soundtrack to My Life and Times

neil peart

ECW PRESS

Published by ECW PRESS
2120 Queen Street East, Suite 200
Toronto, Ontario, Canada M4E 1E2
416.694.3348 / info@ecwpress.com

NATIONAL LIBRARY OF CANADA CATALOGUING IN PUBLICATION DATA

Peart, Neil
Traveling music: the soundtrack to my life and times / Neil Peart.

ISBN 978-1-55022-664-5 (cloth) — ISBN 978-1-55022-666-9 (paper.)
ALSO ISSUED AS: 978-1-55490-666-6 (PDF); 978-1-55490-795-3 (EPUB)

1. Peart, Neil 2. Drummers (Musicians) — Canada — Biography.
3. Lyricists — Canada — Biography. 4. Rush (Musical group) I. Title.

ML419.P362A3 2004   786.9ʹ166ʹ092   C2004-902550-3

Cover and Text Design: Tania Craan and Hugh Syme
Production and Typesetting: Mary Bowness
Printing: Berryville Graphics   4   5

This book is set in Razor Keen, Franklin Gothic, and Minion

The publication of *Traveling Music* has been generously supported by the Canada Council,
the Ontario Arts Council, and the Government of Canada through the
Book Publishing Industry Development Program.

  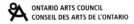

PRINTED AND BOUND IN THE UNITED STATES

ECW PRESS
ecwpress.com

To Carrie

Without music, life would be a mistake

— Friedrich Nietzsche

The music I have written is
nothing compared to the music I have heard

— Ludwig van Beethoven

"Ooh, look at me, I'm Dave, I'm writing a book!
With all my thoughts in it! La la la!"

— Dave Eggers

For this music lover, the concept of "traveling music" evokes several responses. Listening to music while traveling, by one means or another, is the obvious association, and my life has provided plenty of that, in cars, airplanes, boats, bullet trains, subways, and tour buses.

Then there's the "inner radio," when every song I know seems to play in my head, as I perch on the saddle of a bicycle or motorcycle for long, long hours.

"Traveling music" can also be a job description. For thirty years I have made my living as a touring musician, playing drums with Rush in North America, South America, Europe, and Asia, and that has made for a lot of traveling, and a lot of music.

In my other job description with Rush, writing lyrics, I have used many references to modes of travel, from bicycle to boat, sports car to spaceship, airplane to astral projection. My lyrics for our song "The Spirit of Radio" celebrate the simple pleasure of listening to the radio while driving, and inspirations have also come from journeys, and places both exotic and everyday: East Africa in "Scars," West Africa in "Hand Over Fist," China in "Tai Shan," London and Manhattan in "The Camera Eye," small-town Canada and America in "Middletown Dreams."

Most of all, though, I think of "traveling music" as the essence of the music itself — where it takes me, in memory, imagination, and the realm of pure abstract sensation, washing over me in waves of emotion.

Since childhood, music has had the power to carry me away, and this is a song about some of the places it has carried me.

Traveling Music

Driving away to the east, and into the past
History recedes in my rear-view mirror
Carried on a wave of music down a desert road
Memory drumming at the heart of a factory town

Diving down into the wreck, searching for treasure
Skeletons and ghosts among the scattered diamonds
Buried with the songs and stories of a restless life
Memory drumming at the heart of a moving picture

All my life
I've been workin' them angels overtime
Riding and driving and working
So close to the edge
Workin' them angels —
Workin' them angels —
Workin' them angels —
Overtime

Memory drumming at the heart of an English winter
Memory drumming at the heart of an English winter

Filling my spirit with the wildest wish to fly
Taking the high road, into the Range of Light

Driving down the razor's edge between past and future
I turn up the music and smile, eyes on the road ahead
Carried on the songs and stories of vanished times
Memory drumming at the heart of an African village

All this time
I've been living like there's no tomorrow
Running and jumping and flying
With my imaginary net
Workin' them angels —
Workin' them angels —
Workin' them angels —
Overtime

Riding through the Range of Light to the wounded city
Taking the high road —
Into the Range of Light
Taking the high road —
Into the Range of Light

Repeat to fade . . .

Intro

Play through the changes,
Pick up the tempo

"Now what?"

All my life, those two little words have sparked me with curiosity, restlessness, and desire — an irresistible drive to do things, learn things, go places, seek more and always more, of everything there is to do and see and try. My need for action, exertion, challenge, for something to get *excited* about, in turn inspired my ambition to try to capture those experiences, in songs and stories, and share them.

When I was a teenager, sitting around the family dinner table with Mom, Dad, younger brother Danny and sisters Judy and Nancy, I would chafe inside my skin, wishing I just had something *exciting* to say — something I had done, or was going to do.

I guess I spent the rest of my life making sure I always had something to talk about at the family dinner table . . . only I wouldn't be at the family dinner table. I'd be on tour with the band, or away making a record, or bicycling in China, or motorcycling in Tunisia. Then writing a book about it.

My daughter Selena seemed to have inherited some of that itch, for right up to her last summer, at age nineteen, she would climb out of the lake all sleek like a seal, flop on the dock beside me, splash some cold water over my sun-warmed back, look me in the eyes and say,

"Now what?"

I could only laugh, recognizing her own need for diversion, action, something to get excited about — something to talk about at the dinner table. However, in that summer of 1997, those little words came to bear an ominous weight, the menace of imminent tragedy. Selena would not live to find out "now what?"

For a while there, in 1997 and 1998, when everything was being taken away from me — my daughter, my wife, my dog, my best friend, everything I loved and believed in — my own "now what?" became less of an itch and more of a hemorrhage, more like Dorothy Parker's, "What fresh hell is this?"

But on I went, down that healing road, thinking, "something will come up," and as life would have it, something did. In fact, a lot of things came up: a journey to new love with Carrie, new home in California, and because of those unexpected miracles, a new lease on life and work. Back on the high road.

By 2001 I was writing lyrics and playing drums on a new record, *Vapor Trails*, with Rush, writing a book about that terrible part of my life, *Ghost Rider*, and spending most of 2002 traveling and performing in Rush's 66-show tour of North America, Mexico, and Brazil, culminating with a final concert in Rio de Janeiro, in front of 40,000 people, that was filmed for a DVD called *Rush in Rio*.

Early in 2003, all that was behind me, and I was relieved to be taking a break at home, enjoying time with Carrie, relaxed and content in the rhythms of domestic life. I had no ambition to tackle anything more creative or demanding than cooking dinner.

That tranquility lasted for a serene couple of months, until early March, when Carrie started making plans to attend an all-female surf camp in Mexico (a Christmas present from her thoughtful husband). She was going to be away for five or six days, and wheels started turning in my brain about how I might use that solitary time. Before I knew it (*literally*, as so often happens, before I realized my creative unconscious had started spinning its daydreams), every aspect of my life was orbiting into a clockwork vortex around that eternal question:

"Now what?"

Verse One

"Driving away to the east, and into the past"

The Santa Ana winds came hissing back into the Los Angeles Basin that week, breathing their hot, dry rasp through what had once been the fishing village of Santa-Monica-by-the-Sea. The streets around us were littered with dry palm fronds and eucalyptus leaves, and the view from our upstairs terrace reached the distant blue Pacific through the line of California fan palms down along Ocean Boulevard. The incoming waves battled the contrary wind, as dotted whitecaps receded clear back to the long dark shadow of Santa Catalina Island, bisected horizontally by a brownish haze of smog.

More than three hundred years ago, the Yang-Na natives called the Los Angeles Basin "the valley of the smokes," referring to the fog trapped by those thermal inversions. And even then, wildfires sometimes raged across the savanna grasses in the dry season, creating prehistoric smog. Then and now, the air was usually clearer by the ocean, ruled and cooled by the prevailing sea breeze, but the Santa Anas invaded from inland, carrying hot desert air over the San Gabriel Mountains, through the San Fernando Valley, all the while gathering airborne irritants from the whole metropolis and driving them right through Santa Monica, and on out to Catalina.

The Cahuilla Indians believed the Santa Anas originated in a giant cave in the Mojave Desert that led directly to the lair of the Devil himself, and early Spanish arrivals picked up on that story and named those hot, dry winds the *Vientos de Sanatanas,* or Satan's winds. Later arrivals to Southern California were more concerned with Christian propriety and boosting real estate values in this earthly paradise, and the Chamber of Commerce issued a press release in the early 1900s: "In the interest of community, please refer to the winds as 'The Santa Ana Winds' in any and all subsequent publications."

Still, the devil winds were blamed by longtime Angelenos for effects both physical and psychological: Raymond Chandler wrote in *Red Wind* that when the Santa Anas blow, "meek little wives feel the edge of their carving knife and study their husbands' necks." Modern-day urban myths associate the Santa Anas with rising crime rates, freeway gun battles, wild-fires, actors entering rehab, Hollywood couples divorcing, bands breaking up, irritated sinuses, and bad tempers all around.

As a recent immigrant from Canada, I had thought all that was local folklore (or just a regular day in L.A.), but I had only lived in Santa Monica for three years, and spent much of that time working with Rush in Toronto or touring in other cities. Now, though, in late March of 2003, I was feeling the effects of those abrasive winds on my sinuses, and my mood. Along with the brownish haze over the sea and my itchy nose, tension was in the air.

For one thing, there was a war on. The United States and Britain were just into the second week of the attack on Iraq, and no one knew what might happen. The smoke and mirrors of propaganda and the phantom menace of "weapons of mass destruction" had been paraded before us so much that a kind of contagious anxiety had been sown. Dire possibilities seemed to be on everyone's mind, and in every conversation. The chance of a chemical attack on Los Angeles seemed . . . at least worth worrying about. When the war began, I had said to my wife, Carrie, "Let's go to Canada," where I still owned the house on the lake in Quebec, and still had friends and family in Toronto. However, now some mysterious disease called SARS was spreading from Asia to Canada, and people were dying, hospitals were closing, there was a travel advisory against Toronto; it was a bad scene there too.

Then there were the interior battles, and internal "travel advisories" — the "don't go there" areas. I had some serious personal and professional issues weighing on my mind — big questions and big choices to make.

Work, for one thing. After only a couple of months at home, and spending most of 2002 on the *Vapor Trails* tour, and all of 2001 writing and recording that album, I felt I was just catching my breath. But plans had to be made so far in advance. Recently the band's manager, Ray, had been entertaining (or torturing) me with various scenarios of recording and touring possibilities for the upcoming years, and I would have to give some answers soon. In 2004, the band would celebrate our thirtieth anniversary together, so we'd probably want to do something to commemorate that. A party, a cake, a fifty-city tour?

What about prose writing? With a stretch of free time ahead of me in 2003, I felt I wanted to get started on a writing project of some kind again, and friends were encouraging me to write more. But what did I want to write? (Now what?) Maybe try something different from the travel-writing style of my first two published books, *The Masked Rider: Cycling in West Africa* (1996) and *Ghost Rider: Travels on the Healing Road* (2002). Some fiction? History?

I didn't know, but I was thinking about it.

There were a few half-finished traveling books in my files, narratives of journeys I'd taken through the early '90s and never had the time or drive to complete: the third of my African bicycle tours, of Mali, Senegal, and the Gambia; several motorcycle explorations around Newfoundland, Mexico, and North Africa; perhaps I should look at them again. Or, back in the fateful summer of '97, I had abandoned a narrative recounting the Rush *Test for Echo* tour, called *American Echoes: Landscape with Drums*, when my life was suddenly pulled out from under me by tragedy and loss. But I wasn't sure I wanted to take up that story again, or any of the old ones. Something new would be good, it seemed to me.

In another area of my mind (I picture little, self-contained clockwork

mechanisms, slowly grinding through their particular subject of cogita-
tion until they produce the answer, the "right thing to do"), I was thinking
about the house on the lake, up in Quebec. Having lived in California for
over three years now, I didn't get there much anymore, and yet when I did
visit, it remained ineffably haunted to me, after the tragedies. (Selena and
I would stand right *there* in the kitchen, arms over each other's shoulders.
That terrible night Jackie and I got the news in *this* hallway, and Jackie fell
to the floor right *there*. These were not happy memories to continually
relive.) The Quebec property was large and the upkeep was high, and
maybe I didn't *need* it anymore. Maybe it was time to say goodbye to that
place, and to that time.

Another little clockwork mechanism in my head was working on the
problem of our California home, which was feeling increasingly too small,
especially in its lack of a writing space for me. A two-bedroom townhouse,
with Carrie taking one of the bedrooms as an office to run her photogra-
phy business as well as most of our lives, left only the loft above the
kitchen, open to the rest of the house. I would find myself trying to write
against the clatter and chatter of our Guatemalan housekeeper, Rosa, and
one or another of her cousin-assistants, vacuum cleaner and dishwasher,
ringing telephones, and our cheerfully-mad assistant, Jennifer, running
upstairs, all apologetic, to use the fax and copy machine.

It seemed that my years of training at reading in a crowded dressing
room had made me able to concentrate no matter what was going on, and
it had already served me well in writing — much of *Ghost Rider* had been
written and revised in a recording studio lounge, with *Vapor Trails* being
mixed on the other side of the window, the other guys coming and going,
talking, laughing, watching tv, and occasional breaks to approve final
mixes. The work could certainly be *done*, it just took longer.

There were other things on my mind, too. So much percolating
around my poor little brain; I needed some time to *think*.

It seemed like a good time to get out of town.

In early March, knowing Carrie was going to be away for those six days
later in the month, I started browsing through the road atlas (the Book of

Dreams), thinking of where I might go. My favorite destinations always tended to be the national parks of the American West, where I could combine the journey with some hiking, birdwatching, and general communing with nature. While living in California (and not away working), I often made overnight motorcycle trips to Kings Canyon and Sequoia National Parks in summer, or to Big Sur or Death Valley in winter, exploring the myriad of Southern California's backroads with my restless curiosity and love of motion (and giving Carrie some time to herself, too). With a little more time and the opportunity to cover more distance this time, my first inspiration had been to ride my motorcycle to Utah, and wander around the wonderful national parks in the southern part of that state, Zion, Bryce Canyon, Arches, and Canyonlands.

However, a look at the online weather reports tarnished that idea. The overnight temperatures in Bryce Canyon and Moab were still in the twenties, Fahrenheit, and that meant icy roads. No good on a two-wheeler. Even Yosemite was still in the grip of winter, and the only national park in the American Southwest I could think of that might not be under snow was Big Bend. So, I thought, "go there."

I had passed through that area of Southwest Texas once before, by motorcycle, during the Rush *Test for Echo* tour, in late 1996, with my best friend and frequent riding partner, Brutus. That tour was the first time I attempted that novel method of traveling from show to show, with my own bus and a trailer full of motorcycles. During the previous two years, my friendship with Brutus had grown strong as we both became interested in long-distance motorcycling. Exploring the pleasures and excitements of motorcycle touring, and learning that we traveled well together, Brutus and I had ridden tens of thousands of miles around Eastern Canada, Western Canada, Mexico, and across Southern Europe, from Munich down through Austria, Italy, and by ferry to Sicily, and across the Mediterranean to Tunisia and the Sahara.

We developed a comfortable rhythm between us, of tight formation, lane position, relative speed, and overall pace. Apart from being an entertaining dinner companion, Brutus always wanted to get the *most* out of a day — he could *carpe* that *diem* like few people I ever met. On an early ride together, we were motorcycling from Quebec to Toronto, normally a six-hour journey on the four-lane highway. Brutus convinced me to try one of his "adventurous" routes across Central Ontario, along county roads and country lanes that constantly changed number or direction. When we finally arrived in Toronto, I mentioned to Brutus that it had taken us nine hours instead of six, and he said, "Yeah, but would you rather have *fun* for nine hours, or be *bored* for six?"

Elementary, my dear Brutus, and a lesson was learned that reinforced my own tendency to seek out the back roads. From then on, if there was a chance to make a journey I *had* to make into a journey I *wanted* to take, I would seek out the high road, the winding road, and make the most of that traveling time.

So, when I was making plans to take my motorcycle on the *Test for Echo* tour, I convinced Brutus to come along too, as my official "riding companion" (he didn't take much convincing). Credited in the tour book as "navigator," a big part of Brutus's job really did become the plotting of the routes every day, as we moved around the country. He made it his mission to seek out the most interesting roads and roadside attractions, and while I was onstage, thrashing and sweating under the lights, Brutus sat in the front lounge of the bus surrounded by maps, magnifying glass, tour books, and calculator. He worked out the most complicated, roundabout, scenic, untraveled routes possible — that would still get us to soundcheck on time. (From the beginning, I warned Brutus that I tended to get "anxious" on show days, especially about the time, and that if we did not arrive at the venue at least an hour early, we were *late*. To his credit, we never were.)

As the bus roared down the interstates of America, Brutus would tell Dave where to stop for the night, usually a rest area or truck stop near the back road he had chosen for the morning. Sometimes I would go to sleep as Dave sped through the night, then wake to my alarm clock and the steady drone of the generator, in a wonderfully stationary bus. There was never enough sleep, but we were determined to make the most of the day, and sometimes I crawled into my riding gear, unloaded the bikes and rode away — without even knowing where we *were*. If it happened to be my turn to lead (we alternated every fuel stop), Brutus would point me in the right direction, and give me a sheet of handwritten notes on road numbers, mileages, and town names. Riding off into the morning, I followed Brutus's clear directions on the map case in front of me, and gradually discovered my place in the world.

After a show in El Paso, Brutus and I slept on the bus while Dave drove us to a truckstop near Marfa, Texas. We got up early the next morning, unloaded the bikes from the trailer, rode south to Presidio, and followed the Rio Grande to Lajitas for breakfast. (It's a measure of how Brutus and I lived on that tour, making the most of every minute and every mile, that so much could happen before breakfast. Especially on a day off, with no schedule, no soundcheck, and no anxious drummer to worry about.)

Just after Lajitas and Study Butte ("Stoody Beaut"), we entered Big Bend National Park, and crossed through a tiny fraction of it, on the fly. We cut north to Marathon, east to Langtry (made famous by Judge Roy Bean, "The Law West of the Pecos"), Comstock, and Del Rio, and north to Sonora. There we met up with Dave and the bus again, and wheeled the bikes back into the trailer in the gathering dark. (We always tried to avoid riding at night — it was more dangerous, and we couldn't see the point of riding through scenery we couldn't *see*.) I remember falling asleep almost immediately on the couch in the front lounge, as Dave drove us on to the hotel in Austin, for the next night's show. Music played quietly from the *Soul Train Hall of Fame* CD (introduced to me by Selena, as it happened, in her teenage taste for "old school" R&B, echoing one of my own "first loves" in music).

On that tour, Brutus and I were up early every morning and rode a *lot* of miles, often 500 or so on a day off, and maybe 300 on a show day. In 40,000 miles of motorcycling on that tour alone, through forty-seven states and several Canadian provinces, Brutus and I had many adventures together, in every kind of weather, from blistering heat to bitter cold and torrential rain, even snow and ice. A certain amount of pain and suffering kept things interesting, and made for good stories, but one thing we were constantly short of was *sleep*. On show days I used to squeeze in naps whenever I could, sometimes even setting my alarm clock for twenty minutes between dinner and pre-show warm-up.

So often our brief, rapid travels between shows were a kind of "research," checking out places that might be worth a later, more leisurely visit. Even that small taste of the Big Bend area had been impressive, as part of a continent-wide tour in which we had seen so much of America's scenic beauty. I retained a vague memory of majestic rock formations and wide desert spaces, canyons, bluffs, and mountains enclosed in a wide arc of the Rio Grande.

However, Big Bend National Park was 1,200 miles away from Los Angeles, on a fairly tedious, familiar interstate all the way (no time to take the high and winding road all *that* way). There were some areas of dodgy weather out that way too. Even by freeway, I'd have to ride two and a half long days to get to Big Bend, spend a day there, then turn around and make the same long slog home again. It didn't sound like a very appealing motorcycle trip, but it might be fun by car.

And not just any car. Early in 2003, I had become the proud owner of my longtime "dream car," a BMW Z-8, black with red interior (always my favorite combination). Driving that sleek, powerful two-seater through the Santa Monica Mountains, up Old Topanga Canyon to Mulholland Drive, and a longer trip up to Big Sur and back, revived the thrill I used to feel driving an open sports car (usually with music playing). Taken seriously, on a challenging road, driving could really feel like a *sport*, comparable to riding a motorcycle with adrenaline-fueled urgency.

Motorcycles had dominated my garage and travels for the past seven years, and bicycles before that, but I had loved cars since childhood. Mom says my first word was "car," and there's a photograph of me as a baby sitting behind the wheel of our '48 Pontiac, my tiny hands reaching up to the steering wheel and a *beaming* smile on my chubby little face. In my teenage years, drums and music had attracted all my attention (and all my money), so it was not until my early twenties that I bothered to get my driver's licence — and only then after I'd already bought my first car. It was a 1969 MGB, an English roadster of traditional character (meaning it leaked oil and had an unreliable electrical system).

I had it painted purple (always celebrating my individuality), and I *loved* that car, even as it drained its oil, its battery, its radiator, my patience, and my meager wallet. After that came a Lotus Europa (a tiny, very low fiberglass "roller skate," about which my dad once asked, "You really prefer that to a *real* car?"), another MGB, and — once I became a little more successful — a couple of Mercedes SLS, two different Ferraris, a 308 GTS and a 365 GTB/4 Daytona, an MGA, and a 1947 MG-TC. At one point in the early '80s I had four cars at once, and decided that having too many cars, especially *old* ones, was more trouble than pleasure. I trimmed down to running just two, more "practical" machines, including a series of Audi Quattro GTS (the first all-wheel-drive sports car, a real bonus in Canadian winters), and a trio of successive Porsche 911s through the '90s.

I had always loved driving, and listening to music while I drove, especially on a long journey. In the unique zen-state of driving for hour after hour, music didn't just *pass* the time, it *filled* the time, with pleasure, stimulation, discovery, and memories. So, all things considered, the decision was made — I would drive to Big Bend. And listen to music all the way.

After dropping Carrie at the airport in the Audi wagon, I drove home and threw a small bag and my album of CDs in the trunk of the Z-8, checked the oil level and the tire pressures, then drove through Santa Monica to the freeway. Merging with the four lanes of eastbound traffic on Interstate 10, dense as always, I headed toward the towers of downtown Los Angeles.

Eastward and upwind, the view tended to be clearer than usual during the Santa Anas, and behind the city, the San Gabriels and the snowy peak of Mount San Antonio (commonly called Old Baldy Peak) dominated the background against the scoured blue sky. The "steel forest" of antennas high on Mount Wilson, near the observatory, was finely etched and glittering.

Early one morning, a year or two before, I had ridden my motorcycle up the Angeles Crest Highway from Pasadena and stood looking down from Mount Wilson just after sunrise. The morning was clear all the way out to the Pacific, and the landscape of the Los Angeles Basin seemed dominated by green, even though I knew those valleys were actually floored in wall-to-wall carpets of suburbs and freeways, broken only by occasional clusters of tall buildings. From my high vantage point, I looked south and west and tried to identify the major crossroads of the city, from San Bernardino to the San Fernando Valley, from the Downtown to Century City. Overlooking it all from that high vantage, I had the sense that human history was thin and brief, and no matter what we tacked onto the land, it was nature that still ruled. This Basin could endure another ten thousand years, or it could shake to pieces in a few hours — that was an omnipresent dread that seemed to bother immigrants more than natives, for at least once a week I imagined the coming of the Big One, "What if it happened *now?* In this house? This office tower? This elevator?"

Most residents of Southern California seemed to be insulated by the "geological denial" described by geologist Eldridge Moore in John McPhee's *Assembling California:*

> People look upon the natural world as if all motions of the past had set the stage for us and were now frozen. They look out on a scene like this and think, It was all made for us — even if the San Andreas Fault is at their feet. To imagine that turmoil is in the past and somehow we are now in a more stable time seems to be a psychological need.

In Elna Bakker's natural history of the state, *An Island Called California*, she gave a wry twist to describing the action along the San Andreas Fault (one of *dozens* that riddle California),

> The land west of the fault is moving north at a generalized rate of more than an inch a year, and at some time in the future Los Angeles will be where San Francisco is now, a thought not happily received by most residents of that city.

Standing by the observatories at Mount Wilson that morning, I looked down at the constellations of life below me, and tried to imagine the great megalopolis of Los Angeles, what it had been, and how it had grown into today's sprawling mass of humanity, and the place I was now trying to call "home." In 1781, a Spanish supply station for Alta California was established down there, with almost more words in its name than people: El Pueblo de Nuestra Señora de Los Angeles del Rio de Porciuncula — The Town of Our Lady the Queen of the Angels by the River of a Little Portion. Whatever it was a little portion of, it was not lotus-land, but an arid chaparral surrounded by mountains, with no harbor, an unreliable river, and a climate that ranged from Mediterranean to monsoon. According to historian Marc Reisner in *A Dangerous Place*, during the brief rainy season, the nether reaches of the basin — now Long Beach, Culver City, Torrance, Carson, the South Bay cities — were vast marshlands covered with ducks and prowled by bears. (The last California brown bear, the state's symbol, was shot in 1922.)

By 1791 the pueblo boasted 139 settlers living in 29 adobes, surrounded by vast ranchos, like the Rancho Malibu and Rancho San Vicente y Santa Monica (owned by Francisco Sepulveda), that gave their names to modern communities and boulevards (including my adopted home of Santa Monica). The Rancho Rodeo de las Aguas became Beverly Hills; the Mission San Fernando became the warren of communities in the San Fernando Valley; the Rancho Paso de Bartolo Viejo would become the Quaker settlement of Whittier, Carrie's home town. (Richard Nixon's too, and one of Carrie's first jobs as a student was at his one-time law office.)

By the 1840s, El Pueblo de Nuestra Señora de Los Angeles del Rio de Porciuncula had swollen into a rough cowtown, violent and deadly (averaging a killing a day), a place Reisner described as "a filthy, drowsy, suppurating dunghole, a social meltdown of Mexicans, Indians, Americans, various Europeans, Hawaiians, and a respectable number of freed or escaped slaves. Among its vernacular street names were . . ." words this sensitive soul blushes to write: the N-word Alley, and the female-C-word Lane. In any case, when the gold rush struck Northern California in 1849, the population of Los Angeles declined from 6,000 to 1,600 in just one year, as everyone who felt able went north in search of instant riches.

(Interesting to note that by the end of the Civil War, $785 million in gold had been mined in California, making the crucial difference by delivering five or six million dollars a month to the money men of New York and keeping the Union solvent.)

By 1884 the population of Los Angeles had rebounded to 12,000, and it was then that the great land rush began, with boosterism, speculation, development, and outright fraud swelling the population to 100,000 in less than three years, and multiplying land values beyond all reason. The banks eventually pulled the plug, and the boom collapsed; suddenly the trains were arriving empty, and leaving full.

The famed naturalist John Muir visited in 1887, and wrote in his journal, "An hour's ride over stretches of bare, brown plain, and through cornfields and orange groves, brought me to the handsome, conceited little town of Los Angeles, where one finds Spanish adobes and Yankee shingles overlapping in very curious antagonism." *(Plus ça change . . .)*

The population declined (for the last time) to 50,000 by 1890, but rebounded to 100,000 by 1900, then took off again and never looked back. Tripled by 1910, doubled again by 1920, and by the time I drove through Greater Los Angeles in March, 2003, I passed through a population approaching ten million.

Like history, geology came alive when it was *felt* to be true, and as I continued driving east on I-10, I took in the macro-view. In late March, the rainy season was just tapering off, and the hills and mountains were unusually lush and verdant. To the north and east, the Hollywood Hills among the Santa Monica Mountains, and the lower foothills of the San Gabriels by Pasadena and Glendale, were all folds and peaks of green, villa-studded clarity. The white letters of the Hollywood sign glowed against Mount Lee, and I thought of how a little knowledge deepened my appreciation of what I was seeing.

As a recent Junior Geologist, I had been doing some reading in a subject that had once been opaque to me, and starting to build a few elementary facts into some kind of mental picture of how the actual Earth grew and changed, globally, and in the Western United States particularly. The curiosity seemed to have been inspired by traveling so much in the American Southwest, with all that naked geology, and as I so often did, I found books that educated me, by writers who entertained me. John McPhee was especially adept at combining geological information that hurt my brain with images and ideas that delighted it. Titles like *Basin and Range* and *Assembling California* had originally been written as serial articles for *The New Yorker*, and thus were perfectly targeted at the intelligent lay reader — or one who was willing to read the books two or three times until he could begin to apprehend, or at least approach, the concept of geological time, and to interpret the world around him as a whole new, truly fundamental, paradigm.

How could anyone ever be bored in this world, when there was so much to be *interested* in, to learn, to contemplate? It seemed to me that knowledge was actually *fun*, in the sense of being entertaining, and I had loved learning that the hills and peaks I was driving by, the ones supporting that famous Hollywood sign, were all part of the Coastal Ranges, and I had begun to understand how they were created by plate tectonics. The Pacific Plate crunched slowly against the North American Plate to push up the Sierra Nevada where they met, and, like a snow shovel, piled up the Coastal Ranges behind. Somehow, understanding how the earth beneath my feet — or wheels — was created, helped to make me feel more at home there.

Although, those were still difficult words for me to put together, "home" and "Los Angeles." When strangers asked me where I was from, I was more likely to say, "Canada," which conveyed a completely different message, and — true or not — a "friendlier" stereotype.

It is no secret that many people claim to dislike Los Angeles, and no doubt some of them have actually *been* there. For myself, I imagine life always depends on how big your city is — how big your *world* is. My Los Angeles had come to include favorite restaurants and bookstores, the County Museum of Art, the hiking trails in Temescal Canyon and Topanga State Park, and the rock formations at El Matador beach. My Los Angeles included the Mojave Desert, the Sierra Nevada, the Pacific Ocean, the Angeles Crest Highway, Highway 33 north out of Ojai, and Mulholland Highway out past Topanga Canyon.

Within a day's motorcycle ride, my Los Angeles stretched north on the coast highway to majestic Big Sur, the Sierra Nevada national parks of Yosemite, Kings Canyon, and Sequoia, across the enchanting Mojave Desert to Death Valley, or south to the Anza-Borrego desert and all the way into Baja. Indeed, I happened to know that an early start and a fast ride could put you on the South Rim of the Grand Canyon for a late lunch. If Los Angeles was not exactly a "moveable feast," it was certainly a *reachable* feast. And now I was stretching my Los Angeles a little farther yet — all the way to Texas.

Moving slowly eastward in the usual thick traffic on Interstate 10, through the endless suburbs of East L.A., everything blended into a flow of malls, car dealers, warehouse stores, insta-home subdivisions, and fast-food outlets (after reading *Fast Food Nation*, only "In 'n' Out Burger" would ever get my business again). It was difficult to imagine this land had all once been cattle ranchos, then irrigated citrus groves built around separate villages like Pasadena, Whittier, and the Mormon outpost at San Bernardino. During that late 19th-century real estate boom, the developers had soon run out of names for their invented projects, and one of them, Azusa (said to be the smoggiest city in the country these days), whose name seemed to echo native names like Cucamonga, Cahuenga, or Topanga, was actually named for "A to Z in the USA."

All those *real* place names ended in the "nga" suffix, meaning water, which always seemed to be the most common derivation of place names. (Every ancient place name in Canada, for example, seemed to mean either "swift-moving water," or "gathering of huts near water.") Topanga Canyon, which led from the San Fernando Valley to the Pacific, meant "place that leads to water," while Cahuenga, near a natural spring, meant "place of water." The people who gave these names were called the Yang-na, which could well have meant "people of the water."

Some of the names on the exit signs resonated for me in different ways, and at different stages of my life. Trawling back for my earliest impressions of California while growing up in Ontario, Canada, the first must have been seeing Disneyland on television, and TV shows like "77 Sunset Strip," "Highway Patrol," and "The Beverly Hillbillies." Then there would have been the "beach movies," with Frankie and Annette, at the Saturday afternoon matinees — *Beach Blanket Bingo*, *Bikini Beach*, all those, introducing me to the exotic world of surfing, sidewalk-surfing (I built my own skateboard with a piece of plywood and old roller-skate wheels), and inevitably, surf music: the Beach Boys, Jan and Dean, and the hot-rod and motorbike songs too. In later years I learned that some of those, like "Go Little Honda" and "Little GTO," were actually created and paid for by ad agencies, the latter to promote a Pontiac model (named after a legendary Ferrari) marketed by John DeLorean, who wasn't a Californian, but perhaps should have been. (His dream of building his own sports car ended in 1979 when he was arrested at a Los Angeles airport hotel trying to sell a suitcase full of cocaine to save his failing company.)

As an adolescent car nut, those songs resonated with me more than love songs did, reflecting my love for building car models and papering the walls of my room with centerspreads from *Hot Rod* and *Car Craft* magazines. California place names like Pomona, Riverside, and even Bakersfield were legendary to me, the homes of the Southern California drag strips. There were also drag races in a place called Ontario, California, which I had always wondered about, since I lived in the Canadian province of Ontario. I had learned, through reading some California history, that the California Ontario was actually named after the Canadian one. A self-taught engineer named George Chaffey came down from Canada in 1880 to visit, and ended up staying to become a visionary developer. He installed innovative irrigation systems, telephone lines, and a hydroelectric generator, lighting his home with the first incandescent lights west of the Rockies, and organized the Los Angeles Electric Company to make L.A. the first electrically lit city in America. So impressive was Chaffey's design for the community of Ontario that in 1903, U.S. government engineers erected a scale panorama of it at the St. Louis World's Fair.

Just after San Bernardino, I passed the exit for the road up to Lake Arrowhead and Big Bear Lake, high in the San Bernardino Mountains. In September of 2000, just before Carrie and I were married, my younger brother Danny (my best man) and I hiked a section of the Pacific Crest Trail up there, camping overnight for my "bachelor party." Each of us carried at least fifty pounds of gear in our backpacks, and as we set out on the trail we met another hiker coming from the opposite direction. Seeing our heavy packs, she asked if we were hiking the entire trail from Mexico to Canada, and we had to laugh. We were only starting a one-night hike, but included in our provisions were the ingredients for a fine dinner, including a flask of The Macallan, a bottle of chardonnay, a coffeepot, and a decadent dessert.

That Rim of the World Highway was also one of my favorite summer motorcycle routes, climbing up and winding around the mountain lakes to the west, linking with the legendary Angeles Crest Highway through miles of looping road and high pine forests, coming out above Pasadena in La Cañada, where my friend Mark Riebling had grown up. So many connections in the grid of greater Los Angeles.

That Angeles Crest Highway was another memory, for in November of 1996, on the *Test for Echo* tour, Brutus and I rode our motorcycles west on that road over the San Gabriels on our way to the Los Angeles Forum for a pair of concerts. I came around a corner behind Brutus to experience the novel sight of my friend sliding down the road on his back at 50 miles-per-hour. Beside him, his fallen motorcycle was spinning slowly on its side, trailing sparks, the bright headlight rotating toward me and then away. The bike came to rest on one side of the road, Brutus on the other. Fortunately he had been wearing an armored leather suit, as we always did, and his only injury resulted from the bike's luggage case landing on his foot on the way down.

Seeing that probably saved me from a similar tumble, as I backed off the throttle and, heart pounding, held the bike straight up and down over that icy patch. I coasted to a stop beside Brutus, relieved to see him struggling to his hands and knees, shaking his helmeted head. He seemed to be all right, though well shaken up, and we picked up his bike, which also seemed to be all right, scraped but undamaged, and carried on. Later, backstage at the Forum, Brutus was limping around and telling people how he'd "sacrificed" himself to save me, all for the sake of the show — addressing a crew member with a slowly wagging finger, "To save *your* job, my friend!"

Brutus' foot was sore for the next couple of days, but he was able to stay and rest at the Newport Beach hotel while the band played two nights at the Los Angeles Forum. After the second show, I saw that he was still limping and feeling tender, so I suggested an alternative to us riding to Phoenix the next day: we could spend that day off resting in Newport Beach, then ride the bus overnight to Phoenix, arriving in the early morning. As part of the research I wanted to do for that book I was planning, *American Echoes: Landscape with Drums*, I thought it would be good to watch the whole process of assembling the show, hang around all day and take notes, and Brutus decided to video the highlights.

The crew members and truck drivers were very surprised to see Brutus and me walking in at 7:00 in the morning, and spending the whole day watching them at work. I sat out in the arena's spectator seats with my journal, writing down the progress of erecting the show, while Brutus limped around with the video camera.

Back in 2003, driving east on Interstate 10, the skyline ahead gradually came to be dominated by the high snowy dome of San Gorgonio Mountain (11,490') to the north, and to the south, its twin, snow-covered sentinel, San Jacinto Peak (10,804'). Between them, in the San Gorgonio Pass, hundreds of giant propellers on the wind farms churned in the strong Santa Anas, accelerated through the narrowing pass by the Bernoulli effect.

I sped past a solid wall of green tamarisk trees waving in the gusts, then the view opened wide to the Coachella Valley. To the south, Palm Springs lay tucked under the San Jacintos, and to the north, the furrowed, naked brown slopes of the Little San Bernardino Mountains. Cutting west to east, Interstate 10 made an unnatural, but fairly accurate division between the lower Colorado Desert to the south and the first few Joshua trees, emblematic of the higher Mojave Desert to the north: 29 Palms, Joshua Tree National Park, and away over the creosote sea and jagged brown islands to Baker, Barstow, Death Valley, and Las Vegas.

When people asked how I liked living in Los Angeles, I usually answered that while it had its negatives — traffic, smog, crime, racial tensions, earthquakes, wildfires, mudslides, the general disregard for pedestrians, cyclists, or turn indicators (a recent favorite bumper sticker: "World Peace Begins with Turn Signals"), the shallow fixation on *appearance* among many Angelenos, the botox-collagen-silicone-facelift, chrome-rimmed-suv-and-spa culture — it certainly had its compensations. Chief among those was Carrie, of course, who wanted to live near her friends and family, and keep up her blossoming photographic career, especially when I was away so much, but there was also the great variety of nature that abounded in Southern California — the ocean, the mountains, the desert.

I came to appreciate, and glory in, the fabulous variety of trees and plants, native and introduced, and the birds and animals: Joshua tree and creosote, redwood and sequoia, eucalyptus and live-oak, manzanita and bristlecone pine, bright orange poppies and yellow desert senna, black bear, white-tailed deer, golden eagle, Steller's jay, and the emblem of the Southwest, coyote, the Trickster. In the holy trinity for travelers, as I had defined it in *Ghost Rider*, Southern California was prodigal with landscapes, highways, and wildlife.

Carrie's father, Don, a recently-retired history professor, had introduced me to many books of Californian history, from the 1840 account by William Henry Dana Jr., *Two Years Before the Mast*, to Carey McWilliams's pioneering examination, a century later, *California: The Great Exception*, from 1949. Most comprehensive of all was Kevin Starr's six-volume (so far) series documenting the "California dream" through the 20th Century. (One telling quote described Southern California by the 1950s as a place "where men who had arrived did not feel it, and those who had failed felt it too much.")

Starr's fifth volume, *The Dream Endures*, was the book I was carrying with me on this Big Bend journey, to be my restaurant companion.

California history had come alive for me as an endlessly amazing variety of *stories*, of human drama, achievement, artistry, corruption, cruelty, and nobility. What Balzac called *La Comédie Humaine* had played out in Southern California in hyperbolic fashion, then and now, and proved the truth of Wallace Stegner's remark, "California is like the rest of America — only more so."

As the freeway descended into the valley and the traffic began to thin out at last, I relaxed a little and turned on the CD player. The first disc was the soundtrack from the movie *Frida*, with its evocative use of traditional Mexican instruments and melodies. The lush textures and exotic mood were working for me, casting the right atmosphere for the desert crossing, and for the journey. Not that I was headed for Mexico, but literally the next thing to it, the Big Bend of the Rio Grande River also describing the Mexican–American border.

As I started across the Mojave Desert on the long climb to Chiriaco Summit (home of the General George Patton Museum, near where he had trained his troops in the desert to prepare them for the North African campaign against Rommel in World War II), traffic began to bog down again. Generally, I hate passing on the right, but driving habits in North America are such that it is often the only way. Carefully watching my mirrors, and using my turn signals — no matter how unfamiliar *that* custom had become — I threaded between the gas-gulping SUVs and asthmatic Japanese compacts clumping in the left lane, and the roaring, straining semis in the right.

Next up on the CD player was *Sinatra at the Sands*, with Count Basie's band. As always, not only did the music I listened to accompany my journey, but it also took me on sidetrips, through memory and fractals of associations, threads reaching back through my whole life in ways I had forgotten, or had never suspected.

The American writer Ralph Ellison began as a musician, and wrote passionately on the subject throughout his life. In a collection of essays called *Living with Music*, he wrote about the power of music as a part of one's life, and even of one's culture.

Perhaps in the swift change of American society in which the meanings of one's origins are so quickly lost, one of the chief values of living with music lies in its power to give us an orientation in time. In doing so, it gives significance to all those indefinable aspects of experience which nevertheless help to make us what we are. In the swift whirl of time, music is a constant, reminding us of what we were and of that toward which we aspire. Art thou troubled? Music will not only calm, it will ennoble thee.

Sinatra at the Sands was released in 1966, when I was fourteen, and it was one of the records I remembered my father playing on his console stereo. It seemed there was always music playing in our house, and it had to have an influence on me. Dad was the kind of music lover who turned on the radio when he woke up in the morning, and listened to music every waking moment, while he shaved, ate breakfast, in the car, at work, and at home, inside or out. Always there was music.

I had been playing drums for a year or so back then, and as a fan of The Who, Jimi Hendrix and the like, I didn't have much use for "old people's music," but at the same time I was so obsessed with drums and drummers that I would even watch "The Lawrence Welk Show" with my grandmother, hoping for an occasional glimpse of the drummer's champagne sparkle drums in the background.

Obviously I didn't have much choice about hearing my dad's music, and even back then I couldn't help appreciating *Sinatra at the Sands*, especially the fiery arrangements (by a young Quincy Jones), and the energetic, exciting drummer, Sonny Payne. (Sonny was known for his showmanship, twirling sticks, tossing them in the air and catching them between beats. There's a story about Buddy Rich, certainly the greatest jazz drummer ever, but an intense man who preferred to dazzle with his playing rather than his juggling. Buddy appreciated Sonny's drumming, but when sticks were twirling and flying in the air, Buddy commented dryly to a friend, "He'd better watch out — he might *hit* something.")

A few years later, in the early '70s, when I lived in a London bed-sitter with my childhood friend Brad, I rediscovered my father's music, the big band stuff like Duke Ellington, Count Basie, and Frank, and I bought my own LP versions of them. I remember listening to *Sinatra at the Sands* on headphones many times (because our speakers were so poor — because *we* were so poor), and after that kind of intimate listening, even more than thirty years later I still knew every word and every note of that album. As I drove eastward across the high desert and into late afternoon, I was humming and nodding and drumming on the steering wheel as Frank and the band worked through all those great standards: "Come Fly with Me," "I've Got You Under My Skin," "Fly Me to the Moon," "Angel Eyes."

A couple of times Frank paused to deliver a "monologue," and in one of them he mentioned having recently turned 50. I had passed that milestone myself the previous September (behind my drums, fittingly, playing a show in Calgary on the *Vapor Trails* tour), and my reactions had ranged from a sense of the "impossible" (the notion that I had survived half a century, and also thinking back to being 20, say, and what I thought then it would be like to be 50 — ancient and decrepit), to a sense of the number being "meaningless." In an interview with *Modern Drummer* magazine before the tour, I was asked about that upcoming birthday, and said, "I've read that everyone has an inner age that they think they are, regardless of their actual age. I really think of myself as being about thirty. In modern life it's a matter of keeping your prime going as long as you can."

Recently a photographer friend introduced me to his young assistant, saying to him, "Tell him when you were born, Ben!" Ben told me he was born in 1976, and my immediate reaction in thinking about that date, and starting life then, was not envy, but a kind of *sympathy*. I shook my head and said, "You've missed so much."

For me, to have grown up through the last half of the 20th century, to have been a boy in the '50s and '60s, a young musician in the '60s and '70s, and into the '80s, '90s, and now the 21st century, seemed more valuable than being merely young. Perhaps this reaction only marked a kind of turning point of true aging, when the past seemed more important than the future — because at a certain age you suddenly *have* more past than future — or maybe it was the vantage point of a half-century that allowed me to feel what Wallace Stegner called "the very richness of that past."

And listening to *Sinatra at the Sands*, it occurred to me how Frank's singing had spanned my whole life, from childhood on, in a way that no other artist had, and how his music continued to *reach* me on such a deep level.

Many theories had been spun to explain the appeal of Frank's singing through decades and generations (in my own family, from my father to me, then late one night a teenaged Selena and I were driving back to Toronto from visiting friends in western New York, and I was playing *Sinatra and Company*, and suddenly, half asleep, Selena *got* it — and soon actually bought that CD for herself).

In *Why Sinatra Matters*, Pete Hamill wrote, "As an artist, Sinatra had only one basic subject: loneliness. His ballads are all strategies for dealing with loneliness; his up-tempo performances are expressions of release from that loneliness."

Everybody can relate to loneliness. In a Canadian context, when the members of Rush were being presented with our Order of Canada medals (a kind of "good citizenship" award), the governor-general of Canada, Roméo LeBlanc, made an eloquent bilingual speech about the shared experience of being Canadian, "We all know what it's like to be alone in the snow." (When I complimented him on that line later, he shrugged and said, "I have a good speechwriter!")

I once read a comment that Frank's singing was felt so powerfully because he seemed to be singing "to you alone," while others opine that, like Billie Holliday, he was able to convey all the passion and heartbreak of his own life when he sang. It seemed to me that the key to Sinatra's magic was that when Frank sang, he *meant* it. As he said himself, "Whatever else has been said about me is unimportant. When I sing, I believe I'm honest."

Perhaps the key to *any* great performance is just that quality: sincerity.

Of course, many singers become phenomenally successful *without* that magic ingredient. A golden voice and good looks will often appeal, even when it's obvious to a caring listener that when that singer delivers a song, he or she (read "diva") doesn't mean a *word* of it. You'd think that difference would be apparent to the listener, but I guess that is the clearest difference between art and entertainment. If people only want to be diverted and distracted, rather than moved or inspired, then fakery will do just as well as the real thing. To the indiscriminate, or uncaring, listener, it just doesn't matter. Sometimes I have to face the reality that music can be part of people's lives, like wallpaper, without being the white-hot *center* of their lives, as it always seemed to be for me.

All my earliest memories were like pearls grown around a grain of music or traveling. When I was three years old, we lived in a duplex on Violet Street in St. Catharines, and I remember being pulled around the block on a sled in winter. I also remember Dad proudly setting up his new General Electric hi-fi record player in the living room, so I must have picked up on his excitement about it.

A big old house, it had sunken basement windows framed in concrete below ground level, and while riding my tricycle along the driveway, I somehow fell into one of those window cavities and broke through the glass. I remember hanging upside down and looking at my mom, as she looked up in shock from the wringer-type washing machine. My first travel adventure.

Mom worked in a restaurant called the Flamingo while I was still a toddler, and I remember its shiny, lighted jukebox, and in a corner, a floodlit diorama of a pink flamingo, a plastic palm tree, and a reflective chrome sphere on a pedestal. (Perhaps my first travel fantasy.) I also remember the beginning of another lifelong addiction: my first chocolate bar. When the owners went away on vacation and we stayed there to look after the place, after dinner I was given my choice of chocolate bars from the candy counter. What joy to be able to choose, but what sweet torment *having* to choose. I wanted them all. (I still do.)

A friend of Mom and Dad's worked for a company which serviced the jukeboxes, and he gave them a rack of old 45s which hung around our house for years. Among them was "Wheels" by Billy Vaughn and his orchestra (another traveling song), on the flip side of "Sail Along Silvery Moon" (and heaven knows why I remember *that*).

One Christmas, when I was about four, we traveled by car to Virginia, where my grandparents were living, on the first "road trip" I remember. Most of our vacations were car journeys, usually camping in a canvas tent with its evocative smells of baking in the sun or mildewing in the rain. Once we stopped for the night at a motel, and I can still remember the excitement of sleeping in a rollaway cot in an unfamiliar, temporary home. My first motel stay — and far from the last. Fortunately, my reaction was excitement rather than dread, for I would be spending a good portion of my life in temporary homes, like hotels, motels, and furnished apartments. Whenever I checked into a hotel room, I felt a kind of eager anticipation. Good or bad, expensive or cheap, I locked myself into a private, anonymous space, and it felt something like home, and something like freedom.

I first achieved *musical* freedom when I was about ten, and my mother gave me a small plastic transistor radio. She showed me where the "Hit Parade" station was on the dial, and I remember sitting on the front step of our split-level holding that radio in my hands like a holy relic, transfixed by the notion of *my own private music.* (Funny that I didn't know *records* were played on the radio, just like on the jukebox at the Flamingo, and I thought each song was being broadcast live from the studio, with the performers moving from station to station.)

For me, that was really the beginning of *loving* music. I listened to that little radio constantly, searching out all the Top-Forty AM stations, WKBW in Buffalo, New York, CHUM in Toronto, and CHOW in Welland, Ontario. I would even fall asleep with that little transistor playing faintly in my ear.

Also, now that I had my own music, I had an alternative to my *father's* music, and the division began. It would be another ten years until I learned to appreciate Dad's music on my own, but of course once I did, it would stay with me for the rest of my life.

Sinatra at the Sands also featured a couple of slow-tempoed Basie instrumentals, "All of Me" and "Makin' Whoopee!", which showcased the tight discipline of that great band. No session musicians or generic horn section could have duplicated that dynamic swell and punch and kick, the synchronized breathing you hear when Basie's or Ellington's band played, the sound of musicians who played together night after night and really *lived* that music, didn't just *read* it.

From all those years ago, right back to childhood, the repeated snatches of Basie's theme song, "One O'Clock Jump," had so ingrained themselves in my memory that when I was choosing material to play in a Buddy Rich tribute concert and, later, recording, one of my choices had to be Buddy's band's arrangement of "One O'Clock Jump," just so I would have the chance to play that great "shout chorus," the one that appeared repeatedly on the Sinatra record.

A little more traveling music.

Before Buddy's passing in 1987, one of his final requests to his daughter, Cathy, had been for her to try to keep his band working somehow, to keep the music alive, and to "give something back" to American music. Cathy established a memorial scholarship in Buddy's name, and began presenting concerts with well-known drummers "sitting in" with Buddy's band, to raise money for the musical education of deserving young drum students. In late 1990 Cathy approached me about taking part in one of those shows, and my reply to her described my thoughts and feelings about that challenge.

> I am honored that you have asked me to be a part of the Buddy Rich Memorial Scholarship Concert. In the past I have always shied away from participating in events of this nature, partly out of shyness, partly out of overwork, and partly out of a sense of inadequacy. As a rule, I do my work with Rush, and hide behind a low profile otherwise.
>
> But even my own rules are made to be broken, and this seems like a worthwhile occasion to come out of my self-imposed shell. Not only is it an opportunity to "give something back," but also an opportunity to fulfill a long-time ambition of my own — to play behind a big band.

Along with Basie's "One O'Clock Jump," I ended up choosing to perform Buddy's band's arrangement of Duke Ellington's "Cottontail," as a tribute to that giant of American music, and another tune with some nice drum breaks, called "Mexicali Nose." Through the early months of 1991, I practiced those three songs over and over (playing along with Buddy's recorded versions), and in April I drove from Toronto to New York City, and appeared with the Buddy Rich Big Band at a small theater (the Ritz, formerly Studio 54) as part of a concert featuring five other guest drummers.

Unfortunately, it turned out to be a difficult and disappointing experience for me. With minimal rehearsal time, there had been no opportunity to discover that the rest of the band was playing a different arrangement of "Mexicali Nose" than the one I had learned, and during the performance I was unable to hear the brass section at all. I struggled through it, and managed to hold it together, but after, I felt very let down by the experience I had so anticipated, and down on myself about it.

The following day I drove home to Toronto, about a 600-mile journey, and it turned out to be another occasion during which a long drive was a good opportunity to think. I left New York at dawn, feeling sad and disheartened, but as I drove, I found myself thinking about some lines from a song called "Bravado," which I had recently written for Rush's *Roll the Bones* album, recorded earlier in 1991. The song began, "If we burn our wings, flying too close to the sun," and resolved with the repeating line "We will pay the price, but we will not count the cost," which I borrowed from novelist John Barth, with his permission and approval. At least, I sent him a copy of the song, and he wrote back "it seems to work very well," which I chose to take as permission. And approval.

So, if I had "burned my wings" a little, taking on a challenge with all the circumstances against me, I was paying the price, but not even thinking about the cost. I just wanted to make myself feel better, and the only way to do that was to do it *again*, and get it right. (It also occurred to me that this was the first time I had ever been inspired by my own words!)

By the time I got back to Toronto, ten hours later, I had figured it all out. *Someone* was going to have to produce a Buddy Rich tribute album, so that I could play on it, and have a chance to play big-band music under more controlled conditions. Inevitably, of course, that "someone" was going to have to be me, though it took almost two more years to make that happen, between Rush recording projects and concert tours, and my own busy life of writing projects and bicycle tours to Africa.

In December, 1993, I finally wrote to Cathy and formally proposed the idea:

> Recently I've been thinking about a little dream project, and I wanted to run it past you and see what you think. It seems to me it's high time for a Buddy Rich tribute album, with a number of top contemporary drummers playing the band charts — like the Scholarship videos, but with studio-quality recording. I would like to play on a track or two myself, of course, but more than that — I would like to *produce* the project.
>
> Would you be agreeable to an idea like that? Without your blessing (and *help*), I will certainly not go ahead with it, but if, like me, you think it would be a positive thing, I would like to proceed with some plans. We could work together in choosing which drummers to involve, which tunes to feature, the cover artwork and so on. With a little good old-fashioned hard work, I think we could turn out a very nice package.

Cathy was equally excited about the idea, and together with her husband, Steve, and Rush's tour manager, Liam (sharing the executive producer credit with Cathy), we started working on organizing the project, co-ordinating a list of drummers and all the logistics of travel, equipment, accommodations, and studio time.

During two weeks in May, 1994, we did the actual recording at a studio in New York City. Working with a fourteen-piece band almost entirely composed of Buddy alumni, we averaged two "guest" drummers a day, each of them recording two or three songs, mostly from Buddy's "songbook." It was a monumental undertaking, but eventually resulted in a two-volume CD called *Burning for Buddy*, which sold modestly (though I still enjoy listening to it — reward enough!), and even a set of videos documenting the "making of" process.

Every day I walked the ten blocks from the hotel to the studio, through midtown Manhattan and Broadway, taking different routes and enjoying the unmatched vitality of those streets. My feet raced over the pavement, so excited about what the day would bring, which drummers we would be recording with, and what new music we would be capturing. And apart from the day-to-day excitement of those sessions, and the pleasure of becoming friends with many of the drummers along the way, there was another unexpected benefit.

A few years before that project, I had worked with drummer Steve Smith on a recording with virtuoso bassist Jeff Berlin. Steve had always been a great drummer, but on the Buddy sessions I suddenly noticed a *huge* growth in his playing — in his technique, and, especially, his *musicality*. When I asked Steve what had happened to him, he smiled and gave me a one-word answer, "Freddie," referring to his teacher, Freddie Gruber.

Freddie was in his late 60s by then, and had been one of Buddy Rich's closest friends since the late '40s, when they'd met in the vibrant New York City jazz scene of those days. They stayed friends when the path of Freddie's life took him from the streets of New York out through Chicago and Las Vegas to Los Angeles, where he found his own natural calling as a teacher.

During the *Burning for Buddy* sessions, I met Freddie, a nonstop storyteller with a lively mind and ageless hipness, rarely without a cigarette in his hand, lit or not. I sat at dinner with him and some of the other drummers a couple of times, and in the following weeks, I became curious about what a teacher like Freddie might do for *me*. By that time I had been playing drums for thirty years, and was feeling as though I was playing "myself" about as well as I could — maybe it was time to, as Freddie would put it, "take this thing a little further."

The timing was certainly right, as Rush was on hiatus that year while Geddy and his wife Nancy awaited the birth of their daughter, Kyla, so in

October of 1994, I arranged to spend a week working with Freddie in New York City. The first day, he watched me play for about one minute, then started *talking* — telling stories about Buddy and other drummers, anecdotes from his "misspent youth," encounters with Allen Ginsberg, Marlon Brando, Miles Davis, Malcolm X, Stanley Kubrick, abstract-expressionist painter Larry Rivers, and assorted hookers, junkies, and geniuses. Amid all that — look out, here comes the lesson! — he moved around the little rehearsal room, acting out the motions of soft-shoe dancers, pianists, violinists, and so on, showing me how those activities, like drumming, took place largely in the *air*, and ought to be more like a *dance*.

Also, he said, holding up a magisterial finger, "there are no straight lines in nature." Thus our movements should be circular, orbital, smooth and flowing. And, on the drums, we should pay more attention to what happens in the *air*, between the beats. Another of his finger-raised directives, delivered emphatically, with tall eyes, was, "Get out of the way. *Let* it happen! Or worse, don't *prevent* it from happening."

Freddie could best be compared to a tennis player's coach, always watching and correcting movement and physical technique. Freddie didn't try to teach you how to play the game — you were supposed to know that already — but he watched your "serve," or your cross-court backhand, and tried to get you *moving* better. So Freddie was not the kind of teacher you learned from and moved on; you could always use that kind of guidance, and Freddie had built a tight circle of faithful students for *life*, studio legends like Jim Keltner, recently drumming on the Simon and Garfunkel tour, and British journeyman Ian Wallace, and jazzy, rocky, so-called "fusion" (Freddie calls it "con-fusion") masters, like Steve Smith and Dave Weckl.

It was a dizzying week, full of more stories than lessons, it seemed to me, but at the end of it Freddie left me with a written list of exercises for my hands and feet, all designed to affect the motion of my entire body, eventually — though that "eventually" would require a lot of time and effort on my part. It was already clear to me that if I was going to surrender to Freddie's "vision," I would basically have to start all over again on the drums — changing the way I sat, held the drumsticks, set up the drums, and moved my hands and feet. Perhaps most daunting of all, I would have to find time to practice those exercises every day, in a busy life of work, home, and family. Practicing every day was easy and natural enough when I was thirteen and fourteen, but 30 years later, life had grown considerably more *complicated*.

However, I did find myself inspired and dedicated to the task, and every day I made time to go down to the basement of our Toronto house and practice on my little yellow set of Gretsch drums (seen in a drum shop window in the mid-'80s, I thought how I would have dreamed of those drums when I was sixteen — so I bought them, for the part of me that was still sixteen). As an old dog learning new tricks, I was even sitting in front of the television at night with sticks and practice pad, working on those exercises.

Over the passing weeks, I began to feel the benefits in the fluidity of my playing, and after six months, Freddie came to visit me in Toronto for another week, to "take this thing a little further," "start to put the pieces together."

"Get out of the way, *let* it happen."

He left me with more exercises to work on, and the practicing continued. Then again, six months later, in September of 1995, Freddie came to Quebec for another week (as a New Yorker living in Los Angeles, he *loved* it up there, smelling the air, floating around the lake together in my boat). More exercises, more practicing, until finally, I felt ready to actually *apply* those hard-won new techniques.

In early 1996, I started working with Geddy and Alex on what would be our *Test for Echo* album, and I could feel I had brought my playing to a whole new level, both technically and musically. Later that year, I expounded on these new directions, and on Freddie, in an instructional video, *A Work in Progress*.

Throughout this time, Freddie and I became close friends, and during the *Test for Echo* tour, he also met and became close to my best friend, Brutus. During my tragedies and subsequent "exile" in England, Brutus kept Freddie updated on my "condition," and when I was wandering around on my motorcycle in the fall of 1998 and learned that Brutus had been arrested with a truckload of marijuana at the U.S. border in Buffalo, and was likely going "away" for awhile, Freddie understood better than anyone the weight of this latest loss. He said to me, "I thought you'd hit the very bottom of life already, but now you've hit *lower* than bottom — you've hit *lead!*"

Just after a five-day stay at Freddie's house in the San Fernando Valley in November of 1999, I started a letter to Brutus from my accommodations in Show Low, Arizona, to his at the Federal Detention Facility in Batavia, New York. Coincidentally, I was on my way to Big Bend that time too, though I never made it (for reasons that will be revealed), and that letter also happened to contain some "traveling music," and tell of a journey eastward on Interstate 10, near where I was driving in March of 2003.

As I closed in on Blythe, California, the Colorado River and the Arizona line, who should be up next on the CD changer but Buddy Rich, in a sweet coincidence, and a sublime recording with Buddy's band and Mel Tormé, called *Together Again — For the First Time*.

So many connections on this traveling roadshow.

From a letter to Brutus, dated November 15, 1999, telling about my stay with Freddie.

> Anyway, every day there was sunny and warm, and every night was cool and clear. I would lay out in his backyard at night in the one operable chaise longue, and look up at Orion, the Pleiades, the star I think is Arcturus, and all the rest.
>
> Airplanes high and low, shooting stars, a fingernail moon. Eight cypress trees in the neighbor's yard, a shaggy, silhouetted palm. Radio station KGIL, "America's Best Music," plays from the Silvertone radio in the laundry closet, in the half-covered patio, and in the dark living room, coming on every afternoon at 4:00, on a timer. Their playlist could be sublime — an instrumental version of the Ellington-Strayhorn classic, "Don't Get Around Much Anymore," then "He'll Have to Go" ("Put your sweet lips, a

little closer, to the phone"), "Cherish," "I Love How You Love Me," and "Maria," from *West Side Story*.

Or another set which included "Take Five," "Unchained Melody," "Only You," by the Platters, Dusty Springfield's "Wishing and Hoping," and Ed Ames doing a heartbreaker (for me) "Sunrise, Sunset" — "Is that the little girl I used to carry" . . . Ach. Other greats I hadn't known about: Errol Garner, Dick Haimes — or hadn't fully appreciated — Bobby Darin, Eydie Gorme (really!). Altogether, as before, Freddie's "pad" is a timeless oasis of sanctuary, a hideaway, but with the two of us in various "states," and me already a little "beat up" after ten days in L.A.

A bit much, but — that's the way it went down, and if Freddie needed me for a few days to "see him through," then of course I could do that for him. Late yesterday morning I finally got away from there ("Escape From Encino"), feeling pretty used up, groggy, weak, and tired. So I kept it simple — just angled my way over through Pasadena and Glendale to I-10, and across the desert to Blythe, on the Colorado, which at that point was slow, muddy, and about 50 feet wide (as the early settlers used to say, "too thick to drink, too thin to plow").

It seemed I had a bit of *sleep* to catch up on, and today I didn't get on the road until about 10:00, still feeling groggy and fuzzy headed, though I "sharpened up" a little through the day. I *needed* to — though it started off flat and straight, on Highway 60 through creosote, cholla, palo verde, saguaro, ocotillo, and mesquite, you'll remember our ride up 89 to Prescott, and from there to Jerome and on to Payson. Dynamic, right? (And again, we were *spoiled*.) So that helped me to "straighten up and fly right," and also got me back into the *riding* groove. Why, lately my bike has been collecting more *dust* than road dirt. Shameful.

After Payson I stayed on 260, through the high pine forests and mostly gentle curves. All in all, a nice day's ride, and I'm feeling much more "myself" again. (Or should it be "ourselves?")

[A little later] Can't sleep, and tired of reading (halfway through another Saul Bellow epic, *Humboldt's Gift*). And speaking of epics, what a treat it was to pick up your two letters just as I was checking out of the Marquis. As soon as I got to Freddie's I started reading avidly, despite his constant interruptions and demands for attention, with a pile of photographs of him and his jazz buddies from a thousand years ago! You can imagine that it took a while to get through even the *first* letter amid all that — but I persevered, and then, the next day, when he was absent for awhile (like, out of it), I had the luxury of rereading them both, at leisure. (Annoying pen trouble today — even tried changing the refill, but it was still scratching and skipping. Maybe the Mendocino paper doesn't like Arizona? Hey man, I took it through Jerome [another "hippieish" sort of town, likely to have "good energy"]; it should be cool!)

Anyway, just let me say that you done some *fine* letter-writing there, boy. The world around you, and within. You *do* seem to be making the most of this opportunity for reflection, and it was certainly a pleasure (and privilege) to be the recipient of so much soul searching, and to feel the sincerity, clarity, and painful honesty of your reflections. Of course you're too hard on yourself, but the alternative is either blame-shifting, or the usual exculpatory rationalizing that you hear every day.

Reminds me of one night on the bus, when I was giving my performance a critical review, and you said, "You're too hard on yourself," and I said, "Hey man — it's my *job!*"

Somehow it still is, and I'm constantly tormenting myself over some dumb thing I said or did five, ten, or fifteen years ago. Actually flinching at the memory, and cursing myself. Like that helps. But maybe it does, at least, let us see ourselves closer to how we really are. *Evil.*

Or, as you put it, "special."

In answer to a couple of your on-the-fly questions:

- "Get It On (Bang a Gong)" was Marc Bolan and T. Rex, sub-titled like that only in America because a group called Chase had a song called "Get It On."
- Keith Moon did indeed play on *Tommy*, and beautifully, at his absolute peak of inspired, sublime lunacy. And it still sounds great today.
- "Gaia" was the name of the earliest-known deity, a kind of earth goddess in Mesopotamia, I think it was.

  Also, note the limitations of your Spellchecker, amigo — that which is "excepted" is not necessarily "accepted," even if the "censors" have "sensors." (Color me pedantic, but such solecisms can spoil a carefully drawn *effect*, sayin'?)

That letter continued from Tucson the following day, November 16, 1999, and it also happened that in March 2003, I would be passing through Tucson the following day, three and a half eventful years later.

As I drove across the Colorado River into Arizona, the wind remained strong, sending waves of sand drifting across the freeway, and occasional tumbleweeds (despite being emblems of the American West, they were actually Russian thistles, accidentally imported with Asian wheat seeds). The sun was sinking behind me, filling my mirrors, and the creosote, ocotillo, and palo verde trees began to cast long shadows to the east. Up ahead was Quartzsite, Arizona, the neon of truck stops and RV parks illuminating the oncoming night, then passing behind my speeding car, to leave only the red dashlights and pale sweep of headlights before me.

And the music played on. Buddy and Mel's album, *Together Again — For the First Time*, was originally made as a direct-to-disc recording in the late '70s, shortcutting the analog technology of those days. It had been considered an "audiophile" product, for there was no tape involved, and thus no tape noise, with the aim of producing the cleanest, most dynamic sound possible. The mix went straight to the cutting lathe, and no edits or overdubs were possible, so the band had to play an entire side of the LP in one take, as near perfect as humanly possible.

I once talked with a recording engineer who worked on the Buddy and Mel project, and he told me that when an error marred one of the tunes, the producer stopped the band and instructed them to go "back to the top." Some of the musicians went back to the top of the song, and some remembered to start at the top of the *side*, and this apparently caused a hilarious "train wreck." (A musician's term for when the players get out of sync with each other, especially terrifying when it happened onstage.)

Mel himself had written the intricate and accomplished arrangements for the album, with the exception of the tour-de-force on "Blues in the Night," arranged by Marty Paich (father of David Paich, from the band Toto), which featured a brief solo from Buddy that was blistering, highly technical, and yet sublimely musical — in short, a summation of Buddy himself. For anyone who thought Buddy was only about pyrotechnical solos and driving swing, they should listen to his sensitive performance with wire brushes on a lovely rendition of "Here's That Rainy Day," even mimicking the patter of raindrops in a kind of musical onomatopoeia, and showing yet another facet of his consummate musicianship.

Mel sang wonderfully well, too (I particularly love his delivery of my favorite Paul Williams song, "I Won't Last a Day without You"), and the guest soloist on alto sax, Phil Woods, was poetic and kinetic, like swallows in flight. When you listened to the overall performances, and considered that every one of the musicians had to play perfectly through a whole side's worth of complicated material, you had to be impressed. Most importantly, though, it was great music, and a testament to Buddy's excellence as a musician.

As Buddy and Mel wound up their tribute to Ella Fitzgerald, "Lady Be Good," the next CD began with a rich female voice framed in exotic percussion and tight background harmonies, "Where love goes, I will go too/ Up twenty-nine flights of stairs." Ah yes, haven't heard this for awhile. The Mint Juleps, singing the first song on a favorite of mine from the mid-'90s, a side project by one of the Grateful Dead's drummers, called *Mickey Hart's Mystery Box*. He brought together some of the all-stars of "world music," American, African, and Latin, and composed a similarly international, percussion-based blend of musical styles, working with evocative lyrics by one of the Dead's frequent lyricists, Robert Hunter.

In 1990, Mickey had cowritten a book (with Jay Stevens) on the history of drums and rhythm, artfully interwoven with his own autobiography and some of the Grateful Dead's history, called *Drumming at the Edge of Magic*. When Selena was looking for a topic for a junior high science project, I suggested something I had learned about from the book, the "Theory of Entrainment." The theory held that any two mechanisms, including humans, tended to synchronize their rhythms, to "prefer" them, as compared to beating against each other. Thus two analog clocks placed in proximity would eventually begin to tick in sync with each other, neighboring heart cells tended to pulse together, women living together often synchronized their menstrual cycles. And thus, thought Mickey, he and the other Grateful Dead drummer, Bill Kreutzmann, should (and did) link their arms before a concert, to try to synchronize their biorhythms with the Theory of Entrainment. Selena put two old-fashioned alarm clocks, with keys and springs and bells, beside two digital bedside clocks, and made a poster to describe the principle. I think she got a good mark.

For my part, I was so impressed with the scholarship and artistry in the book that I wrote Mickey a letter of appreciation, and we began to correspond a little. Later that year, in 1991, it happened that both our bands were playing at the Omni arena in Atlanta on successive nights, the Dead one night and Rush the next, and Mickey and I invited each other to our shows. On our night off I went to see the Dead play, accompanied by our tour manager, Liam, and what an experience *that* turned out to be.

Liam and I arrived just as the show was starting, and gave our names at the backstage door. One of their production crew gave us our guest passes and escorted us to our seats — right behind the two drum risers, in the middle of the stage! Liam and I looked at each other with raised eyebrows as we sat down, and noticed that right behind us was the production office, with telephones, fax machines, and long-haired, bearded staff dealing with communications and logistics (presumably, though the production office is normally a room backstage, where such work can go on *apart* from the concert), and we also heard there was a telephone line run through the crowd to the front-of-house mixing platform. Catering people walked across the oriental rugs that covered the stage, delivering salads and drinks to various musicians and technicians, even during songs, and meanwhile, the band played on. Lights swept the arena, reflecting off white, amorphous "sails" suspended above the stage, and clouds of marijuana smoke drifted through the beams and assailed our nostrils with the pungent, spicy aroma.

My familiarity with the Grateful Dead's music really began and ended with their first album, back in '67, when my first band, Mumblin' Sumpthin' (I'm not sure, but I think the name came from a "Li'l Abner" comic), used to play several of their songs, "Morning Dew," "New New Minglewood Blues," and "Good Morning, Little Schoolgirl." (Other gems in our repertoire included songs by Hendrix, The Who's "I Can't Explain," a couple by Moby Grape, the Byrds, the Animals, Cream, and Blue Cheer.) In later years, my musical taste and the Grateful Dead's music had drifted apart, but no one could be unaware of their immense popularity, and the subculture of "Deadheads" that followed them around the country. Now I was seeing that subculture in action, as the whole arena full of devotees raised their arms and waved in a kind of trance-like unison, or raised their voices and sang along with every song the band played.

And they played and sang really well, too, augmented by the soulful keyboards and accordion of Bruce Hornsby. The two drummers, Mickey and Bill, became an interlocking, mutually complementary rhythmic unit, right out of the Theory of Entrainment. Bands with two drummers emerged in Ontario around the mid-'60s, just when I was starting to play, and later showed up in the "big time," with bands like the Allman Brothers, the Doobie Brothers, and the Dead. Very often they combined complementary styles, a solid, rooted drummer who laid down the time, and another whose approach was more "decorative," even flighty, adding counterpoints and percussive textures, then locking into a tight, compelling unison that was powerful and effective. (In later years, when Phil Collins took over the frontman position with Genesis, they featured some great double-drummer work with him and Bill Bruford, then later with Chester Thompson.)

Liam and I couldn't see much of the "front line" guys, the guitarists and vocalists, because of the wall of amplifiers, but occasionally, on the stage-left side, the spotlights caught an unmistakeable bush of gray hair that could only have been the legendary Jerry Garcia.

During intermission, Mickey invited Liam and me to his dressing room in the familiar backstage corridors of the Omni (each band member had a separate room, which hinted at certain "divisions" among them; after Jerry Garcia's tragic death, I read a story asserting that he hadn't enjoyed touring very much, and when the others wanted to go on the road again, he responded, "What, they need *more money?*"). Mickey was a friendly, outgoing man, with an engaging smile and an intense, joyful enthusiasm for percussion. With all my African travels and interest in African percussion music, and Mickey's musical explorations in print and on records, we shared a few things we knew and cared about, and had a good conversation until they were called to the stage to begin their second set.

Liam and I returned to our center-stage reserved seats, and I noticed that not only did the band members have separate dressing rooms, but the wings of the stage were lined with small tents of black cloth, one for each of the musicians to retire to during the songs on which they didn't play, and have some privacy. During an acoustic number in the second part of the show, Mickey disappeared into his little tent, then motioned for me to join him. We talked for a few minutes about drums and drumming, and I told him how much I was enjoying their performance, then he went back up to the riser and started playing again.

Next night, the positions were reversed. That tour (probably *Counterparts*, in '93), we had a metal gridwork runway (dubbed the "chicken run" by the crew) about four feet high, running across the width of our stage behind my drum riser, where Geddy and Alex could wander while they played. During the show, I looked back and saw Mickey, under the chicken run, smiling out between its black curtains. He was just as close to me as I had been to him, and he seemed to be enjoying himself.

And now Mickey was playing in front of me once more, but in the speakers of my speeding car on dark Interstate 10 eastbound, and his divine backing vocalists, the Mint Juleps, sang in close harmony and tight phrasing, as night began to darken over Western Arizona, over creosote, ocotillo, and the trademark saguaro cactus. The driving part of my consciousness had settled into a speed of 90 mph, which seemed to suit the conditions, the traffic, the car, and its driver. The limit in Arizona was already a reasonable 75 mph, and you could generally count on a 10 mph buffer zone, so I was hoping the radar detector wouldn't be necessary. But I had it on anyway, just in case.

As Mickey's record came to an end, suitably, with "The Last Song," suddenly the speakers lit up with a series of loud, percussive smashes, then a crash of breaking glass that segued into a harsh, aggressive drum-machine rhythm. This major dynamic shift announced the new album by Linkin Park, *Meteora*, which I had just bought the day before.

Linkin Park's first record, *The Hybrid Theory*, in 2000, had been hugely successful commercially, and, for this listener, musically as well, bringing together heavy guitar riffing and rock rhythms, vocals ranging from pop melody to metal screaming, and an ultra-modern hip-hop influence of turntable scratching, sampling, and rap-style verses and backing vocals. One song on that first album, "In the End," was particularly emblematic of that "hybrid theory," and brought together all those influences in a dynamic, melodic, and powerful combination. A modern masterpiece, I felt.

Typically, that blend of influences had been a long time reaching the popular ear, going back to the early '90s and bands like Faith No More, Rage Against the Machine, and Cypress Hill. Those bands and others like them had certainly found an audience, but never the "mainstream," just as reggae had slowly made its way into pop music in the late '70s, but not through the *original* artists, and rap had appeared in Jamaican reggae *long* before it morphed into so-called "urban" music. Likewise, punk music seemed to be reborn every decade, and find its audience of pimply wannabe English boneracks with epoxied mohawks and bits of metal studding their anatomies. By early in the 2000s, though, the rock/rap hybrid had become mainstream rock, with Linkin Park among the best. My only reservation was that the style seemed to adhere to strict rules of rhythmic simplicity and repetition, so it wasn't really "drummer's music," in the sense of being active or adventurous. The great jazz drummer Tony Williams once remarked that rock drummers didn't play *drums*, they played *beats*, and that was too often true.

However, those simple, repetitious rhythms were certainly *effective*, and as I listened to Linkin Park's new album for the first time, my head was soon nodding in time, liking it. By the third track, "Somewhere I Belong," I knew they had beaten the sophomore blues, and had made another great, fresh record. Their chosen blend of influences and abilities seemed to reach a perfect balance in "Easier to Run," and as I rocked along with it, I smiled with the recognition of sincerity, youthful energy and excellence in action (thinking as I listened to the one vocalist who shredded his voice so alarmingly, "He won't be singing *that* part when he's 40" — but of course he wouldn't, and shouldn't, care about that now). The Real Thing. The *Brave* Thing.

Despite the formulaic cynicism of modern entertainment, real, brave music could still be made, and become successful, and it was obvious even from the cover art and liner notes on *Meteora* that Linkin Park were trying to make *art*, not just entertainment. Their previous album, *Hybrid Theory*, had played regularly on my bus after shows during the *Vapor Trails* tour, and that was another critical type of traveling music.

At the end of a show on the last two tours, when I was traveling with my own bus and motorcycles, at the end of the show I performed what is called "a bolt." After the burnout ending and final crash of the encore, I put down my sticks on the floor tom to my right, waved to the audience, then ran straight off the stage, through the backstage corridors and stairways, and into the bus. Dave the driver followed the police escort out of the congestion of the parking lot and onto the freeway, while I balanced against the wall of the rear stateroom, struggling out of my sweaty clothes and into dry ones, then returning to the front lounge to join Michael, my riding partner for that tour.

My riding partner from the *Test for Echo* tour, Brutus, had not only suffered through two years in various jails in the U.S. and Canada, but was now labeled as a "convicted felon," and banned for life from entering the United States (even while, as Brutus was released in 2001, dozens of soon-to-be terrorists were moving freely around the country, and taking their pilot training). When we started planning the *Vapor Trails* tour, I wondered what to do. I was certainly used to riding around America on my own by then, but on a concert tour, the risk of having a breakdown or flat tire that might make me late for the show (or even late for soundcheck) was too great — I needed a backup, a riding partner, if for no other reason than to "commandeer" his machine if necessary, and get to the show.

When I first moved to Los Angeles in early 2000, a friend recommended Michael to help me set up a "secure" home there, to protect my privacy from invasive fans, and to keep my address, phones, utility bills and such anonymous. In his early 30s, Michael was a private detective specializing in such security matters, as well as computer crimes, and he and I became friends. Michael had done a little motorcycling in past years, and was thinking about getting into it again. Seeing a possibility, I encouraged him to buy a BMW R1150GS like mine (replacing the *Ghost Rider* bike, an R1100GS, which had passed 100,000 miles, and would serve as backup on the tour), and arranged for him to be hired for the *Vapor Trails* tour as the band's security director — and my riding partner.

That last job description was a difficult position to fill, in many ways. Not least, by the time I came running onto the bus, he should already have poured me a glass of The Macallan over three ice cubes. Dried off and changed, I would sip that glass of whiskey and light that first delicious cigarette, and slowly, as we roared down the highway, begin to come down from the adrenaline of the physical effort, the mental focus, and the sheer fatigue of the three-hour show. That's when the right music was *really* important. Sometimes I needed the soothing mood of one of Frank's records, other times I'd be all vibed up and want to hear Linkin Park, or Michael's and my official theme song on the *Vapor Trails* tour, Limp Bizkit's "Keep On Rollin.'"

Michael and I also sometimes listened to a series of CDs of mixed tunes I had programmed to be played over the P.A. system in the venues before our shows, and during the intermission between sets. Called "walk-in" music, it was another very important kind of traveling music.

I started making those mixes back in the late '70s, mainly because we had a sound man with questionable taste, and after hearing our audiences assailed by mindless heavy rock every night (even before *we* went on!), I decided to do something about it. It is a measure of the passing decades that the "ShowTapes" were made on cassette at first, then DAT (digital audio tape), and for the most recent tour, on CDs (now I call them, with tongue in cheek, "ShowTunes"). Next tour, no doubt they'll play straight off a computer.

I always thought of that platform as my own private radio station, a chance to reach thousands of people with songs and artists I liked at the time, especially the more obscure ones an American audience wasn't likely to hear on their local mainstream rock station. I also tried to program the music to follow the dynamics of the evening, from the time the doors opened until the anticipation was building just before show time, or for the intermission between an opening act and our show, or on the last two tours — when we had stopped having an opening act, to give more time for our ever-growing songlist — between our two long sets.

On those first ShowTapes, in the late '70s, I was mixing in a lot of the so-called "new wave" music of the time, Talking Heads, Ultravox, Japan, Joe Jackson, and the Police. We were touring in Britain once around that time, and our sound engineer told me that when a song by the Police came over the P.A., the English audience actually *booed*. Hard to believe, but so it was.

The cassettes from the *Signals* tour, in 1982, neatly hand-labeled on the spine, "Rush Radio," and with my drawing of the fire-hydrant logo from the album cover, offered a selection of lesser-known songs from that era, by New Musik, Simple Minds, King Crimson, U2, Ultravox, Max Webster, Joe Jackson, Japan, Thinkman, Go, XTC, Talking Heads, Jimmy Cliff, a couple of Pete Townshend's solo songs, Bill Bruford's jazz-rock excursions, and the ponderously-named-but-ethereal-sounding Orchestral Maneouvres in the Dark.

Ten years later, on the *Counterparts* tour in 1993, I was broadcasting DAT tapes with that tour's bolt-and-nut logo drawn on the spine. These ones included songs by Nirvana, Alice in Chains, Pearl Jam, Soundgarden, the Tragically Hip, Faith No More, Urge Overkill, Smashing Pumpkins, Roger Waters, Gene Loves Jezebel, Tom Cochrane, Curve, Big Country, Chapterhouse, and Temple of the Dog.

For the *Vapor Trails* tour, in 2002, I changed my programming style (or what the radio programmers call "format"), for the first time. As much as I had always resisted any form of nostalgia, the prevalence and popularity of "classic rock" radio were undeniable (at least one in every city), and it had somehow become more than just nostalgia. At its best (say 25% of what such stations played), it was the *heritage* of rock music, and might even be called *history*. There was also the splintering of modern music into narrow factions, especially on the radio. Compared to the variety of pop music I used to listen to on my transistor radio in the '60s — when AM stations tried to be all things to all people, from teens to old folks, and you might hear Louis Armstrong, the 1910 Fruitgum Company, and the MC5 on the same station — modern radio was fiercely segregated by demographics and "market segments." The gap between rock and hip-hop may have been invisible to a fan of Limp Bizkit or Linkin Park, but it remained *vast* between a fan of those bands and, say, Led Zeppelin, Radiohead, Madonna, and Frank Sinatra — you weren't likely ever to hear them on the same radio station.

Unless it was programmed by me. I wanted to juxtapose what I thought was the best of modern music with what I considered to be *real* classic rock — not just because I liked it in 1969, but because it sounded great to me *now*. This music was for a *rock* concert, and I left off the Sinatra and Madonna, but alternated The Who with Linkin Park and Radiohead, Led Zeppelin with Tool and the Tragically Hip, Jimi Hendrix with Vertical Horizon, and Pink Floyd with Coldplay. Once again, I was programming my own little radio station, to my own "format." Hopefully the audience appreciated the "ShowTunes" during the shows, and Michael and I certainly enjoyed them on the bus afterward.

As I drove toward the western suburbs of Phoenix, Linkin Park wound up their portion of the evening's entertainment, the last disc in the changer, and I decided I might as well stop for the night. It was getting late; I'd covered over 350 miles, and if I made an early start the next morning I could get through the congestion of Phoenix and make a good, long day.

On my "Ghost Rider" travels I had stayed at a tolerable Best Western in Goodyear, thirty miles west of Phoenix, but when I stopped there I learned their restaurant was closed. The man at the front desk said I could eat in the bar, but it was not inviting — a loud, busy place with lots of television screens blaring a basketball game.

I drove on to the next exit, saw the sign for a Ramada Inn, turned off and verified that it had a restaurant next door, and stopped there for the night. It was the kind of place where you park right in front of your room, which is always convenient, and I carried in my small bag and the CD case. As I relaxed and toasted the day with a glass of The Macallan from my well-traveled old flask, I removed the last six CDs from the cartridge and returned them to the album, flipping through and choosing the first six discs for the next day's ride.

Considering where I was, the lyrics to one song were already playing in my head:

"By the time —
I get to Phoenix . . ."

Chorus One

"Drumming at the heart of a factory town"

My song really begins on the family dairy farm, near Hagersville, Ontario, in 1952. Mom tells me they used to wrap me in swaddling clothes and lay me in a manger, but this was no messiah story; they just wanted me out of the way for the milking. Still, the dimly lit barn, redolent of straw and cow manure, was an early imprint, and later in life a dairy farm always seemed to smell like "home." Wherever I traveled, from Switzerland to Senegal, my deepest memories were triggered by . . . cow dung.

After a couple of years, our little family moved about 50 miles away to the "big city," St. Catharines, where my father became parts manager at the International Harvester farm equipment dealer. We settled briefly into an apartment on the east side, then into a duplex on Violet Street, in the Martindale area. Our '48 Pontiac had a circular chrome rim framing the plate-sized radio speaker in the middle of the dash, and I remember sitting in the front seat between Mom and Dad and "steering" the car with it.

In January of 1955, the stork brought my brother Danny, and sister Judy a year after that, and soon we moved to a brand-new split-level in the lakeside suburb of Port Dalhousie. (Youngest sister Nancy was a later arrival, and apparently something of a "surprise," born April of 1964, when I was eleven.)

St. Catharines is on the northern edge of the Niagara Peninsula, on the shore of Lake Ontario, with Lake Erie to the south, and the Niagara River to the east. The weather was tempered by all that water, creating a micro-climate around the fertile alluvial soils, a "banana belt" of orchards and vineyards. Its proximity to power and transportation also created an industrial belt, and many St. Catharines men carried their lunchpails to factories like General Motors, Hayes-Dana, Stelco, or Thompson Products, then, at the end of their shifts, drove their Chevies and Fords home to the ever-expanding suburbs of the postwar years.

Because of that common level of relative income, our subdivisions allowed more-or-less classless societies, in which most of the kids I went to school with had similar, modest homes, durable clothing, and simple, inexpensive toys. Of the two other classes, the relatively wealthy lived mostly in the privileged enclaves at the south end of St. Catharines, called Glenridge, while one of the poorer areas of town was a part of Port Dalhousie called "the Avenues," a warren of streets crowded with tiny, ramshackle houses that had once been summer cottages. Although most of us were part of the same blue-collar socioeconomic class, there did seem to be some kind of distinction; I once brought home a boy named Brian Jayhen, from the Avenues, ragged-looking and unkempt, and sensed that my mother seemed cool toward him, while welcoming other friends of mine, like Tommy Corbett, whose father was a traveling salesman, and Doug Putman, whose dad was a postman.

(One memory that demonstrates our economic status was the time my Dad gave Mom a choice of a vacation in Bermuda or an automatic dish-washer, and she chose the dishwasher.)

As my new hometown of Santa Monica was to Los Angeles, so my old hometown of Port Dalhousie was to St. Catharines (given fractions of scale of about a hundredth, as St. Catharines had a population of fewer than 100,000 in those days). Like Santa Monica, Port Dalhousie had grown as a waterside village, though for shipping rather than fishing. The Welland Canal was built in 1829 to allow sailing ships to travel between Lake Erie and Lake Ontario, bypassing Niagara Falls on the eastern end of the Peninsula, and the canal opened into Lake Ontario at Port Dalhousie. In the 1930s, the canal was made deeper and wider to handle larger ships, and moved eastward, bypassing Port Dalhousie. In 1961 Port Dalhousie was absorbed into St. Catharines, just as Santa Monica had been overtaken by Los Angeles.

For those hundred years, though, Port Dalhousie's small business area had catered to the needs of ships and sailors, and even when they were gone, some of the rough character survived. The bars in the hotels — the Austin, the Port, and the Lion House — were not frequented by the respectable citizens of Port Dalhousie, those who raised their families in the new housing tracts spreading to the west.

Our block had formerly been an orchard, and four pear trees remained at the end of our yard. We ate so many of those pears I have never been able to eat them since. Just behind us was Middleton's cornfield, a few acres in the middle of the block which, in late summer, became a cool green labyrinth, wonderful for hide-and-seek in the long twilight hours, or stealing through in the dark when we slept out in a tent in the backyard. My dad built us a swing set and a sandbox (painted International Harvester red), and with those pear trees to climb and the cornfield to run through, our yard was nearly perfect. We needed a pool and a trampoline, and maybe a roller coaster. But life was pretty good in our single-digit years.

In those days we didn't know about daycare centers or nursery schools, but Grandma Peart moved from the family farm in Hagersville to a house on Bayview, right across the cornfield, and she often looked after us, especially when Mom started working at Lincoln Hosiery, when we were still small. Grandma played hymns on the pedal organ, baked amazing pies and buns, taught me all about birds, made quilts with her friends from the United Church Ladies' Auxiliary, and wore her long gray hair tucked in flat waves under a net. She was a classic Puritan grandmother: wiry and iron-hard, a stern disciplinarian. Her chosen instrument was the wooden spoon, applied to my backside with enough force to break more than a few of them, but I also remember a thousand acts of kindness. And if she believed the injunction against sparing the rod, she could still "spoil the child" in other ways, and we also knew her innate softness, her pure gentleness of heart.

I remember staying at Grandma's house on the farm when I was very young, three or four, and at bedtime she would emerge from the bathroom totally transformed: leaving behind the severe cotton dress, the hard black shoes, and the strict hairnet, she tiptoed into the dark room on bare feet, wearing a long white nightgown, her hair down in a rope of gray braid, and the smell of Noxzema skin cream on her face. She seemed so frail and girlish as we knelt beside the big wooden bed to say our prayers: "Now I lay me down to sleep . . ."

I started kindergarten at McArthur School, under the gentle tutelage of Miss Olive Ball, and the class photograph shows me sitting in the front row scowling resentfully at the camera. My mother says I was upset because I wasn't allowed to stand beside Miss Ball, and when Carrie saw that old photograph, she claimed that exact same expression still darkened my face whenever I felt slighted by the world. (Yeah, so?)

The first time the school had a fire drill, and all the bells started ringing, I ran straight out of there, right past the ranks of students lined up in the playground. The older kids were waving and shouting at me to stop, but I kept running, speeding through the gate, and I didn't stop until I got home.

At the age of six or seven, I remember pushing my little red wagon down the street, one knee in the box and steering with the tongue as I pushed with the other foot (the way you do), pretending to go visit Brad when I had actually been infatuated with his sister, Pam, since kindergarten. I was singing "Tell Laura I Love Her," which was one of that strange genre of late-'50s "death songs," like "The Last Kiss," about a guy who doesn't have enough money to marry his girlfriend, so he enters a stock-car race with a "thousand-dollar prize," but alas, he is killed, and his last words are . . . "tell Laura not to cry, my love for her, will never die."

That same summer, my dad worked on the pit crew for a neighbor, Jordie, who raced a stock car at the local dirt track, Merrittville Speedway (with its big sign promising "Thrills! Chills! Spills!"). Our family went to the races at Merrittville every weekend that summer, and I loved the noise, the dust, and the spectacle of the brightly-painted jalopies racing around under the lights. The neighborhood kids used to gather in Jordie's driveway and watch the men work on the racing car, and make fun of Jordie's low-riding pants, pushing our own pants halfway down our hips to reveal our little butt-cracks and giggling, "Look at me, I'm Jordie!"

From Grades 1 to 5 I attended Gracefield School, just two blocks from our house. Gracefield's playing fields were still surrounded by farmlands and orchards in those far-off days, and a copse of trees which we called, poetically, "Littlewoods." Once I fell out of one of those trees, landing on a broken branch and tearing a gash in my inner arm, big enough that I could see the white bone. An older boy from down the street, Bryan Burke, had the presence-of-mind to rip off his T-shirt, wrap it around my arm and get me home to my shocked mother. Once Mom got me to the hospital and had it stitched up, the only permanent damage to my future drumming limb was a long, ragged scar.

My earliest effort at versifying was written in Grade 2, a four-page epic poem about a fox hunt, "The Little Red Fox." It hung on the wall of Gracefield School for years after that, on display mainly because it was so *long*, I always thought; it didn't seem to have any other special merit. I remember it began, "Once there was a little fox/ And he had the chicken-pox/ He was covered with red spots/ And all he ate was pans and pots." Acceptably lame for a seven-year-old, I suppose, though there was one line I still admire, "The fox woke up in the early morn/ You would too if you heard that horn!"

Reading became a big part of my childhood, and I would devour anything put in front of me — cereal boxes, comic books, Hardy Boys and Enid Blyton adventures (a good example of a Canadian childhood's blend of American and British influences), *Mad* magazine (which encouraged me to learn how to laugh at people and popular culture), Nancy Drew books borrowed from girl cousins, my parents' *Readers Digest* (always reading the jokes first, "Laughter Is the Best Medicine" and "Life's Like That," though life-patterns were also established by "Quotable Quotes," and "It Pays to Increase Your Word Power"). Our skimpy home bookshelves contained a set of Collier's "children's classics" that came with our encyclopedia, including fairy tales, King Arthur, and Greek myths, and I liked some of those.

One summer we shared a cottage on Lake Erie for a couple of weeks with some of my parents' friends, and one of the women left out a paperback called something like *Doctors' Wives*. Of course, I picked it up and started reading — an eight-year-old trying to comprehend why a woman named Grace would be looking at her breasts in the mirror and saying to her husband, "Mine are better than hers." Mom caught me reading it, and had words with the other woman who had accidentally left it out for me to find.

During that same vacation, I found what I thought was a bar of chocolate squares in a bathroom cabinet. I had never heard of a chocolate bar called Ex-Lax, but I ate it all, with predictable results. I learned another lesson about how all was not as it appeared in the grown-up world.

My grandmother started buying me the Thornton W. Burgess books about Paddy the Beaver, Danny Meadow Mouse, Reddy the Fox, and the rest, and I also remember loving some animal stories that were set in the ravines of nearby Toronto: *Wild Animals I Have Known*, by Ernest Thompson Seton. Again, lifelong enthusiasms started so early, and you can never tell which influences are going to be important — in Grade 8 I won a public-speaking medal with a speech about General Douglas MacArthur (opening with "Old soldiers never die"), which had been adapted from a comic book of stories about World War ii.

Every Tuesday I visited the little Port Dalhousie library, where I discovered and read through a series of books about Freddy the Pig, a bumbling detective and excruciatingly bad poet created by Walter Brooks (who also gave us, more famously, Mr. Ed, the talking horse). Freddie's humorous adventures were told with wit, irony, and sympathy, and I learned from those too. (After not hearing anything about Freddy the pig for forty years, and never hearing anybody else mention him, I had almost begun to think I'd imagined Freddy and the other characters on the Bean farm, like his human friend whose name also stuck with me all those years,

Mr. Camphor. Then around Christmas of 2002, I found a reissued collection of Freddy stories, and bought a copy for my niece, Nancy's daughter, eleven-year-old Hannah. And one for me, too. They were still good.)

All in all, Port Dalhousie in the late '50s seemed like a magical time and place, perfect for boyhood. Quiet streets for ball hockey, the lake for swimming, skating on Martindale Pond, the library, and hordes of other baby boomer kids around to share it all. We measured our lives not by the seasons, but by the ancient festivals — children are natural pagans. Winter was centered by Christmas; spring was Easter, and autumn was the magic of Halloween: dressing up as Zorro, or a pirate, or a hobo (I doubt that's an acceptable costume these days), and wandering the cold, dark streets with flickering pumpkins at the doorways and people filling our bags with loot. Whispered words passed among the ghosts and goblins about which houses were giving out fudge or candy apples (no fear of needles or poison in those innocent days — so tragic, and so *mysterious*, that it changed).

Summer, of course, was a long pagan festival all its own, triggered each year by the change from flannelette sheets and pajamas to cotton ones, and by going to Gus the barber for our summer crew cuts. When school was out, I would get together with a friend or my brother Danny, and we would hike or ride our bikes to Paradise Valley, out by Ninth Street Louth, or farther, to Rockway and Ball's Falls. Somehow nothing was more attractive than "the woods" — a bit of leafy forest, a stretch of running water, maybe a shallow cave in the ancient rocks of the Niagara Escarpment. This was Romance and Adventure.

Sometimes we would ride to the railway crossing at Third Street Louth, and just sit in the culvert all day with the smell of damp concrete and earth, listening for trains and running out to watch them go by. Perhaps that sounds as exciting as watching grass grow, except for those apocalyptic seconds when we stood by the track and felt that power speeding by so close, so loud, and so mighty that the earth shook and the wind roared.

We could explore along the wilder parts of the lakeshore, the steep, eroded brushy banks, and maybe sneak into old man Colesy's orchard to pilfer some apples or cherries (risking his fabled pepper gun), or just spend our days messing around down by the old canal and the Henley Regatta grandstand, or over by the sandpiles and the lighthouse. We would often see old mad Helen walking fast across the bridges, a blade of nose, protruding teeth, and a thatch of gray hair racing ahead of her old overcoat and blocky shoes. Helen was always muttering to herself as she stalked along, and adolescent boys, hiding under the bridge to listen, could imagine as much profanity in her gibberish as we did in the lyrics to "Louie Louie."

Then there was riding in the back seat of the red '55 Buick hardtop, squirming against Danny and Judy, all of us excited to be on the way to a drive-in movie. One time I remember we were allowed to watch the first movie of the double feature, but had to lie down on the car seats and go to sleep for the second movie, which was "only for grown-ups": it was *Splendor in the Grass*, starring Natalie Wood and Warren Beatty — which came out in 1961, so I would have been eight.

We were unrestrained by then-unknown seatbelts or car seats, and if we were driving home from visiting relatives or the drive-in, Danny, Judy, and I used to stretch out in the back: one on the floor, one on the seat, and one on the parcel shelf. Even if we woke up when the car pulled into the gravel driveway, we would feign sleep so Dad would carry us all to our beds.

But the rarest, most exciting luxury was going out for dinner at the Niagara Frontier House, a diner on Ontario Street which was modest enough, but seemed like the Ritz to me. Red upholstered booths, lights glinting on wood, Formica, and stainless steel, the Hamilton Beach milk-shake machine, the multilevel tray of pies and cakes on the counter, and the chrome jukebox beside each booth, with those metal pages you could flip through to read the songs. Although the highest luxury of all was being allowed to choose from a menu, I think I always ordered the same thing: a hot hamburg sandwich and a chocolate milkshake, and nothing has ever tasted so good.

Simple joys, and simple sorrows, yet felt as deeply as they will ever be. Like the old Animals song, "When I was young it was more important/ Pain more painful, laughter much louder, yeah."

Perhaps the greatest "pain" for me early on was the Canadian institution of hockey, for my skinny little ankles bent right over in ice skates, I couldn't skate backwards, and I never made a hockey team. A Canadian boy who couldn't play hockey, or any sport, was already beyond the pale. Still, I always had a friend or two: Tommy Corbett, Rick Caton, Brian Unger, Doug Putman. The real pariah at Gracefield was a poor little second-grader named Betty-Jane Prytula. For no reason other than childish cruelty, it had been decided by consensus that she "smelled," and every day she had to endure being the Untouchable, and witness the schoolyard game of passing around "B.J. germs." I still remember her sad, uncomprehending little face.

I did manage to get into a few schoolyard fights in my first couple of years at Gracefield — of the "Oh yeah?" "Yeah!" variety — all of which I lost. My very last fist fight ever was in Grade 3, under the tall, gloomy spruce trees (filled with grackle nests) near Gracefield School. With a crowd of kids around us yelling, "Fight! Fight!" I went at David Carson with my arms flailing until, in seconds, I was exhausted, and he pinned me down. When he let me up, I trudged home, tearful and ashamed.

Around that time I stayed home from school one day with a stomach ache, which became severe enough that my mom took me to the hospital. They wheeled me straight into surgery for acute appendicitis, my mom crying above me as she told me I had to have an operation (when I reminded her of that in recent years, she shook her head and said, "I thought I'd *killed* ya!"). However, for me to learn that in another hour or two my appendix might have burst and I would have been *dead* somehow made me feel *important*. The few days I had to spend recovering in that hospital were lonely and frightening, and I remember the bell tolling from the college across the valley, and calling my dad at work (Mutual-55091).

The man in the bed beside me was campaigning for a Canadian political party called Social Credit (a depression-era theory of governmental control of the economy), and he showed me a trick cartoon of a smiling man who had voted Social Credit, then turned it upside-down to reveal a sad-faced man who hadn't. For some reason I became enthused with his cause, and though I failed in convincing my parents to vote Social Credit (I couldn't understand why they wouldn't vote for his party — he was my *friend*), a few weeks later I listened eagerly to the election results on the earpiece of my little homemade crystal radio (a revelation when I put it together and it actually *worked*), and was disappointed when my friend's party lost.

Then there was television, in the days when we only got five channels, three American and two Canadian, all in glorious black-and-white. I remember Jackie Gleason's catch phrase, bellowed across the stage to his bandleader, Sammy Spear: *"A little traveling music, Sammy!"* Then spreading his arms and singing out, *"And awaaaay, we go-o-o!"* (The morning after his show, or Red Skelton's, all the kids at school would be acting out their skits.)

On "Ozzie and Harriet," I always hoped the episode would end, as it sometimes did, with Ricky Nelson singing in front of an audience of screaming girls, him looking all glamorously shadowy, in dramatic black-and-white (like a prototypical rock video), with stage lighting making it a magical fantasy. I especially used to love the song, "Travelin' Man," and though I haven't heard it since, in over forty years, some of the lyrics come back to me yet: "My pretty Polynesian baby, over the sea." Watching that performance, I was galvanized, and somehow I felt I *wanted* that — to be on that stage, in those lights, singing songs about traveling while girls screamed. That was 1961, I was nine years old, and, in the fullness of time, it all came true. (Except for the singing part.) (And the screaming girls.)

My mom was a big Elvis fan, and sometimes took me to see his movies (because my father wouldn't go), but I never wanted to be Elvis — especially the *movie* Elvis. Around that time I was taking piano lessons, first from our teenage neighbor, Donna Pirie, then from big old scary Miss Latcham, who lived in a big old scary mansion at the other end of town (in later years our family lived in what had once been the coach house for the Latcham mansion). I didn't enjoy the piano lessons much, and eventually started calling in sick and spending the lesson money on chocolate bars, but I still absorbed a grounding in basic theory that served me well in later years, especially after the mid-'70s, when I began to dabble in keyboard percussion with Rush.

When that magical little transistor radio came into my life, I began to hear "modern" music, mostly the pre-Beatles white pop music of 1962 and 1963. Danny Gould, next door, was a year older than me, and he talked me into my first record purchase — going halves with him on a Four Seasons LP, a greatest hits collection with "Sherry," "Big Girls Don't Cry," and all that.

In another early response to music that presaged my interest in the words, right from the beginning I began copying down the lyrics to my favorite songs from the radio, keeping pen and paper handy and waiting for a certain song to come on the air so I could catch another verse or chorus and scribble it down. Rhythmically, among my first impressions was the pure, physical *compulsion* in the response I felt listening on my transistor radio to the shuffle beat of a song called "Chains," by an early '60s girl group called the Cookies.

From music back to traveling, from transistor to bicycle, it was Danny Gould who taught me to ride a two-wheeler, running behind and pushing me across the lawn of his backyard, then letting me go on my own before I knew it. I'll never forget that feeling (though I couldn't know how much of my life I would spend balanced on two wheels).

It was also Danny Gould who imparted to me the mysteries of life, from a book his father had given him (maybe called "The Mysteries of Life"). He would have been twelve, and I was eleven, and in those innocent "Ozzie and Harriet," "Leave It to Beaver" days, I had no clue about sex. Thus I was shocked and appalled at the things he was telling me, all in such dry, anatomical words. ("Our minister does *that*? Our teachers? Our *parents*? Impossible.")

One summer, when I was eleven or twelve, Mom and Dad talked about getting me a summer job. Dad and I drove out Lakeshore Road and up the lane to Mr. Houtby's farm, and Dad got out to talk to him. In retrospect, I have to wonder if Mr. Houtby had some grudge against my Dad's farm equipment business, for next morning, when Dad dropped me off at the

farm on his way to work, I found myself sent out to weed a potato field —
by hand. After three days of crawling through the dirt on my hands and
knees under the baking sun, I received the princely sum of . . . three dollars. Even in 1964, that wasn't very much, and I didn't go back.

Next I tried a morning paper route, for the Toronto *Globe and Mail*,
which I took over from a local boy, and kept for two years or so, until I
handed it down to Danny. In the pre-dawn darkness of frigid winter, or the
early promise of a summer day, I carried my heavy bag of papers through
the alley and into the open beside Lakeside Park, exposed to the north wind
in winter, or the rising sun in summer. Passing the huge fans outside the
bars that expelled the night's collection of sour beer and stale tobacco
smoke, I left the folded papers in the hotels, whose upstairs rooms had
become musty-smelling residences for silent old men. When I told my
mom that one of them, old Archie, had come to the door naked, she looked
worried, but whether it was from innocence or intuition, I knew Archie
was okay. Then to the rough-looking little diners, and Latcham's grocery
store, then up the steep hill behind the bank to Mayor Johnston's house.

The Johnstons were the minor aristocracy of Port Dalhousie, with several branches of the family prominent in the town. Farther down Main
Street was the home of the kid I probably envied most when I was seven
or eight. Colin Johnston lived in a big house (no mansion, just a little
grander than our bungalows and split-levels), rode in his mother's white
Cadillac convertible (the classic '59 with the big tailfins and rocket tail-
lights), and sailed in his father's motor yacht out of the Dalhousie Yacht
Club, over on the "Michigan side" (so-called because many cottages on the
east side of the old canal had once been owned by Americans from
Michigan). One time Colin had showed me around that cabin cruiser, taking me aboard where it was tied up along the old canal.

The cabin of varnished wood and polished trim seemed like the ultimate luxury, a self-contained house inside a boat, and seemed to promise
such fun and adventure that I was overcome with the desire to be *part* of
that experience. I knew Colin was best friends with Bobby Lyons, but I
couldn't resist asking if I could be his best friend. He must have sensed my

shallowness, and stayed friends with Bobby Lyons. Colin's older brother, Roger, eventually took over their father's insurance and real estate business, and forty years later, still handled my Canadian insurance needs from the same little office on Main Street.

On Bayview Avenue, overlooking the lake, a modern ranch house on a large, open lot was owned by another Johnston, a legendary character called Captain Johnston, who was said to be retired from the big Great Lakes freighters. That was a job of unimaginable grandeur to us Port kids, who sometimes watched the huge ships go through the locks of the canal, feeling that strange sensation that the ships were stationary, while the ground beneath us was moving. Out on the lake in front of Captain Johnston's house, a few hundred yards offshore, a wooden raft had been moored.

We had all learned to swim at Mrs. Stewart's classes on the beach, and even in summer, the waters of Lake Ontario could be chilly on a breezy, overcast morning. Among a crowd of bony little kids, I stood shivering as rafts of green algae and rotting silver fish brushed my trembling knees. The lake was a toxic mess in those days, but nobody seemed to "know" yet. Bigger kids were taught to dive and swim off the pier, gradually moving out from First Lamppost to Second Lamppost to Third Lamppost. There was still a tall white lighthouse on the Michigan side, and in the corner where the beach met the pier, the water heaved with a solid mass of algae ("seaweed," we called it), dead fish, and pale, rubber tubes the older kids snickered at and called "Port Dalhousie whitefish."

The word "pollution" hadn't passed into common parlance yet in the early '60s, and it was only later in the decade when signs suddenly appeared on the beach, stern and scary messages warning swimmers that the water was polluted, and swimming was prohibited. Back then, everybody seemed to take for granted that the cause was *industrial*, from the steel mills in Hamilton, on the western end of the lake, or the paper mills in Thorold, but of course the problem was *sewage*, as it still is when the Great Lakes beaches have to be closed in hot weather.

On summer afternoons, some of the bigger kids used to swim out to that big raft off Captain Johnston's house, and one day, at the age of ten or so, I decided to brave the chilly waters and try to make it. I had done it once before that summer, but I was not a strong swimmer, and as I dog-paddled out from shore, shivering added to the exertion. Choppy waves broke in my face, and I choked a couple of times on mouthfuls of water. Finally I made it, and I paddled up to the raft, gasping, arms aching.

A bunch of the neighborhood bullies was playing there, boys from McArthur who were a couple of years older than me, wrestling and throwing each other into the water. They thought it was a good joke not to let me on the raft, and, exhausted, I paddled around it, from side to side. They would only taunt me, laugh, and push me away. I gave up and started to swim back to shore, while they lost interest and turned away again, back to their rough play.

It was too far. About halfway I ran out of strength, and in a panic realized I was going to drown. I couldn't move my arms and legs anymore, and I felt myself sinking. While I was going down that last time, I actually experienced the old myth: I saw my life pass before my eyes. I was so young there wasn't much to replay, but episodes, still vignettes like a slideshow, flashed in sequence through my mind.

I suppose I must have struggled and called out, as the next thing I knew I was lying in the sand at the water's edge. Two other kids I went to school with, Kit Jarvis and Margaret Clare, were standing over me, and I guess they must have pulled me out; I never really knew.

As for those bullies who nearly killed me, I owe them a different kind of debt, for that episode left a deep, lasting scar. For a long time, I thought I had all but forgotten about the experience, but years later, in my 20s, when the pressure and demands of touring with Rush began to weigh me down, I learned how the pathogen of stress attacked the weakest areas, physically (heart arrythmia, tooth and ear infections, lowered immunity), and psychologically. In airplanes, and even onstage, I would be overwhelmed by a sudden wave of anxiety, a morbid sense of being trapped, isolated, and unable to escape, and it would take me straight back to the memory of that traumatic episode. I would simply feel "too far from shore."

An obvious response was being uncomfortable swimming in open water without a boat nearby, but the association also materialized whenever my freedom of movement felt restricted. It was irrational, but irresistible, and the only good thing was that it forced me to learn to minimize stress and learn to *control* it for the rest of my life, as the only way to prevent those waves of anxiety from ruling me.

More anxiety was sown in my ten-year-old soul later that year, in the fall of 1962, when I began to hear about missiles in Cuba, our black-and-white television screen suddenly filled with deadly-serious speeches, threats, and warnings. The whole world seemed to have gone crazy. The grown-ups around me, parents and neighbors, were talking about the likelihood of a Russian attack on our neighborhood, because we were near Niagara Falls, which supplied hydroelectric power to much of the Eastern Seaboard. "They'd hit that for sure," I remember the man next door saying, and the image of bombs falling on Niagara Falls seared into my memory forever.

Movies about World War II were constantly shown on late-night television and Saturday afternoon matinees, as they were so much a legacy of the postwar era, but they tended to be bloodless and heroic, more propaganda than documentary. Up to that dramatic fall of 1962, the scariest thing I had ever seen was the flying monkeys in *The Wizard of Oz*. But I felt something different in the air, as I watched my father making preparations that now seem so touchingly futile: filling a corner of the basement in our split-level house with sleeping bags, canned foods, water, flashlights, batteries, and radio, as he tried to make preparations for his family to survive a nuclear bomb exploding 30 miles away.

The documentary film, *The Atomic Café*, gave a humorous spin on the early nuclear age, and on growing up in the '50s and early '60s with school drills to prepare for nuclear attacks ("Duck and Cover"), but I can now imagine how it must have felt to be a husband and father at that time, responsible for defending and protecting your family; it must have been *serious*.

And for those of us who were children then, we were surely scarred by that memory, by our introduction to that level of pervasive fear and incomprehensible threat. We couldn't understand it, but we certainly *felt* it, even the wordless vibrations, as only children can.

Similarly, I was standing on the steps of McArthur school when I heard about President Kennedy's assassination, in November of 1963. Although we were all proudly Canadian, and had even begun singing "O Canada" instead of "God Save the Queen," JFK's youth and charisma had impressed us too. I had made a project for school, a folder of words and photographs called "My Favourite President" (using the British spelling we were taught back then), and when my Mom asked why he was my *favorite*, I could only shrug — of course he was the *only* president in my memory.

So the thought that someone would, and could, kill the president of the United States was confusing, frightening, and terrible. After school, we watched it all on television, again and again, and a dark pall seemed to cover the world through the days leading up to the funeral, the black caisson, and John-John's salute to his dead father.

There was fear and darkness even in the idyllic small town of Port Dalhousie, and even in the schoolyard at McArthur. Anytime I hear sentimental nonsense about the innocence of childhood, I think of not only my own near-drowning, but the same gang of adolescent boys marauding through McArthur schoolyard, seizing some poor unfortunate victim and carrying him, spread-eagle (as the cry went up, "The pole! The pole!"), to ram him, crotch first, into the basketball upright. (Still makes me wince to think about that.)

Inevitably, that climate of fear in the schoolyard would influence my lifelong worldview, and brutes like that would color my impression of humanity forever.

Around that time, though, other events were about to transform the world, mine and everybody else's. I saw an 8" x 10" glossy photo of a group called the Beatles behind the counter of the Music Fair record store in the Fairview Mall (the first indoor mall in St. Catharines, greeted with excitement and novelty, it was even a new destination for hikes). The Beatles photo showed the Fab Four all cute and smiling, in their collarless suits and Beatle boots and "long hair," but it didn't look to *me* like a revolution — not until I watched the hysteria on television when they arrived at the New York airport (disillusioned later to learn the event was orchestrated from behind-the-scenes), and then on "The Ed Sullivan Show," in February of 1964. Then came the subsequent flood of British and American groups, introduced by Ed each week as "something for you youngsters out there." I was too young to be really enthralled by the *music*, but I was certainly impressed by the *excitement*.

In our little town of Port Dalhousie, the Catholic, Anglican, and United churches took turns holding dances for the teenagers and preteens, playing the pop records of the time, and providing a wholesome outlet for adolescent energies. I remember scraping up my nerve to ask Doris Beedling to dance, and I guess my childhood ornithophilia made me too "inventive" in my dance moves — at school the next day, the cool guys made fun of me, calling me "Birdman." As a general thing, I had learned to keep quiet and try to slip below the radar around the schoolyard, but the cool guys made a lot of sport out of me, even that early in my career as a misfit. For one thing, I had accelerated through two grades of elementary school, from four into five, then from five into six, and thus was two years younger than my peers, at that all-important cusp-of-adolescence phase, so fragile and insecure. I was definitely two years too young to be starting high school, a week short of my thirteenth birthday, and immature even for my *true* age. Not to mention self-conscious, uncoordinated at sports, and not equipped with the proper wardrobe.

A new style of teenage fashion, called "hellcats," was spreading from the teenagers down to the adolescents. The necessary uniform included madras shirts, white jeans, penny loafers (or high-top versions called British Walkers), hooded parkas, and certain "right" colors for sweaters and socks: bottle green, whisky, and cranberry. Expensive, fashionable clothes were not in our family's household budget, but one evening my mom traipsed all over downtown St. Catharines with me, searching for the holy grail of a pair of cranberry socks, so I could be *cool*. Eventually we settled on the closest we could find, but typically, they were not quite right.

On Saturday afternoons, preteens were allowed to attend the Castle (a "Knight Club for Teenagers"), where we danced to records — if a boy were brave enough to ask a girl, and if a girl were asked — and they sometimes had bands playing. (My reading habits paid off one afternoon when I won a door prize, a movie pass, for knowing the name of James Bond's American friend: Felix Leiter.) My mom made vests out of fake fur, like Sonny and Cher wore, for me and my friend Mike Lowe, and we wore them proudly to the Castle. Somehow, though, I knew that Mike looked cool, but I only looked like I was *trying* to look cool.

Educational theory has changed since those days, at least, and school boards no longer push kids ahead just because they are *bored* (wearing that "now what?" expression, no doubt), but they did have one enlightened idea: one afternoon a week a group of seventh and eighth graders, one from each school, it seemed like, took the bus to another school for a Major Achievement Class, where we were taught Shakespeare, French, and more advanced literature and poetry. The biggest advantage for me was being exposed to these other bright misfits, in the sense of affirmation, as well as being inspired by their relative sophistication. I learned from their talk about B-movies, apartheid, schoolyard references to the American presidential candidate, Barry Goldwater, as "Au-H2O," and my first dirty jokes.

With some other neighborhood kids, I spent a Saturday trying to sell subscriptions for the Toronto *Globe and Mail*, and sold enough to win two 45 records, one the Beatles' "And I Love Her," backed with "If I Fell," the other "World without Love" by Chad and Jeremy, and I played them anytime I was allowed near Dad's hi-fi. Even then, I was attracted by the dreamy sentimentality of the songs, the vocal harmonies, and their plaintive, wistful earnestness, but I seemed to feel the melodies more than the rhythm. As yet the drumming did not impress itself on me — I don't remember wanting to be Ringo; I think I still wanted to be Ricky Nelson.

The first time I was inspired with the idea of playing the drums was from watching *The Gene Krupa Story* on late-night television, at the age of eleven or twelve. The film's dramatization of Krupa's life (though far from factual) and Sal Mineo's convincing portrayal (coached by Gene himself) managed to make the idea of being a drummer seem exciting, glamorous, elegant, and dangerous. Even better than being Ricky Nelson.

My uncle Richard was only a year older than me, by some trick of familial timing, and I got all his hand-me-downs that smelled of my grandfather's cigars — but he was also a drumming inspiration. Richard played drums in a band called The Outcasts, young white guys playing Sam and Dave, Wilson Pickett, Otis Redding, and James Brown songs, in the "blue-eyed soul" style that was popular in Southern Ontario in the mid-'60s. Most of the "big" Toronto bands that we saw play in our high schools and dance halls, the Ugly Ducklings, the Mandala, Dee and the Yeomen, Jon, Lee, and the Checkmates, and a few years later, Nucleus and Leigh Ashford, combined Hammond organs, funky guitar players, bass players, and drummers, and James Brown-influenced singers.

Perhaps a certain Motown influence had spread up Highway 401 from Detroit, just as it had affected white rockers there like Mitch Ryder, Rare Earth, and Bob Seger. In any case, it might be said that for those of us raised on the painfully white pop music of the late '50s and early '60s, R&B music was the underground music, the alternative music of the times. I didn't think of it as listening to "black music"; I just knew I liked the rhythms, the intense, passionate vocals, and the way my pulse rate increased when I heard that horn line in "Hold On, I'm Coming," even played by a teenage white boy on a Fender Telecaster in my uncle's band.

R&B was definitely my "roots" music, the first music I responded to that way, and the music I played in many of my first bands. Interesting that my first favorite band, The Who, billed themselves early on as "Maximum R&B," and included a couple of James Brown songs on their first album.

But for me, the fire was definitely lit by *The Gene Krupa Story*, and there's often a clear difference in the playing and musical values of drummers who traced their inspiration to Gene Krupa or Buddy Rich, compared with those who set their childhood sights on emulating a simple rock drummer, like Ringo Starr, and stopped there. A matter of taste, perhaps, but also a matter of ambition — an accomplished drummer can play simply if he chooses, but it's quite a different thing from playing simply because that's all you know. As a young person attracted to the idea of being a musician, do you want to play the role, or do you want to *play the instrument?*

Obviously quality is not a popularity contest, and I often think of how Buddy Rich must have felt during the '60s and '70s, looking at the various musician polls and seeing himself way down the list behind so many callow beat-keepers, even as he struggled to keep his big band working. John Bonham, on tour with Led Zeppelin during the '70s, bewailed his own ranking in the *Playboy* polls behind Karen Carpenter (who, may she rest in peace, didn't even play on the Carpenters' records; it was Hal Blaine, a legendary session drummer, who, after playing on so many hit records that sold millions and millions for Phil Spector, the Beach Boys, the Byrds, the Mamas and the Papas, Frank Sinatra, Simon and Garfunkel, John Denver, and so many more, now lives on social security in a small town in the California desert).

The summer I was eleven, about to turn twelve, our family camped for a month or so at Morgans Point on Lake Erie, my Dad commuting the thirty miles back to St. Catharines for work. That's when I saw my first rock band play, through the raised shutters of a dance pavilion. Called the Morticians, they wore long-tailed, funereal suits, and traveled in an old hearse. I was too young to go inside the "teen dance," but I remember wondering why the drums sounded so *metallic* — I didn't know what cymbals were, but the drummer must have been heavy on them.

In any case, the seed had been planted by *The Gene Krupa Story*, and I started beating on the furniture and my baby sister Nancy's playpen with a pair of chopsticks (great attack on those plastic-covered rails). After all that, and my constant talk about wanting drums, on my thirteenth birthday my parents gave me drum lessons, a practice pad, and a pair of drumsticks. They said they wouldn't buy me *real* drums until I showed I was going to be serious about it for at least a year.

Every Saturday morning I took the bus uptown to the Peninsula Conservatory of Music (a rather grandiose name for a few paneled rooms above St. Paul Street). Taught by Don George, I practiced my rudiments and my sight reading, and at home, I arranged magazines across my bed to make fantasy arrays of drums and cymbals, then beat the covers off them.

One of Don George's other students was Kit Jarvis, the kid who saved me from drowning, and with whom I attended grade school and Cub Scouts (his father was "Bagheera," one of the leaders). After I had studied with Don for about six months, he told me that of all his students, only Kit and I would ever be drummers. That encouragement meant more to me than any I ever received.

Some of these memories were revived for me when I wrote a story for my hometown paper, *The St. Catharines Standard*, in the mid-'90s, called "Memories of a Port Boy." I included the near-drowning episode, and my rescuers, Kit and Margaret, and Kit wrote to me through the *Standard*. He had ended up working as an officer at the Fort Erie–Buffalo border, but still played drums part-time in local bands, though he had recently had to sell his drumset. I was glad to be able to show my appreciation to him by sending him a brand-new set of Ludwig drums. I wish I had found a way to thank Margaret Clare some way as well.

For my fourteenth birthday, after I had demonstrated my "seriousness" about playing the drums with a year of lessons with Don and nonstop beating on magazines and practice pad, my first set of drums arrived at our house. It was a three-piece, red-sparkle Stewart outfit (I still remember it cost $150), bass drum, snare drum, and tom-tom, with one small cymbal. It was one of those unbearably exciting days in life, waiting for them to arrive, then setting them up in the front room and playing and playing the only two songs I knew, "Land of a Thousand Dances" (as played by the number-one local band, the British Modbeats) and "Wipeout" (a young drummer's necessary calling-card in those days — the first thing other kids asked was, "Can you play 'Wipeout?'").

I rattled the house for a few days (and made my parents reconsider the wisdom of their supportiveness, I'm sure), then moved the drums up to my room, setting them up beside the pink-spackle plastic AM radio on top of the steam radiator. From then on I came home from school every afternoon and played along with whatever song came on (probably a good enough course of study, really, to build versatility, and to understand song construction), playing until Mom and Dad couldn't stand it anymore. (Though when any neighbors commented, they took *my* part, which felt good.)

I continued my lessons with Don George every Saturday morning upstairs at the Peninsula Conservatory of Music, and my Gene Krupa inspiration, using Slingerland Gene Krupa model drumsticks. When I broke the tips off them by playing too hard, and couldn't afford new ones, I would turn them around and use the so-called "butt-end," giving me the advantage of a heavy impact from lighter sticks. That became part of my playing style for the next thirty years, until, while working with Freddie Gruber in '94 and '95, I eventually switched back to the "proper" end of the sticks, as I developed a more subtle technique. (Plus, they were *giving* me drumsticks by that time, with *my* name on them.)

By far the most important experience I had at Lakeport Secondary School was my first public performance on drums, playing in a variety-show trio called the Eternal Triangle, with Don Brunt on piano and Don Tees on saxophone. I was fifteen, with my red-sparkle Stewart drums (though I had a hi-hat and floor tom by then), two Ajax cymbals perched way up high, and a "racing stripe" down one side of the front of the bass drum, made with electrical tape. We practiced evenings in a room at the high school, picked up and driven home by Don Brunt in his father's '65 Pontiac (often with a detour out to Middle Road, where he could get it up to a hundred and give us all a dangerous thrill), and then we performed in the annual variety show.

The atmosphere backstage was chaotic and electric, a bustle of people in makeup and costumes for the skits, everybody nervous and excited. In retrospect, I realize even that "backstage" feeling was addictive. One friend of mine from the MAC classes of Grades 7 and 8, Paul Kennedy, performed in a skit with Barbara Budd, and both of them ended up in show business too, broadcasting for CBC radio.

When the Eternal Triangle took the stage, one of our songs was an original number entitled "LSD Forever" (as if we had any *idea*), and I performed my first public drum solo. This changed everything. As a miserable failure at sports and "coolness," I had felt inferior, like a complete outsider, but for the first time I did something that actually *impressed* people, especially my parents and some of the other kids, and that experience illuminated something inside me for the first time.

When I told Paul Kennedy that I was auditioning for a group in his neighborhood called Mumblin' Sumpthin', he said, "They should audition for *you*," another encouragement I never forgot.

After the variety show triumph, when I had joined a "real band," I was able to convince my parents that I needed a new set of drums. I used the usual family strategy in such matters — I talked to Mom, and she talked to Dad. One Saturday, Dad met me at the Peninsula Conservatory of Music to look at a small set of Rogers drums, in a gray ripple finish. They were *so* beautiful, but they cost a fortune: $750. Dad agreed to sign for the loan if I would make the payments, $35 a month, and of course I agreed immediately. I still had the paper route, mowed neighbors' lawns, worked for Dad at the farm equipment dealership on Saturdays and holidays, and played with Mumblin' Sumpthin' every week or two at YMCA dances or Legion halls (our equipment often transported in Dad's pickup), so I managed to make most of those payments.

These days people sometimes ask me if I ever dreamed that one day I'd be playing in big arenas in front of thousands of people, and the answer is, "of course not." Sitting at the family dinner table, I was excited just to be able to announce that Mumblin' Sumpthin' was going to be playing at the roller rink in a couple of weeks, or a Battle of the Bands at the YMCA— that was "big time" enough for me. The way I thought the world worked, I just had to get *good*, and success would come, pretty much automatically.

I stopped taking formal lessons around then, when Don George quit teaching at the Peninsula Conservatory. His replacement didn't seem as "inspiring" to me, except for the day he showed me an album by a group called the Jimi Hendrix Experience, and said, "This changes everything."

Don had given me a good foundation for all I needed to know, and I carried on practicing and learning from all the great drummers I heard on records, and even in local bands. Moving into the late '60s, rock music was growing, *progressing*, and there were so many good players to learn from, especially in the Toronto bands, who *all* seemed to have drummers who were light-years beyond me.

Having started drum lessons just as I started high school, the two paths began to diverge radically. In the wake of my near monomania about drums and rock music, my academic career went straight down at the beginning of high school, from effortlessly being at the top of my classes, to the bottom — with the same amount of effort. I squeaked through Grade 9, but failed Grade 10, then squeaked into Grade 11, then failed it (though at least I was finally the same age as my classmates). I had stopped reading, except *Hullabaloo* magazine (later called *Circus*), my rock "bible," which I picked up the day it arrived at Mrs. Thompson's store every month. I had no interest in school, books, birds, or even cars, just drums and rock music. Mom and Dad were perplexed, but kept hoping I would "adjust."

I dutifully continued to attend Lakeport Secondary School, but I was always thinking about drums, drawing pictures of drums, and playing drums on my desk. I did have a few teachers who could make English or history interesting, and one English teacher, Miss McLaughlin, seemed delighted that I cared enough to argue that Mark Antony was the bad guy in *Julius Caesar*, not Brutus. That was an important lesson — it was okay to *disagree*.

But there were others, like Mr. Adams, a science teacher and self-important martinet who used to roam the hallways in a quest to eliminate the evil of untucked shirt-tails. Mr. Adams was disturbed by my tapping on the desk in class (as more than a few people were, including fellow students; a girl named Donna once threw a book at me), and when I told him that I really couldn't help it, it just "happened," he said, "You must be some kind of *retard*." He sentenced me to a detention in which I had to sit for an hour and drum on the desk. Some punishment. I had fun playing the whole of *Tommy* from memory; he had to leave the room.

I would also be unexpectedly rewarded by two subjects I chose as "options" in Grade 10, mainly because they sounded easy: Latin and typing. Later in life, when I began traveling the world, a rudimentary knowledge of Latin gave me a boost into the Romance languages of French, Spanish, and Italian, and when the world of computers and word processors dawned, I became forever grateful for that one year of typing instruction (the only boy in the class, I think, in those days).

I collaborated with one of the other "freaks," Joel Rempel, a Grade 10 classmate (who later began calling himself Iggy Stooge), on a music-review column called "Sound System" for the school newspaper. We championed our favorites and pilloried the rest as bubblegum merchants or mercenaries, and I remember one of the members of our little smoking-area gang, Margaret Ashukian, saying she was surprised to learn that I had "principles" — one of those back-handed compliments that can leave you wondering, "What *did* she think of me, and why?" When I met Margaret again, years later, as a successful musician, she didn't remember saying that.

Another important setting in my childhood and early teens was Lakeside Park, in Port Dalhousie. By the piers of the old canal, overlooked by the white and red lighthouse, amid lofty weeping willows and poplars, picnic grounds and pavilions, the black asphalt midway ran between dense rows of ten-cent games and rides. A merry-go-round, bumper cars, bingo, catch-a-fish, catch-a-bubble, little wooden airplanes spinning out from slender cables, trampolines, the "Caterpillar" ride, the "Hey Dey," the "Tilt-a-Whirl."

When I was fourteen and fifteen, I worked summers at Lakeside Park as a barker ("Catch a bubble, prize every time," all day and night), and for the old English couple who ran the catering for the picnic pavilions, scrubbing out huge urns of coffee and tea, hating the smell of both, and setting them up for family reunions, company picnics, and most dramatic of all, "Emancipation Day," a strange tradition when every summer the African-American families from Buffalo and Niagara Falls, New York, thronged to Lakeside Park.

There were no black people (African-Canadians?) in Port Dalhousie then, and only one or two families in all of St. Catharines. As John Steinbeck wrote in *East of Eden* about his hometown of Salinas, California, we were all more *proud* of them than otherwise, but we small-town kids were a little wide-eyed and curious at these "aliens" (as much because they were *Americans* as because they were "colored," as some people still referred to them, for despite being only about twenty miles from the American border, and growing up with American television and radio, we still considered Americans to be different, the "other," louder, brasher, richer, and — just maybe — cooler). We peeked at the crowded tables of black people from a distance, hearing the music and laughter, and were a little afraid, but there was never any trouble, except occasionally among themselves, with the odd fistfight and once, we heard about a knifing.

One summer I ran the bumper cars, which was exciting, but best of all was being part of the community of teenagers working there; for the first time I felt almost part of a "group" of friends. Even if I was on the fringes, and not accepted as one of the "cool" ones, I was still allowed to hang around with them. And there was music: some of the kids brought transistor radios to work, and the music of that summer of 1966 played up and down the midway. Bob Dylan's "Like a Rolling Stone" stands out as emblematic of that summer to me, and that song still comes up on my mental transistor radio sometimes. It was the longest single ever released at that time, more than six minutes, and was glued together so well by Al Kooper's rolling organ part and the elegant, enigmatic lyrics in Dylan's abrasive sneer, "Ah, how does it *feel?*" (What an influence Dylan had on *everybody*, though it often seems underrated now; the uncompromising intelligence, the poetic sophistication he brought to popular music, the pioneering use of electric instruments in so-called "folk music," and even the famous story of him turning the Beatles on to marijuana.)

We worked barefoot all day, walking around on that sunbaked asphalt until we could stub out our Export A cigarettes with the calluses on our bare feet. At night, when the midway closed, we gathered around a fire on the beach, singing along with red-haired Arthur's acoustic guitar, and — interesting to note — without drugs or alcohol. It was just before "all that," drug-wise, and the drinking age in Ontario was still twenty-one (though we could buy our Export A's freely from stores and vending machines).

The Lincoln Curling Centre was another social magnet in the mid-'60s, becoming the "roller rink" in summer, catering to younger kids on weekend afternoons, older teens at night. We skated to records, racing around the rink to fast songs for "Boys Only," or skated backwards to slow songs for "Couples Only" or "Ladies' Choice" (again, if you were chosen), and the roller rink also had live bands on weekends.

Once I was walking home from the roller rink, my skates around my neck, and I stopped at the A & W for Coney fries and a root beer. A carful of guys pulled up and one of them called me over to the passenger-side window, then punched me in the face. It was a glancing blow, but still: what was that for?

The Lincoln Curling Centre was owned and ruled by Jack Johnson, a steam-driven Armenian tyrant. With a short, powerful physique, fearsome temper, loud voice, and red-veined forehead, he cursed out hooligans and troublemakers in a hoarse bellow of profanities. All of us in Mumblin' Sumpthin' were so excited to play our first Friday night at the Roller Rink, but after the first set Jack Johnson came into the dressing room (the ice-making room with leftover benches from the rink) and gave us a memorable lecture.

He bellowed out a monologue about how we needed to play more familiar music, and when our guitar player, Eddie, said that we played the music we liked, Jack proceeded to explain why we should *forget* about doing what we wanted. He illustrated this intended life-lesson to us sixteen-year-olds with a loud, colorful parable about a prostitute he said he knew. "She says to me, 'Jack, I love to fuck, but I have to keep my tits and ass nice, so I can only do it when I get paid.'"

We looked at each other, bewildered by both the advice and the story.

Jack Johnson pointed at our bass player, Mike, and his fraternity jacket, and growled, "I was talkin' to one of your brothers out there. That guy shook his head and said, 'Jack, the guy's in our frat, but get yourself another band.'"

When the once-proud members of Mumblin' Sumpthin' climbed up onto that stage to play our final set, the crowd had dwindled to a few friends, and we were discouraged, dismayed, and crestfallen.

Unknown to me, though, a guitar player from Niagara Falls, Felix Elia,

had seen me play that night, and called a few weeks later, just as Mumblin'
Sumpthin' was drifting apart. He said that his band, Wayne and the
Younger Generation, was looking for a new drummer, and they played a
lot of the R&B music I liked: "In the Midnight Hour," "Knock on Wood,"
"I Feel Good," "My Girl." My mom drove me and my drums the 30 miles
to Niagara Falls and back for the audition, and then sometimes after that
for band practices.

The band's name was soon changed to the Majority, and thanks to the
keyboard player's father, a Niagara Falls policeman, we had a Hammond
organ and obligatory Leslie speaker, a P.A. system and small light show,
and not one, but *two* vans painted in the stars and stripes "Join the
Majority" logo, to carry us and our equipment to high school dances in
small Ontario towns.

The old dance pavilion in Lakeside Park had been closed since the days
of the big bands, in the late '40s, when steamers used to cross from
Toronto on summer weekends, but it was reopened for awhile in the summer of 1967, when I was almost fifteen, as the Beach Ball. Graeme and the
Waifers, a band that had moved to St. Catharines from the Prairies, used
to rehearse there in the afternoons, and they didn't seem to mind if the
local kids watched.

They were a "mod" group, and played the music that would become
mine. Through them, I first heard the songs of The Who, the Hollies, the
Small Faces, the Yardbirds, and others of that mid-'60s era, the "second
wave" of the British Invasion that reached me in a way the Beatles and
Stones hadn't. Graeme and the Waifers particularly emulated The Who,
and played some of their great early singles like "Substitute," "I'm a Boy,"
"The Kids Are Alright," and "My Generation." Sometimes they even kicked
over their equipment at the end, though carefully, I imagine, not wanting
to break anything they couldn't afford to replace. (Even The Who didn't
make money on tour for *years* on that account.)

One afternoon I watched Graeme and the Waifers work through an
original piece of music, conducted by the singer, Graeme (who seemed to
be authentically English, with an accent and everything, which gave him

great local credibility). This music was apparently going to be a dramatic opening theme for their shows, and again and again, Graeme counted the band through a series of tight, staccato punches and into a muted eighth-note bass part with guitar and drum accents, and I was forever impressed by the idea of creating your own music like that, and by how many times they repeated it until Graeme was satisfied they had it right (and until I could remember it to this day).

On April 7th, 1968, when I was fifteen, my parents drove me to Toronto and dropped me off at the Coliseum arena. I had wanted to get there in the morning, so I could buy my ticket (I think it cost $9), then wait all day and run in to get as close to the stage as I could for my first big-time concert. A local Toronto band called Rajah opened, combining East Indian members and influences, with electric sitar and such. Next up was the outrageous Detroit band the MC5 (Motor City 5), and they wailed with a kind of hysterical energy, sweat and noise and cool clothes, wild hair (especially Rob Tyner's proto-Afro), the scarecrow figure of "Brother Wayne Kramer," and at the end, a saxophonist with a mic stuffed down the bell of his horn.

Today the MC5 are considered a prototypical punk band, and their first album (which I bought when it came out later in 1968), *Kick Out the Jams*, is still celebrated as a kind of garage-band classic. At first the MC5 were all tied up in some political nonsense about the "White Panthers," dreamed up by their manager, John Sinclair, and I was proud to have the early "uncensored" version of the LP, which had "Kick Out the Jams" introduced by a yell of "It's time to — it's time to — *kick out the jams, motherfuckers!*" Later that was censored to "brothers and sisters."

The CD package for the MC5's *Kick Out the Jams* reissue, in the early '90s, included a radio chart from February 20th, 1969, for a Detroit AM station, which said much about the musical climate of those days. The playlist ranged from the bubblegum music of "Dizzy" by Tommy Roe and "Indian Giver" by the 1910 Fruitgum Company (the "teenybopper" songs my friends and I despised so much), the old-people's-music like Glen Campbell, Frankie Laine, and Dionne Warwick, to the "cool stuff" like "Hot Smoke and Sassafras" by Bubble Puppy, the Zombies, and

Steppenwolf. In the middle of all that, number two in fact (after "Dizzy"), was "Kick Out the Jams" by the MC5. Strange days.

The Troggs seemed relatively tame after the MC5, even playing the bump-and-grind anthem, "Wild Thing." They had nice, matching pin-stripe suits and neatly-trimmed hair, unlike the wild animals of the MC5, but of course they still moved the audience, especially with their summer-of-love anthem, "Love Is All Around," when the guitar player switched to an electric twelve-string, probably the first I ever saw.

Then came The Who, dressed in Late Mod, Keith Moon with the exquisite "Pictures of Lily" drum kit, black lacquer with artful psychedelic panels around each drum, including one reading "Patent British Exploding Drummer," and with the Victorian-circus-style logo on the bass drum heads. He played like a demon, making lunatic faces and throwing sticks and drums around, while Roger Daltrey lassoed his microphone, Pete Townshend windmilled his white Stratocaster, and John Entwistle just stood there and played. Pete Townshend did the talking between songs, opening with, "'ere we are in this . . . gawbage can," and introducing "I Can't Explain," "Substitute" (cheekily calling it "Prostitute," making the audience titter), "I'm a Boy," and still more R&B classics, like "Young Man Blues," "Shakin' All Over," and "Summertime Blues."

Then the climax, "My Generation," with Townshend silhouetted atop his tower of Hiwatt amps and smashing the white Stratocaster until the neck broke off, Keith Moon kicking his drums all over the stage as smoke bombs exploded and feedback roared. At that age I had never experienced any mind-altering drugs, or even been drunk, but when the houselights came up and I walked out of that arena, past the tiled fountain in the lobby and out to find my parents, my consciousness was *altered*.

Maximum R&B, indeed. (And that's one band that was never asked to do encores.)

So much I learned from The Who, from Pete Townshend's sense of song construction, the way he put together verses and choruses and his excellent "middle eights" (an interlude set apart from the rest of the song, so-called because it often consisted of eight bars), and his grand thematic ambitions and intellectual approach to life and music — he smashed guitars *and* read books! — to Keith Moon's way of framing the vocal parts with his manic, yet instinctively musical drumming. The sheer, unrestrained *energy* he introduced to rock drumming was stunningly different from anything that came before.

But perhaps the most valuable lesson came to me when I started to play Who songs in cover bands in my early teens, and discovered that I didn't *like* playing like Keith Moon. His style simply didn't suit my temperament, my sense of organization and precision, and although I loved the action and unpredictability of his playing, I didn't like the *chaos*. This would start me on the road to playing like *myself*.

As I approached my sixteenth birthday, I was the proud owner of ten LPs, lined up cover outward on a shelf in my room, alternating the one on display in front: the first three Who albums, *My Generation, Happy Jack,* and *The Who Sell Out;* two by Jimi Hendrix, *Are You Experienced* and *Axis; Bold as Love;* Cream's *Disraeli Gears;* Blue Cheer's *Vincebus Eruptum;* Traffic's *Reaping;* and the eponymous debut albums by the Grateful Dead and Moby Grape (I could reproduce their loopy, psychedelic logo *perfectly,* and did, along with the other bands', all over my schoolbooks).

Certainly I love music now, as an adult and professional musician, but these days music is only *part* of an active, busy life, filled with wide-ranging interests and activities. When I was a teenager, music was *all there was.* Recently I went back and listened to *The Who Sell Out,* after something like thirty years, and everything about that record reminded me how I *used* to love music — from the inside out, every note, every beat, every word, every *sound.* Beyond the melodies and rhythms, the actual sonic textures of the music had an effect on me that was transcendent — sensory, emotional, cerebral, physical. While I listened, it was the whole *universe* to me, and listening to that album again, I felt a connection to me then, what I loved and why, and how central that music was to my very existence. Some things are diminished by time, and by greater knowledge and sophistication, but not the memory of that love.

My walls were covered with posters of The Who, and drawings and mobiles I made of them, and I drew pictures of Keith Moon's drumkit on my schoolbooks, listened to their records constantly, and was as fanatical as a "fan" could be. I went to see them again in May of 1969, with a guitarist I played with in the Majority, Terry Walsh, and his wife Jill (with whom I also watched the moon landing that July), at the Masonic Temple in Toronto (called the Rockpile, for concerts). We arrived early in the day, then went running in when the doors opened, thrilled to be so close to the stage we were actually squeezed up against it by the crowd behind us. Later that year, in October, I saw The Who again, back at the Coliseum, when they launched the *Tommy* tour.

My fellow music reviewer and Who fan, Joel "Iggy Stooge" Rempel, was there too, and after the equipment-smashing finale, he managed to get a piece of one of Keith Moon's cymbals off the stage. Heroically, he broke it into three pieces, gave one to another "freak," Kevin Hoare, and one to me. I wore that jagged little piece of bronze around my neck for years.

In later life, when I complained aloud about young fans invading my privacy and upsetting my life (*knowing* no one ever wants to hear about that, but desperate for someone to understand *how I felt*), or about parents driving up to the door of my family home on a Sunday morning and dropping off their kids to get my autograph, thoughtless and uncomprehending people would ask, "Oh come on now, weren't *you* ever a fan?" Obviously, I was, even in the true sense of fan as "fanatic," but I never imagined trying to approach my heroes, never even *dreamed* of hanging around a backstage door, or trying to find their hotel. It was about the music and the image and the magic of it all, not about trying to invade their *lives*. So no, sorry, I don't understand.

Another life-altering experience occurred when I was about seventeen, and my Dad gave me an old minibike that had been kicking around his shop for a few years. I had my first adventures on a motorized two-wheeler, but alas, it ended badly. Riding along the sidewalk (wearing no helmet, gloves, or anything protective) down to Lakeside Park and along the deserted midway, still closed for the season (the Port kids all kept watch and passed the word when the rides were being prepared for opening day

— you could get free rides as the mechanics checked them out), I rode that little orange minibike to where the asphalt ended at the pier. I saw that a few cars were parked there, as I went to turn around and go back, but I hit a patch of drifted sand and slid sideways, my wheels rolling right across the side of a Volkswagen Beetle and dumping me on the beach (sand rather than pavement, luckily). As I traversed the Beetle's door, I had seen a young man through the window, reading a newspaper, then looking up in shock. I stood up, unhurt, he got out, disgruntled, and we regarded the damage: a bent strip of chrome hanging off the vestigial running board.

Fortunately I had a little money from my paper route and the occasional high-school gig with the Majority, and I was able to arrange to keep it secret, meet the guy the following week and pay for it myself. Forty dollars, I think it was. In any case, that episode had the result of making me afraid of motorized two-wheelers for the next 25 years.

Lakeside Park resonated in my life in so many deep ways, especially those fundamental exposures to music that would be forever important, and scaring me away from a mode of travel that would also figure so largely in my future.

It's all gone now. All that's left, apart from memories, is the old merry-go-round, the brightly-painted horses still cranking up and down to wobbly organ music, still giving five-cent rides of traveling music to new generations of children.

✪

Certain species of birds, like cuckoos and cowbirds, are called "parasitic nesters," and lay their eggs in the nests of other birds. Human sympathy tends to go to the hapless parent birds who exhaust themselves trying to feed the overgrown nestling. But what of the misfit young bird itself, growing up so different from all the birds around it? The old "Ugly Duckling" story, I guess.

(When I first brought Carrie to Toronto to introduce her to my friends and family, she had afternoon tea with my Mom, and asked her what I had been like as a boy. Mom sighed and said, "He was *always* weird.") Being a "cuckoo" in that atmosphere made me turn even more rebellious, more of a non-conformist and contrarian, firing in me a combination of native willfulness and an angry response to that stifling environment.

In those high school hallways in the mid-'60s, the conformity *was* stifling. Everyone dressed the same, in a uniform-of-choice — Sta-Prest slacks, penny loafers, and V-neck pullover vests over Oxford shirts — and at Lakeport High, the jocks and frat-boys were king. To be both a jock and in a fraternity was the ideal, to be neither, unthinkable. Even by 1967 and '68, when I was fifteen and sixteen, in our whole school there were only about three guys who dared to have long hair (below the ears, that is — though I combed mine up and pushed it behind my ears when I was around my disapproving dad). I was starting to wear bright-colored "hippie" style clothes, long-sleeved striped T-shirts, floor-dragging flared jeans, and in the hallways we endured constant verbal abuse: "Is that a girl?" "Hey sweetheart!" "Let's give *it* a haircut!" and other intelligent remarks. (For a while they called me "Scarecrow," I guess because of my bony frame, mismatched wardrobe, and scruffy hair.) Outside in the parking-lot smoking area, it was worse, feeling tense and watchful as the frat boys passed, with bullying threats and casual elbows and punches thrown at us. All because we were "freaks."

Conformity seemed to be everywhere in the St. Catharines of those days. Until I was in my late teens I didn't know a single black person (even then it was one guy our age, Ralph, who made everybody laugh by making jokes like, "Quick, get me some chocolate milk, I'm fading!"), and there was one Chinese boy at Lakeport, Ron Wong, and one Japanese guy, Ernie Morimoto (who I bonded with, as another "different" kid — he sat behind me in one class, and I made him laugh by wiggling my ears, while he could make his nostrils quiver). I didn't know what it meant to be "Jewish," and didn't think I knew any of them either (turns out I did, of course, but their Jewishness apparently wasn't considered "significant," or blameworthy). The Catholics were different somehow, with the Star of the Sea church so much more ornate than the plain Protestant churches, and I wondered why their kids were kept apart in a "Separate School," behind the chain-link fence I walked past on my way to McArthur, but it didn't seem to mean much; we all played together in the streets. A half-Chinese family lived across from us, and my mom once warned us never to tease their kids with remarks like (she whispered) "chinky chinky Chinaman." We had never thought of anything like that, but she must have heard other kids teasing them and wanted to make sure her children wouldn't. Well done Ma! But really, I never knew about racism or homophobia or anything antagonistic like that; there was simply no one to fasten it on, because nearly everyone was the same. Or pretended to be . . .

Like the town of Gopher Prairie in Sinclair Lewis's *Main Street*, people in St. Catharines in those days were nearly all decent, kind, and friendly — as long as you filled your part of the "social contract" by fitting in; as long as you weren't willfully different. It wasn't just the high school kids who made fun of me; as my hair got longer and my "get-up" wilder (running shoes painted in psychedelic designs with fluorescent paint, purple bell bottoms, a long black cape) I was stared at, laughed at, and jeered at by people all the time on the streets of St. Catharines. Nonconformity seemed to be taken as some kind of personal *reproach* by those willing conformists, and they would close ranks against you, and shun the "mutant." As Nietzsche wrote, "The surest way to corrupt a youth is to instruct him to hold in higher esteem those who think alike than those who think differently."

One cold winter afternoon I went into the Three Star Restaurant, across from the courthouse bus stop in downtown St. Catharines. When I sat down, the waitress said she couldn't serve me, and gestured toward the owner. I stood up and confronted him, a balding man with a European accent, and he said he didn't want any "longhairs" (again, below the ears) in his restaurant. Being naïve and idealistic, I couldn't believe what I was hearing, and I stood up and made a scene, called them Nazis, went and complained to the police and everything. Rebel without a clue.

Of course, other small towns were equally "intolerant," and when the

Majority traveled out of town to play high schools in Mitchell, Seaforth, Elmira, even as far as North Bay and Timmins, we sometimes ran into trouble with the local "greaseballs" (also referred to by us junior hippies as "lardheads," or "auger-bits," after their coiled and oily forelocks). Late one night, after stopping at an all-night restaurant along the highway just north of Toronto, we had to get a police escort to escape from a gang of such atavistic thugs waiting outside for us.

After a couple of years playing in various versions of the Majority, the band self-destructed for the last time, and I evolved a new strategy. I thought the best musicians in the area were in a band called J.R. Flood, but I didn't think the drummer was as good as the rest of them (I didn't think I was either, but that didn't affect what I *wanted*). I began urging the other members of J.R. Flood to give me a try, and finally we gathered in guitar player Paul Dickinson's basement and played together, and we really clicked. Not wanting to kick the other drummer out of the band, they decided to tell him they were going to break up, then later get back together again — only with *me*. Perfect!

Keith Moon joined The Who in a similar fashion, the story goes, though typically more flamboyantly than my quiet scheming. Apparently he went dancing up to the bandstand of a club in London dressed all in red, with hair dyed to match, and shouted to the band that he could do a better job than "that bloke," so they gave him a try. He bashed away madly, making a mess of the drummer's kit, but made enough of an impression on the other members to get the job.

I had started "skipping out" from school whenever I could get away with it, riding the bus uptown to hang around Ostanek's music store, talking with other would-be musicians about equipment, our favorite musicians, and the brilliant careers ahead of us. One time the conversation turned to drugs, at a time when hashish and LSD were just starting to circulate a little, and a prominent local singer named Alex Piccirillo, a little older and more experienced than the rest of us, told us how he had tried heroin once, and would never take it again, because "It was *too good*." I never forgot the power of those words, so much more effective than an adult saying it was "bad," and he scared me away from that vicious drug forever.

And around then, at seventeen, I was old enough to consider leaving school. J.R. Flood was working most every weekend, and the other members had quit school to be full-time musicians, so I began lobbying my parents to let me try being a full-time musician, "just for a year." If it didn't work out, I promised I would go back to school (looking back on that time, I can see how hard it must have been for Mom and Dad to deal with this latest weirdness). One day they came to the school for a meeting with the vice principal, Mr. Higgins, who was feared as a stern disciplinarian. I was nervous and inarticulate, but to my amazement, Mr. Higgins came out and said that I wasn't accomplishing anything there — wasn't "living up to my potential" — and he said that maybe I should be allowed to follow my own path.

Whoa! Yeah! Right on! I am out of here! Bye Bye!

And so my career as a professional musician began, with my bandmates in J.R. Flood, and we did work hard, practicing every day and playing weekends at high schools and small arenas. To get to band practice at Paul Dickinson's house, I had to take two buses, and the one over to Western Hill, a tough part of town, always had some *charming* characters — greasy-haired thugs with football-pad shoulders and shoe-size IQs. By then I was roaming around with a frizzy Hendrix perm, long black cape, and purple shoes — but I wasn't hurting anybody. I was just different, and they didn't like it.

To make matters worse, at a time when I was just starting to gain some confidence, virulent acne afflicted me for the next four years (what J.R. Flood's organist, Bob, jokingly referred to as my "adolescent complexion problem"). This only reinforced my self-consciousness and insecurity, and, I suppose, the Ugly Duckling story.

We began writing our own songs: intricate, quirky, often extended excursions in the Hammond organ, funky guitar style that was coming out of Toronto in the late '60s, growing out of the earlier "blue-eyed soul." Returning to my second-grade roots in versifying ("The Little Red Fox"), I tried writing some lyrics, and was thrilled to hear my words being sung for the first time. "Gypsy" was a slow song about a magical heart-healer

("Gypsy comes, Gypsy goes, wandering near and far, healing wounds, patching the scars"), and the other, up-tempo number was called "Retribution" (when I showed it to my always down-to-earth mom, she said, "what are you trying to do, write songs for college professors?"). That one was about a karmic afterlife, I suppose ("Retribution comes slowly, while death is so swift/ On a sea of retribution, my soul is adrift").

J.R. Flood had a fairly slick and ambitious manager, Brian O'Mara, who managed to arrange "demo sessions" for us with a couple of Canadian record companies in 1970. It was certainly exciting to be in a real recording studio (first at Toronto Sound Studios — coincidentally, where I would later work with Rush on our first three albums together — the other at RCA, later called McClear Place, where so many of our later albums would be recorded and mixed), but nothing came of that — the record companies "didn't hear a single."

Recently I dug out those ancient reel-to-reel mono tapes and had them "resurrected" by an archival specialist. How funny to hear myself at eighteen, with more ideas than skill, more energy than control, and more influences than originality — a raw blend of Keith Moon, Mitch Mitchell, Michael Giles, and Toronto drummers Dave Cairns from Leigh Ashford and Danny Taylor from Nucleus. The band was actually pretty good for its time, with complex, ambitious arrangements, and epics like the eight-minute "You Don't Have To Be a Polar Bear To Live in Canada."

Through the late '60s, FM radio had become a major influence on the music we *heard* at that time, but not yet on the music we could expect to *sell*. It was usually the big, successful AM stations that owned the obscure little FM stations, and apparently they used them largely as a tax write-off, and thus didn't interfere in whatever weirdness the FM jocks got up to — and they got up to plenty. The jocks tended to be individualists and "characters," and there was no such thing as "programming" or "format," they just played what they wanted, usually obscure album tracks and bizarre, "trippy" music, from Pink Floyd and the Moody Blues to Frank Zappa and Captain Beefheart. It was a strange and wonderful time for radio, and for music.

Gradually the FM audiences grew to where the advertisers caught on, then the programmers, then finally the record companies (always last to know what's *really* going on, and to jump on the wagon of bands as it passed by), and a new "formula" was born in the mid-'70s: "Album Oriented Rock," or AOR. This, at least, would give more bands a shot at precious airplay, without having to fit into the two-minute-and-thirty-second, widest-possible-common-denominator, keep-it-simple-stupid parameters of AM radio.

Not yet, though, in Canada in 1970, and the lack of a perceived "single" spelled the end of any larger opportunities for J.R. Flood. Local popularity wasn't enough to get a record contract, though that September we did play for 10,000 people at a rock festival at Brock University in St. Catharines, with headliners the Guess Who and Mashmakhan, the top Canadian bands at the time (they had hit singles). After my drum solo in Santana's "Soul Sacrifice," I was told there was a standing ovation (typically, I didn't notice — I was busy *playing!*). Later in the day, the bass player from one of my favorite bands, Leigh Ashford (a Toronto band who had been one of the opening acts for The Who the second time I saw them, in May of '69), stuck his finger in my chest and said, "You . . . were great." That felt good.

But, now what?

Nothing seemed to be happening for the band, and the other guys didn't seem to share my aching ambition. By early in 1971, we had built a local following who trailed us from gig to gig, but eventually what seemed like half of those "fans," boys *and* girls, were hanging around in our dressing room before the show. Even at eighteen, I thought that was unprofessional and distracting. When I suggested that we ought to *do* something, move to Toronto, or New York — hell, even *England* — no one took me seriously, or wanted to actually make plans.

At that time I was still under the naïve misapprehension that all I had to do was get *good* and I would be successful, but I began to think all that wasn't going to happen in St. Catharines, not with this band. Nobody else seemed to want to go places, do things, to *escape* that narrow world.

As Brian Wilson sang so poignantly on "I Just Wasn't Made for These

Times" (a fitting title for the soundtrack to my teenage years), "No one wants to help me look for places, where new things might be found."

No one wanted to help me look for those places either, and if I wanted to take that high road, I would have to go alone.

Verse Two

"Diving into the wreck, searching for treasure"

"By the Time I Get to Phoenix" was the day's opening song, but not just any version would do for this drive. I wanted none other than the eighteen-minute-and-forty-second, totally-over-the-top, horns and strings to the max, overarranged, overproduced, Mack Daddy, Isaac Hayes and the Bar-Kays, deep-voice-rapping, *Hot Buttered Soul* version.

I pulled onto the dark highway and accelerated gently, warming up the car's vital fluids, shifted up to sixth gear, then pushed the button to start the CD and bumped it forward to track four. A low, bubbling organ chord and a slow dirge of drums and bass introduced Ike's rich, evangelical voice, and he began telling the sad story of a young man "from the hills of Tennessee," who moved to the West Coast and married a lying, cheating woman. As Ike tells it, "She tripped out on him." He came home early from work one day, and, "I don't have to tell you what he found — *oh* it hurt him so!" Seven times he caught that evil woman cheating, and seven times he left her, and came back again. This time, though, he says he's going for good.

When I was an adolescent, riding to work at the farm equipment dealership with my dad driving the red and white International pickup, I remember hearing that song on the radio (probably Glen Campbell's version) and thinking that at the end, it ought to be revealed that the guy was on his way *back* to her. I guess I thought that would have been an ironic twist, but at that age I wouldn't have understood that she was a *bad* woman. But even then, long before I ever thought of writing lyrics myself, I seem to have been fairly critical — I remember telling my dad I thought it was dumb when Perry Como sang, "And I love her so/ The people ask me why/ I tell them I don't know." (I still think that's pretty lame.)

By the timetable implicit in the verses of "By the Time I Get to Phoenix" (written by one of the great American songwriters, Jimmy Webb), our hero from the hills of Tennessee, now living in California, was going to get to Phoenix when she was rising, Albuquerque when she was stopping work for lunch, and Oklahoma by the time she was sleeping. So he must have left Los Angeles about midnight, and he might have been trying to get through Phoenix at the same time I was, about 5:30 in the morning, only to find himself in bumper-to-bumper traffic crawling through the darkness toward the city. I had thought I was leaving early enough to beat the morning rush hour, but apparently Phoenicians started their morning commute exceptionally early.

I passed the exit for the Desert Sky Amphitheater, where we had played the previous summer on the *Vapor Trails* tour. The show before had been in San Diego, with a day off between, and I had wanted to try to get to the Grand Canyon and spend the night there, then ride down to Phoenix on the show day. Michael and I slept on the bus in a truck stop near Yuma, then got up and rode north toward Lake Havasu.

On a desolate stretch of two-lane highway, surrounded by the brown dirt of the cactus desert, Michael suddenly signaled, slowed, then pulled well off the road, behind a barrier of cactus and mesquite. He parked his bike on its sidestand and motioned to me to follow him. I was feeling tired and stiff that morning after a long, difficult show the night before, and I just wanted to sit on that bike and *ride*, so I was not very interested in whatever else Michael had in mind. He started walking into the desert, smiling and saying, "Come on — let's go shoot up a dead tree or something," and though I followed, I was downright crabby, sullen, and grumbling as my tired body trudged through the dry, heavy dirt.

"Don't be so enthusiastic," Michael said.

As a licenced private investigator, Michael was also licenced to carry a handgun, and I knew he always kept it with him, though I rarely saw it, and never touched it. I had never owned a gun, and had always had a healthy fear of them (like I used to have for motorized two-wheelers, though not because of any traumatic experience — they just scared me). But I must admit it was a kind of solace, traveling around well-armed America, to know that even if I didn't have a gun, I was traveling with a friend who *did*.

A hundred yards from the road, screened by ranks of saguaro, mesquite, palo verde, and cholla, Michael bent down and uncased his Glock, then began filling the clips with bullets. We agreed on a dead mesquite tree about fifty feet away, and took turns trying to plug it.

The elemental, boyish fun of it, and the sheer *American-ness* of it began to make me smile, and I fired away at that dirty, rotten, no-good dead tree. A year or two before, Michael had taken me to a shooting range in Los Angeles, my first real experience with a handgun, and had shown me how to hold the weapon, how to aim it, and how to squeeze the trigger and let the gun rise with the powerful kick as it fired. During a couple of early-'90s Rush tours I had carried around a hunting bow and a portable, straw-filled target, and show-day afternoons (riding into the arena by bicycle, so purposefully always early) I would find a back hallway or empty dressing room and shoot arrows for an hour or so, a relaxing and enjoyable pastime that helped to calm my pre-show anxiety. The shooting range had been like that, engrossing and challenging, only more explosive, less "zen." Being outdoors, in the desert, shooting that dirty, rotten, mother-raping villain of a dead mesquite tree was boyishly enjoyable.

Farther up the highway, in the pretentiously (or wishfully) named strip mall called Lake Havasu City, I led Michael across the reconstructed arches of the original London Bridge, and when we paused at the far end to put our feet down astride the bikes and take in this monumental anomaly, Michael turned to me and said, with good-ol'-boy enthusiasm, "Kin we *shoot* it?"

I shook my head sadly. "We ought to be able to."

Picking up Old Route 66 near Needles, we followed that storied "Mother Road" through Oatman and Kingman and Seligman, then cut north to the Grand Canyon. So late in the summer season, we were able to get rooms at the Bright Angel Lodge, right on the South Rim, and enjoyed our post-ride cocktails sitting on the canyon's edge and watching the sunset over that breathtaking view, the impossibly vast, luminous maw of brown and pink strata seeming to gather light and radiate it back, like heatwaves.

John Muir described it like this:

> In the supreme flaming glory of sunset the whole canyon is transfigured, as if the life and light of centuries of sunshine stored up in the rocks was now being poured forth as from one glorious fountain, flooding both earth and sky.

The sheer majesty of its size, depth, and range of colors hit my senses in a way I can only compare to a deafening, monster power chord, so vertiginous and overwhelming that I almost reeled backwards. Its sheer magnitude seemed to rise up at me, not like a chasm, but a sea of light, and "grand" seemed the proper word (though it was actually named after the original name of the Colorado, the Grand River).

Visiting that fabled scenery for the second time (the first had been with Brutus, on the *Test for Echo* tour, in late '96), I realized that my memory of its scale had diminished, as if mere memory couldn't hope to retain what the senses could hardly contain, for it was bigger, grander, and more spectacular than I had remembered.

The following morning, Michael and I made an early start, so we would have time to ride along the South Rim, then south through Flagstaff to a winding route through the mountains from Jerome to Prescott. We spent the last hour bogged down in the far-reaching suburbs of Phoenix, which always seem to sprawl over an unbelievable distance. In *Ghost Rider* I quoted Edward Abbey about Phoenix, "the blob that ate Arizona."

He was speaking as an adopted Arizonan, but I too have long had issues with Phoenix. One reason stems from a concert we played at the arena there in the mid-'80s. It was early in the show, and we had just started the song "Distant Early Warning," when I noticed that Geddy had stopped playing. I looked over and saw him staggering back on the stage, his hands hanging at his sides. Puzzled, I played on for a few seconds, thinking maybe it was equipment failure, but the fast-thinking Alex ran over to Geddy and guided him to a chair at the side of the stage. I stopped then too, and went around the amp line to stage left and learned that Geddy had been struck in the middle of the forehead by a disposable lighter, thrown by someone in the audience. Fortunately he was okay, just stunned, and after a few minutes he collected himself, we restarted the song, and finished the show. Some other audience members turned in the idiot who had thrown the lighter, and he was held backstage until after the show, when Geddy was asked what he wanted to do.

A moral dilemma, because of course you just want to have the guy *killed*, but if stupidity were a capital offence . . .

Over 30 years of touring, many things have been thrown onto our stages: tapes, letters, flowers, glow-sticks, CDs, a brassiere (once, at Alex), and worst of all, bottles. One of my drums used to wear a deep dent from where a heavy, square-edged Jack Daniel's bottle had been hurled out of the audience — imagine what *that* would have done to one of our heads. The weirdest thing is that these were all "friendly fire"; not thrown by enemies or critics, but by *fans*. It has been theorized that these demented individuals are motivated by a warped idea that such an act will bring them *closer* to their "heroes" — help them make some kind of contact. More insidiously, though, I believe it's an act of too-excited vandalism, and they don't really believe those figures onstage are actually *human*, and could be *hurt*. To the unthinking perpetrators, it's more like throwing a bottle at a billboard, say, or a distant streetlight.

In the end, Geddy just told the security people to let the guy go. He would have liked to confront him and perhaps share a few choice words, but therein lay another dilemma — it would have given the guy the satisfaction of actually *meeting* Geddy, a twisted reward for his idiocy, and a story to tell his friends. Best just try to forget about it. Only, as this story demonstrates, you never do.

Starting with the *Grace Under Pressure* tour, in the mid-'80s, I began to carry a bicycle with me on the tour bus, and enjoyed getting away from "the touring machine" and out into the countryside on days off, or even around the different cities on a show day. Having never been athletic as a boy, I had found that the stamina I had built up as a drummer suited me to endurance sports, like cross-country skiing, long-distance swimming, and bicycling. On that tour I accomplished my first Century (a hundred miles in one day), finally learned to repair a flat tire (a big confidence-builder), and started to ride from city to city sometimes on days off, if they were within a hundred miles or so, or hop off the bus at sunrise and ride the rest of the way into whatever city we were approaching (all-time favorite: Evanston, Wyoming, to Salt Lake City, by the "back way," Highway 150 to Guardsman Pass and Cottonwood Canyon, with two ten-thousand-foot passes over the Wasatch Mountains — a grueling day's ride, but so memorable I did it twice, on two separate tours). I especially liked having the whole entourage drive off to the next city after a show and leave me behind to make my own way. On the *Power Windows* tour in 1986, we had a day off between Phoenix and Tucson, about a hundred miles away, so I decided to stay behind and ride it.

It must have been late in the year, maybe November, because the streets of Phoenix were still dark when I set out from the hotel, around 6 a.m. And of all things, it was *raining*. That's one thing I hadn't expected, but I was prepared, and wore my rainsuit. However, the streets were slick, and when I had to cross some railway tracks, my wheels went right out from under me, and boom! — I was lying in the dark, wet street. Fortunately I was wearing long pants and a sweatshirt under the rainsuit, so I wasn't hurt, and there was no other traffic to run over me, but I was rattled, and it was a bad beginning.

I had thought there would be plenty of light from the city streetlights, but the way the south side of Phoenix was splayed among hills and mesas, there were some pitch-dark stretches where I could barely see the road, and could only *hope* the few approaching cars could see me. In the graying dawn, I finally made it to the other side of Phoenix, and onto the "back road" to Tucson, the Pinal Pioneer Parkway, a lonely two-lane through a desert of tall saguaro cactus. It might have been a lovely ride, except it was raining and cold, and *everything* seemed to go wrong. I got a flat tire, and crouched in a culvert under the road, out of the rain, to fix that, then the rain turned to sleet, and even snow. Though I had the rainsuit, I only had short-fingered gloves, and my hands became so cold and stiff that if I wanted to move them to a different position on the handlebars, I had to stop and painfully lift one hand with the other hand and physically *move* it. When I eventually reached the hotel in Tucson, I was as tired and miserable as I have ever felt.

Almost twenty years later, as I drove through that region, I thought I would retrace that route, this time in the comfort of my warm car. It had already occurred to me how different this was from two-wheeled, *al fresco* traveling of the bicycle or motorcycle kind; for one thing, I didn't watch the Weather Channel half the night trying to figure out what I was in for and how to dress for it. If it was cold, I turned the knob one way; if it was warm I turned it the other way, and if it rained, I turned on the wipers. All in the same wardrobe.

By the time I got *out* of Phoenix, the rest of Ike's *Hot Buttered Soul* had played through. I started back at the opening track, a lush, twelve-minute arrangement of another great song, "Walk on By," and the equally over-the-top, though less enduring song called, "Hyperbolicsyllabic-sesquedalymystic." (The poor back-up singers actually had to *sing* that.)

Selena once told me about a black friend at high school telling her he liked Isaac Hayes, and when she told him her father liked him too, the friend said (with ebonic gusto), "Your pops knows what's *happenin'!*" One of my proudest testimonials.

Now came a rolling, synthesized bass line with drum machine, and a crooning female voice mixed over keyboard pad, turntable scratching, samples, and proto-rap backing vocals. As ultramodern as all that might sound, the record was from 1991, *Blue Lines*, by Massive Attack.

(Interesting to note it was released in America during the *first* Gulf War, and out of record company nervousness, the band's name was briefly changed to simply "Massive.") The credits have a telling list under the heading "inspired by."

Isaac Hayes is on that list, coincidentally, as are less likely musical influences such as the Mahavishnu Orchestra, a '70s jazz-fusion group, their virtuoso drummer Billy Cobham (a big influence on me around that time), Herbie Hancock, John Lennon, the Neville Brothers, and Johnny Rotten's post-Sex Pistols group, Public Image Limited. Then there are the cinematic "inspirations," like Martin Scorsese and movies like *Taxi Driver, Blood Simple, Dog Day Afternoon*, and *Body Double*.

In any case, *Blue Lines* was a rare, cutting-edge piece of work that still sounded fresh and satisfying twelve years later, and I particularly loved their remake of the '70s R&B hit, "Be Thankful for What You've Got," opening with the line, "You may not drive/ a great big Cadillac," and the backing vocals chiming in, "Diamond in the back, sunroof down, diggin' the scene with gasoline, ooh, ooh, ooh." That wonderful slice of urban America "back in the day" always put a smile on my face.

There were a couple of other minor masterpieces too, like that opening track, "Safe from Harm" (the wailing chorus sung by Shara Nelson, "If you hurt what's mine/ I surely will retaliate"), and the same great singer on the haunting tour-de-force, "Unfinished Sympathy." (The word "haunting" seems apt, for some time in the late '90s I was walking down a London street near Hyde Park, and heard a few seconds of that song blaring from a passing car. It was one of those moments where I knew I *knew* that song, and liked it, but I just couldn't place it, and those few seconds of music played in my head for *months* before I finally identified it.)

The Pinal Pioneer Parkway, on a *sunny* day this time (compared to the cold, rain, sleet, and snow of the time I'd bicycled it), was a scenic delight, with little traffic. I cruised south at a moderate speed, taking in the wide views of saguaro cactus jutting up from the creosote bushes in tall, rounded spears, and thinking about that long-ago bicycle ride. I was also thinking about breakfast, for I had left the Ramada Inn without eating, wanting to get through Phoenix as early as I could, so I was on the lookout for a likely-looking place. I stopped at "Sunny Side Up," in Oracle Junction (near Oracle, where Edward Abbey had spent his last years, and where the Biosphere 2 project was centered, which I had visited late on my "Ghost Rider" travels).

The little restaurant was fairly busy on this Friday morning, with a few tables of tradesmen in work clothes, businessmen in short-sleeved white shirts, some older couples, a couple of rancher-types in bolo ties and cowboy boots, and a pair of cyclists in bright, road-racing outfits and cleated shoes. I sat at a small table and enjoyed what the menu described as the specialty of the Sunny Side Up — not fried eggs at all, but blueberry pancakes. Orange juice, coffee, and friendly service, and I was on my way again.

A jagged, ambient drum fill settled into a rhythm-section groove and eccentric guitar part: a Canadian group called the Philosopher Kings, another "old favorite," from the mid-'90s. Lots of great songs, interesting lyrics ("Now, she moved like a liquid/ through the boys of Mason City"), soulful vocals, some nice playing (like any music *this* listener is going to enjoy, the drumming is fine, solid and dynamic), intricate arrangements, good sound; it had it all. The Philosopher Kings (clever Platonic name, too) had been a serendipitous discovery for me; around 1996 I saw their video for "Charmed" as a between-show filler on the cable TV channel, Bravo. Immediately charmed myself, I took note of the group's name and bought their self-titled CD.

I don't know how it is for other music lovers, but it's rare for me to have a "committed relationship" with a piece of music. So many times I become briefly infatuated with a record, listen to it regularly for a few months, then grow tired of it, and never feel like listening to it again. Of course, I have a long list of "timeless classics," those I will always appreciate and speak well of, but even with many of those, once I come to know them by heart, I don't necessarily feel compelled to listen to them again. They are held in memory, complete in every detail of song and sound, like digital recordings. The exceptions seem to be the "aural feasts," the

Philosopher Kings, Massive Attack, Isaac Hayes, all that stuff, where the recordings simply sound so good, musically and sonically, that they are a pleasure to hear repeatedly, just as a *sensual* experience. And more, it's when the actual *construction* of the music — the composing, arranging, performances, and recording — is artful and subtle enough to bear repeated listening. Perhaps the difference is that you can't get to know such music "by heart," because it brings your heart, and your ears, something different every time, in line with the saying that you can't step into the same river twice.

Insights I gained from books on art criticism by E. H. Gombrich have served me well in deciding how I feel about artists of any kind. Professor Gombrich suggested judging a piece of art by two basic criteria: "What are they trying to do?" and "How well did they do it?" Simple, yet so profound, and the starting point for a reasonable assessment of any artist's work.

In music, the same principles apply, and the same two questions are asked. Expert listeners, appreciative but objective, respond to and assess the particular forms and expressions of music they are knowledgeable about and often love, and come to their best and most objective conclusion, which can range from "a masterpiece" to "a failure in almost every respect."

For expert music critics, well-informed and passionate fans, and those who love music as much as I do, as the old saying goes, "Taste is an acquired luxury." You have to care enough to *learn* to judge those qualities with some intelligence and discrimination. Early in my career I found it frustrating, and often hurtful, to be judged, misunderstood, and insulted by people who, if they were going to *help* me, ought to know more than I did about the music I wanted to make. Sadly, they did not.

In 1990, I wrote to the novelist Tom Robbins (*Even Cowgirls Get the Blues, Still Life with Woodpecker, Jitterbug Perfume*, etc.), to tell him I had enjoyed his latest novel, *Skinny Legs and All*, and hoped he hadn't been bothered by an idiotic review I had seen in the *New York Times*. He wrote back saying that he had long ago stopped reading reviews, and I understood. There were so few good, helpful reviews, that it was better not to read them at all than to spend too many hours sorting through the ignorant and nasty ones. I decided to do the same, and I've been spared a lot of grief since then.

The most objective, and perhaps useful, review I've ever read said simply, "People who like this sort of thing will find this the sort of thing they like." The most succinct was, "Nothing — well done."

Approaching Tucson, I cut back over to the interstate to try to take the quickest way through the city, but found myself bound up in a solid mass of slow-moving traffic again. Though Tucson had only a quarter of the population of Greater Phoenix, it was still a sizeable city of a half million people, and growing fast. Among its growing pains was highway construction, which slowed me to a claustrophobic crawl, surrounded by the hot brassy glare of cars and trucks. Not the ideal listening environment for Pink Floyd's mid-'70s epic, *Wish You Were Here*, with its long, textural movements that seemed to breathe open space and menacing skies.

The title song, and two of the album's longest pieces, "Shine On You Crazy Diamond" (Parts One and Two), were apparently addressed to one of the band's founding members, Syd Barrett, who had left early on, after becoming mentally unstable as a result of his overenthusiastic use of LSD. Other songs, like "Welcome to the Machine" and "Have a Cigar," reflected Roger Waters's increasing cynicism about the music industry ("You gotta get an album out, you owe it to the people/ we're so happy we can hardly count"). These themes would eventually grow into Pink Floyd's, and Roger Waters's, greatest work, *The Wall*.

As a musician who lived through the kind of touring life Waters used as background in *The Wall*, I knew too well the combination of exhaustion, confusion, alienation, and fragility he described so masterfully (even the "swollen hand blues" he writes into one song, so symptomatic of the touring musician's version of repetitive stress syndrome). Great lyrics and songwriting, wrenching vocals, and David Gilmour's sublime guitar work all came together on that one, and are certainly evident on their earlier records, too, notably their all-time best-selling classic, *Dark Side of the Moon*.

A show from that tour which I attended in Toronto in 1970 or '71 stands as one of my greatest concert experiences, along with another Pink Floyd show at the Rainbow Theatre in London in 1972. The chart-busting popularity of *Dark Side of the Moon*, and the subsequent arena and stadium tours, were the proximate causes of many of the responses described in "Welcome to the Machine" and "Have a Cigar" on *Wish You Were Here*, and later, *The Wall*.

At any rate (a *slow* one, crawling through Tucson), I had time to think about previous visits to Tucson, which in recent years had so often been a hub for different journeys. Back in 1999, I had been attempting my first return to Big Bend, on my "Ghost Rider" wanderings, working my way across Northern Arizona. One morning I rode out of Show Low (named for the poker game in which ownership of the town was won and lost, the story goes, and the main street was named after the winning card, "Deuce of Clubs"), riding south through pine-forested mountains, on a clear, cool day, following the fantastically curvy Coronado Trail Scenic Road, or Highway 191.

Then suddenly — I wasn't riding anymore, I was *coasting*. The clutch had failed (no fault of the bike's, it turned out, but a mechanic's error during a recent service in Montreal), and I was a long way from anywhere. Amazingly, my emergency cell phone worked way out there, and after a fruitless attempt to use the AAA service, I was able to reach the friendly service manager at the BMW dealer in Tucson, where I had stopped for oil changes a couple of times. When I told him my story, he responded cheerily, "Well, *that* sucks!" Then he gave me the number of a local "recovery service," who would come to the rescue and carry the bike and me to Tucson.

Though not for a while.

While I waited, I continued that letter to Brutus I had started in Show Low.

Nov. 16, '99
somewhere on U.S. 191

Dude —

We done *broke down!* A Brutus-in-the-Sahara type of dead clutch thing. All of a sudden, the bike was *dead*, the engine still running, but the driveline just making some nasty scraping sounds, and goin' *nowhere*. Up till then this had been one of the best roads *ever*, winding and winding through high pine woods (6–9,000 feet), with amazing views, and clean, fresh pavement. I was loving it, riding a smooth groove, thinking of our future recommendations, and — now this.

Bless the cell phone, but not AAA — who, I learn now, "don't cover motorcycles!" The number they give me for local towing rings off the hook. Thanks for nothing. My buddies at Iron Horse in Tucson come through, and somebody's on the way. But it's pretty far, so, while I'm waitin' here — on a *very* lonely road, ten miles north of Morenci (apparently — back a long way I passed a sign "Next Services 90 Miles," which would be about ten miles from here. Another sign said "Sharp Curves and Mountain Grades Next 90 Miles," and so it was. And in all those glorious 80 miles, I passed *one* car).

You can nearly always say, "It could have been worse" (*nearly* always), and this is no exception. Two o'clock on a sunny Tuesday, when the dealer is *open*, unlike, say, yesterday when I was riding into Show Low in the cold late afternoon, with darkness coming on [many dealers are closed Mondays]. Or — lots of other times, of course.

And there are worse places than Tucson to be stuck for a few days too, and hey — I've been wanting to see more of that town. Here comes my opportunity.

Sun falling behind a ridge, half moon in the east, occasional train horn in the distance, heavy machines working what appears to be an open pit mine way over there, and — *you're* with me, no? I've been here an hour now, and *two* vehicles have passed. We are, like, *out there*. And will be a while yet, I reckon. Wind picking up, time to dig out a sweatshirt. (And some whisky?)

Sure, why not. I'm not going to be riding! It's the good stuff, too, from the Gelson's market near Freddie's, in Tarzana (named after Edgar Rice Burroughs's ranch, which lay under the endless stores, restaurants, and services along Ventura Boulevard — impossible to imagine now). Freddie is banned from that Gelson's because he once bought a bottle of booze for some underage guys! What a character . . . Fortunately there's another Gelson's nearby, for it's *way* better than the other choice, Ralph's.

A couple of questions left over from your letter: tell me more about the Quiet Room. You haven't explained that to me, only that you were waiting for your "turn." What is it — the can? (I loved the way you described the Window, by the way, and your various "special moments" in the Yard. Funny they don't let you out when the weather is bad — afraid you'll get sick?)

Nov. 17, '99
Tucson

Well, three hours I waited out there, darkness coming on by 5:00, my cell phone battery dead by then. I was actually starting to look around for a place to set up my tent, when Chris with his little pickup and trailer showed up. "Am I glad to see you," I said, and he said, "I bet you are — I didn't know you were so far *out there*." I saw what he meant after we loaded up the bike and drove back — in the dark now — over about another 20 miles of *very* twisty road (fortunately my guess had been accurate; I was *exactly* 10 miles north of Morenci — the massive open-pit mine I mentioned — so he could find me, with my phone gone dead), then down out of the mountains to I-10, and still 90 miles to Tucson. About 180 miles altogether.

Since I'd always wanted to have a look at the *real* Tucson, I decided to stay at the downtown Holiday Inn, but I needn't have bothered. "Downtown" is nice enough, but there's nothing *here*. Banks, state and federal buildings (saw a "con-bus" at the courthouse, ach!), coffee bars to serve the bureaucrats, bus terminal, Amtrak station, a couple of music stores, piercing and tattoo parlors, and Walgreen's the only actual *store*, among a bunch of boarded-up windows. A little park nearby has yet another equestrian statue of our old buddy Doroteo Arango, a.k.a. Francisco [Pancho] Villa, which was apparently a present to Arizona from a former Mexican president.

Um — why?

In memory of his famous cry, "Let's go kill some gringos?" Or maybe because apparently he then bravely stayed *away* from that attack on Columbus, New Mexico, and ran away and hid from General Pershing's pursuing army?

Anyway, never mind that — I just learned that it looks like I'm going to be stuck here until at least Saturday (it's now Wednesday), and that's kind of scary. However, they offered to lend me a bike, so maybe I'll go to the Desert Museum, and up to Oracle to check out "Biosphere 2," and . . . read *Moby-Dick*.

In any case, I want to get this mailed to you, so you'll know whassup with me. Longadioso for now, amigo.

Down and out in Tucson
Ghost Rider

During my three days in Tucson, I had plenty of time to explore the city. I rented a car and visited the Saguaro National Park, the two historical museums at the university, and did some book shopping to keep me busy in the evenings (Tom Wolfe's *A Man in Full*, which I could hardly put down), and even found an unexpected treat on the wasteland of television, the three final episodes of the excellent documentary, "New York." The third one culminated in some great old black-and-white footage of the construction of the Empire State Building, which was part of my own family saga.

My maternal grandfather, Alec, emigrated from Ontario to New York in the late '20s in search of work, and ended up working as a rivet-tosser on that project, throwing red-hot rivets with a pair of tongs through the empty air between the girders to the catcher, his brother, who had to catch them in a bucket — all of that hundreds of feet above the ground. Gramps never talked about that much, though he never talked about *anything* much; from childhood I remember him calling me "Noyle," calling their dog, Toby, "Bunghole," and when he was irritated with my uncle (one year older than me, he was more like a cousin), he'd say, "Kee-*ripes* Richard!"). Years later, I bought Gramps the book of Lewis Hine photographs of his fellow builders, and when I visited New York City on the "Ghost Rider" trip, just a few months before his death (aged 93), I sent him a postcard of the Empire State Building. I wrote that they were looking for someone to do a few repairs on it, and were still paying $4 a day.

After being stuck in Tucson for three days in November of '99, I had some family commitments in California closing in, and I realized I was running out of time, and would have to give up on making it to Big Bend, and head back west. Things were also getting serious with Carrie at that time, and I soon found myself back in Los Angeles to spend some time with her. Then I was off again, riding back to Tucson to meet up with brother-in-law Steven, in his father-in-law's Hummer, and head down to Baja California. He and I had decided to kill off the dreaded Christmas season by four-wheeling around Baja for a couple of weeks.

During that Baja trip, and after, when I flew to Quebec to host Carrie for the Millennium New Year, I stored my motorcycle at the BMW dealer's shop in Tucson. In January of 2000, I moved to Santa Monica, first staying in

Carrie's small rent-control apartment, then, until we could find a bigger place to live in together, I moved into a tiny furnished apartment near the Santa Monica Pier (so often seen in movies and TV shows), beside the Hotel California (one of them, anyway). I could just glimpse the ocean from my kitchen window, and I could walk to the stores, to the Y, to Carrie's apartment. It was as simple as my life has ever been, and my possessions were simple too; apart from a few clothes, all I had were a portable stereo and a yellow mountain bike. (Two constants in my life, again: music and motion.)

My whole life had changed so miraculously ("Oh, sweet miracle"), and later that month I flew to Tucson once again, from my new home in Santa Monica, to pick up my motorcycle and ride it . . . home.

New home, new love, new life, and now, new car, and in March of 2003, I headed into a long stretch of open desert through eastern Arizona and New Mexico. Settling into a comfortable cruising speed of around 90 (with the radar detector on guard, though rarely needed), it was time for some more Big Frank, this time *Sinatra in Paris*, recorded live in 1962 with a small, six-piece group.

The liner notes tell the history of this show, which was part of an international tour for children's charities, apparently designed to restore Frank's public reputation after a "snub" by President John Kennedy, during Kennedy's visit to Palm Springs, California. Instead of staying at the home of his friend Frank Sinatra, a lifelong Democrat, highly effective fund-raiser for the presidential campaign, and Master of Ceremonies for the inaugural celebration (who was said to have built a new guest house and helipad in expectation of the visit), Kennedy stayed at the home of Bing Crosby, a Republican. Apparently this was advised by the president's brother, Attorney General Robert Kennedy, who disapproved of Frank's alleged links to organized crime. More realistically, perhaps he disapproved of the *public's* disapproval — there are enough stories of the Kennedy family mob connections, starting with the patriarch himself, Joe, who is said to have made his fortune on "liquor futures" during Prohibition, and rigged the Chicago vote in JFK's election (one quote of the day: "They stole it fair and square"). It also seems well enough documented that the Kennedy brothers contracted with mobster Sam Giancana, who also shared a girlfriend with JFK, to assassinate Castro.

In any case, even with Frank's small, charity-sized sextette (though not small in talent; they were all great musicians, including his longtime drummer, the solid and impeccable Irv Kottler, and the celebrated guitarist, Al Viola), *Sinatra in Paris* must be his finest live recording. All the classic songwriters are represented: Cole Porter, the Gershwins, Cahn and Van Heusen, Rogers and Hart, Johnny Mercer, and on and on. Songs I hadn't even known I *liked*, such as "Moonlight in Vermont," become radiant, lyrical gems, and proof again of Frank's ability to make any song his own, because he doesn't just *sing* it, he *lives* it. I think of another song I used to hear on my Dad's radio station that I thought was "dumb," "Little Green Apples," but when I heard Frank sing it, it was suddenly transformed into a sensitive, moving tribute to American family life. An even more striking example is the version of "Ol' Man River" on *Sinatra in Paris*, where Frank becomes the first-person storyteller of a black stevedore on the Mississippi, and wrenches the listener's heart as if he were.

The renditions of "My Funny Valentine," "Night and Day," and (of course) "April in Paris," are superb as well, and when I hear a live recording like that, even with its technical flaws (like Frank's microphone not turned up yet for the first few words of the opening song), or the occasional voice break, I am always amazed to think that this performance occurred just that once, just that night, and happened to be captured on tape. Pure magic. There is also something about it being recorded in Paris, that most magical of cities, back in 1962, that gives it a special patina of romance.

As Dean Martin once said, "It's Frank's world; we just live in it." For most of his life Frank Sinatra was the living epitome of "cool," and he even *died* cool, buried with a bottle of Jack Daniel's, a pack of Camels, a Zippo lighter, and ten dimes (his daughter Tina said, "He never wanted to get caught not able to make a phone call").

Cruising along, cruising along. There's the exit for Sonoita, where I turned off one time on my motorcycle when I had been intending to ride north, but was advised by the Tucson BMW people that the weather was cold and snowy up there. Then the exit for Tombstone, where I had ended up riding instead, and Bisbee, where I had spent a night and written part of a letter to my friend, Brutus.

Other memories were tormenting me that day, too. (And again I have to cite the Spanish word for storm: *tormenta*.) Sometimes when I was driving along a highway like that, I couldn't help but think of another highway, in Canada, on August 10, 1997, when Selena had been driving home from the house on the lake to Toronto. Something had gone wrong, and her Cherokee had veered into the median, and rolled and rolled. I had never wanted to know too many details about the accident, but that didn't stop my mind from *imagining* it, and for months after I had been tortured by endless replays of it every day, seeing that car rolling and rolling. From time to time it still happened (especially if I had to pass an accident scene — oh god), even after more than five years of grieving and healing, and I would have to try to shake myself out of it, steer my mind in some other direction.

During that journey I was also wondering whether I could ever stand to be a parent again, which Carrie and I had been considering. I knew it was the right thing to do, on every level, but I was still tangled in conflict over the fears, the anxieties, the fear of fears, the imagination of facing all that without my former faith that life was going to be *nice* to me. Normally a parent's natural fear is buffered by the equally natural reflex of disbelief — "It won't happen to me" — but I was no longer protected by that spurious defence.

As always, I could only try to Do the Right Thing, the criterion I tried to apply to every knotty decision, and I have yet to find any problem that wouldn't *eventually* yield to that process (though it might sometimes require a lot of thought). Certainly Carrie should never have to live with *regret*, not if I could help it. John Barth again, as quoted in the song, "Bravado," "We will pay the price, but we will not count the cost."

And alas, continuing that dark storm of imagination and memory, a cloud of sorrow loomed ahead of me on the calendar in late March of

2003. Selena's birthday was only a few weeks away, April 22nd, and I knew it was going to be an especially bad one (not that such desolate anniversaries are ever any good). She would have turned 25 that year, and it felt unaccountably different. She had died at nineteen, so the distance was increasing between the young woman, girl, child, and baby I remembered, and the full-fledged (ready to take flight), independent woman she would have become. I had always been able to picture her as she had been that last day, but now she would have grown beyond that, and I was tormented by how different that "imaginary reality" would be. I could no longer even *imagine* how she would be now, and that somehow took me down to a new level of grief.

The music helped lift me out of this abyss. It was "rock time" again on my CD changer, and guitars and drums lit up the speakers with another of my enduring favorites, *Fully Completely*, by the Tragically Hip. I remember the first time I heard them; it must have been 1989, September I think, and I was staying at my old log cabin in Quebec, working on the narrative of a bicycle trip over the Canadian Rockies from earlier that summer, taken with my brother, Danny, and some other good friends. *Raindance over the Rockies* was one of many privately-published travel-writing projects in my apprenticeship since about 1985, each more-or-less an "experiment" (this one pushing the limits of description — too far, but it was also the last step on that learning curve). Just a month later, in October of 1989, I would take the Cameroon bicycle trip that resulted in my first published book (though not until 1996), *The Masked Rider*.

Rush had just released *Presto*, and someone from the office told me CHOM-FM in Montreal was playing one of the songs, "Show Don't Tell," on a "Top Ten at Ten" feature, where listeners called in to vote for their current favorites. I turned on the radio one night to listen to the countdown, and I think we were number three that night, but it was number four that struck me: a Canadian band I'd never heard of, the Tragically Hip, and a live recording of a song called "New Orleans Is Sinking." As the band played a slow groove, the singer, Gord Downie, told a long, rambling tale that was thoroughly weird and bizarre — about throwing bodies out of his girlfriend's apartment window or something — and yet riveting.

Through the '90s the Hip became very successful in Canada, but never seemed to find the audience they deserved in the United States. That remained a mystery to this listener, for their music seemed accessible enough, smart and yet deceptively simple in construction, rhythmically straight-ahead, and lots of guitars; it certainly *rocked*, but regrettably, the Hip remained largely a Canadian phenomenon.

I think it was for our *Roll the Bones* tour in '91 that I lobbied our manager, Ray, to book the Hip as our opening act on a major tour of the U.S. and Canada, a tour that would have put them in front of more than a million potential fans. However, their manager turned the offer down, saying there was a "buzz" starting for the band in Europe, and the record company wanted them to go there. I don't know, but that may have been a missed opportunity for them.

The Hip's music was especially admirable because it had so much *Canada* in it, in Gord Downie's excellent lyrics, unique, intriguing, and sometimes obscure. Probably my overall favorite record of theirs, *Fully Completely*, from 1992, had some classic examples, from the opening track, "Looking For a Place to Happen," with references to the French explorer, Jacques Cartier, who visited Canada in 1534 ("Jacques Cartier, right this way/ I'll put your coat up on the bed/ Hey man, you've got a real bum's eye for clothes"), to the verse in "Fifty Mission Cap" about Bill Barilko, a hockey player with the Toronto Maple Leafs in the early '50s, down through "Wheat Kings" ("Sundown in the Paris of the Prairies"), and the song title "Courage (for Hugh MacLennan)" (MacLennan was the Canadian author of great novels like *Barometer Rising* and *The Watch That Ends the Night*). The Tragically Hip were as Canadian as . . . hockey and beer. And donuts.

In Wilcox, Arizona, I stopped for gas and refilled the CD changer, then carried on eastward, past the exits for Fort Bowie National Historic Site, and the Chiricahua National Monument, both of which were on my endless mental list of places to explore one day. Right now, though, I was making some miles, wanting to get well into Texas before that day was through. "Miles to go before I sleep," as Robert Frost put it in one of my favorite poems.

Time for another musical interlude with an old favorite, Roxy Music's *Avalon*, from the early '80s. It had been a long time since I had listened to that one, and again, it was unusual for a piece of music to endure so long for me. But, once in a while *Avalon* could still weave just the right spell, as much for its overall *texture* as the songs or performances (though they were good too, of course). I knew from people in the recording world who had worked on that project that infinite care had been taken in the making of it, in the sound and blending of instrumentation, muted guitars and mellow keyboards, soft-edged percussion, the warm drum sound and solid playing of Andy Newmark, and the velvety crooning of Bryan Ferry, in his mature transformation from "lounge lizard" into the ultimate "jaded sophisticate."

The easy groove of "More Than This" and "The Space Between," and the gentle, Latin trance of "Avalon," carried me into New Mexico, past Lordsburg, where I had spent a sad, lonely night after leaving Alex's place in Santa Fe, back in November of '99, and Deming, where I had spent a night earlier that same year, after riding up from Mexico. Both places had been datelined in "letters to Brutus," and he was on my mind that day too, for I was approaching his old territory, around Las Cruces and El Paso.

I had never wanted to know too much about Brutus's former enterprises (nor did he seem particularly keen to tell me, perhaps for my own protection), but I had gathered that his ill-fated choice of "career paths" had begun way back in his college days, in Newfoundland. Early on he had decided to confine his activities to moving the "herbal" product, and stay away from the guns, gangsters, and overall nastiness of the heroin and cocaine trades, so whatever he was up to seemed innocent enough to me. Brutus had also let on that while plying that particular trade, and arranging shipments from Mexico to Canada through the United States, he used to spend large periods of time in the El Paso area.

Since Brutus's long, harrowing incarceration that was part of the series of tragedies recounted in *Ghost Rider*, he had turned his talents to other, more legitimate fields, like carpentry, cabinet work, and building sets for photographic shoots, and became fairly successful at what Freddie would call "straight life." But during the years before, when we traveled together so much and became so close, Brutus had gradually revealed some of his past life, coming out in stories about his adventures and the other characters he'd worked with. When the band played El Paso on the *Test for Echo* tour, he took me on a tour of his old haunts, and to me, that netherworld — truly, the *underworld* — was kind of fascinating, and kind of frightening too.

Strange how I had ended up with no fewer than three friends who are convicted felons. None of them for violent crimes, but two for various kinds of corporate fraud, and Brutus with his "victimless crime" of organizing shipments of marijuana. In each case, they were my friends *before* they were convicted felons, but still, there must be some "fascination" there, some shared sense of being "outlaws," of rebelling against authority, conformity, and what used to be called the Establishment.

And how easily one can be led astray in youth. My childhood was littered with the usual puerile peccadilloes: throwing snowballs at buses, blowing up anthills with firecrackers, spending my Boy Scout dues on cigarillos (with my friend, Rick Caton, on a winter night, hiding behind a frozen tree and shivering as we puffed away and got dizzy), maybe pilfering a little money from my paper route, but nothing too hurtful or "delinquent." As a teenager, I was mostly a Serious Young Man, devoted only to drums and music. I never drank alcohol ("uncool" to us, anyway, in the late '60s), and my experience with drugs was limited to smoking lousy hash a couple of times, and pretending to be stoned (though I didn't know how you were *supposed* to act if you were stoned, so I just acted goofy, like everybody else was doing).

However, when I was about sixteen, I played in a band with a singer who was, I realize now, about the worst influence in my young life. He was a good singer, in the "blue-eyed soul" fashion of the day, charismatic, attractive to the girls, both conceited and deeply insecure, vain, a snappy dresser (an agent once remarked that he could wear jeans and a T-shirt and make them look like a thousand-dollar suit), and funny (though mostly in a cruel way). Also, he was pure *evil*. Or at least, he was a true sociopath, completely amoral — he had no sense of right or wrong.

He had endured a knockabout childhood, moving from Toronto to small Ontario towns with his divorced mother, and had ended up living in Niagara Falls. His mother's suitor at the time tried to win his approval by buying him an old MGA sports car, and one winter night he drove me around Niagara Falls on his "rounds." First he stopped for gas at Ralph Sauder's gas station, made fun of the poor guy's cleft palate, then drove off without paying. He parked at a church hall, in a lot full of frost-rimmed cars, where a week-night meeting must have been going on. He told me to come inside with him, and to my horror, he went along the line of winter coats in the cloakroom, rifling the pockets for wallets, and told me to start at the other end. *Jesus!* I was terrified and appalled, *knowing* this was really, really wrong, but such was his power that I pretended to do it, glad he didn't find anything. Later in the night he parked on a suburban street, and told me to follow him, only to start jimmying the lock of a basement door. *What?*

He led me into a low room crammed with musical equipment, and told me it was the home of another local musician, whom he called "Pizza Face," because of his severe acne scars. Striking a match, he looked around, then shook out the match and unscrewed a couple of Electrovoice microphones (ironically, the kind that had often been stolen from high school auditoriums by young musicians), and stuck them in his pocket. We heard a noise from upstairs, and beat it out of there, but man — was I scared! And *lucky* not to be caught, unlike another mutual friend of ours, who *was* arrested with him for stealing change out of a newspaper box. I never let myself be roped into one of his "adventures" again, but I never forgot what it was like to be influenced by evil, and even *attracted* by it.

I have also never forgotten a chilling vision I once had in his room in his mother's house in Niagara Falls. He turned to the little record player that sat on his dresser, maybe changing Mandala's *Soul Crusade* to the first Led Zeppelin album, and as I looked at his back, I had a vision of a knife planted in it. I didn't know what to make of that, but it scared me.

Girls were certainly attracted to that sociopathic lead singer, which puzzled me then as similar "bad boy" attractions do now. Despite women often claiming to be smarter and less shallow than males, when sexual attraction is involved, they are obviously no better at judging character.

In the early '90s, a particularly beastly criminal was captured in St. Catharines, after a horrific spree of kidnapping, raping, torturing, and killing young girls, and one of his former girlfriends was interviewed on television, saying, "It couldn't have been him, he wasn't like that." She was certain of his innocence because, as she said, she "would have known." That scenario has been played out many times, "when good girls fall for bad boys."

At one time in our teens, that evil singer went out with my girlfriend's best friend, who went all starry-eyed when he wrote maudlin, vacuous love songs for her ("I worship Melinda, she is my way of life," and who could ever forget the verse ending, "You will surely lose your mind, on some strange anvil block"); then when they had a fight, he actually kicked her *between the legs*. Unbelievable. And of course, she went back with him after that. Even more unbelievable.

Typically, he was also the first to start bringing drugs around. First it was marijuana, though I don't remember it having any effect other than feeling "naughty," but he also turned me on to LSD for the first time, when I was sixteen or seventeen. The two of us spent a whole June night on the open deck above the porch of an old house on Duke Street in St. Catharines, and it was a *powerful* experience. The world dissolving into patterns, my face touched by gentle rain, wide eyes enraptured by droplets on a perfect rose growing out of the vines on the wall, hearing the sounds of the night, the thoughts coming out of our mouths, all of it seeming *alive* in a whole new way.

But then, next morning I had to go to school and face a *math exam*. That is what is popularly called "a bummer." I failed miserably (though I always did at math).

When I last saw him, in the mid-'70s, I was playing in Austin, Texas, with Rush. I was easy to reach in those days, still staying in hotel rooms under my own name, and he called me. He was living in Austin then, still trying to get his singing career going, though supporting his girlfriend and her young child by driving carloads of pot between Florida and Texas. About fifteen years later, in the early '90s, I received a phone message from him, through the office, and, out of some twisted confusion of honor, guilt, and — I suppose — fascination, I called him back. He was still trying to launch his career, which had been his real motive for contacting me, it seemed, to send me his video and management information and see if I could help him get "discovered." I had to watch the video, just out of curiosity, and he was still playing the Jaggeresque, Jim Morrison (his idol) "bad boy" role.

Of all the so-called criminals I've known personally, he was the only one who was truly *evil*. You could see it in his eyes, even in photographs, a cold, dispassionate, reptilian glaze (maybe he *was* the Lizard King), and he was always the kind who wouldn't hesitate to hurt somebody else, if it served his desires, or even got a laugh. The others were all "loveable rogues," who just happened to live by different rules. Nobody would get hurt, except maybe some faceless corporation (in the case of the two convicted of fraud), and as human beings, and as friends, they remained as good as anybody, or better. Not the way I would choose to be, but I didn't feel the need to *judge* them. (Society took care of that, for they all did time behind bars — with the ironic exception of the sociopathic singer, as far as I knew. Maybe he eventually got that knife in the back I had envisioned.)

At a truck stop near Las Cruces, New Mexico, I stopped for a sandwich and a Coke to go, and carried on driving, crossing the Rio Grande as it flowed south from its headwaters in Colorado, through the middle of New Mexico, then curved southeasterly between Texas and Old Mexico, forming the Big Bend I was on my way to see.

Driving past Las Cruces brought back some touring memories too, as we had often played there in past years, in the university arena. Las Cruces also summoned the memory of an unpleasant fan encounter, and though it had occurred in the mid-'80s, it still made me feel . . . uncomfortable. After a long night's bus ride, I had dragged myself into the motel room around dawn, only to be awakened, what seemed like a minute later, by a knock at the door. I looked out through the peephole, saw no one, and opened the door a crack. There was a brown paper bag sitting there, with my name on it, and when I brought it inside I saw it contained a half dozen bottles of beer, and a note. As I unfolded the note, the phone rang, and a male voice said, "You got my present."

How did he know that unless he was watching my door? How did he get my room number, when I'm staying under a phony name? (One of a series of esoteric aliases I used over the years, mostly from old televisions shows: Larry Tate, Darren's boss in "Bewitched," Hank Kimball, the endlessly tangential agricultural agent on "Green Acres," Johnny Gilbert, the faceless announcer on "Jeopardy," Waylon Smithers, Mr. Burns's abused and adoring manservant on "The Simpsons" — that sort of pop culture icon.)

"Oh . . . yes. Um, thank you." (Alarms already going off in my head.)

"How do you like the beer?"

"Well, I haven't tried it. You know — it's early in the morning, I was sleeping, and I have to work tonight." (How should I handle this one?)

"I thought maybe we could get together today." (Why did he think that?)

"Oh? Well, no, thanks. I need to rest."

His voice cracked with emotion as he said, "But I gave you a present. I . . . I'm your *friend*. I can't believe you're treating me like this!" (Oh-oh.)

"I don't *know* you, do I?"

"Your, your *songs*, they're about *me*. And I know *you!* And I gave you a *present*." He was almost in tears now, and I was getting nervous.

"Well," I said carefully, trying to improvise a polite-but-stern brush-off, "I said thank you, and if you had left me alone, like you should have, I would have written you a nice note, like I always do. You gave me your address."

"But I bought you that beer."

I breathed a soft "*Jesus*," and tried to steer this away from me, a little angry now (or at least tired and crabby). "Look, to tell you the truth, I don't really like beer. I guess a 'friend' of mine would know that, but never mind — you can have it back if you want. I'll leave it outside the door."

And I hung up and put the brown paper bag outside again, then tried to get some more sleep.

But all that day I felt nervous and watched, spied on — *targeted*, as it were, by an obviously unbalanced, deluded person. (John Lennon was killed by a *fan*, after all, who was unhappy with the autograph Lennon had signed for him.)

When I carried my bicycle out of the motel and rode to the university arena, I felt tense and wary, the kind of helpless paranoia that wears at a sensitive soul. I hated the feeling of being "under siege" by strangers, especially on tour, when I was conspicuous and such people could figure out where to find me. Again, as a young fan myself, I had never dreamed of chasing after my own heroes, but as Rush became more successful, there were more and more young males lurking around hotels and backstage, waiting to pounce on me with feverish eyes, embarrassing adulation, and vague "expectations" that a forced encounter with me was somehow meaningful.

During our first years of touring in the '70s, our dressing-room door was always open to anyone who wanted to talk to us — we had no security guards or barriers around us. We still joke about the time a guy came to the door and said, "Is this Rush's dressing room?", and when we said it was, he marched in and said, "Well, I gotta piss!"

As our popularity gradually increased, it still felt wrong to ourselves to start putting up barricades, literal and metaphorical, between us and our fans. For three suburban Canadian kids, it seemed a self-important, elitist way to behave, alienating and unnatural, and we resisted that decision as long as we could, until the situation became impossible — until our audiences contained thousands instead of hundreds, and they all seemed to want to be in our dressing room. As I wrote in the liner notes for one of our early live albums, "*We* didn't change, everybody else did!"

Sometimes the encounters were scary like that, or like the time in Minneapolis when I arrived at the arena by bicycle, and I was alone in the dressing room in the afternoon, changing out of my riding clothes and getting ready to take a shower. A catering worker, a young man in his twenties, came into the dressing room with a tub of ice or something, and when he spied me, he froze and stared at me, silent and wide-eyed. I felt vulnerable enough, standing there in my socks and underwear, and then he said, "Apparently psychic powers run in my family."

He just stood there, staring at me, and again, the mental, "Uh-oh." I was all alone, and this guy was *weird*.

I struggled into my pants, as he went on, "I have always felt a psychic connection with you."

Slipping on my shoes, I got the hell *out* of there.

Sometimes, though, the encounters with strangers could be amusing. During my "Ghost Rider" travels, I had visited a BMW repair shop in Vancouver a couple of times without any fuss, when the third time one of the mechanics looked carefully at my name on the work order, and made the "connection."

He moved in closer, staring at me. "Say, are you who I *think* you are?"

Up until that moment, he had been a normal, pleasant young man to deal with, but now, I knew, things were going to change. I felt that strange combination of embarrassment and wariness, looking down and shuffling my feet, mumbling something like, "Oh, well, I guess so."

I could see his excitement growing, until he was all wide-eyed, tense, and shaking, "Oh my god, I can't believe I didn't recognize you! Oh my god!"

"Well . . . you know, it's no big deal. I'm just a regular guy."

He was trembling, his head shaking from side to side. "You might be just a regular guy, but . . . you *rock*, and . . ." He paused for a second, trying to think of something even more profound, but failed, "And . . . you *rock!*"

That made me laugh, and was a good story to recount later. When I traveled from Vancouver down to Los Angeles to visit my Canadian expatriate friends, a bunch of us were sitting around comedian Dave Foley's kitchen table one night, and he turned it into a catchphrase, turning to me at perfectly-timed moments and deadpanning, "You know, you rock . . . and . . . and you rock!"

On the eve of my 50th birthday, Michael and I were staying at the Chateau Lake Louise, having a drink after dinner, when the waiter said,

"Are you who I think you are?" With a wave of my hand, I said, "I'm not even who *I* think I am!"

Other such encounters could be innocent and friendly, like when someone came up on the street, stuck out his hand and said, "I don't want to bother you, but I love your work." Pleasant enough, and not at all "freaky," so it was simple to shake the guy's hand, say "Thank you," and move on.

For the most part, though, I preferred to simply avoid the whole issue — remain anonymous, if I could. Easier in a truck stop or small-town motel, or inside a motorcycle helmet, than backstage at a rock concert, and it was only on the *Test for Echo* tour, in 1996–97, that I started to evolve a touring style which allowed me both privacy and freedom. For a few years Geddy and Alex had been wanting to stop traveling by bus and start flying, which I had resisted, but if I had my own bus with a trailer for my motorcycle, the other guys could travel by airplane, and everyone would be happier. I could stay completely apart from the "circus," except during the actual show, then leave straight off the stage and drive away from the rest of the band and entourage, and the ever-widening ripples of hangers-on, to sleep in a truck stop or rest area, maybe with a day off ahead for Brutus and me, or Michael and me, to explore some back roads and offbeat destinations, like Punxsutawny, Pennsylvania; Deals Gap, North Carolina; or Teec Nos Pos, Arizona (the hot spots).

From Las Cruces it was only another forty miles to "the West Texas town of El Paso," where Marty Robbins sang about falling in love "with a Mexican girl," which somehow cost him his life, I forget why. Rush hadn't played El Paso on the *Vapor Trails* tour, but on the one before, *Test for Echo*, Brutus and Dave and I had eaten great barbecued ribs on the bus after the show, riding to Marfa to sleep and then motorcycle through the bit of Big Bend that would make me want to return someday to explore and enjoy it more fully.

Cruising through El Paso this time, the freeway ran along the Rio Grande and the Mexican border for a few miles. I passed a tall, glittering American city on my left, and a squat Mexican shanty town, Ciudad

Juaréz, tumbling down to the river on my right. The shabby little boxes crowded up against the border like a flood against a dam, against an artificial barrier to life's natural desire to move. The border as condom, controlling the passing of an unwanted population.

As I continued on Interstate 10 into the plains of West Texas, the final mellow chords of *Avalon* drifted away into the humming of the tires and the rushing wind. Back to guitars and drums now, and something a little more recent: *Everything You Want*, by Vertical Horizon. I had first heard the single of the same name on the radio back when I moved to Santa Monica, in January of 2000. I had just started to listen to modern music again, on the pop station in Los Angeles, KYSR, and one day I heard "Everything You Want," and immediately liked it — the music, the lyrics, the vocals, and the all-important "sound." I bought the CD, and discovered a variety of different songs, all good, and all with the same compelling quality of *sincerity*.

Years later, there would be an unexpected connection between that band and the car I was driving. At the time of first hearing them, I had told our manager, Ray, about this band I liked called Vertical Horizon, and not long afterward he happened to meet their singer and songwriter, Matt Scannell, at an industry function. Ray told me later that when he commented to Matt that I liked their music, "he was very pleased." Then he concluded the story in inimitable Ray-style, "You'd think I'd told him Pamela Anderson liked him!" Not long after that, the guys from Vertical Horizon had a dinner meeting with our Alex, to discuss the possibility of working together, because Alex was interested in producing other artists while we weren't working. In the end, that hadn't worked out, probably because the three of us were back together and working through 2001 and 2002 (thanks to Carrie helping to put *my* life back together). But I knew Matt had attended a couple of our shows on the 2002 *Vapor Trails* tour, and had said hello to the other guys afterward, when I was already on the bus and gone.

The automotive connection came about early in 2003, when I bought my Z-8 (through eBay) from a BMW dealer in Texas, who agreed to take my

Porsche 911 Speedster in trade. The sales manager asked if he could send a Los Angeles photographer over to take some pictures of my car for their advertising, and a couple of days later a woman called to make an appointment for the photo shoot. She asked if it would be all right if she brought her boyfriend, saying that I knew him; he was Matt, from Vertical Horizon. Well, I didn't actually *know* him, I said, but sure, I would be pleased to meet him, so Leah and Matt showed up at our house one afternoon.

Assuming she was a professional photographer, I suggested we use the back alley, where the light was better at that time of day, and said they could bring the equipment through the walkway. Matt held up a tiny digital camera, and said, "Here's the equipment," and I had to laugh. It turned out Leah was actually an actress (considering Ray's comment, ironic that at the time she was working on a show called "VIP," with Pamela Anderson), a friend of the owner of the Texas BMW dealership, who had called her and asked if they could do this as a favor. Matt, a fellow car-lover, took the photographs, while Carrie, who *is* a professional photographer, came out to say hello, and she and Leah were soon talking together.

I noticed the Rolex Submariner on Matt's wrist, and showed him the Patek Philippe I was wearing (my ultimate "dream watch," and a 50th birthday present from Carrie), and we learned that the first things each of us had bought after achieving a little success were a good car and a good watch. Leah wondered what it was about "musicians and mechanical things," and Carrie pointed out, perhaps correctly, that we just "liked toys."

Matt and his band were going through the follow-up blues, after having a successful record (their third) and touring for a couple of years behind it. They were trying to assemble a new album, but in the interim, Matt explained, their record company had been through two changes of "regimes." All the people they had established working relationships with were gone, and the band found themselves being micromanaged by the latest president, Clive Davis, through his "minions" — as the great mogul would never deign to meet with Matt personally.

For this listener, and perhaps for many others who made *Everything You Want* a multimillion-selling album and number one single, they had straddled the perfect line between rock and pop, both in Matt's song-writing and singing, and in the band's performances. However, now they found themselves being urged to be more "pop," to conform to the current state of pop radio — which, by 2003, perhaps reflecting the increasing tension in the "real world," had cycled into a saccharine, almost Muzak, state of blandness. (Driving along and first hearing a slow, pseudo-jazz ditty by Norah Jones, for example, I looked down at the radio, thinking I had accidentally switched to an easy-listening station. Nothing wrong with the *music*, if that's what she wanted to do, but it said something about a youth-oriented pop station's audience, and the times.)

At the record company's urging, Matt kept writing new songs, but Davis's yes-men kept sending him back to write more, saying they needed another "money track" (meaning the kind of simple, catchy, easily-accessible songs that were the staple of pop radio). As a listener, I had been struck by my first hearing of the song "Everything You Want" precisely because it *wasn't* the usual pop fodder, but was simply a great song, with a great sound, that happened to *accidentally* fit the radio format of the day, and was part of a well-rounded album of good songs. I was tempted to say these things to Matt, but I didn't feel it was my place to interfere. I sensed that perhaps he was trapped by being a genuinely nice and agreeable person, who wanted to please everybody, and would likely resist making demands or insisting on doing things *his* way.

As Carrie and I stood in the alley talking with Matt and Leah, each of us thought of inviting them into the house for a drink, but didn't like extending invitations without consulting the other, so we let them go. However, when Matt was thoughtful enough to send me digital copies of the Porsche photographs, I let him know that Carrie and I would like to get together with the two of them sometime. It took a while to synchronize all of our complicated schedules, but finally in March, not long before my journey, Matt and Leah invited us to Leah's house high in the Hills of Beverly. We had an enjoyable evening of good conversation, an excellent meal cooked by Leah, and red wine (when I e-mailed Matt about "what color wine" we could bring, he answered, "the preferred color of wine in this house is red!").

After another close listen to the Vertical Horizon CD on that driving trip, through Las Cruces and El Paso and into the plains of West Texas, I felt I had to speak out to Matt, and I sent him an e-mail about it.

> Speaking of art and music, I must confess that in our previous conversations, when you've been telling me about your troubles with the record company, the "new boss," and the constant dictates to go back and redo things in search of "another money track," I've had to bite my tongue a few times to stop myself from suggesting that you tell the record company to shut up and let you make your *own* record.
>
> Of course, it was right for me to bite my tongue — it's not my place to offer that kind of advice — but on the other hand, I like you *and* your music, so please accept these as thoughts from someone who *cares*.
>
> It seems to me that if anyone is going to decide what you should release to your audience, it's *you* (and the band, of course). And equally, if anyone is going to screw up your career, it should be you!
>
> All this meddling just seems *dangerous* to me, flying in the face of the obvious *sincerity* of your previous record, when it seems like you just made the best record you could, then hoped people would *like* it. I was listening to *Everything You Want* on my way across New Mexico and Texas, and it remains a really fine piece of work, with lots of great songs. For my money, they're all "money tracks."
>
> Maybe you're just *too* nice a guy, and want everyone to be happy? I can understand that, and again, it's not my place to judge or dole out unwanted advice. Forgive me if this seems presumptuous — I almost deleted it, but it has been on my mind quite a lot since we met, and it demonstrates the kind of meddling of the "business" in the "music" that always bugs me. But if this bugs *you*, please forget I ever said anything!

Fortunately, Matt took my thoughts in the spirit in which they were intended, and his answer expressed a healthy, *creative* response to the situation:

> Let me first say that I sincerely appreciate your thoughts on my current situation and in no way am I offended by your "two cents." In fact, I'm grateful for your insight. You're absolutely right — I do indeed find myself at times wanting to please everyone else, leaving me to be the unhappy one. I am constantly aware of how fortunate I am to be able to make music for a living, which sometimes keeps me from asserting myself as much as I could, or perhaps should. That's not to say that I haven't voiced my objections to this "record-making by committee" method. Indeed I have, and I find it incredibly frustrating to have my music become such a product. And yet that product is the very thing that sustains me. What a strange balancing act. I absolutely agree with you that if anyone screws up our career it should be us! We recorded a new song last week called "I'm Still Here" that is getting some passionate responses from The Powers That Be at RCA, and it may indeed become the first single. It's ironic that many of the lyrics were written out of distaste for this whole process.
>
> It means a lot to me that you would care enough to write down your thoughts on the matter, and I will keep your words in mind as I continue to deal with this complicated situation. Thanks.

What Matt said about the lyrics for "I'm Still Here" being inspired by *resistance* to the record company's meddling sounded a chord with me that was hopeful for their future, and echoed my own experience too. Early in Rush's career, in the summer of 1975, we made our second record together (the band's first, self-titled album, with another drummer, had been released just before I joined, in the summer of '74, then six months later we made *Fly by Night* together). Our second record was called *Caress of Steel*, and we loved that record so much we were sure everyone else was going to love it too. Only, they didn't.

In retrospect, I can see that *Caress of Steel* was opaque and obtuse, bizarre and esoteric, experimental and stylistically "all over the shop," as the English would say, and its sincerity was perhaps its only real virtue. We believed in it with all our hearts, and blamed the record company, whose people seemed completely apathetic, for its lack of success. We had a meeting with them to try to figure out why there had been so little response in radio play and sales, and I remember one of the "promo guys" saying, "Maybe it's just not in the grooves." We were outraged at such a lack of faith.

The tour that followed *Caress of Steel* was the lowest point in our career, a string of club dates and small-time opening slots across the U.S. and Canada that, even at the time, we dubbed the "Down-the-Tubes Tour." By the fall of 1975 we were unable to pay our crew's salaries, or our own, and as we convened to start work on our next album, things were grim. I was sharing a house in the country with some friends, driving a borrowed car to the studio in Toronto, and sleeping on friends' sofas between sessions. Management was grumbling that "We might have to talk about material," and we learned later that the American record company, Mercury, had written us off — literally. We did not figure at all in their financial projections for the following year. The fact that they didn't simply "drop" us, terminate our contract, was not an act of generosity or faith, but simple disorganization in the company.

Up to that point we had stubbornly resisted any compromise in our music, naïvely trusting that if only we could make it *good* enough, people would like it. We were certainly aware that other bands tried to mold their songs to the lowest common denominator, to make their music more radio-friendly, but we were idealistic and innocent, unable to imagine being so mercenary or cynical. We hated it when the business people called our music "product," talked about selling "units," and referred to a city as a "market." When other bands picked up that attitude, and even that language, we called it "the sickness." I remember hearing a "musician" we were touring with being interviewed on a local radio station before a show, and actually saying, "We haven't played this market for a while, and we have some new product."

In the face of all that negativity, our faith and determination were shaken. If something didn't happen soon, our careers could well have been over, and we didn't know what to do. However, instead of caving in and trying to make our music more "commercial," we got mad and decided to *fight*. That anger and rebellion went directly into our next record, implicitly and explicitly, and *2112* became our first real success. The lyrics of the side-long title track told a story about individual resistance to oppression (I remember management warning us, "The record company doesn't want a concept album," and thinking sardonically, "Oh, well then"), and the music was so imbued with that emotion of angry rebellion, it seemed to communicate itself to a young audience in a way no other theme (except sex) can do.

We had decided to stay on the high road, and fortunately, *2112* took off, selling more than 500,000 copies in the United States, earning us our first gold record. Now we had the foundation of an audience that was large, and loyal, enough, to insulate us from corporate interference, and allow us to keep recording and touring for at least another 27 years. Unconcerned about why we were successful, or how we could be *more* successful, we were driven by musical ambition and creative synergy, and the only question we worried about, as always, was "Now what?"

I could only wish the same for Matt and his band, who were now winding up on my CD player with a melodic, mid-tempo rocker, "Shackled." The traffic around El Paso had slowed me down a little, but now I was on the open road again, still pushing eastward. It was late afternoon, cool, windy, and overcast, and I had covered 500 miles since morning. The next major junction on the map looked to be Van Horn, Texas, which might be a good stopping place for the night. I'd have a choice of routes for the morning, and a relatively short run of maybe 300 miles south to my destination, Big Bend National Park.

Once again, I selected my current favorite CD, Linkin Park's *Meteora*, nodding my head to its insistent rhythms and enjoying it more with every listen. I set the cruise control on 90, radar detector on guard, and its sudden series of warning beeps saved me once, as I slowed and another car went racing past me — only to be pulled over a few miles later. When you're committing an innocent offence, it's good to have a good defence!

Cruising the I-10 "business loop" through Van Horn, I checked out the motel possibilities. A couple of Best Westerns at one end, and at the other, one of the old-fashioned, independent motels called The Sands. It had the requisite restaurant next door, and I thought, "What the heck," I'd give it a try.

When I stepped into the lobby, I saw that it was attached to the living room, with a television playing, and an old couple on the sofa. It wasn't a Mom and Pop place so much as a Grandma and Grandpa place, and Grandma came out to greet me. Well, "greet" was a stretch, for she just stood behind the counter and looked at me, without a word or a smile. When I asked if she had a room available, she said "twenty-nine dollars," and pushed the registration card toward me.

While a little concerned this rate sounded maybe *too* cheap, I decided to take the chance, and nodded okay. I went out to the car to get my reading glasses to fill in the card, and when I returned I tried to joke with her, saying, "When you get to be my age you'll find you need glasses for *everything*."

She only frowned, and growled, "Don't talk to *me* about *age*."

I tried to protest, "But — I was making *me* older than *you*," but the moment was lost. She didn't want to joke.

I parked in front of the room and shifted my stuff inside, noticing that the room was a *little* scruffy, but clean enough, and I decided I could endure the soft, springy bed for one night.

I turned on CNN to see if anything unthinkable had happened in Iraq, or anywhere else, and saw the usual bombs over Baghdad and succession of war experts and "embedded reporters" giving their opinions. The visual image of this war seemed to be through night-vision lenses. One general commented, "We need to attrit the Iraqi forces." The meteorology department gave a "Battlefield Forecast."

The reports were anchored by Aaron Brown, who, like all CNN "personalities," had risen to prominence during a crisis — in his case, the days following September 11, 2001. His on-camera presence came across as sincere, sympathetic, and down-to-earth, but what most impressed me was that he wasn't afraid to think out loud, rather than speak verbatim off the TelePrompTer, like most network news robots.

A political insider commented on the White House's reaction to all the second-guessing these experts brought to the day-to-day conduct of the war, saying they were greeted with "words you can't say on television."

Brown remarked that "The notion of 'words you can't say on television' is slightly ironic, when we're showing a *war*." Final analysis from *this* "embedded reporter": WAR IS MADNESS.

Brown also commented on the ever-growing SARS story, centered in Asia and, lately, Toronto, and how it would have been a "huge story" in other times.

I turned off the TV and went back to ask the cheery lady for some ice, then enjoyed a plastic cup of The Macallan while I cleaned the bugs off my windshield, then emptied the CD cartridge and thought about my music for the following day's drive. Those seemed to be the important priorities: a clean windshield and a full CD player. Music, and a clear view of the road ahead.

And The Macallan.

And dinner.

Chorus Two

"Drumming at the heart of a moving picture"

It is difficult now to imagine a time when it was rare to see rock music performed on television — an antediluvian era, as it were, before a flood of music videos became available 24 hours a day.

During the 1960s, if you lived in a small town, or were too young to go to concerts in a larger city, the only way to see a rock singer or band perform (or even *pretend* to perform) was on a variety show like "The Ed Sullivan Show," on Sunday nights, or weekly pop music shows like "American Bandstand," or later "Shindig," "Hullabaloo," and "Where the Action Is." ("Soul Train" was also great, for "alternative music," and for the dancing.)

As a young would-be drummer in St. Catharines, Ontario, with no easy access to rock concerts, and no such thing yet as instructional videos or concert DVDs, my attention was riveted on *any* drummer I saw, from Jack Teagarden on Dick Cavett's late-night talk show to occasional shots of Ed Shaughnessy on the "Tonight" show. Buddy Rich often appeared on the "Tonight" show (given an open invitation by Johnny Carson, an amateur drummer and admirer), but at that time he was so beyond the reach of my drumming knowledge and ability that I hardly understood what he was doing. (Gene Krupa once said, "There are all the great drummers in the world — and then there's Buddy.") Years later, I realized how his music had impressed itself on my mind, and certainly on my ambitions, but in reality, every drummer I saw or heard did something I could learn from, even if it was what *not* to do. When my first teacher, Don George, moved on, I decided to carry on learning alone, and thus all those drummers became my teachers.

In the early '60s, there were a few pop-music movies around, like the Beatles' *A Hard Day's Night*, but that had little to do with *music;* it was really more of a cartoon. There was an animated Saturday-morning Beatles cartoon too, but it seemed cheap to me even then (no reflection on John, Paul, George, and Ringo, I'm sure; the amount of Beatles merchandise, from lunchpails to dolls, that suddenly flooded the western world was another whole new phenomenon, and no doubt it was *way* outside their control, and even their awareness). And again, I was only eleven and twelve years old then; too young for the Beatles. I liked some of their songs, and emulated the hairstyle and clothes like every other kid, but I never really caught the "bug" of Beatlemania. Other than the 45 single of "If I Fell" that I won by selling newspaper subscriptions, I never even owned a Beatles record (still don't), never sang Beatles songs in my inner transistor radio (still don't), and never cared to see *Help!* or *Yellow Submarine* (still haven't). "My" bands would come later.

Another movie around the same time was a much stronger musical influence on me — in fact, in retrospect, it was *the* influence. *The T.A.M.I. Show,* or "Teen Age Music International," was shown as a Saturday matinee in my old hometown of St. Catharines in early 1965, when I was twelve-and-a-half, and was filmed in October 1964 in my *new* hometown, at the Santa Monica Civic Auditorium (where Rush played around 1976 or '77, with our friends Thin Lizzy opening, before the tragic death of Phil Lynott, another heroin casualty). *The T.A.M.I. Show* was an early "package" performance, bringing together widely varying strands of early '60s pop music, an all-star lineup including Marvin Gaye, Chuck Berry, the Beach Boys, Jan and Dean, the Barbarians, Lesley Gore, Smokey Robinson and the Miracles, the Supremes, Gerry and the Pacemakers, Billy J. Kramer and the Dakotas, James Brown, and the Rolling Stones.

It had been surprisingly difficult to see that movie again, to see if what I *remembered* had any relationship to what I *saw* in that dark theater on a Saturday afternoon almost forty years before. Web sites referred to it as "often cited but rarely seen," "never released on home video," and apparently the Beach Boys segment had been removed immediately after the theatrical run, as part of father Murry Wilson's often self-defeating machinations. Eventually I found a rough, but complete, DVD version of the show.

Shot over two days by director Steven Binder in black-and-white "Electronovision" (basically high-definition video transferred to film), the production values were impressive, then and now, with great sound, elaborate sets and lighting, and choreographed "go-go" dancers (including a young Teri Garr) bouncing onstage all loose-limbed and energetic, with frenzied versions of the dances of the early '60s: the Watusi, the Frug, the Mashed Potatoes, the Jerk. (They remind me now of the kids dancing in a "Peanuts" cartoon; maybe that's where Charles Schultz got his inspiration.)

Even the opening titles presaged how pop music was to be presented visually in the future, from the Beatles (who apparently didn't appear in *The T.A.M.I. Show* because they were working on *A Hard Day's Night*) to the Monkees to the age of rock videos. The opening theme song, "They're Coming From All over the World," was performed by Jan and Dean, the show's hosts, over a fast-paced film pastiche of the two of them (wearing long-sleeved, striped T-shirts) riding Hondas, sidewalk surfing, and driving go-karts, intercut with shots of the other performers arriving by bus and car (the Miracles pretending to climb out of the trunk of a taxi).

The doors were opened to a surging crowd of Santa Monica teenagers looking more '50s than '60s in their hairstyles and clothes, and although the performers were remarkably integrated for the times, the audience was mostly white, with only a few groups of black girls clapping along. Black or white, the girls in the audience seemed to go into fits of screaming hysteria about *everybody*, from the driving soul music of James Brown to the lightweight British Invasion ditties of Gerry and the Pacemakers (though

I confess, "Don't Let the Sun Catch You Crying" played on my youthful heartstrings — still does).

Smokey Robinson's performance was very strong, and I remember the tight choreography with the Miracles impressed me then, and became a part of singing-group showmanship I would always admire, from the Pips to 98°. Smokey was especially good on "You Really Got a Hold on Me," which clearly demonstrated his influence on the Beatles, too, especially as they covered that very song.

Likewise, Marvin Gaye's performance was impressive, with "Can I Get a Witness," and "Hitchhike" (and still the girls kept on *screaming!*), and it occurs to me now how much R&B I was exposed to in that movie, and how it would affect me in later years.

In contrast, I would never be a fan of slick Motown, which was (I know now) quite literally *manufactured* by an assembly line of writers, producers, and session musicians, who often created a backing track without even knowing who would be singing on it. Watching the Supremes on *The T.A.M.I. Show* movie forty years later, they struck me as "basically insipid." Diana Ross, soon to go solo and become the original "diva," so obviously didn't *feel* what she was singing, but just *performed* it (though I did note "nice gowns and choreography").

Lesley Gore was only seventeen in 1964, but she was almost an anachronism already, with her "girl group" sound records (her own voice double-tracked, and produced by a young Quincy Jones), '50s hairdo, makeup, and skirt suit, but she was so poised and professional, and what a *big* voice she had. She belted out "It's My Party" and the follow-up answer song, "It's Judy's Turn to Cry," and was particularly great on the proto-feminist ballad, "You Don't Own Me." Those dramatic key changes and heartfelt lyrics grabbed me even as a twelve-year-old, "Don't tell me what to do/ Don't tell me what to say/ And baby, when I go out with you/ Don't put me on display."

Interviewed years later about *The T.A.M.I. Show*, Lesley Gore said the audience was so loud when she sang it was difficult for her to hear the orchestra, but the overall sound was remarkably good. The bands, by all accounts, played live, sometimes augmented by the excellent orchestra that accompanied the singers. The orchestra was assembled, arranged, and conducted by Jack Nitzsche, and included musicians like Glen Campbell, Leon Russell, and drummer Hal Blaine.

Jack Nitzsche said he tried to make the arrangements "sound like the records," which he certainly managed (even though many of the songs were cut to a minute or less), and those musicians played so well, especially Hal Blaine, who just laid the tempos *down*. The nervousness of some of the other bands, and their drummers, showed in their tendency toward "speediness," especially when it made the vocals hurried and breathless — but not when Hal was playing. His drums sounded so great too, which was certainly a testament to his "touch" rather than the recording technology of the day. Now I realize that the way I heard those drums all those years ago, before I'd ever touched a drumstick, became my ideal of how drums *ought* to sound.

Chuck Berry's role as one of the pioneers of rock 'n' roll in the '50s was undeniably important, but some say he was never the same after his imprisonment under the Mann Act — transporting a minor across state lines for immoral purposes — in 1962. By 1964 he displayed no edge, no cockiness, no aggression, just ingratiating smiles, and seemed content to be an "entertainer" (one definition of the distinction might be "performing" as opposed to "playing"). He performed a lounge-act sort of duet with Gerry and the Pacemakers on his song "Maybellene" (apparently inspired by his feckless tour bus), and from then on he would thrive on a series of more-or-less novelty songs like "Driving Around in My Automobile" ("Can you imagine the way I felt?/ I couldn't unfasten my safety belt"), to his lowest point, and biggest hit, "My Ding-a-Ling."

The Barbarians, though, were a real *rock* band, with their wild-man drummer who played with one drumstick held in a hook, and they would soon have a hit with "Are You a Boy, or Are You a Girl?" They actually played once at our local "Knightclub for Teenagers," the Castle, but I was too young to go.

Billy J. Kramer and the Dakotas and Gerry and the Pacemakers were the representatives of "Merseybeat," and not only was Billy J. Kramer managed by the Beatles' manager, Brian Epstein, but several of his hits, including "From a Window," had been written for him by Lennon and McCartney. Given their prodigious output in those early years, for themselves and others, it occurred to me that this song was perhaps an example of their method, being thematically similar to the older doo-wop hit, "Silhouettes" (which Herman's Hermits covered in that era). Perhaps they sometimes used other songs as "templates," in the way that John Lennon described modeling "Norwegian Wood" after Leonard Cohen's "Suzanne." Not copying, but *emulating*, as in, "Let's write *that* kind of song."

The Beach Boys definitely used Chuck Berry's "Sweet Little Sixteen" as the model for "Surfin' USA," and would eventually be forced to pay him a cut of the royalties for it. They played and sang very well, though, all in their matching striped shirts, and unusually, the camera spent a lot of time on the drummer, Dennis Wilson, as he shook his thatch of blond hair and pounded his drums while the girls screamed for him. That must certainly have impressed a preteen like me, just starting to get interested in pop music, and especially the drums, and his influence on a young English surf-music fan named Keith Moon was also obvious.

Dennis's older brother Brian, though looking nervous and awkward (a hint of the "stage fright" that would soon compel him to retire from performing into his infamous seclusion), delivered his strong, affecting falsetto on "Surfer Girl" (which, that summer of '65, I danced to over and over again with red-haired Doreen Porter in her basement rec room). Watching Brian Wilson as he was then, young, slender, fresh-faced and smiling shyly, was so poignant in the knowledge of how life would unfold for him in later years, as his grand visions led him to the edge of insanity, and beyond. When I introduced my younger friend Matt to *Pet Sounds*, he said he thought you could *hear* a man on the edge in the music, and by the time that masterwork was completed (when Brian Wilson was only 23!), he was already descending into prodigious drug abuse and severe mental illness.

Steven Gaines's biography of the Beach Boys, *Heroes and Villains*, is a harrowing story of "squandered talent and ruined lives," as one back-cover blurb put it, and likewise, Jon Stebbins's biography of Dennis Wilson, *The Real Beach Boy*, documents that golden-haired surfer boy's downward spiral into alcoholism, drugs, reckless, self-destructive behavior, and early death — by drowning, probably during an alcoholic seizure, in the Pacific Ocean, at Marina del Rey. Some part of Brian Wilson still lives on, making music, but younger brother Carl died of cancer in 1998, and Dennis drowned in 1983, at the age of 39, by which time he had become a pathetic skid-row alcoholic.

Like the Beatles, the Beach Boys had never been a big part of my musical history, but I liked a lot of their songs, certainly appreciated the best of Brian Wilson's work, and what a *story* they were — what a *California* story. The Wilson brothers, Brian, Carl, and Dennis, grew up in the Los Angeles suburb of Hawthorne (Dennis the only one who actually surfed or raced the fast cars their songs celebrated). Their early career was masterminded by their abusive father, Murry, and it was their mother, Audree, who had insisted that if Brian and Carl and cousin Mike Love were going to form a group, Dennis had to be in it too. So Dennis became the drummer (and, some say, Brian's muse to a certain degree, as Dennis was certainly the inspiration for the surfing and hot rod songs, and an early title for the projected followup to *Pet Sounds* was *Dumb Angel*, said to refer to Dennis).

Despite Dennis's later growth as a singer and composer, his drumming skills were limited, and, like everybody else, he was overwhelmed by his brother's talent and vision. As Brian's composing, arranging, and producing became more ambitious, and he began to stay home and make records while the rest of the band went on tour, he began using legendary session master, Hal Blaine, to play drums on the Beach Boys' sessions. Obviously there would be psychological conflicts for Dennis, in the family dynamics and in the sense of "unearned success" that has tormented many a performer, but he enjoyed the star's life, fulfilling his insatiable appetite for admiration, money, fast cars, and women. Unfortunately, that appetite was equally keen for drugs and alcohol, and like his early British fan, Keith Moon, Dennis Wilson spiraled inexorably downward. Also like Keith

Moon, Dennis Wilson the *man* was loved more than he seemed to feel he deserved, and he just seemed *helpless;* he tried to pull himself together many times, but could never do it.

In his biography *Moon: The Life and Death of a Rock Legend,* Tony Fletcher wrote that Keith Moon's favorite ballad had been the Beach Boys' "Don't Worry Baby," and suggested that perhaps what Keith had really needed was for someone to hold him and sing that song to him. At first I thought that suggestion was simplistic and shallowly sentimental, but after listening to that song a lot lately, maybe that's what *everybody* needs: someone to hold them and sing, "Don't worry baby, everything will turn out all right."

The revelation of the whole *T.A.M.I. Show* movie for me, though, and a performance I would never forget, was James Brown, who gave an intense, theatrical demonstration of what soul music was all about. As his band funked it up in the background (another great drummer, with a great sound, and another important "impression" on me, I realize now), James Brown gave an amazing performance, with wailing horns, tight choreography with his backup singers, working out on a fast song with indistinguishable lyrics, but for the chorus, "You're outasight!" then a powerful repeating call and response, "Are you ready for the night train?"

Then came the show-stopper, "Please, Please, Please," when James seemed to sing and dance himself to exhaustion, falling to his knees as if he had collapsed completely. A "handler" came out and put a cape around his shoulders and tried to lead him offstage, while the band played on, funky and driving. Just as James reached the wings, he threw off the cape and exploded once more into song and dance, as if possessed by an irresistible power. Then, he collapsed to his knees again, and once more, the handler and one of the backup singers tried to lead him away. James shook them off again, tore off his jacket, and, supported by one of the backup singers, he started up again, dancing feverishly, only to fall to his knees and be helped up and led off *again.*

This time he came back from the wings and did what can only be described as a break-dance routine — in 1964! The whole performance was just part of the show from the Godfather of Soul, of course, but for this twelve-and-a-half-year-old in the summer of '65, it was all *for real*, and I was simply amazed, and never forgot it.

(Recently I was at a party in Los Angeles, and James Brown's *Live at the Apollo* album was playing. It sounded so good that I found myself retreating from the guests and standing beside one of the speakers, just listening. He and his various bands were always *so* good.)

The Rolling Stones closed *The T.A.M.I. Show*, with a leaping, charismatic Mick Jagger sometimes imitating James Brown (who they had been worried about having to follow), a remarkably *alive* looking Keith Richards, and a smiling, perfectly-coiffed Brian Jones looking not at all like a young man who would overdose and drown at the bottom of his swimming pool in a few more years. Charlie Watts sounded really good, as they worked through "Round and Round," "Off the Hook," "Time Is on My Side" (a song I always liked, with that "talking blues" rap section in the middle), "All Over Now," and the grand finale, "It's Alright," with the whole cast of performers and dancers thronging the stage. Watching it now, I was moved to note, "The Stones *rock* (don't know why that's a surprise or a revelation!)."

My take on the whole film, in retrospect, was summed up in one emphatic word: MAGIC. And I realize now that it was absolutely my formative musical experience.

During my search for *The T.A.M.I. Show*, I found some interesting background history that resonated through the years after that landmark event.

The opening theme, "They're Coming From All over the World," was written by a pair of high-school students named P.F. Sloan and Steve Berry, who would later compose the early "protest song," "Eve of Destruction," for Barry McGuire. The arranger and orchestra leader, Jack Nitzsche, who had done a lot of work with Phil Spector, would later work with the Rolling Stones and Neil Young, and score films like *One Flew Over the Cuckoo's Nest* and *An Officer and a Gentleman* (with the hit "Up Where We Belong" cowritten with his second wife, Buffy St. Marie). So many *stories*, everywhere I looked.

The orchestra members Leon Russell, Glen Campbell, and Hal Blaine would all work on later Beach Boys recording sessions (Campbell even filled in for Brian Wilson on tour for a few months), and the director, Steven Binder, had been directing Steve Allen's late-night talk show, and brought his crew from there to the Santa Monica Civic Auditorium. Binder would later direct Elvis Presley's famous "Comeback Special," and he recounted a telling difference in that experience compared to the sweaty close-ups of James Brown's face in *The T.A.M.I. Show* — NBC didn't want him to show Elvis actually perspiring, or with his carefully-designed hair disarranged.

In an interview in the 1990s, Binder said that when they were assembling the footage for *The T.A.M.I. Show*, they encountered a difficult audio problem in their mono mix: how to disguise the unmistakable sound of the young girls in the audience chanting *"Fuck me!"*

That seems unbelievable in the context of the times, but maybe that perceived "context" needs re-examining. Perhaps all along the older generations had been *right* to fear the sexual power of rock 'n' roll (a phrase, incidentally, said to have been an African-American euphemism for the sex act). But of course rock wasn't really to blame; there is a basic relation between *any* kind of music and sex — sensual, emotional, and physical — and even that degree of pubescent-female mania predated rock 'n' roll by a few years (if not so baldly stated). It seemed to have been born out of nowhere during World War II, with the male-deprived Bobby-Soxers suddenly wildly hysterical over Frank Sinatra (it hadn't happened with Rudy Vallee, or Bing Crosby!). Then successive waves of young girls began screaming and swooning for Elvis, the Beatles, and right up to the boy-bands of the present day. When Selena was thirteen, I took her and her friend Mishka to see New Kids on the Block at Toronto's Maple Leaf Gardens, which, apart from other dutiful parents, was filled with 10,000 pubescent girls. I swear you could *smell* the sex in that building, a kind of estuarine electricity.

Puberty and pop music had a cathartic reaction to each other, as those hormonal changes also alter one's relationship with music, but boys and girls responded in different ways. It is a music business truism that young girls are the most *fickle* of audiences, being fanatical about the teen sensation of the day for a year or two, then losing interest suddenly, and completely. The summer Selena was fourteen, she came home from camp and took down all her New Kids posters, and they were *over*.

In attempting to understand the paucity of female musicians (as opposed to singers) in rock music, Camille Paglia has pointed out that men are simply more obsessive, for both evil and good, and in mentioning that her hero was Keith Richards, she said there would never be a female Keith Richards because "they simply won't spend the time with the instrument." (Though it should be noted that one of the most in-demand bass players in Los Angeles in the '60s was Carol Kaye, who worked with Hal Blaine's group of session musicians, "The Wrecking Crew," on many great recordings, including such legendary projects as *Pet Sounds*.)

On the bulletin board in front of my desk there's a newspaper clipping I've held onto for many years, describing the "fantasy careers" of men and women in little pie-charts. It is a clear illustration of the complicated, much-disputed story of the "differences," the dream-lives of men and women. Among several thousand adult Americans surveyed, almost half the men fantasized about being an athlete, followed by business leader and musician, while the women were divided evenly among singer, author, and doctor. Therein hangs many a tale of fantasy, if not reality.

The raw sexuality in early rock music was also apparent in a video compilation I found in my search for *The T.A.M.I. Show* movie. Called *That Was Rock*, the video was hosted by Chuck Berry, and contained a few performances from *The T.A.M.I. Show* and some from another multi-act show presented by Phil Spector at the Santa Monica Civic Auditorium the following year, 1965, called "TNT."

That video also had some interesting performances to see and hear now, notably a noisy, savage, mesmerizing performance by Bo Diddley, accompanied by a trio of female backup singers in long gowns, one playing electric guitar (a sexy visual, and probably somewhat shocking for the time), and a long-limbed bass player repeating a graceful dance step while he and the drummer pounded out that trademark "shave-and-haircut, two-bits" Bo Diddley rhythm. The beat became trance-like in its ceaseless repetition, and the sheer *presence* of the man himself was riveting — not arrogant so much as *careless*, as if to say, "Here I am; dig me, or don't"). In my early years, I had never paid much attention to the early "wild men" of rock 'n' roll, like Little Richard and Jerry Lee Lewis, but I was beginning to understand the stripped-down, authentic *accomplishment* of what was a real musical and cultural revolution.

Among the pictures and posters that used to hang in the psychedelic "art installation" that was my bedroom when I was a teenager, I remember a page from *Eye* magazine with a pop-art layout of live photos of The Who, and a quote from Pete Townshend to the effect that "Rock needs to go back to the power, glamour, and insanity of the Elvis Presley age."

That quote came into my head, all those years later, watching Bo Diddley, and thinking that what we needed now was more of the power, glamour, and insanity of the *Bo Diddley* age. He was no pale imitation of the hypnotic, primal pulse of rock music; he was *it*.

The Ronettes also appeared in that TNT show, produced by Phil Spector, and his then-wife, Ronnie Spector, was cute and smiling as she belted out one of his early pop masterpieces, "Be My Baby" (a song Brian Wilson claimed to have listened to so many times he wore out the grooves of copy after copy). Ronnie and the other two pant-suited, bouffant-hair-doed singers seemed much more "there" than the Supremes had, less cool and aloof as they moved through their dance routines in the exuberant, up-tempo anthem, "Shout."

The Ike and Tina Turner Revue seemed to be the knockout performers that year, though, and Tina put out amazing energy and sexuality. In later years, Janis Joplin was said to be the first female rock star, but in retrospect, Tina would seem to wear that crown. It can't be a question of *color*, as Janis certainly sang "black music."

And Janis Joplin would be a big part of the next Big-Screen epiphany in my musical development, *Monterey Pop*. In June of 1967, the first true rock festival took place in northern California, a three-day event called

"The Monterey International Pop Festival," and I saw the subsequent movie at an "art-house" cinema in Toronto when I was fifteen. That, for me, was the movie that put it all together. This was something I wanted to be part of — indeed, *felt* part of.

Even now, *Monterey Pop* stands as the ultimate document of the late '60s, both musically and sociologically, and when I looked back with 50 years of sophistication and opinionated taste, once again I was curious to see if what I admired *then* still stood up 35 years later. Those bands whose names I drew so artfully on my schoolbooks, and whose records I bought and loved, were they really any good?

I decided to find a copy of *Monterey Pop* and watch it again, to see what I might learn from the past.

As the titles and opening shots of the crowd were shown, the first thing I noticed was that these people, the early hippies, really *were* beautiful people. The "flower children" were young and innocent and free and idealistic; they were the sons and daughters of what Tom Brokaw called "the greatest generation," as their parents had lived through and fought the Depression and World War II. The generation that followed, the true "baby boomers," lived through and fought the next age, the Eisenhower years of conformity and suburban boomtimes, through inexplicable wars in Korea and Vietnam which continued to draft the young boys, but this time allowed no "heroes," and through the pervasive Cold War which held everyone under the threat of nuclear annihilation for almost fifty years — almost my whole *life*.

Not surprisingly, youth responded with existential abandon, idealistic rebellion, social nonconformity, Dionysian hedonism, and flamboyant creativity. They were something like the "lost generation" that emerged in the 1920s from the devastation of World War I — disoriented, disaffected, and dismissive of the past, living somewhat desperately in the moment. And in their own way, the hippies were a tough generation too. They survived their own times, they were hardy and adventurous, traveling rough, hitchhiking around and "crashing" any old place and eating any old thing, experimenting with communes and drop-in centers, and new attitudes to sexuality (though "free love," as T. C. Boyle implied in his '60s novel, *Drop City*, may have been more about masculine guile in taking advantage of early feminists who wanted to appear "liberated").

The hippies also famously experimented with recreational drugs (*dozens of different drugs* — marijuana, hashish, mescaline, peyote, LSD, MDA, STP, angel dust, heroin, uppers, downers, amphetamines, barbiturates — some of them, unfortunately, too often destructive, and even deadly), and in the middle of all that inner and outer ferment, or perhaps because of it, they were able to create an entire *culture* of style: clothing, music, hairstyles, décor, graphics, even organic foods — throwing a whole psychedelic *light* on the rest of the world, that soon pervaded all of western society.

And it still seems as though at the beginning, at the time of *Monterey Pop*, that culture had an integrity and beauty that were not yet tarnished by commercialization and drug casualties.

The opening theme to *Monterey Pop* was "San Francisco (Be Sure To Wear Flowers in Your Hair)," sung by Scott Mackenzie, and written by John Phillips of the Mamas and the Papas. Phillips was one of the promoters of the event, inspired by the annual Monterey Jazz Festivals, along with record producer Lou Adler (who produced the Mamas and the Papas, as well as that Scott Mackenzie song).

The homemade basis of the festival was evidenced by early shots in the movie of Phillips and his then-wife Michelle personally dealing with phone calls and business arrangements (John on the phone to Dionne Warwick, who backed out at the last minute, as did the Beach Boys, citing Carl Wilson's draft-evasion charges — a sign of the times — though apparently it was really because Brian Wilson feared they would not be appreciated by that audience — another sign of the times).

The first live appearance in the movie was by the Mamas and the Papas, who looked and sounded *great*, their voices blending naturally into the rich harmonies of their recordings. "California Dreamin'" was especially poignant, in that time and place. And once again, there was Hal Blaine (heard but not seen), who had played on all their records, and often their live performances as well.

Next up in the movie were Canned Heat, rocking out with the Willie Dixon blues song, "Rollin' and Tumblin'." Apparently it was their first gig outside Los Angeles, and watching them made me think of the autobiography, *Living the Blues*, written years later by their drummer, Fito de la Parra, who joined just after Monterey, was there for Woodstock, and eventually became the last survivor. Three members of that band died from drug-related causes, but more from habitual abuse than the accidental overdoses that had struck down others, like Janis Joplin, in ways that just seemed *unlucky*. It was also notable that the Canned Heat guys all seemed to start *out* on shaky ground, psychologically.

Simon and Garfunkel also sounded really, really good, both of them singing beautifully on "The 59th Street Bridge Song (Feelin' Groovy)." I was reminded of their song "America," which my friend Tuck and I used to play over and over in his basement. That song still came up in my "helmet transistor" from time to time, and I still remembered every word. Another classic song of the American road.

The outtakes on the DVD version of *Monterey Pop* also revealed wonderful versions of "Homeward Bound" and "Sounds of Silence," showcasing Paul Simon's place as one of the great songwriters of the age. (Hal Blaine comes to mind once again for his great drumming on the recorded versions of those songs, as well as the Mamas and the Papas, Scott Mackenzie, the Association, Johnny Rivers, and the Byrds — just from that festival!)

South African bandleader Hugh Masekela helped to make Monterey truly an *international* pop festival, with his beautiful trumpet playing fronting a mixed-race band (which must have pushed contemporary mores, in South Africa and in the U.S.) performing a song by Miriam Makeba, "Bajabula Bonke (Healing Song)."

Jefferson Airplane highlighted the emerging style of true psychedelia, and the two songs shown in the movie made it clear that Grace Slick could really *sing*. The bass player, Jack Casady, was also a standout, and when I was first auditioning for Rush and we were discussing influences, Geddy told me Jack Casady was one of his favorite bass players. I was pleasantly surprised to recognize the gentle ballad "Today," from their album *Surrealistic Pillow*, which I had owned and loved as a teen, and it still stood up as a fairly sophisticated love song.

(The other psychedelic San Franciscans, the Grateful Dead, played at the festival, but didn't appear in the movie because, according to the director, D.A. Pennebaker, every one of their songs was longer than ten minutes. Too long for the reels on the film crew's portable cameras, they could never capture a full song.)

Next came the show-stopper, then and now: Janis Joplin. This was the performance that launched her career, with the band Big Brother and the Holding Company, and it's not hard to see why. "Ball and Chain" was the consummate white blues performance, with Janis completely *possessed*, hair flying and feet pounding, wailing out the desperate sorrow of "everywoman," whose love of a careless man is an insupportable burden. Cass Elliot is shown watching her in open-mouthed astonishment, and as I watched the power of Janis Joplin's total abandonment to the emotion she expressed so unstintingly with her raspy, Southern Comfort-fueled voice, and knowing she had only another year or so to live, I found myself in tears. Such an unbelievably powerful performance, and such a tragedy to have lost her.

Next there was a long violin intro to the Rolling Stones song "Paint It Black," leading into a vocal by Eric Burdon, who was then on the cusp of leaving behind his roots as an English blues-rock singer in the Animals, and becoming a kind of champion of the San Francisco scene. He had spent the winter of '66–'67 in San Francisco, and put together a new version of the Animals which recorded the great song "When I Was Young" (with a B-side called "A Girl Named Sandoz," an acid-rock ode to the pharmaceutical company which originally made LSD), then "San Franciscan Nights," and, later in 1967, the song which celebrated the Monterey Pop Festival experience, "Monterey."

One line of that brief epic, in which many of the performers were cleverly mimicked instrumentally as they were sung about, goes "His majesty, Prince Jones, smiled as he moved among the crowd," and the movie showed Brian Jones (who also acted as occasional M.C.) dressed in a fantastic pale-blue outfit, doing exactly that, walking through a crowd of music fans who could still let a legendary musician stroll among them, unmolested.

(Jones also apparently applauded loudly for Burdon's version of his band's song, "Paint It Black," and it occurs to me now that the Stones never really recovered from his loss — there seems to have been a whole *dimension* of their music, a depth, that was lost with him.)

During rehearsals for Rush's *Vapor Trails* tour, in the spring of 2002, the three of us discussed the idea of each of us choosing an old song by bands from our youth, to have something different we could play in the show, perhaps as encore songs, or alternating "treats" to spice up the set.

For a few years, Eric Burdon's "When I Was Young" had been playing back in my mental transistor radio, and I imagined a slowed down, heavier version, with those impassioned, defiant lyrics, "When I was young, it was more important/ Pain more painful, laughter much louder, yeah . . . When I was young" (written when Burdon was twenty-five). Wanting to check out the original version, I found a "Best Of" collection and discovered some treasures, largely forgotten but for the occasional oldies station playing "House of the Rising Sun" or "Don't Let Me Be Misunderstood."

For a native son of Newcastle, England, Burdon had one of the most authentic and enduring blues voices, gravelly and soulful, with particularly fine phrasing and a natural style that seemed *felt* rather than *imitated*. The drumming of Barry Jenkins was solid and sometimes inventive, as in a single bass drum beat he dropped in the middle of "When I Was Young" that was just *perfect*, and some of his snare rolls as well.

But it was the bass player, Danny McCulloch, who really impressed me. In the song "Monterey," his playing was so energetic, melodic, and driving that I could listen to the song for the bass part alone, which is a rare tribute.

Then came the performance that totally galvanized me at age fifteen, and still gets my blood racing, The Who doing "My Generation."

Although I was already a fan, thanks to Graeme and the Waifers covering their early singles, The Who were not well known in North America at the time, having only toured as an opening act for Herman's Hermits. But all that was about to change. Pete Townshend stepped to the mic and said, "This is where it all ends," and they went crashing and thrashing into that ultimate punk anthem, "Why don't you all f-f-fade away."

As with Dennis Wilson in *The T.A.M.I. Show*, the camera paid unusual attention to the drummer, Keith Moon, locking on him and capturing a sequence of lunatic facial expressions, as he thrashed away at a rented Slingerland kit (he always played Premier drums, but their own equipment couldn't be shipped there in time).

Then came the total anarchy of the ending: microphone whirling, drums kicked over, smoke bombs igniting, Townshend's guitar smashing against mic stands, amplifiers, and finally the stage, as he broke the neck off the body and left the stage while feedback squealed and hummed. (All while the stagehands scrambled onto the stage and tried to save the sound company's microphones for the rest of the festival.)

Nothing could follow that, of course, and in the movie, they cut to the proverbial "something completely different," a daytime performance by Country Joe and the Fish, called "Section 43." It was ambient, psychedelic, early "trance" music, which my modern-day notes could only describe as "weird as hell." In the mid-'70s, their guitarist, Barry Melton, would share a bill with Rush at a club in Southern California, when I would be playing Slingerland drums, in a chrome finish inspired by Keith Moon's Premier drums on the *Tommy* tour.

So many connections in this musical roadshow.

Next up was Otis Redding, who was *so* cool and sang so well, first on an up-tempo number called "Shake," and then on a classic ballad, "I've Been Loving You Too Long," building to a powerful climax. His band (Booker T and the MGs) was also great, particularly the drummer, I noted, and I summed up my modern response in a single word, "Wonderful." Alas, Otis Redding was to be another tragic casualty, dying in a plane crash later that same year. (In fact, after Monterey, Otis Redding spent some time in San Francisco, where he wrote "Sitting on the Dock of the Bay," recorded just before his death and released posthumously.)

Next, Jimi Hendrix, about whom my replacement drum teacher had said that very year, "This changes everything." Like my other idols, The Who, his music was not well known in North America, and Monterey was the time and place that changed all that. Brian Jones introduced him as "the most exciting guitar player I have ever heard."

The argument between Hendrix and The Who over who would go on before the other is well-documented (one story has Hendrix calling Pete Townshend a "honky"), and Hendrix, losing the deciding coin-toss, set out to do all he could to overshadow the explosive finale of "My Generation." First of all, there was the way he looked, described by a contemporary writer, Michael Lydon, who attended the festival and described it at length for *Newsweek*.

> Hendrix is a strange looking fellow. Very thin, with a big head and a protuberant jaw, Hendrix has a tremendous bush of hair held in place carelessly by an Apache headband. He is both curiously beautiful and as wildly grotesque as the proverbial Wild Man of Borneo. He wore scarlet pants and a scarlet boa, a pink jacket over a yellow and black vest over a white ruffled shirt.

In his final number, the Troggs' "Wild Thing," Hendrix played the melody of Sinatra's "Strangers in the Night" (a current hit) as a guitar solo — with one hand — then played the next verse behind his back, raised the guitar to his face and played it with the pick between his teeth, and then went into his own anarchic finale, with drummer Mitch Mitchell rolling around the drums and accelerating into a frantic pace. Jimi, down on his knees and straddling his Stratocaster, doused it in lighter fluid, set it on fire, and *then* smashed it.

Another tough act to follow, and again, the movie used an abrupt change of mood, segueing to Cass Elliot's sweet solo version of "Got a Feeling." However different their moods, Hendrix would be dead in September of 1970, and Cass in '74. Alas, drugs and booze again.

Suitably, somehow, the grand finale of the movie version of the

Monterey International Pop Festival was Ravi Shankar, who played a long sitar raga in astonishing unison with a virtuoso tabla player, Alla Rakha, and a woman named Kamala playing another stringed instrument called a taboura. Apparently Shankar had asked the audience not to smoke during his three-hour afternoon performance, and the photographers not to take pictures, and he wondered aloud to the audience, "What am I doing at a pop festival when my music is classical? I knew I'd be meeting you all at one place, you to whom music means so much. This is not pop, but I am glad it is popular."

The audience seemed to be completely rapt in the spell cast by the music, floating along with the intricate melodies and rhythms as they swelled and whirled through strange, exotic movements, finally rising to a frenzied climax of prestidigitation and seemingly telepathic communication among the musicians.

Jimi Hendrix and Micky Dolenz both looked awed as they watched and listened, and it is interesting to note that after seeing Hendrix play at Monterey, Dolenz lobbied for the Jimi Hendrix Experience to be the opening act on a Monkees tour later that year. Predictably, Jimi's music was not a success with a teenybopper audience, and he soon left the tour. (Chris Welch's Hendrix biography told of a story being invented that the Daughters of the American Revolution had protested the "sexuality" of his act, which was a fabrication apparently dreamed up to get some publicity out of the situation.)

Another celebrity in that audience, Tommy Smothers (also an occasional M.C.), was impressed by The Who's performance, and invited them to appear on the weekly comedy show he hosted with his brother, Dick: "The Smothers Brothers Comedy Hour." My fellow Who fans at school (all three of us) were thrilled that after doing the autodestruction act in "My Generation," Townshend grabbed Tommy Smothers' guitar, and smashed it too. We thought that was cool.

A few interesting bands played at Monterey who didn't appear in the movie, for various reasons, some of them included as outtakes on the DVD release. (One not shown was an early Canadian rock band called the

Paupers, who had recently been signed by Bob Dylan's manager, Albert Grossman.) Buffalo Springfield featured David Crosby filling in for a recently-departed Neil Young, to the displeasure of Crosby's own band, the Byrds, who also played Monterey — a chain leading to the various permutations of Crosby, Stills, Nash, and Young, the Association, Laura Nyro (excellent, though apparently her "soul revue" presentation didn't go over well with the audience), Quicksilver Messenger Service, and another important group of bands: the electric blues tour-de-force outfits like Paul Butterfield (I missed out on his music somehow the first time around, back in the day, but he was great), the Blues Project, Al Kooper, and the Electric Flag (the contemporary reporter, Michael Lydon, wrote colorfully about their drummer, who would later play with Hendrix: "Drummer Buddy Miles, a big Negro with a wild 'do' who looks like a tough soul brother from Detroit and who is actually a prep school-educated son of a well-to-do Omaha family, sings and plays with TNT energy, knocking over cymbals as he plays").

Such anachronistic racial terms told a story of the times, and the back-stage political dramas told some stories too, and hinted at others. The festival was incorporated with an honorary board of governors that included Donovan, Mick Jagger, the Stones' manager Andrew Oldham, Paul Simon, John Phillips, Smokey Robinson, Roger McGuinn, Brian Wilson, and Paul McCartney (who apparently recommended The Who).

Among other things, there were racial tensions. Phillips said later, "Smokey was completely inactive as a director. I think it might be a Jim Crow thing. A lot of people put Lou Rawls down for appearing. 'You're going to a Whitey festival, man,' was the line. There is tension between the white groups who are getting their own ideas and the Negroes who are just repeating theirs. The tension is lessening all the time, but it did crop up here, I am sure."

The Grateful Dead's manager was quoted as saying about the organizers, "Of all the shifty schemes and scaly exploitations of the hour, this is the most nefarious." Paul Kantner from Jefferson Airplane expressed the divide that existed even then between San Francisco and Los Angeles, saying that

Monterey was "totally ruined by Los Angeles interests." Another musician said, "Does anybody really know where these L.A. types are at?" Country Joe McDonald called the festival "a total ethical sellout of everything that we'd dreamed of."

It's not clear exactly why they felt that way, for even the honorary "board of governors" showed the idealistic spirit of the event, and all the artists were paid only expenses, the proceeds going to a charitable foundation which *seems* to have been legitimate. (Phillips talked about inviting Chuck Berry: "I told him on the phone, 'Chuck, it's for charity,' and he said to me, 'Chuck Berry has only one charity and that's Chuck Berry, $2,000.' We couldn't make an exception.")

"The San Francisco groups had a very bad taste in their mouths about L.A. commercialism," the co-promoter, Lou Adler, reflected, "and it's true that we were a business-minded industry. It wasn't a hobby. They called it slick, and I'd have to agree with them. We couldn't find the link. Every time John [Phillips] and I went up there, it was a fight — almost a physical fight on occasions. And that was right up to the opening day of the Festival, with the Dead — the Ungrateful Dead, as we called them — threatening to do an alternative festival."

And that was the beginning of the Summer of Love. It continued with *Easy Rider* in 1968, then the ultimate expression of '60s rock festivals, Woodstock, in the summer of 1969. How close I came to attending that one. Almost seventeen, I was playing in the final version of a band called the Majority (ever-shifting personnel in that embattled band), and the four of us heard about the upcoming festival down in New York State. Bob, Rick (the only guitarist I ever knew who played "air guitar" by holding his right forearm across his chest, like a guitar neck, and "fingering" the imaginary fretboard with his left as he "played" along with the radio or record), Paul, and I decided to go together in the band van, and two of the guys went over the border to Buffalo to buy tickets, only to be told that the festival had been canceled. I don't know how or why they were told that, but it was a shame. As a consequence, I remember exactly where I was when I *didn't* go to Woodstock: at our keyboard player's aunt's cottage, on a lake in Ontario.

That's where I was when I was *not* watching and hearing The Who, Jimi Hendrix, Janis Joplin, Santana, Joe Cocker, Crosby Stills and Nash, and the rest.

But even watching the movie, first when it was released in 1969, and now thirty-four years later, it is apparent that something had changed over the two winters since Monterey. The unselfconscious innocence and idealism were giving way to bitterness and resentment about Vietnam, the draft, civil rights, and other social and political issues, disillusionment with the commercialism and, perhaps, even the increasingly universal *acceptance* of the hippie aesthetic, and a weary kind of cynicism with the "youth movement."

After Monterey, Brian Jones said, "I saw a community form and live together for three days. It is so sad that it has to break up." After Woodstock, Pete Townshend said he had "hated" it, and told one reporter, "Listen, this is the fucking American dream, it's not my dream. I don't want to spend the rest of my life in fucking mud, smoking fucking marijuana. If that's the American dream, let us have our fucking money and piss off back to Shepherd's Bush where people are people."

At Woodstock, there were infamous warnings over the P.A. system about staying away from "the brown acid," and people were learning that getting high could be more than a "bummer." Earlier that same year the terrible roll call of rock drug casualties had begun with Brian Jones, overdosing and drowning in his swimming pool.

The Summer of Love, and the '60s, ended later that year, too, when the Rolling Stones performed (with Jones's replacement, Mick Taylor) at a "free concert" in Altamont, California. Tour photographer Ethan Russell wrote, "The frightening thing at Altamont, and everyone noticed it, was how much of the audience wasn't just high, they were *gone*. Their eyes were not entranced, but vacant."

The Hell's Angels motorcycle club claimed to have been hired as security by the promoter, Bill Graham (who later found it prudent to deny that), but in any case, they became the eye of a chaotic storm of tension and violence. As the intoxicated mob closed in around the stage, the

Angels' precious motorcycles were pushed over, and the bikers struck back with pool cues. Mick Jagger tried unsuccessfully to calm the situation, but violence continued to erupt throughout the show, until, while the Stones played "Under My Thumb," a member of the Angels stabbed a black teenager to death right in front of the stage. (Some written accounts end the story there, making it seem like an act of racist brutality, but it was not until I watched the movie again that I remembered the victim was clearly out of control and waving a *gun* around in the middle of a huge crowd. Not something he should have been *killed* for, of course, but a tellingly different scenario.)

The whole out-of-control event, including the stabbing, was caught in the movie *Gimme Shelter*, originally planned to be a documentary of the Rolling Stones' 1969 tour. Fate provided a chilling climax to that tour, to that movie, and, as a symbol, to the generation who came of age in the '60s. It was the end of something.

From the inspiration of *The T.A.M.I. Show* at twelve, I had grown to the affirmation of *Monterey Pop* at fifteen, but when I was seventeen and saw *Gimme Shelter* for the first time, what I felt was *shame*.

Music and life taught me a lot during those few years, and what a cast of *teachers* I had. It is said that the man who claims to be self-educated has a fool for a teacher, but I have learned from literally hundreds of people, in music, in reading, and in life, and they became part of a continuum that continues to inspire and drive me onward and upward.

At different periods of my development as a drummer, I was directly guided by Don George and Freddie Gruber, but indirectly, my inner sixteen-year-old would forever be inspired by, among countless others, such lifetime exemplars and touchstones as Buddy Rich's virtuosity and dedication, Hal Blaine's masterful musicianship, and Keith Moon's exuberance and abandon.

Looking back on my development as a *person* (in Bill Bruford's excellent phrase, "life beyond the cymbals"), so many names and faces come surging up. Old friends and neighbors, of course, but more important: so many people who made a positive mark on my life: schoolteachers, drum teachers, life savers, guitar players, grandmothers, and even Mom and Dad.

In a world so desperate for heroes that we have to *invent* them, buying and selling super-humans made from the common clay of actors, athletes, or artists, then turning on them when they betray us by being, as old Fred Nietzsche put it, "human, all too human," maybe the role models we really need are found all around us, right in our own neighborhoods. Not some remote model of perfection which exists only as a fantasy, frustratingly unattainable, but everyday people who actually show us, by example, a way to behave that we can see is good, and sometimes even people who can show us what it is to be excellent.

Here's to all my teachers.

Verse Three

"Workin' them angels overtime"

On my way across the Sands Motel parking lot to the attached restaurant, I noticed a pair of well-traveled touring motorcycles, an older BMW and a Honda, parked in front of one of the rooms, and imagined the two motorcyclists had taken refuge early. The temperature in West Texas was only in the high forties, and the winds remained strong and gusty. Not great motorcycling weather, and once again I was content to be driving.

Motorcyclists sometimes refer to four-wheelers as "cages," and though I have shared that sense of superiority when mounted on a two-wheeler — bicycle or motorcycle — of feeling freer, more in touch with the scenery, the weather, and the world around me, it was hard for me to think of this car as a *cage*. It felt more like a "module," maybe, a space ship, a speeding cocoon of sensual peace, fragrant with fine leather, insulating and pampering me as we arrowed through the day. If not quite as open or agile as a motorcycle, it still felt responsive and ready, still an extension of mind and body. Even when I wasn't driving the Z-8, it was a pleasure just to *look* at (true love), and as I walked to the restaurant I couldn't help pausing and looking back to admire its flowing lines, still shiny black under the patina of a thousand miles of dust and splattered insects.

And I wondered, not for the first time, if it was possible to love a machine. Males in particular were often belittled for their frequent fascination with mechanical things, and those of us with pretensions to being more evolved or sensitive could be made to feel guilty about such shallow, materialistic instincts, as if they were the mark of an atavistic brute. But the feeling could be more like that felt for art, the resonance of beauty *felt*, and more, it rested on shared *experiences*. Sometimes at the end of a long day on my motorcycle, I would walk past it in front of the motel and feel moved to give it a pat of appreciation and affection. The machine and I would have shared a long, hard, dangerous journey together, and come through it all; if the machine had been stalwart and reliable, I would feel grateful. Appreciative.

The hardcover, large-format book that came with my Z-8, describing its evolution and craft, was designed and produced like a work of fine art itself (wrapped in a swatch of the actual red leather used in the interior, and containing a Polaroid of the actual finished car in the Munich factory), and included a poem called "Ode to an Automobile," by Wolf Wondratschek.

It's like love.
We want to marvel. And,
Whether for ever or not,
We want to touch
Things we don't understand.
We want to grasp everything,
Even the invisible.
What might it be,
Besides being a car?

Dismantle its parts
Screw by screw.
Where could the secret lie?
Outside, inside, below,
Or under the hood?

Are miracles back in fashion?
Does the Garden of Eden now have
A race course? What does it feel like to
Fill the tank of a dream?
It's like love.
Any exaggeration is allowed,
But please: no big talk.

Instead, just let the motor run
And mingle what you hear
With the pounding of your heart.

Poetry aside, the Sands restaurant, next door to the motel, was another in my lifelong series of cultural experiences, a humble local place of cheap paneling, Formica, and everyday fare of meat and potatoes. A couple of vastly-overweight old ranchers sat at the table next to me, looking as over-stuffed as the beef cattle they probably raised. Their polyester cowboy shirts were bursting at the sides and over their formidable belt buckles, and their big, round heads were topped with giant Stetsons. Strangely, there was something about their bearing that made me smile to myself, and take to them. Perhaps just their obvious *authenticity*. I thought about the reaction I often felt toward strangers when I traveled, watching them with their friends or family in a restaurant, and either liking or disliking them on the most fleeting observations, seemingly intuitively, and I wondered how reliable those first impressions might be.

Perhaps not very, though there was something more than "superficial prejudice" about observing the way people presented themselves to the world, something more than "judging a book by its cover" in, for exam-ple, riding my bicycle past a slack-jawed, dull-eyed punk slouching lazily down the street with an arrogant sneer, or a woman defining herself by a spare-no-expense illusion of youth and beauty. More than appearance or clothes or grooming was being seen there; in the largest sense, it was the *face* these people wore.

If I indulged in shameless presumptions and stereotypes, these two good ol' boys from West Texas may well have been as opposite to me as humanly possible. No doubt they cared little about books or art or music, and quite likely they shared the cultural biases of their environment, with at least a tendency to be racist, sexist, homophobic, and narrowly religious and reactionary. Yet despite all that, I sensed they were probably good men at heart, and if I had a problem and asked for their help, they would probably give it willingly.

The Sands Restaurant in Van Horn, Texas, reminded me of the Cowboy Cafe, in Tilden, Texas, just a few hundred miles away, where Brutus and I had stopped one morning in December of 1996. The Cowboy Cafe had been like a Sam Shepard play or a Cormac McCarthy novel, showing us something of the changes in "the state of being Texan."

The Dallas show (December 3rd, 1996) had gone well, and the audience clapped, sang, whistled, and roared their appreciation. They were a happy bunch, and it was a nice feeling to look out and see people enjoying themselves like that — especially when I was sweating and straining so hard for them. A guy in the middle, back a few rows, was holding up a cellular phone, its keypad lit up green when the arena was dark between songs. The green light jerked up and down as he talked into the phone, then as we started another song, he held it out toward the stage again, perhaps for a friend who couldn't make it to the show, listening in from work, or from his bedroom.

(Many years ago in Dallas I was sent a custom-made cowboy hat, a discreet, sleek little "five gallon" model, by a member of a local hat-making family. That hat often served as my "lyric-writing hat," for I liked to say it was impossible to take yourself too seriously while wearing a cowboy hat. When I sent a card to thank the young fan and his family, I mentioned how perfectly the hat fit my head, saying, "most people think my head is *bigger* than it actually is!")

I could feel I was playing well that night, but it was never easy; I could never relax and take it for granted, or let down my professional *intensity*. And as always, I was aiming higher. In the end it was a solid nine-out-often show, but I wanted eleven. Journal note: "tried hard to make it great, but just wouldn't happen!"

A couple of hours out of Dallas, Brutus and I were already asleep when Dave parked for the night in a truckstop in San Marcos. When my alarm went off in the morning, I peeked through the bus window to see wet trucks, wet pavement, dark cloudy sky. Muttering "rain gear again," I pulled on my riding clothes and went out to help Brutus unload the bikes.

We headed south through intermittent rain, but the mild temperature made for pleasant, relaxed riding. The narrow country roads were signed "Ranch Road" or "Farm Road," but the distinction was often unclear. Certainly they smelled the same — manure, that redolence of my infancy — and this suggested a kind of scatological symbiosis which might be a happier way for vegetarians to view cattle ranches: fertilizer factories for the vegetable farmers.

In any case, these aromatic roads were plain, narrow strips of two-lane pavement, with no shoulders and no power lines marring the view over fields of manicured earth. Somehow the open spaces on the map of south Texas had led us to expect a desolate land, but it was obviously fertile, and artfully cultivated. Plow and disk harrow had combed the brown soil into neat contours and swirls, like a Chinese garden, and the fields lay in elegant fallow. With my farming heritage and farm-equipment background, I had to admire this example of deft tractor-handling, and "excellence on earth."

The farms gave way to arid, rolling ranchland, and dark herds of cattle hunched under the dull sky. A pair of hawks flew between the few bare trees, their plumage dramatically patterned in dark and light, like magpies. The scrubby ground cover was green with the recent rain, and occasionally dotted with small oil wells, a prehistoric-looking "dipper" rising and falling in slow-motion rhythm.

Long stretches of empty road carried us through crossroads towns, little more than a gas station and convenience store, and maybe a farm equipment dealer or feed store. The drivers on the Texas back roads seemed wonderfully alert and polite, actually seeing us when we came up behind them, and pulling as far to the right as they could, even onto the shoulder if there was one, to let us pass. Old guys in Cadillacs, white-haired ladies in Buicks, cowboys in pickups, and big-rig drivers all waved us by cheerfully. Road manners were different around Houston and Dallas, of course, where territorial aggression (and traffic volume) were considerably greater, but we appreciated the back-road customs in south Texas.

At Freer we stopped for gas, and felt warm enough to take off our rain suits and unplug the heated vests. A few drops splattered my visor as we set off again, and I wondered if packing away the rain suits had been foolish bravado, tempting the gods to give us a good soaking. But the rain held off.

Thoughts of breakfast were beginning to gnaw, and I was tempted by signs pointing toward towns a few miles off our route, where we might find a diner. Many of the towns in that part of South Texas had names like Peggy, Nell, Rosita, Alice, Christine, Charlotte, Marion, Helena, and Bebe, and I imagined lonesome cowboys pinin' for the girls they left behind. (The female population of frontier Texas, like all the West, was probably half wives and daughters, and half prostitutes.)

Brutus and I rode on, pinin' for the diners we'd left behind. Finally we came to another little crossroads town, called Tilden, the seat of McMullen County. A new brick courthouse with a tiled roof stood on one side of the road, and opposite it, the Cowboy Cafe.

The walls inside were lined with rows of well-worn cowboy hats, each tagged with a name and year, and a poster for a '50s Western movie starring Rex Allen, the "Oklahoma Cowboy." A framed black-and-white glossy of Rex himself was autographed with folksy good humor, testifying that the Cowboy Cafe "filled us up real good."

Brutus and I peeled off a few more layers of clothing as Willie Nelson played on the radio, then sat down to the strains of "Don't Come Home A-Drinkin' with Lovin' on Your Mind." This late in the morning, the Cowboy Cafe had only one other customer, a silent man in a straw cowboy hat hunched over his plate. A tiny Mexican woman shuffled to our table, her crippled body barely as tall as we were — sitting down. She wore a large, shapeless T-shirt reading "Always a Lady," and her toothy smile and good-natured banter soon had us laughing with her. We looked at each other and smiled; this place was the real thing.

I asked Brutus how he was feeling, and he told me his injuries seemed to be migrating through his body. This was a week or so after his crash on the Angeles Crest Highway, when he'd hit that patch of ice and slid down the road at fifty miles an hour. The worst injury had been caused by the bike's luggage case coming down on his foot, but of course the rest of him had taken a hit too. The smashed foot was feeling better, and his back wasn't quite so stiff, but now his knee was seizing up, and sometimes collapsing when he came to a stop and went to put his foot on the ground.

I shook my head and pointed my finger at him, like an accusing mother, "It's always *something* with you, isn't it?"

A tall, lean man came in, dressed in neat denim jeans and jacket, and a collared work shirt. He sat at the table beside us, saying "Morning, Gloria," and after a bit of banter with her, he leaned over to us. He looked to be in his fifties, his smooth-shaven face refined-looking, only mildly weathered by an outdoor life.

"I see by your licence plates that one of you fellows is from Ontario."

I raised a hand, "That's me."

He stood and introduced himself, shaking our hands. "I'm Johnny Nicholls, and I run a ranch just down the road here. The man who first settled it was John Fitzpatrick, who come down from a place called St. Catharines. You know it?"

I laughed, "Sure do — I grew up there!"

"Right near Niagara Falls, right?"

I nodded, smiling.

"See, I've looked into it *all*."

Johnny Nicholls sat down again as Gloria brought his coffee, then continued. "Uncle John, we called him, he come over to Canada from Ireland in the 1860s. He wanted to come down here then, but the Civil War was on, so he started farmin' up there. Then once the War was over, he worked his way down the Mississippi on the log booms, all the way to New Orleans, then made his way over here, and started runnin' sheep. A coupla years later, his younger brother Jim followed him down, but one cold morning his horse was kinda skittish, and it reared up on him. Jim was tryin' to hold on, and his hand come down on the hammer of his gun and he shot himself in the leg. Died of blood poisoning."

We made the appropriate grimaces of sympathy and shook our heads.

"Then old Uncle John, he'd been battlin' with this neighbor of his for a long time over water rights, and things started gettin' bad. They all used to stay out on the range in tents, you know, and one day this neighbor come ridin' into Uncle John's camp, shootin' and hollerin', and Uncle John shot him out of the saddle, dead."

He paused for effect, then added, "But he got off for self-defence."

Johnny Nicholls had our attention, and sensing our interest, he showed himself to be a fountain of local history. This had been Mexican territory before the Texas War of Independence, in 1836, and the Mexicans had barred American settlers from moving in. The Irish Catholics, however, went through the Church in Mexico City, and received permission to settle there. When the other settlers and ranchers in Texas began to agitate and organize against the Mexicans, the Irish stayed out at first, thinking their "special relationship" with the Church would result in better treatment for them. However, they soon found that they too were being exploited and ignored, and joined the fight for independence. Apparently several battles had been fought in the surrounding area.

We asked about the reservoir we'd seen on the map, so big and blue on paper, but which had turned out to be a wide, dry hollow full of skeletal trees, drowned long ago then left to slowly weather in the dry air. Johnny told us they'd dammed up the river back in '85, the reservoir had filled up in '87, then had been dry ever since. Water was obviously a critical matter in this area, for Johnny discussed the relative merits of the local rivers. He said they'd had some dry years, but it was better in this area than farther north. "Down here, it don't take much rain to make something turn green enough that a cow can eat it!"

Johnny Nicholls also warned us to watch out for wild pigs on the road, and I wondered if he meant the ones I'd read about called "javelinas" (I pronounced it like the thing you throw).

"*Havelinas*," he corrected me, then said no, these ones were bigger and meaner. Then Gloria brought his breakfast, and a couple of other ranchers came in and joined Johnny Nicholls at his table. All of them looked the part of ranchers and cowboys in their denim jeans and jackets, high-heeled boots, and hats. One of them asked another what was going on "across the road," nodding toward the courthouse, and the other said only, "The judge isn't in, and no one seems to know what's going on." Sounded like a scandal brewing in Tilden. Trouble in River City.

As Brutus and I finished our coffees and our journalizing, I heard bits of their conversation, and suddenly realized they were talking about *golf.* Different types of clubs, and courses they had played on. Texas ranchers talking about golf? As I noted in my journal, "Don't seem right!"

Then they went on to talk about oil, which seemed a more proper topic of conversation, according to my Texas script. Their conversation was sprinkled with the relative merits of petroleum, its color, pressure in pounds-per-square-inch, and the percentage of water they were pumping. Johnny Nicholls shook our hands again as we left, and just south of Tilden we saw the sign arching above a sideroad, "Johnny and Maggie Nicholls."

Their ranch had been established by "Uncle John" Fitzpatrick, who had made his way down to Texas from St. Catharines, Ontario, my hometown, way back in 1866. From then on that little crossroads town and county seat of Tilden, Texas, took its place on our "mental maps" for good, and we would never forget the Cowboy Cafe, or Johnny Nicholls, or Gloria, or even Rex Allen, the "Oklahoma Cowboy."

The Sands restaurant was not quite so memorable, but it "filled me up real good," and the following morning I was back there for an early breakfast. No hurry to get on the road today; there were no cities ahead of me now, and it was Saturday, too — no worry about beating the morning traffic to Big Bend National Park, just a few hundred miles away now. In the cool overcast, I filled up with gas at the truck stop, then headed east again on I-10.

I started my day with the Miles Davis classic, *Kind of Blue*, probably the all-time greatest improvisational jazz record. Apart from the big band stuff, I had never been much of a jazz fan, except for a flirtation with so-called "fusion" music in the '70s (much of that rock-oriented, really, Brand X, Bill Bruford, Jean-Luc Ponty, Weather Report's all-time great *Heavy Weather*, the CTI catalog, that sort of thing), but I liked to think I could recognize excellence when I heard it, regardless of genre. As with country music (which we'll "drive through" later), most modern jazz blew right by me (maybe Ralph Ellison was right in feeling that jazz died when people stopped *dancing* to it), but the few true masters were undeniable, and irresistible. The great Duke Ellington said, "There are only two kinds of music: good music, and bad music," and he was certainly one of the immortals who demanded my admiration, regardless of personal taste. Among other singular artists who compelled such appreciation, I would definitely number Miles Davis.

Though Miles and his cohorts had a lot to answer for — or at least his *imitators* did.

In the same way that Ernest Hemingway changed literature forever by chiseling his prose down to spare, almost taciturn phrases that could still convey deep emotions (while also licencing generations of would-be imitators), and the lush, carefully-orchestrated paintings of Jackson Pollock allowed too many hacks and dribblers to call themselves Abstract Expressionists, the legacy of Miles Davis and other adventurous jazz musicians (perhaps beginning with another great original, Louis Armstrong) was to unleash a flood of self-styled improvisational instrumentalists who figured that an aloof soloist noodling scales over an arbitrary set of chord changes — or a Disney showtune, or a sappy easy-listening ballad — put them in the same arena as Miles Davis.

It has been pointed out that a true abstract painting is still *of* something, and similarly, the minimalist credo of "less is more" includes the tacit understanding that less has to *mean* more. It takes a certain subtlety of taste to *understand* what a master has accomplished, let alone to imitate it. There was nothing random about what Miles Davis achieved with *Kind of Blue* — the musicians were a carefully chosen ensemble of masterful players who could help him achieve the sound, musical content, and overall mood he envisioned: Cannonball Adderley on alto saxophone, the legendary John Coltrane on tenor sax, Bill Evans on piano, Paul Chambers on bass and James Cobb on drums.

The recording was made over two days in 1959, and in the liner notes Bill Evans described the background to the sessions. "Miles conceived these settings only hours before the recording dates and arrived with sketches which indicated to the group what was to be played. Therefore, you will hear something close to pure spontaneity in these performances."

Spontaneity, perhaps, but these musicians were not "flying blind," playing any old thing whenever they felt like it. The vision of their leader gave them a road map, and Miles Davis was surely guiding every step of the journey, and the environment. He had hired the vehicle (the players), mapped the highways and background scenery (the musical structures), and conjured the weather (the bluesy, muted mood) he envisioned. Bill Evans went on to describe the pieces as "frameworks which are exquisite in their simplicity and yet contain all that is necessary to stimulate performance with a sure reference to the primary conception."

Key words there: "sure reference to the primary conception." Evans also mentioned that in each case, the first "complete take" became the master, and perhaps they simply stopped when things went awry, calling it a "false start." That's another difference in trying to create something so delicate and risky in the studio, rather than in front of an audience. In the recording studio, an uninspired performance can be redone, or attempted another day, but onstage you live and die by what comes out in the moment (or you *should;* for good or ill, most musicians seem to judge their self-worth by the credo, "You're only as good as your last show").

At that Grateful Dead concert Liam and I attended in Atlanta, Mickey Hart told me he didn't expect to have a good show that night, because the band had played an inspired performance two nights previously, and the good ones tended to come in cycles of four, for some reason. So even for a band celebrated for their improvisation (I once heard a young stagehand at a theater in New Jersey nod his drooping hair and say, "Yeah man, I dig a Dead jam"), it was not only hit and miss, but more *miss* than hit.

As with so many aspects of honest music, the balance of arranged music and improvisation to be performed ought to be determined by what the musicians *like* (Jack London wrote that the two most powerful words in the English language are "I like" — though an argument could be made for "I want"). The character of a group's music ought to be a reflection of their shared character, presented in a framework they were all truly *comfortable* with, musically and personally.

My partners and I never wanted to improvise too much in front of a paying audience, just because of that lack of consistency, and because we liked to know where we were going, in a given song, and on a given night. As live performers, we preferred to have a strong foundation that would always be at least *good*, and then on the occasional "inspired" perform-ance (whether every fourth one or not), have the freedom to stretch out from there. Even my drum solo was constructed in that mold, so that I had an arranged series of movements to work through, with set patterns to make the transitions, but there was always room for variations, and an ongoing series of experiments under development. From night to night I kept the same basic structure, length, and content, but as a whole, it was never the same twice.

Pure improvisation had been an important part of my musical educa-tion early on, though. In St. Catharines in the late '60s, the Niagara Theatre Centre was a downtown coffee house, its walls plastered with day-glo Che Guevara posters. They occasionally screened underground movies like Bob Dylan's *Don't Look Back* and John Lennon in *How I Won the War*, and also featured performance art by such local cultural insurgents as the Perth County Conspiracy and the Nihilist Spasm Band. On Thursday nights, there were open jam sessions, and members of the half dozen or so local rock bands were paid $10 each for taking part (a welcome payday in those days, when we were lucky to have one or two high school gigs per month).

There were some good players among us, but we were young and relatively clueless, and I suspect the whole thing was pretty pathetic. (Fortunately the audience was young and relatively clueless too.) I remem-ber lots of endless twelve-bar blues rambles ("Stormy Monday" every

Thursday), psychedelic excursions, and that sociopathic singer doing his Jim Morrison "I Am the Lizard King" routine. But I guess we were learning.

In *Living With Music*, Ralph Ellison wrote of the jam session as the jazz player's "true academy," and of the place of improvisation in the education of a musician, and in the eventual development of a "unique voice."

> Here it is more meaningful to speak not of courses of study, of grades and degrees, but of apprenticeship, ordeals, initiation, ceremonies, of rebirth. For after the jazzman has learned the fundamentals of his instrument and the traditional techniques of jazz — the intonations, the mute work, manipulation of timbre, the body of traditional styles — he must then "find himself," must be reborn, must find, as it were, his soul. All this through achieving that subtle identification between his instrument and his deepest drives which will allow him to express his own unique ideas and his own unique voice. He must achieve, in short, his self-determined identity.

These concepts carried equal weight in rock music, for the serious practitioners; an individual voice was likewise valued, as were technical fluency and eloquence on the instrument. If rock tended to be more vocal than instrumental, then the voice could be considered another solo instrument, along with electric guitar, and that iconic six-string had its own pantheon of expressive and passionate voices: Hendrix, Santana, Jeff Beck, Dave Gilmour, and so many more.

The guys on my bus during the *Vapor Trails* tour, driver Dave and my co-rider, Michael, were talking one night as we drove away from a show about what an underrated guitarist our Alex was, and I had to agree. In the crowded hierarchy of electric guitar-slingers, speedy exhibitionism and "bad boy" attitudes often seemed more admired than purely *musical* values, and Alex's highly original sense of melody, phrasing, orchestration, and rhythmic ensemble work did indeed seem underrated. His solos, especially, flowed out as the genuine expression of ineffable emotion, yearning, and exaltation.

Watching Alex record his solos in the studio was a powerful musical experience, a process so different from the methodical, painstaking way the rest of our records were made. Lights dimmed, he stood behind the mixing console, between the speakers, and played to the prerecorded backing track, ripping out a completely spontaneous performance every time. He played with total abandon, total surrender, his body nodding and twisting like a puppet to his own fingers, rapt in the physical expression of his soul. Again and again he would play to the same track, recording each pass, and every time through the solo was entirely different, hardly repeating a single note.

In the truest sense, Alex was completely unselfconscious, hardly *aware* of what he was doing, and the objective ears were provided by our other bandmate, Geddy, and the coproducer. After four or five takes, they would send Alex out of the room and listen through what he had done, making note of the finest passages from each take. Usually a finished performance would be edited together from several sources — the beginning of take three, cutting to take four, then back to take one, for example. In any case, the performance was still *spontaneous*, but selected from moments of inspired, sublime spontaneity. As Somerset Maugham wrote, "Only a mediocre man is always at his best."

In my instructional video, *A Work in Progress*, I quoted producer Peter Collins's response to my own efforts to combine careful preparation with a spontaneous performance: "Don't leave spontaneity to chance."

Significantly, on our most recent album, *Vapor Trails*, Alex had rejected the whole tradition of obligatory guitar solos, choosing to develop instrumental sections of the songs with layered creations of textured sounds, backwards guitar notes, and background vocal effects.

A lot of our songwriting had been based on improvisation, too, and in much the same selective way. During our concert tours, we often begin our afternoon sound checks with an "excursion," where one or another of us starts playing something, the others join in, and off we go. (If Alex was in the mood, he would sometimes step to the microphone and deliver amazing comedic performances, long-winded, bizarre stories about crew members and current events, which culminated most recently in his rants during "La Villa Strangiato" on the *Vapor Trails* tour — never the same twice, and ranging from the sublimely hilarious to the merely funny.) Over the years those jams and explorations were often recorded for future reference, and at the end of the tour, when we were back in the songwriting mode, they were mined for golden nuggets.

Similarly, when we began the songwriting for *Vapor Trails* in 2001, after five years of not working together (following my personal tragedies, as recounted in *Ghost Rider*), Geddy and Alex set up in the studio and just started playing together, recording everything, then going back later to search for interesting pieces of inspiration. After nearly thirty years, the three of us had worked together in many different ways, the "group method" gradually refined over time to accommodate each of our specialties and preferences, to allow me to work on the lyrics and the drum parts slowly and methodically, on my own; Alex to be both spontaneous and obsessive with his guitar parts; and Geddy to be painstaking in endless refinement of the arrangements and vocal parts.

I have always liked the saying, "No work of art is ever finished, it is only *abandoned*," but in regard to recording and mixing, Geddy prefers the other version, "No work of art is ever finished, it is only *taken away*."

And oh, is there a metaphor for life in that. I don't think any life is ever truly considered *finished*, in the sense of completed and ready to give up, but some lives are certainly abandoned, one way or another (out of resignation, fear, surrender, grief, insurmountable limitations, even suicide), and some are definitely taken away — too soon, too soon.

And so it was with popular music too, that a particular style never seemed to be really finished or used up, but more often taken away, somehow — not by the artists themselves, but by external forces. Rock 'n' roll had no sooner been born than it was co-opted by marketers and fakers and reduced to a slick formula, as it would be again and again, forcing the rebels and visionaries to play along, fade away, or fight back. Fortunately, some of them were willing to fight, and there were also occasional revolutions from the "garage bands" that brought back sincerity. As soon as popular music became too difficult for teenage beginners to emulate, whether technically or technologically, there would be a rebellion: punk, grunge, even rap. As soon as a pimply-faced kid with a second-hand guitar or microphone couldn't play what was on the radio, before long he would put something *new* on the radio.

The record companies seemed to think they controlled the music business, but the reality was much more reactionary, and more like bankers gambling with venture capital. They could, and did, spend millions trying to *create* a hit (a long article by John Seabrook in the July 7th, 2003 issue of *The New Yorker*, called "The Money Note," examined the state of the modern-day record business — as distinguished from the *music* business — and captured the cynical, artless mechanics of this process), but when the Next Big Thing came blaring out of a scruffy club in New York, or a garage in Seattle, all the salesmen could do was scramble all over each other trying to capitalize on the new revolution.

In jazz, for example, the big bands had faded away in the late forties, and their decline was variously blamed on artistic exhaustion, economic conditions, or a changing audience. Ralph Ellison had an interesting perspective on that, and how the same forces governed rock music by the early '60s:

> Cultural forms, especially forms of popular music, become trivialized through the efforts of promoters to package novelty. This has a negative effect on art. The jazz of the thirties and forties was not exhausted artistically; they were supplanted by promoters who were more interested in making money than in art. The big bands were broken up by agents who convinced sidemen that they would make more money by going on the road as members or leaders of small combos. We can't overlook the economic conditions that made it difficult to maintain a big band, nor the war, but the agents were largely responsible. In this country the direction of culture is always being tampered with by people who have little concern for art, and yet their manipulations have conse-

quences in other areas of the society, often leading to chaos in our lifestyles and moral disorientation. As with the Beatles, who with their Liverpool-accented rebellion and Afro-American influenced music hit this country and its young like a ton of bricks. I think that some of the attitudes promoted by the boppers, their discouragement of the dancers, the legend of [Charlie] Parker's drug habit — such things helped make the Beatles phenomenon possible. The artistic quality of the Beatles' music was masked by their irreverent behavior. It sounded easier than it actually was and this was helped by the use of electrified instruments and their costumes. Such details made many white kids believe that they could create a do-it-yourself type of music. As I indicated in the Minton's piece, so many who didn't grasp the agony of Parker or the music he created imitated his drug-taking and irresponsibility. Suddenly you couldn't visit friends who had adolescent children without having to listen to them bang on guitars and little electric pianos. And yet for all its tastelessness, at a time when Johnny Hodges was hardly making a living, such noise became the source of great wealth and facile celebrity.

On one of the Rush tours around 1980, we had a night off in Evansville, Indiana, at the Executive Inn, and a few of us from the band and crew, and from our opening act, Max Webster, went down to the "show bar" to see Woody Herman perform. Like Buddy Rich in his later years, Woody Herman had kept his big band going in difficult economic times by hiring young musicians fresh out of college music programs, but Woody's band played his charts competently, and like Buddy again, he had always included a lot of modern arrangements in his repertoire.

Also like Buddy, Woody Herman had had serious problems with the IRS, had even famously lost his home, so he was out there on the road from necessity, not desire. He was almost seventy, stooped and sagging, but he tootled his clarinet well enough, and the band sounded good. However, it was sad to see that by the time of his second show, at 11:00 on a Sunday night, there were barely a dozen people in the audience, most of them long-haired rock people — us.

Visibly disgusted, Woody finally walked off the stage while the band played, only to reappear wearing a trench coat and standing on the dance floor in front of the band, frowning and gesticulating as he stormed off, leaving the band to fill in their time with a little impromptu "rehearsal." The one time I'd seen Frank Sinatra perform live, in Toronto in the late '70s, Woody Herman and his "Thundering Herd" had been the backing orchestra, but those kinds of gigs were rare for a big band in modern times, and it was sad to see one of the all-time great bandleaders obviously reduced to a struggle for survival.

Back in 2003, after a thousand miles of Interstate 10, I was finally able to get off the freeway, at Kent, Texas, where I turned off onto Highway 118, a two-lane headed south. Looking over the map the previous night, I had decided it looked like the most scenic, circuitous route down to Big Bend, through what was obviously the emptiest part of all Texas, crossed by the fewest roads. A scattering of ranches bordered the lonely road, dry, hilly country under a gray sky, and I settled into a fast, yet relaxed pace.

Kind of Blue came to an end, and a lush, waltz-time string arrangement heralded a completely different piece of work, in every way: Dusty Springfield's cult classic, *Dusty in Memphis*. Dusty was a British pop singer known for what she described as "big, ballady things," and this record combined her with American producers and the legendary Memphis R&B musicians who had backed artists like Wilson Pickett and Aretha Franklin (though apparently Dusty was never actually *in* Memphis, as her vocals were overdubbed in a New York studio). Recorded in 1968, *Dusty in Memphis* produced the hit single, "Son of a Preacher Man" (later featured in the movie *Pulp Fiction*, which gave it a brief revival in her lifetime — she died of cancer in '99), but the album seemed to languish in obscurity for many years. I kept hearing or reading about it here and there through the '70s and '80s, then ended up searching out the CD in the early '90s, not from hearing the music, but because I kept hearing so much *about* it.

If I read a well-written book review, sometimes I feel pretty sure I'll like a book before I ever read it, and similarly, *Dusty in Memphis* must have been spoken of by people whose opinions I trusted, or in terms that spoke to me, for I always had a feeling about it. At that time it remained difficult to find, and I enlisted a friend of mine, Skip, who collected obscure CDs, to track it down for me. Once I heard it, sure enough, it became one of my perennial favorites, especially for "morning music" (the first song rather racily celebrates early-morning eroticism, opening with the lines, "Just a little lovin'/ Early in the morning/ Beats a cup of coffee/ For starting off your day").

The whole album has a certain *easy* mood, as comfortable as the companionship of an old friend, and is also easy on the ears (despite the primitive use of stereo, which shoves the drums way off to the right channel with the horns, backing vocals on the left, and bass and voice down the middle), with so *many* great songs. Just reading down the list of composers is impressive: no fewer than five by Gerry Goffin and Carole King, and the rest by Mann/Weil (another former couple as well as songwriting partners, like Goffin and King), Bacharach/David, Bergman/Legrand, and two great songs by Randy Newman, "Just One Smile" and "I Don't Want To Hear It Anymore."

Great songs, great musicians, great arrangements, especially the horn and string charts by Arif Mardin (who wrote the arrangement of "Picking Up the Pieces" drummer Steve Ferrone played with Buddy's band on *Burning For Buddy*), and backing vocals by the Sweet Inspirations, while soaring over it all was Dusty Springfield's incomparable voice, sometimes light and ethereal, sometimes edgy and narrative, then growing big and bold and opening to a wide vibrato.

The road ahead of me began to wriggle as it climbed into the Davis Mountains, and I didn't pass another car for miles. Feeling the Z-8 balancing power and grip so effortlessly, the series of linked curves tempted me to step up the pace, attack those corners, smooth them off, then accelerate to the next one, brake, turn smoothly while the tires "gave" just a little. Falling into a rhythm and keeping the car always balanced, like skiing through a series of carved turns, I took my right hand off the shifter and pressed the button on the console marked "Sport," and felt the accelerator become more sensitive, more responsive, following a different electronic "map" in that intelligent, adaptable car (the difference was described in that hardcover book that came with the car as "smooth and easy or sporty and eager"). Thank Munich it still had a manual transmission, though most modern supercars had Formula One-style "paddle shifters" on the steering wheel, where a flick of one hand or the other could upshift or downshift automatically.

It wasn't just hidebound nostalgia, I hope, that made me cling to the notion that balancing clutch, brakes, gearshift, steering, and throttle with hands and feet and mental concentration was a satisfying, graceful act of coordination and control. Something like playing drums, I suppose, and likewise, who cared if electronic drums could play more precisely, more "efficiently," than any human drummer? They were not more *fun*. Maybe an electronic control unit could program and instantly update the engine's ignition and fuel delivery, but not its driver — he, like I was, should be driving quickly along a curvy road and rowing up and down the gears, right foot dancing between gas and brake as I worked on my heel-and-toe downshifts.

That was a technique one didn't get to use everyday, especially in Los Angeles. Just as on the motorcycle I had learned the racer's technique of squeezing the brake lever hard with my right two fingers, and at the same time rotating the throttle quickly as I blipped down the gears, at a racctrack driving school I had learned the traditional heel-and-toe method for making smooth, rapid-fire downshifts. Like another near-obsolete technique that had challenged me for years, telemark skiing (a traditional technique of downhill skiing using cross-country bindings, with one ski initiating the turn while the other follows, heel raised, both knees bent, in an elegant crouch which rises then bends again to carve the next linked turn), it wasn't easy to do, but it was beautiful and satisfying when you got it right. Back off the throttle and brush the brakes to shift the car's weight forward, simultaneously dab in the clutch pedal with the left foot while the right foot swiveled to keep braking with one side while raising the engine revs with the other side of the same foot, downshift to second, then let out the clutch and feed in the gas. The motto of *Automobile* magazine in its early days was *cogito ergo zoom* — I think, therefore I speed — and that was how I felt about it.

During the *Test for Echo* tour in '96, Brutus and I were riding cross-country one time, and stopped at a Cracker Barrel restaurant in Tennessee on a Sunday morning. A black couple came in behind us, the woman large with a flowered dress and hat, the man small and skinny in a suit and tie. He was smiling kind of sheepishly as she harangued him with a pointing finger, presumably about his driving: "You workin' them angels overtime — you workin' them angels *overtime!*"

From then on, Brutus and I often used that line on each other, to describe the way we lived, on and off the bikes, and it had continued to be a metaphor for my life. I didn't *think* I was foolhardy, or irresponsible, but a certain level of risk in life seemed worthwhile for the promised return — excitement and treasured experiences — and though I didn't really believe in "them angels," if I had them, I guessed I kept them pretty busy.

In a seldom-visited corner of my mind, I knew I probably couldn't get away with carrying on like that forever, but it still seemed the right way to live — as if every day were my last, though hoping desperately that it might not be. My five decades so far had been filled with a serious amount of risky behavior: bicycling, fast driving, smoking, drinking, recreational drugs, motorcycling, and even a vast number of journeys by air, by bus, or worse, by ferry (the most dangerous mode of public transport). Someday, I had to realize, one of those might *get* me.

The only consolation was that I could only die of *one thing*, and there was no knowing what that would be, or when it would strike. Earthquake, aneurysm, plane crash, any of the dark multitude of cancers — who knew?

Carrie sometimes type-casts me as a "risk-taker," even a "daredevil," talking of the way I drive, motorcycle, and *live*, and I guess it's true. How do I equate being "intelligent" with being moderately (I say) self-destructive?

Thrills? Yes. Sensuality? Yes. Sheer cantankerousness? Yes.

One morning not long ago I was riding my motorcycle along Santa

Monica Boulevard in West Hollywood, just on my way to the dealer for
some service work, when I stopped at a red light and smelled something
burning. I looked all around, then finally down, where my mind went *electric* at the sight of a ball of flame around my right cylinder head. With an
astonished curse, I kicked down the sidestand and got off, circling warily
around front to see that a sheet of newspaper had wrapped itself around
my exhaust pipe and caught fire. I kicked the charred paper away, and
everything was fine, but the flames had been right beside the fuel injector,
and right under the gas tank, and it certainly could have been a deadly disaster, one of those "freak accidents" you hear about.

As I bicycle to the YMCA down Wilshire Boulevard in Santa Monica, riding between parked cars and two lanes of oblivious traffic, avoiding buses
and signal-free turners, I often think that bicycling is actually the most dangerous thing I do — especially when I read the story about the English
musician, Mary Hansen, from Stereolab, being killed on her bicycle in
London. Not your typical "rock star" death, but it happens. Everything does.

On the wall of my Quebec house hangs a beautiful lithograph on plexiglas of an artfully interpreted, multicolored bicycle wheel. It was created
by Canadian artist Greg Curnoe, who was killed by a truck while riding his
bicycle on an Ontario country road, and the artwork was dedicated to his
friend, "Doc," who was also killed while riding his bicycle.

So no sense playing it *too* carefully, at the cost of missing out on worthwhile experiences, opportunities, or simply *fun*. Like Jack London's credo,
"The proper function of man is to live, not to exist. I shall not waste my
days in trying to prolong them. I shall use my time."

Or Fred Nietzsche again, "'Was that life?', I want to say to death. 'Well
then, once more!'"

The reward I felt for "workin' them angels" was not about conquering
fear, or getting away with being foolhardy, but simply the quest for *excitement* — the kind of excitement you live to tell, or write, about. I do not
like fear. On my motorcycle, for example, anytime I felt a thrill of fear,
even as a result of someone else's sloppy, careless driving, I would blame
myself, and make a silent vow not to let that situation happen again.

My friend Mendelson Joe taught me that lesson, when I first started riding a motorcycle, in 1994 (finally getting over that teenage minibike trauma!). After I had been riding for a few months, I wrote to Joe and told him I felt I had achieved a reasonable competence on the machine, "from now on, if anything happens, at least it won't be *my* fault."

Joe wrote back and said, "It's *always* your fault," and I realized he was right. It was up to me to be vigilant, and not to put myself in a position of *vulnerability* — where that guy could cut me off, or that woman could turn left in front of me — and it was up to me not to take a corner too fast to deal with a patch of gravel or a stalled truck.

There's a motorcycle safety acronym called SIPDE, for scan, identify, predict, decide, and execute. Scan your surroundings at all times, identify potential dangers and the apparent intentions of other traffic, predict what they *might* do, decide how to protect yourself, then execute the necessary maneuver. The key element of this process might be said to be *imagination*, in being able to observe a situation in the present, picture several possible scenarios in the future and evaluate them, then imagine a course of action to fit each possibility. Similarly, when I see someone riding a motorcycle in shorts, sandals, and a tank top, I can only wince at their vulnerability, and put it down to a failure of *imagination:* they are apparently incapable of picturing what *might* happen.

So, the mission was to seek excitement, but minimize vulnerability, and avoid fear.

And, as I experienced excitement, minimized vulnerability, and avoided fear on that narrow, curvy highway in Texas, after about twenty miles of that enjoyable dance with car and road, the highway divided ahead of me. I paused to consider the alternatives. A light rain had started to fall, and on the map the right fork showed as a longer loop through the Davis Mountains. Both routes ended at Fort Davis, and both were marked with the dotted lines of a scenic road. The right road was signed "Scenic Loop 166," and though it was longer, I was in no hurry that day, and I decided to take it, despite the rain. It was, after all, the high road.

The narrow two-lane curved higher into the mountains, among tall yellow grass, dense green junipers, and distant rounded hills and rocky outcrops. As I drove, I glanced down at the outside temperature on the display screen and watched it fall from the 40s down through the 30s, and then all the way down to a frigid 28°F.

By then the rain had turned to sleet, filling the air with driving pellets of ice, and the roadside was bordered in a clumpy white blanket of snow, which must have fallen overnight. I slowed down in such slippery, curvy conditions, and in some areas I felt the car's traction-control kick in, controlling wheelspin as my wide tires scrabbled at a crumbling surface of gray ice. Once again I thought about what I would do if I were on my motorcycle in those conditions. Turn around, I guessed, and try to go around another way. Though I couldn't help sometimes feeling a twinge of guilt for doing it "the easy way," that day I was again glad to be driving.

Paul Young's *Other Voices* kept me company through the Davis Mountains and the snow and ice, another one from the library of music that endures. I had been listening to this one from time to time for more than ten years, since first hearing his version of the Chi-Lites hit, "Oh Girl," and the theme from the movie *Baghdad Café*, "Calling You."

Other Voices was definitely a product of its times, having been recorded in the halcyon late '80s on what must have been a sizeable budget, in studios in London, New York, and Los Angeles, with several producers and an all-star assemblage of musicians, including Dave Gilmour, Stevie Wonder, Steve Winwood, Pino Palladino (one of my favorite bass players, who took over John Entwistle's demanding job following his tragic death from a heart attack, apparently cocaine-related, just before The Who tour in 2002), and two of my favorite drummers as well, Vinnie Colaiuta and the wonderful Manu Katché.

Manu's unique style seemed to be at least partly a result of his heritage — a mother from France and a father from the Ivory Coast — and he incorporated the rhythmic, syncopated stabs of West African pop music into the driving backbeat of American funk. Manu's drumming had been showcased on several landmark recordings, with Peter Gabriel, Robbie Robertson, Sting, and several of the songs on this Paul Young album. I had the pleasure of working with Manu on the Buddy Rich tribute sessions, in May of '94. Like most of the guest drummers, Manu played on one of Buddy's signature arrangements, a tune called "No Jive," joined by Brazilian percussionist Mino Cinélu, who had worked with Miles Davis and Weather Report.

Together they wove a rhythmic spell that began with subtle insinuations of the pulse, locking into a syncopated introduction, then melding into the driving, rock-funk meat of the song. Toward the end Manu played a solo that was utterly, head-shakingly amazing — so sophisticated technically, yet so exciting viscerally, that for this listener (and drummer) it represented the kind of seemingly effortless mastery we were honoring in Buddy himself.

Like many drummers, Manu was a quiet, gentle soul away from the drums, and a nice person to work with, so warm and personable. He was living in Montreal at the time with a French-Canadian girl, so we had some "common ground," too. The Brazilian percussionist, Mino, was equally sweet, and both of them pressed their home phone numbers on me before we parted.

Among musicians, it is generally accepted that drummers are "different," particularly in their sense of community. Perhaps that is partly a shared humility from being relegated to the "background" most of the time, and from the lack of respect they were sometimes given by other musicians. (Including a myriad of "drummer jokes," like "How many musicians in your band?" "Four musicians, and a drummer," or, "What do you call someone who hangs out with musicians?" "A drummer.")

The fraternity among drummers was often warm and real, and when Gene Krupa was sick with leukemia later in his life, Buddy Rich arranged a celebration in New York to bring together Gene's friends and former bandmates, growling, "It seems to me you should give flowers to the *living.*" Whenever Buddy and Gene played their traditional "drum battles," friends could see that Buddy, despite his reputed ego, actually held *back*, so as not to make his friend look bad.

The Buddy Rich tribute project was another example of the brotherhood of Planet Drum, when we had many of the finest drummers of the day working for union scale to pay tribute to another drummer. Nearly everyone we asked to take part showed up ready to play, excepting only a few (Vinnie Colaiuta, Terry Bozzio, Louis Bellson) who were out of the country during our brief two-week window of recording time. Even with two drummers coming in and out of the Manhattan studio each day, a bond was forged, and by the time we worked together, and maybe broke bread together later, nearly every one of those drummers became a friend.

Manu's drumming on "No Jive" took the central role in a driving ensemble, with ample space to "play out," but his playing on the Paul Young record was more typical of his work as an accompanist — restrained and sensitive, yet no less exciting. I especially loved Manu's compelling, aggressive-but-relaxed (an alternate definition of "menacing?") backbeat and lyrical, dynamic fills in "Right About Now," and he offered subtle nuances to "Stop On By" and "Softly Whispering I Love You."

The other drummers on the record, Vinnie Colaiuta and Neil Conti, were also very accomplished players, and with star turns like Dave Gilmour's guitar work and Stevie Wonder's virtuoso harmonica solo on "Calling You," all creating a frame around Paul Young's raspy, soulful vocals, it added up to a satisfying musical meal.

I slowed through the small town of Fort Davis, and then the road ahead of me became flat and straight, a line leading away to the vanishing point, not another car in sight. I had been watching for a stretch of road like this, to really let out the horses and see how fast this car would go. The owner's manual claimed its top speed had been "electronically limited" to 155 mph, as most German cars seemed to be (in a bow to the European Union, in return for the German insistence on retaining their stretches of autobahn with unlimited speed limits), and I had also read that this cut-off point had been established because the BMW engineers felt the car's front end became too aerodynamically light beyond that speed. For me, it was time to find out.

I reached down and turned the stereo off, then gripped the wheel firmly at the ten-to-two position, and pressed my right foot *down*. The engine roared, the wind roared and the blurry pavement and smeared landscape came rushing at me. In a matter of seconds the speedometer hit 155, and just held it, the car hardly straining, and the front end feeling completely stable and "planted." Unrestrained, the car would willingly have gone faster, but as another car appeared in the distance and grew rapidly closer, I decided that was fast enough, and I had been there. Workin' them angels again. I eased back to 100, which now seemed a leisurely pace, and turned the music back on.

Parachutes, by the British band Coldplay, was their highly successful debut in 2000. A restrained, reflective series of moody songs, enhanced texturally by guitars and keyboards, and driven by a solid, dynamic rhythm section, created an overall listening experience of *luxe, calme, et volupté*. The songs were woven into one another like a series of Impressionist paintings unfolding one into the next, and I once read an interview with one of the band members saying they had intended to make a piece of music you could sit down with your girlfriend and listen to all the way through.

The morning remained cold, in the mid-forties, even in the lower elevations, and through Alpine I noticed a Saturday gathering of motorcycles outside restaurants. A couple of Harleys cruised the main street, the riders wearing sweatshirts, scarves, and heavy gloves with their leather jackets and chaps. As I continued south, the roadside was dotted for miles with a spread-out line of dozens of bicyclists, all wearing rain gear, plastic hoods drawn up under their helmets, long-fingered gloves, and neoprene booties over their shoes. They looked *cold*, and I turned up the heater.

For the next 80 miles I fell into a kind of trance, lulled by a long, empty road, a brisk, but vigilant pace under heavy gray skies, and my current favorite CD of all, *Grace*, by Jeff Buckley. I had been saving this one for just such a time and place, and I smiled and nodded along as he and his great band launched into "Mojo Pin." The voice of a tortured angel, a rich palette of electric guitar sounds and styles, an overall variety of rhythmic, melodic, and dynamic shifts, and a first-rate production job by Andy Wallace (perhaps best known as a wizard mixing engineer, brought in at the final stage of a project to bring it all to life again, from Nirvana to

Linkin Park to our own *Test for Echo* album) and recording engineer Clif
Norrell (who had also worked on *Test for Echo*, and became known to us
as "Wee Kiltie," after we saw a photo of him as a child wearing a kilt; this
also led to weeks of haggis jokes).

Grace was the first and only album completed by Jeff Buckley, son of
the '60s folk-rocker Tim Buckley, who died young of an accidental
heroin-morphine overdose right in my adopted hometown of Santa
Monica. Jeff would also die tragically young, in Memphis, drowning
rather mysteriously in the Wolf River just as he was about to start recording his second album, in May, 1997. According to David Browne's *Dream
Brother*, a biography of both Tim and Jeff Buckley, their deaths had both
been accidental, yet almost inevitable in other ways — their shared personality traits of obtuseness, willfulness, and a kind of stubborn naïvete.
They had both wrestled with the principles of "artistic integrity" (a
phrase that seems sadly quaint these days) against the juggernaut of commerce, but too often they chose the wrong battles, the wrong lines to
draw. For example, Jeff had fought hard to have Tom Verlaine produce his
second album, although the record company was against it, and when the
demo sessions with Verlaine turned out to be disappointing, even to
Buckley, he insisted on working with him, out of some quixotic resistance
to "caving" to the record company. Meanwhile, of course, only his own
work was going to suffer.

Jeff Buckley's short life also stood as a testament to the twin principles
of success, at least artistically, for he was both gifted *and* dedicated (the
pillars of greatness). He had concentrated on his guitar playing in his
teens and early twenties, studying at the Musician's Institute in Los
Angeles, practicing incessantly, and paying his dues in bands and as a solo
performer long before he made *Grace*. (I was surprised to read that when
he was twelve, his prized possession was a Rush *Hemispheres* picture-disc
hanging on his wall, and that in his high school bands he played "Tom
Sawyer" and "The Spirit of Radio" — how nice to feel like a small part of
the musical development of such an artist.)

On the subject of dedication to a craft in *addition* to talent, I was struck by the words of Ralph Ellison, about his transition from trying to be a musician to trying to be a writer.

> **Interviewer:** Do you think your musical training gave you a discipline or an understanding of a need for discipline in order to approach a new artistic craft?
>
> **Ellison:** Yes, you didn't expect to be able to play because you felt something. You were taught very quickly that there were ways in which the body had to be taught to react, to project itself, to relate to the instrument and to the score. So you began to discipline yourself that way. At Tuskegee I had to get up at five o'clock in the morning and stand in an open window and blow sustained tones on the trumpet for an hour before breakfast. So when I got to writing I said, "Well, if it worked for music it must work the same way for writing." And therefore I wrote many short stories, and in fact I attempted a novel six months after I decided I was going to try to write. But I put these things aside because I looked upon them as what they were: just exercises which would allow me to learn something of the nature of the craft. You see, with writing people get the feeling that a writer is someone that feels things passionately; that all you have to do is go to a typewriter or pick up a pen and pencil and put your feelings down. And of course nothing is done that way.

Important lessons for the would-be musician *or* writer there, and what Ellison describes very much mirrors my own growth from music into prose writing — attempting stories, essays, even a novel, all of them merely exercises to learn *how* to express myself in words, and later put aside).

Grace had been out for a few years, but somehow I missed hearing it at first, and then, in the wake of my tragedies, I wasn't hearing anything new for a while. As with *Dusty in Memphis*, though, I seemed to keep hearing *about* Jeff Buckley. During the *Test for Echo* sessions, I remember Andy Wallace and Clif Norrell talking about working with him, and later, Geddy asking me if I had heard him, and Alex nodding in agreement. Jeff Buckley's name just seemed to pop up from time to time in "better circles." He drowned in 1997, just before my own losses began, but I remember hearing about that, too, and that he was the son of Tim Buckley. I particularly associated the father with the beautiful song "Morning Glory," covered on the first album by Blood, Sweat and Tears (the Al Kooper version of the band, on a well-crafted, pioneering album from 1968 that still sounds remarkably good).

Not long before my Big Bend journey, Carrie and I had attended a dinner party at the home of some friends over in the San Fernando Valley, with two other straight couples and a gay couple (always a good combination, for this hetero homophile). During after-dinner show-and-tell, one of the gay guys showed a sampler from a film he was directing. The moody footage of sex and romance in Singapore played out over the most beautiful soundtrack, a song so great I had one of those "How did I not hear this before?" moments. "Hallelujah," it was called, by Jeff Buckley, and everyone in the room seemed equally transfixed by the haunting song, possibly offending the director by gushing more over the music than his film-making (though as ever, such great music only made the visuals more powerful). I also had to laugh when he mixed up his Buckleys, and said Jeff was the son of *William F.* Buckley.

In the film's credits I noticed the song was written by one "L. Cohen," and guessed (correctly) that it would have been Canada's Leonard Cohen, a long-running institution of folky, intellectual, quirky, lugubrious-voiced songs like "Suzanne" and "I'm Your Man," and a body of work that, if not mainstream, was widely admired enough to have spawned a tribute by other artists doing his songs, called *I'm Your Fan*. From *Dream Brother*, I learned that Buckley had picked up on and learned "Hallelujah" from John Cale's version in that tribute.

The next day I went to the record store and bought *Grace*, and took it with me on a two-day trip up to Big Sur in the Z-8. I played it once, and I turned it up. I listened to it again, and fell more in love with it every time. So many great songs — all of them — and the songwriting, the playing, and especially the *singing*, were so original, so powerful, and so accomplished, that the tragedy of his loss, after making only the one record (though a flood of demos and live recordings was released in his wake), seemed ever more poignant. It was clear to me that Jeff Buckley had been one of the few Great Ones, a one-in-a-billion talent, a true voice of his generation, and at thirty, he had hardly begun. Whatever is left behind in the passing of a rare talent, so much is always lost.

Asked in a 2003 interview what he was listening to lately, Jimmy Page replied, "Nothing that's had the impact on me that Jeff Buckley did," and coincidentally, in the same issue of *Mojo* magazine, Elton John was asked about his favorite all-time record, and he cited either *Nina Simone at Town Hall* or Jeff Buckley's *Grace*: "Like an album made by someone from another planet." (Also interesting that Nina Simone was one of Buckley's many influences, which ranged from Nusrat Fateh Ali Khan to the MC5.)

The real avatars of popular music over the years seemed obvious to me, but like everybody's list of such all-time greats, it had to remain arguable. I never included those who were merely *popular*, or even just *talented*, but the true artists who were lightning rods, signal fires, receivers and amplifiers and transmitters — those who held their audience, heart and soul and *zeitgeist* in their very being, and sang it back to them. Flaubert said a novel should be "a mirror moving down the road," and that's a fair ideal for a song, a musician, a band, and a career.

Another French writer, Émile Zola, said, "A work of art is a corner of nature seen through a temperament," and if we dissect that sentence with Aristotelian precision, and give proper weight to the idea of "temperament" — *soul* — then it speaks of something true and profound.

A thought which I picked up somewhere and used about Buddy Rich, "Genius is the fire that lights itself," seems apt in the context of the *true* souls, the ones who were helpless to pour themselves out, to give everything they had, to burn like a comet — and indeed, some of those fires disintegrated on contact with the atmosphere, became an *auto-da-fé*.

Any pantheon has deities of greater or lesser magnitude, but my art-history avatar, Professor Gombrich, felt an artist should be judged by his or her best work, and thus I would nominate the best work of artists like Duke Ellington, Frank Sinatra, Billie Holiday, Patsy Cline, Brian Wilson, Bob Dylan, Joni Mitchell, Pete Townshend, Jimi Hendrix, Janis Joplin, Bob Marley, Roger Waters, Kurt Cobain, and my latest nominee, Jeff Buckley.

There are some obvious "institutions" missing from my list, like Elvis Presley and the Beatles, and though it is not my purpose to quarrel with others' tastes, that just reflects a feeling about Elvis and the early Beatles being *reactionary* talents, repackaging other people's fires (original black music, in both cases, rock and R&B), and making it palatable to a white audience.

Elvis's first producer, Sam Phillips of Sun Records fame, said he had been "looking for a white boy who could sing black," and many early Beatles songs were covers of black American hits, from "Twist and Shout" to "Please Mr. Postman." Interviewed during the Beatles' first American tour, in 1964, John Lennon stated that their influences were all from American music, especially, as he termed it, "colored American music."

Elvis Presley had a golden voice, and certainly John Lennon and Paul McCartney wrote an unbelievable number of catchy pop tunes, many of them truly great, but they also skillfully adopted the trends occurring around them: American music, from Memphis to Haight-Ashbury.

In Nick Hornby's *Songbook*, he wrote a series of thoughtful essays on songs he loved, and produced one of the few books on a personal love for pop music. Reading *Songbook*, it occurred to me that Hornby's feelings about pop music so paralleled my own that I agreed with nearly everything he had to say — except the music. I liked almost *nothing* he liked, except his own work, and it seems probable that he would like nothing I liked, including my own work.

In discussing a song called "Smoke," by the Ben Folds Five, he drew an incisive bead on the Beatles as emblems of the '60s.

> It's possible that this sort of craft goes unnoticed because "Smoke" is "just" a song, in the way that "Yesterday" or "Something" weren't "just" songs. The young men who wrote them were also, unwittingly or not, in the process of changing the world (or

— to attempt to cover all the arguments in one clumsy parenthesis — in the process of being given credit for changing the world, unwittingly or not). This inevitably means that an awful lot of attention was focused on their talent — which, after all, was ostensibly the only world-changing tool at their disposal. If you're singers, and you're changing the world, then people are bound to look pretty closely at what you're singing — because how else are you doing it? As a consequence, some very good, very pretty, very sharply written, brilliantly produced and undeniably memorable songs have been credited with an almost supernatural power. It's what happens when people are deified. The eighteenth-century British scholar Edmond Malone calculated that Shakespeare "borrowed" two-thirds — 4,144 out of 6,033 lines — from other sources for *Henry IV* parts I, II, and III. And though *Henry IV* is a minor play, the point is that this stuff was out there, in the world, and Shakespeare inhaled it. What he exhaled was mostly genius, of course, but it was not genius that came out of the blue; it had a context.

The Beatles had a context, too, but they seem to have inhaled that along with everything else: they have hoovered up and become the sixties, and everything that happened in that extraordinary decade somehow belongs to them now. Their songs have therefore become imbued with all sorts of magic that doesn't properly belong to them, and we can't see the songs as songs any more.

The word "inspiration" comes from the same root as the French *inspirer*, to breathe in, and the Beatles certainly breathed in what was around them, were *inspired* by it, from Buddy Holly (after whose band name, the Crickets, they chose their own name) to Chuck Berry to Smokey Robinson to Phil Spector to Bob Dylan to Brian Wilson.

Considering the brief span in which the Beatles actually *worked* (from their first hit in 1963 until they stopped touring in 1966 and broke up completely in 1969), they definitely had a context, though it has indeed been "hoovered up" by baby-boomer nostalgia and oldies radio stations. Their more ambitious works, like *Sergeant Pepper*, were clearly influenced by the work of other pioneers, like Brian Wilson and Pete Townshend (as Lennon and McCartney admitted, citing *Pet Sounds* and *The Who Sell Out*). Their prolific songwriting and appealing voices combined with George Martin's adventurous production (an often underrated part of the Beatles chemistry) kept them at the forefront of popular music for those few years, but the Beatles have echoed down the subsequent decades like a sonic boom, deafening people not only to what else was going on, but even, as Hornby pointed out, to the songs themselves.

As George Martin wrote, "without *Pet Sounds*, *Sergeant Pepper* wouldn't have happened. *Pepper* was an attempt to equal *Pet Sounds*," and McCartney stated, "No one is educated musically until they've heard *Pet Sounds*. It is a total, classic record that is unbeatable in many ways."

Martin also wrote that when they were working on John Lennon's "Strawberry Fields Forever," Paul McCartney was worried that it was "too weird," and wrote "Penny Lane" to be released with it, and be more widely appealing.

After their break-up, Lennon wrote a vicious song about McCartney called "How Do You Sleep?", and that angry *ad hominem* attack ("Those freaks was right when they said you was dead/ The one mistake you made was in your head") showed the depth of his contempt for his former partner. Although McCartney went on to produce some good work on his own (*Ram*, particularly), it is interesting that neither of their solo efforts seemed even half as good as the Beatles. Despite their differences, and Lennon's wish to follow an artist's vision, they seemed to feed each other.

Their separate comments about their manager, Brian Epstein, also told a tale. John Lennon once said, "Brian put us in suits, and we made it very, very big. But we sold out. The Beatles' music died then." Paul McCartney seemed to deny anything negative ever said about the Beatles: "People used to say we were manipulated. We were never manipulated." An interviewer mentioned to McCartney that some people had criticized *The White Album* by saying that it ought to have been a single album rather than a double (something this sixteen-year-old reviewer had said at the time, in a scathing review in my high-school newspaper), and he replied, "Shut up — it's the Beatles' *White Album*," as if that's all there was to say about it.

As a teenager in the late '60s, I remember being confused about what the Beatles were supposed to *be*. I liked "rock" music, but they seemed more like "pop" music, sometimes almost the dreaded teeny-bopper, bubblegum music my young-musician friends and I so despised. I was growing into a sense of the principle of "artistic integrity" in music, and it didn't feel as though the Beatles shared that defiant rebellion and desperate sincerity.

Similarly, I remember being disappointed when the Rolling Stones yielded to censorship and management pressure and changed the lyrics of "Let's Spend the Night Together" to "Let's Spend Some Time Together," so they would be allowed to sing their latest single on "The Ed Sullivan Show." It seemed to me then, and still seems now, that if they couldn't change the reality of censorship, they could certainly have sung a different, less-offensive song. Or chosen not to appear.

Conversely, when the Doors performed "Light My Fire" on the Sullivan show and were asked to change the line, "girl we couldn't get much higher," they agreed, but when Jim Morrison got to that line, he sang it *louder* instead. They were banned from the show after that, but the statement had been made — the Doors were rebels, while the Stones, despite their image, were not.

A few years earlier, when Elvis first performed on "The Ed Sullivan Show," his hip gyrations were considered so outrageously sexual that the cameras only showed him from the waist *up*. That tells a story about the changing mores of the past 50 years, and at least he didn't agree to change his movements for the camera. However, as Elvis's career went on, the power of his manager, Colonel Tom Parker, took away whatever genuine rebellion he might have possessed. What thoughtful listener can hear Elvis sing "My Way" in his later years without a wince of embarrassment? From the cheesy movies and Vegas-style spectacles, to his descent into drug addiction and physical decay, it's hard to believe Elvis ever did *anything* his way. And as for, "I've traveled each and every byway," Elvis never left the United States except to serve in the army in Germany for 16 months — he was never "allowed" to perform in other countries because Colonel Tom was an illegal immigrant from the Netherlands. A great singer, perhaps, but no kind of an *artist*.

Again, I'm sure everyone has their own list of immortals, but those are mine, and Jeff Buckley was the latest addition. And the more I listened to "Hallelujah," the more I appreciated the skill of Leonard Cohen's songwriting, too. The lyrics, especially, were so well crafted. The first stanza sets up the character perfectly, evoking a romantic, idealistic-yet-resigned, bittersweet persona that imbues the whole song. "Well, I heard there was a secret chord/ That David played, and it pleased the Lord/ But you don't really care for music, do ya?"

Then it steps up a register, with lovely irony and metaphor, "It goes like this, the fourth, the fifth/ The minor fall, and the major lift/ The baffled king composing Hallelujah." The following three verses develop a continuing series of images and metaphors into an examination of religious experience ("Your faith was strong, but you needed proof/ You saw her bathing on the roof/ Her beauty and the moonlight overthrew ya"), a fading relationship ("There was a time, when you let me know/ What was really going on below/ But you no longer show that to me, do ya?") which builds in turn to a poignant celebration of intimacy ("But remember when I moved in you?/ And the holy dove was moving too/ And every breath we drew was Hallelujah"). Simply gorgeous poetry, especially when delivered by the expressive instrument of Jeff Buckley's voice, already, at such a young age, able to embrace and express that combination of romanticism, idealism, resignation, and bittersweet irony.

One night in Big Sur I went out for a late drive on the Pacific Coast Highway, top down in the cold wind, wearing a hooded sweatshirt, leather jacket, and driving gloves, with the heat turned up (the usual Canadian style of convertible-driving, even in July), and the stereo turned *way* up, playing "Hallelujah" over and over, as I followed my racing headlights along the dark, winding highway.

The other songs in the collection ranged from the hard-driving

"Eternal Life" to Nina Simone's wistful "Lilac Wine" to a reverent, soaring *a capella* delivery of Benjamin Britten's "Corpus Christi Carol."

So, on the Texas trip, I had saved *Grace* for just such a special part of the drive, finally away from the interstate and driving an empty two-lane through a wide landscape, under a big gray sky. Occasionally I wafted through a spell of light rain, but not enough to disturb visibility or traction, so the conditions allowed me to drive and listen comfortably.

I stopped in the tiny roadside settlement of Study Butte for gas ("Stoody," again, where Brutus and I had stopped back in '96), and as I took the winding road toward the park itself, a sudden flurry of snowflakes swept in, and by the time I reached the park gates, it had settled into a veritable blizzard. I saw a solid mass of something gray and prickly beside the road, and I slowed down to see my first wild *javelina*, or collared peccary, resembling a wild, bristly, snow-speckled pig as it grazed at the roadside, then trotted into the misty brush.

As I pulled up at Big Bend National Park's entrance gate to pay my fee, the ranger leaned out of the booth and I asked her, with a wave at the snow filling the air around us, "Is this *usual?*" She said no, and apparently it hadn't even been predicted by the weather service, but up to eight inches had already fallen in the highest part of the park, the Chisos Basin (about 5,000 feet), and the road up there was closed. On March 29th, I might have expected that in Canada, a thousand miles north, but not in West Texas. As I drove along the park road, visibility was down to a hundred feet or so, and the snow began to blanket the roadside. Even the limited view made a dramatic contrast, the white blanket beneath the desert flora in spring bloom, a bright frosting on the branches of the creosote, green with tiny yellow flowers, and the slender stems of the ocotillo hung in red blossoms.

In these lower elevations, the snow melted on contact with the pavement, so the park road remained dark and wet as I drove slowly along, sensing rather than seeing the rising scenery around me. Big Bend was among the largest of America's national parks, covering eight hundred thousand acres, and it also had the advantage of being one of the least visited. Apparently Big Bend received about three hundred thousand visitors a year, compared with, for example, Grand Canyon, which had to accommodate five million.

At the visitors center in Panther Junction, I parked among a few other cars and RVs, already powdered with snow. My first mission was to collect the national park "passport stamp" for the front of my journal, and then I looked around the displays of the park's natural history (especially loving the three-dimensional tabletop relief map of the area), and at the racks of books. National park visitors centers often had good reading for a junior natural scientist, and among them I had discovered wonderful nature-loving guides with wider scopes, like Edward Abbey and Wallace Stegner, and passionate naturalists like Joseph Krutch *(The Desert Year)*, Ann Zwinger *(The Mysterious Lands)*, Edmund Jaeger *(The California Deserts)*, and the granddaddy of them all, Aldo Leopold *(A Sand County Almanac)*.

The other travelers milling around the visitors center looked chilled and a little bewildered by the cold and snow, and I listened to their conversations with the rangers behind their map-covered counter. Some of them were trying to reach the lodge in Chisos Basin, at the top of the steep, winding road which had been closed because of heavy snow. I had been planning on taking that Green Gulch Road too, as it led to the only restaurant in the park, up at the lodge. The rangers said the road up to the Basin would likely be closed for a few hours, until the plows got the snow cleared away, but they seemed confident it would be open later.

I had originally tried to get accommodations at the lodge, but the rooms and cabins had been fully booked. An internet overview of other accommodations in the area had led me to Lajitas, twenty miles west of the park, which I remembered from when Brutus and I had stopped there for breakfast. I decided to drive over that way, and if the weather didn't improve, I would check into the Badlands Hotel, and see where I would be living for the next two nights.

With no lunch available, I stopped at the Panther Junction gas station and picked up some peanut butter cups and a bottle of water, then drove back to the west. The weather seemed to lighten a little, the snow tapering away, and the sky less bruised. The volcanic peaks to the south formed a monumental, snow-streaked chalice around the Chisos Basin.

I passed a sign for a turn-off to the south, and pulled over to look at the park map. Seeing the meandering line of the Ross Maxwell Scenic Drive leading down to the Rio Grande, past Burro Mesa, Mule Ears Viewpoint, and the Santa Elena Canyon Overlook, I decided to go that way.

The musical accompaniment for this relaxed scenic excursion was Isaac Hayes again, this time the soundtrack from *Shaft*, a perennial favorite since I saw the movie back in '71, when I was living in London. I remember seeing it with a couple of European friends, and how differently they viewed what I saw as a campy, humorous, maybe even satirical look at American life. The European kids saw it as a serious expression of American street brutality and gun-happy violence, and yet they also seemed to admire it as an image of ultimate coolness, black American style.

Shaft had a rich, luxurious sound, both in the orchestrations and the recording quality, with a bright sparkling top-end on the drums and cymbals (especially the emblematic hi-hat part in the main theme), a punchy, rounded bass, and a full-bodied presence to the strings and brass. For many years I had used *Shaft* as one of my test records, to audition a stereo or the sound system in a new car, and it remained an audio feast as well as a relaxing flow of music for a scenic drive.

Although the gray clouds stretched from horizon to horizon, the moisture seemed to have fallen mostly in the mountains, which generally received twice the annual rainfall of the surrounding desert. The plains to the west seemed unaffected, and the road was smooth, dry pavement. During the stretches of bad weather, I had put away the radar detector, but now I plugged it in again, knowing I wouldn't be able to stick to the park's 45 mph speed limit. In a fast car on a perfect road, with hardly any other traffic, that would be inhuman.

I stopped a couple of times at roadside overlooks to admire the scale of the scenery without distraction, looking far across the creosote plains, punctuated with yucca, mesquite, and acacia, to ancient, eroded volcanic cones, mountains of rubble, distant blue bluffs and isolated formations of gray rock, and up close, the yellow-flowered yucca and red-blossomed ocotillo. My memory had retained but a small sense of the vast scale of the landscape, both horizontally and vertically, and I felt as I had on that second visit to Grand Canyon, as though the distances and dimensions were too overpowering for the mind to hold, or for memory to retain.

A delightful thirty-mile cruise brought me to the Santa Elena Canyon Overlook, and I parked the car and walked across a dry wash of sand and gravel. Following a trail through tamarisk, prickly pear, mesquite, and ocotillo led me to where the high rocky walls formed the narrow canyon, and a thin stream of greenish-brown water ran between sandy banks, maybe forty or fifty feet wide. This modest flow seemed anything but "grande," and I couldn't believe I was looking at the famed river, the border between two great countries, and that the opposite wall of the canyon was actually Mexico. I remembered seeing a reference to Terlingua Creek, and saw on the map that it was a tributary of the Rio Grande, flowing in near where I stood, and I thought perhaps this narrow canyon and thread of water were the creek, not the river.

But no, this was it. Apparently in modern times much of the river's flow through the park actually came from the Rio Conchos, on the Mexican side, while the American water was largely diverted for irrigation or lost to evaporation. The river must have been much greater before those man-made changes in the 20th Century, and as for how such a mighty canyon was formed, the national park brochure pointed out that if you paddled an aluminum canoe in the river, you would hear the hissing of abrasive particles against its hull. "The river is like a relentless, gravity-powered belt sander that has been running for millions of years." Perhaps this gorge had evolved something like the Grand Canyon had, the land slowly rising *around* the river, resisting the flow and intensifying its abrasive drive to the Gulf of Mexico.

Late in the afternoon I pulled into the small settlement of Lajitas and parked behind the main part of town, which had been made into an imagined replica of a western main street. "Old Town" was closed to traffic, with a row of buildings in unfinished timber along an unpaved street, watering troughs, hitching posts, boardwalks covered with simple balconies in front of the Badlands Hotel, a row of small art galleries and gift shops, and an adjacent complex of restaurants and meeting rooms. In the seven years since Brutus and I had been there, the project had been moving upscale, adding a nine-hole golf course, a hunting preserve, a recently-opened spa, and more accommodations in Old-West-style annexes called the Officers Quarters (still under construction) and the Cavalry Post. Now calling itself a *resort*, its slogan was "The Ultimate Hideout," and the Web site touted the location of Lajitas on the Comanche "Great War Trail," and its accessibility by private jet. Both may have been wishful thinking.

The Badlands Hotel continued the Old West theme inside, with a two-story, galleried lobby, and a large Tiffany-style light fixture above one of those four-sided central sofas. My room had dark wood wainscoting and beamed ceiling, patterned wallpaper, and simple wooden furnishings. The plumbing seemed "authentic" as well, for I never did get hot water out of it.

I pulled the heavy, old-fashioned wooden chair out onto the balcony, overlooking the wooden buildings and the backdrop of dry hills, furrowed mountains, and a clearing blue sky. Pouring a finger of The Macallan over some ice, I sipped and reflected on the day, then found myself compelled to get up and dig out my notebook. I hadn't thought to make this a "journal" sort of journey, and so far had only used it to continue my collection of national park passport stamps inside the cover. But at the outset I had been thinking about a new writing project. Now those clockwork wheels seemed to be carrying me toward an answer to that "Now what?" question.

"Thinking today as I drove through majestic scenery in my 'dream car,' music blasting, that I'm a lucky guy these days!"

That was certainly an unusually bright notion for me, viewed through the lens of my recent history, and thinking about that feeling, I have to hope other people have shared it, however rarely, however fleetingly. For all of us, life is mostly a gray matter, with occasional patches of blue, and maybe a few of black, and the starburst flashes of yellow are the eternal diamonds we hold in memory to show that life is precious.

By saying that life is mostly "a gray matter," I don't mean a cynical dismissal of life as colorless and boring, but rather a description of the more-or-less neutral, undramatic, comfortable rhythm of the regular, humdrum, neither-up-nor-down procession of ordinary days — work and play. There is a quiet happiness, a contentment, in that gray which more often shines in memory than in the momentary present, but sometimes I pause and appreciate its steady warmth and light — the hearth.

Blue represents the sad days, the bad days, the nights when sleep won't come. And black is when you are weighed down by the worst of life, real or imagined — impending doom, the feeling of being cursed, wretched, and utterly miserable. When you were truly "in the black," that succession of gray days seemed like a bright, happy place to be.

Yellow, though, were the brief flashes of existential joy, comets of exultation, the lightning bolts of pure excitement that seem to sizzle through your nerves and veins like electricity. Yellow was the supernova of ecstasy, the sensation that perhaps embodied a rarely used word like "glee."

Those moments in my own life have been so few, so memorable, that I can remember each of them as discrete vignettes, brief interstices of epiphany, as film clips of moments that reach right back to my teens.

Slouching through the mean hallways of Lakeport Secondary School in 1969 with The Who playing in my head, and feeling a sudden desire to do a Pete Townshend jump right there. So I did. Walking through Golden Square in London in 1971, and a sudden flurry of snowflakes filled the air. All at once I felt like running, and my feet seemed to fly above the pavement. I was in London, pursuing my dream, and life was good.

Sitting down at the end of 1986 and writing a little list, just for myself, called "Why It Was the Greatest Year!" The *Power Windows* tour from January to May, playing well and enjoying many bicycling adventures between the shows; then a June bicycle tour with friends from Munich over the Alps to Venice, fulfilling my quest to see all six Bugatti Royales (two in Reno, one in Costa Mesa, one in Detroit, and two at the former Schlumpf collection in Mulhouse, France); a family summer on the lake in Quebec with friends and relatives visiting, a solitary lyric-writing week in September, then starting work on our *Hold Your Fire* album, getting my first Macintosh and using it to write lyrics, a short story, and several magazine articles; and learning to use the new-fangled sampling gear for electronic drums and writing a solo marimba piece called "Pieces of Eight." (It *was* a good year!)

September 14, 1987, I stood at the summit of Mount Kilimanjaro, having passed my 35th birthday during the ascent. From the glaciers and barren rocks of Uhuru Peak, at 19,340 feet the highest point in Africa, I looked down to the clouds far below, broken only by the distant peaks of Mount Meru and Mount Kenya. I recorded a message on my microcassette recorder: "I'm bringing this to you live from Uhuru, the highest point in Africa, the top of a continent, and it feels like the top of a world. So exciting, and I'm so proud to be here."

On a motorcycle trip in Newfoundland in 1994, Brutus and I were walking out to the bikes after stopping at the Visitors Centre in Gros Morne National Park. For some unknown reason (combination of reasons, more likely), I felt a sudden wave of such perfect *contentment* sweep over me that I would remember that moment forever.

And now I had spent the afternoon driving through Big Bend National Park in my dream car, majestic scenery passing before my speeding windshield, and long-loved music pouring out of the speakers. Another yellow day, to remember on a gray one.

But there was always a balance. I had been luckier than most, no question, but I had also been *un*luckier than most, and just as I tended to go to extremes, so, it seemed, did my life. As I put it in the song version of "Ghost Rider," "From the lowest low to the highest high."

I have the job I used to dream of, and I wouldn't trade it for anything, but sometimes it has been too demanding — those endless tours, those long stints in the studio, separated from home and loved ones, alienation, illness, relationship troubles, the distressing intrusions from strangers — and there have been times when I have hated it. I still enjoy the simple act of playing the drums as much as I ever did, just sitting down and playing whatever comes out, or even rehearsing by playing along with our records, as I used to do with the radio. But of course that's not the same as pounding out a three-hour Rush show night after night, at a predetermined time and place, with the weight of reputation and expectation, from myself and others, on every performance.

Still, there are the golden moments: fiddling with a song lyric for days on end, each day thinking it's going nowhere and tempted to throw it in the trash, when suddenly there's a turning point, a brief flash of *faith* — "It's going to work" (though that flash of exultation is quickly forgotten as I apply myself to *making* it work).

Or grinding through day after day of pre-tour rehearsals with Geddy and Alex, struggling with technology and technique, until suddenly it all comes together, and we lock into the transcendent synergy of playing as a *band*.

Overall, I have to say it's a pretty hard job, but it is counterbalanced by commensurate rewards: creative satisfaction, lots of time off (in recent years, anyway), and . . . good benefits.

When Bob Dylan was asked how he justified his wealth, he said, "For every dollar I've made, there's a pool of sweat on the floor."

Being a professional musician was the dream of my youth, and it was still like that for me, work I would truly describe as a dream job. But that had not made getting there, or staying there, easy.

Though after fifty years of living, I am sure that *no one's* life is easy.

Another Rush song, called "Mission," from 1987, was inspired by a conversation I had with Geddy about people we knew in our age group (mid-30s, at the time) who remained dissatisfied with their lives, unfulfilled, and asked us questions like, "How old were you when you knew what you wanted to *do?*"

It seemed like we had *always* known, but I decided to try writing a song from that point of view — not as someone who already had a mission, but someone who was *searching* for one (or, if not actively searching, at least *waiting*).

In praising great works of art, music, books, painting, architecture, and movies, the "narrator" of the verses says, "I wish I had that instinct, I wish I had that drive." The chorus celebrates the heroes — "Spirits fly on dangerous missions, imaginations on fire" — then, in the middle-eight section (really a middle-thirty-two), I pulled the focus back to the struggle and suffering some of those artists had gone through to live their lives and produce their works: "If their lives were exotic and strange, they would likely have gladly exchanged them/ For something a little more plain/ Maybe something a little more sane."

I had been thinking of people like Vincent van Gogh, Virginia Woolf, or F. Scott Fitzgerald, people who lost *themselves* in the struggle for their art, but in the conclusion of the stanza, I tried to step all the way back and speak for *everybody*, in a line that Geddy put his whole heart into singing: "We each pay a fabulous price, for our visions of paradise."

I am married to a dream girl, but the path that brought me to her was harsh and paved with broken glass. It left me cut and bleeding and scarred for life, and the price I paid for where I am now was almost more than I could survive.

I knew how it was to feel lucky, but I also knew how it was to feel cursed. On a winter's day back in 1999, I stood in my snowshoes on a point above the frozen lake, looking out across the grayish-white landscape through the whirling snow. I felt a sudden urge to howl like a wolf, and suppressed it at first, then thought, "Why not?", and let it sing out. A primitive wail of solitude and existential loneliness.

If I was driving my dream car, to earn it I spent six months away from home, rehearsing for months and then traipsing around the Americas, playing 66 long, hard shows, and again, passing my fiftieth birthday pounding and sweating on a stage in the Calgary Saddledome. None of that was a dream.

But it was also not really a *choice*. I had to keep doing those things, even the touring, because that's what I do — that's what *musicians* do.

When I first began to encounter the German word *schadenfreude*, which I now know refers to that ignoble human tendency to take pleasure in another's misfortune, I couldn't find the compound word in my little German dictionary. I tried to decipher its meaning by looking up the component words, and from *schaden* and *freude* I worked out my own home-made translation of "tarnished joy," interpreting it to mean something predominantly good that also included a dark shadow as its necessary component, like adventuring through China or Africa — with dysentery.

Becoming successful, but giving up your peace of mind, or even your previously-unappreciated anonymity.

A wonderful new life, at the cost of a previous life shot to hell. ("We will pay the price . . .")

That definition of *schadenfreude* was not accurate to the word's accepted larger meaning, but the concept was sound, and I might use it as a metaphor for my life: "tarnished joy." Possibly everybody would.

But still, I won't deny it, overall I am a lucky man, and once in a great while I even *feel* that way.

There are things I still wish for, but I envy no man.

After making that happy journal note, "I'm a lucky guy these days!", and reflecting for a few minutes on all the reasons why, I had another thought, and wrote down the first inspiration for that elusive next writing project I'd been fretting about:

"A story could be written just around the music I've listened to on this trip."

Chorus Three

"Drumming at the heart of an English winter"

It used to be said that if you stood in London's Piccadilly Circus long enough, you would meet everyone in the world. I doubt if that's true anymore, but in July of 1971, I had a fateful meeting in Piccadilly Circus that changed the course of my stay in England, and, in far-reaching ways, my whole life.

The month before, I had flown into Gatwick Airport, south of London, on a $200 charter flight. I was eighteen, had never flown in an airplane before, never lived on my own, never been more than a few hundred miles from home, and the only "foreign countries" I'd ever visited were a family camping trip to Montreal for Expo '67 (which only *felt* foreign, being a World's Fair, and in French-Canadian Quebec), and the Finger Lakes region in Upstate New York.

My parents, my girlfriend, and the guys from J.R. Flood and their girlfriends had gathered at the Toronto airport to see me off, resplendent in my red corduroy double-breasted jacket and bad, shoulder-length perm. After the all-night flight, I was met at Gatwick by my childhood friend, Brad, and his two English "mates," tall, cadaverous Bill and short, puckish Pete. Brad had moved to England with his mother and her husband a couple of years before, and when they returned to Canada after a year, Brad decided to stay. He worked as a "fitter's mate" (plumber's apprentice) and lived in a bedsitting room in a northern suburb of London called New Barnet.

Carrying my brand-new, plastic, folding suitcase with the inevitable Canadian flag stickers on the side, I followed the streetwise young lads onto the train. Once it was underway, they led me from our second-class seats to a first-class compartment, then promptly lit up a huge English-style "spliff" — as a welcome-to-England gesture, I guess. A little shocked, I declined, trying not to appear rude (or worse, uncool), but I was already so excited I had stayed awake for the whole flight. Plus it was about 8:00 in the morning.

As the train rolled through the countryside, so lush and green, and into the sprawling suburbs of south London, I stared around at all the *strangeness:* the narrow little "terraced" houses all in rows of brick and chimneypots, the tiny back gardens with clotheslines and garden sheds, the little cars all on the wrong side of the road — it was all so delightfully foreign, and exotic. My first lesson that the rest of the world really *was* more different than I knew or imagined.

When we reached Victoria Station and changed to the underground, we were issued a small yellow ticket, but Pete and Bill told us to throw them away; it would be cheaper if we said we'd lost them, and paid the "lost ticket" rate. Once again a little shocked, I did what they said, and rode the old Northern Line (smelling of coal, as much of London still did in those days) to its very end, the High Barnet station.

In letters we exchanged during the months before my arrival, Brad and I had agreed that I could stay with him for awhile, and we pulled the mattress off his single bed and made it into two. We spent that day, a Sunday, walking around nearby Hadley Wood, and the next day Brad went to work, and I started learning my way around. Before leaving home, I had gone through the credits in my record collection and made a list of the addresses of record companies and management agencies in London. I looked them up in the *London A-Z* atlas and tracked down the addresses, walking around in the rain and marching into these offices dripping wet, clutching my manila envelope of 8" x 10" photos of me playing with J.R. Flood.

Certainly I was naïve, and also painfully shy, but I was just so *determined*. It wasn't as though I thought I was all that great of a drummer (I wasn't), or that the London music scene was just *waiting* for my arrival (it wasn't); the thing was, I just *wanted* it so bad. I followed the map of the underground, the "Tube," all over the vast, rainy city, and never got past a single receptionist — though some of them were sympathetic. I'll always remember one of them hearing my story, and saying, in her chipper English way, "Well . . . you're very *brave*," with a rising note on the end suggesting, "brave, but *daft*."

The other possible avenue for finding a band was the weekly music papers, the musicians' want-ads in the back of *Melody Maker* and the *New Musical Express*. I didn't have any drums yet, because my dad had built me a wooden crate containing my little set of Rogers drums and my record collection (what else did an 18-year-old music fanatic need?), and sent it to England by boat, so it wouldn't arrive for six weeks or more. But in my naïvete and determination, I decided I would go to some auditions, and try to borrow drums from other drummers. (Why I thought they would be willing to help another applicant, I don't know, but it seemed reasonable to me. I guess because we were all "brother drummers," and, again, because I *wanted* it so bad.)

My first audition was held in a relatively affluent part of West London (exceptional for its detached houses and leafy streets), at a suburban house belonging to the bass player's parents. I "rang up" and made an appointment, then showed up early and asked the drummer before me if I could use his drums. Not surprisingly, he was a little reluctant, but finally relented, after asking, "You're not a basher, are you?"

I assured him I wasn't (though I probably was), and while we waited for all the band members to show up, I listened to their conversations about obscure American and British jazz musicians I had never heard of. They seemed dismissive, even contemptuous of the English rock bands I liked: The Who, Deep Purple, Jethro Tull, King Crimson, Pink Floyd, and Led Zeppelin. Other young English musicians would echo this kind of snobbery, a confused mentality of being chauvinistically British, and thus generally anti-American, yet feeling American music was innately superior to their own. The other drummer mentioned Jon Hiseman, the drummer in an adventurous jazz-rock English band of the time, Colosseum, that I liked, but the bass player sniffed, "He's so *busy*."

The other band members arrived, seeming aloof and snobby to me, and when the other drummer finished his audition, I went into the small room jam-packed with equipment, and sat down behind his drums. The keyboard player announced, "This first tune is in seven," which meant absolutely nothing to me at the time, but I kept quiet and just tried to join in when they started playing. The keyboard player, bless him, was kind and patient, and said that I seemed to have a good "feel" for odd times, and I stumbled through a few more complicated bits before they brought the audition to an end.

Knowing it had all been over my head, I was crestfallen and humbled, yet somehow not discouraged; a week or so later I actually called the bass player to see if the position had been filled. Of course, it had, but I simply pushed on, pursuing my dream. And from then on, I set out to learn everything I could about playing in odd times, encouraged by that keyboard player's kindness, and it would become an important part of my musical development, even as that kind of complexity became so much a part of the music of the day, in explorations and experiments by what would one day be called "progressive rock" (or, more dismissively, "prog rock") bands like Yes, King Crimson, Genesis, Gentle Giant, Emerson, Lake, and Palmer, the Strawbs, Caravan, Kansas, and so many more.

During the late '60s and early '70s, the qualifications for what it took to be a rock drummer seemed to keep ramping up exponentially. Until that time, all you had to know was how to keep a simple 4/4 backbeat and play "Wipeout," but suddenly you had to be able to play all these complicated arrangements, odd time signatures, and even exotic percussion instruments. It seemed the bar had been raised awfully high, and it was all a bit daunting — and yet, for this ambitious young drummer, it was exciting, both challenging and rewarding.

My second audition was a whole other thing. Held in a room above a pub in North London, it was for a band entirely made up of handicapped musicians. I didn't need any drums for this one, as the audition was conducted by the band's current drummer on his drums, as he had to leave to have an operation on his legs. He had polio, with leg braces and crutches, and pointed to his double-bass-drum setup, and told me, "I use two bass drums to do what other chaps do with one." There was a trumpet player with one arm, the keyboard player was in a wheelchair, and the guitarist and bass player were blind (guided around by their girlfriends, who apparently dressed them with a certain sense of humor — I remember you needed dark glasses, like they wore, to look at their *shirts*).

Some of the hangers-on were equally "specially abled," blind and crippled and stunted, and amid this Felliniesque scene, I began to feel uncomfortable, even kind of guilty. I waited through a few of the other drummers, and decided: a) This band isn't very good, and b) This is all really weird. I slipped away.

Meanwhile, weeks were passing, and at the end of a month in London, I was running out of money. I had arrived with $200 to live on (my ever-supportive parents had agreed to match whatever money I could raise, and when they paid for the charter ticket, that's what I had managed out of my savings and selling my record player), and it was getting low. I had become well acquainted with the London Transport system as I rambled through my list of record companies and management agencies, but I hadn't found any opportunities, or any promising "drummer wanted" ads in the music papers. I decided not to waste my dwindling resources, but just try to wait until my drums arrived, and something would come up.

By early July, when Brad went off to work in the morning in his dirty boiler suit, I was going out for walks around the neighborhood and Hadley Wood on the rare fine days, or staying in our room to read. I found a couple of paperbacks in the closet that Brad's former roommate had left behind, and that got me started again. It was time for books to become part of my life once more.

Especially one of them: a science-fiction epic called *Fall of the Towers*, by Samuel R. Delany, which would have a profound effect on my life, in so many unexpected ways, both in my future reading and early lyric-writing, such as *2112* and *Cygnus x-1*. In retrospect, how amazing I should come across that particular book, so poetic, richly-imagined, and original, by that particular writer, who still ranks among the best in the genre, I think. My only previous exposure to science fiction had been a short story I studied in high school called "The Ruum," written by Arthur Porges (and what an interesting web-search *that* was!) in 1953. Similar to the way a few novels and plays were drilled into my head at the time without much seeming effect, or affect, later they would resonate in ways I could never have suspected — I actually did learn to *read* properly, or at least I learned that there *was* a way to read properly. Along with *Julius Caesar* and *A Tale of Two Cities*, I still remember the plot line of "The Ruum" in great detail, after more than thirty-five years.

As the weeks went by, Brad and I had adjusted to living together pretty well, and decided to move into a larger room in the same house. Soon I was spending my days curled up on the tiny settee, watching the rain come down and reading book after book. The corner shop took trades, two for one, out of their rack of used paperbacks, and I started plowing through Agatha Christie mysteries and adventure stories from "The Saint" series, and even some more science fiction, classics like John Wyndham's *Day of the Triffids* and *The Midwich Cuckoos* (made into a movie, *Children of the Damned*, which I had seen as a Saturday matinee back in St. Catharines). In one of Wyndham's books I read his definition of what he felt the genre should be: "Extraordinary things happening to ordinary people," which I still think is pretty good, and transcends the genre to cover *all* storytelling, as the best science fiction can do.

My money continued to dwindle, and I was down to my last few pounds on the Sunday in July when I had that fateful meeting in Piccadilly Circus. Brad and I took the Tube into Central London, to the Tottenham Court Road station, then walked down Shaftesbury Avenue to where it opened out among the neon-lighted buildings, the circling black taxis and red double-decker buses, the statue of Eros, and the milling crowds of tourists and Londoners. There, in Piccadilly Circus, I suddenly recognized a familiar face — Sheldon Atos, from St. Catharines, who had once built a primitive light show for my first band, Mumblin' Sumpthin', for our "Battle of the Bands" performance at the YMCA. Sheldon was living in London, married to an English girl, and working for a chain of tourist shops in Carnaby Street and Piccadilly. And, he thought he might be able to get me a job.

Sheldon's boss, Bud, employed him mainly as a handyman, and always called him "Stan," for the toolmaking company, Stanley, and soon that's how I knew him too. Bud was another Canadian, thirtyish, with piercing gray eyes, sharp features, and a longish, late-mod hairstyle that, like his expensively casual wardrobe, was always perfect, every hair in place. Bud had started a "Print Your Name in Headlines" concession near the Houses of Parliament, and built it into a wide-ranging tourist-milking empire (the "S. Morgan Jones Group," an anglophile appellation that was apparently some version of Bud's real name). He owned several shops around Carnaby Street, and souvenir and printing concessions in Piccadilly Circus, Coventry Street, and across from the Houses of Parliament.

Carnaby Street's fame as a symbol of "Swinging London" had made a deep impression on the world during the early '60s and the mod era, a brief explosion of fashion that had burst out of a couple of clothing shops on that previously-obscure backstreet. Like the hippie era that supplanted them, the mods created and adapted their own fashions, music, and attitude, and as with hippies, beatniks, punks, rappers, and every "new" youth movement (an oxymoronic pattern recurs in the notion of young people expressing their individuality by following the latest fashions), there seem to have been two different kinds of mods: the working-class, street-level teenagers celebrated in The Who's *Quadrophenia* (especially the film version, which I watched for "research," but appreciated for its gritty realism), and the kind of shallow dilettante dryly satirized in the Kinks' mod-era song, "Dedicated Follower of Fashion" ("one week he's in polka dots, the next week he's in stripes"). Through all that, the international myth of Carnaby Street endured, and even by the early '70s (and for years after), it remained the second most-visited tourist attraction in London, after Buckingham Palace.

Carnaby Street was nothing special to look at: a humble, narrow little street, only a few blocks long, tucked behind Regent Street. Historically, it was noteworthy only for being described by Charles Dickens in *Nicholas Nickleby*: "A bygone, faded, tumbledown street, with two irregular rows of tall, meagre houses." He also wrote about the street's inhabitants in a way that was strangely recognizable a hundred years later, "The fowls who peck about the kennels, jerking their bodies hither and thither with a gait which none but town fowls are ever seen to adopt, and which any country hen would be puzzled to understand, are perfectly in keeping with the habitations of their owners."

By 1971, both sides of the street were lined with shops, many still selling stylish, youthful clothes, like the original John Stephen outlets, with many more capitalizing on the tourist traffic, like Kleptomania, Pop Shop, and I Was Lord Kitchener's Valet (whose owner demonstrated the street's profitability by cruising to work in a Lamborghini Espada, a fantastically low-slung exotic that remained my idea of a "dream car" for many years).

My new boss, Bud, drove an Aston Martin, then later a Ferrari Dino, from his estate in the country. His most recent business acquisition was a large shop from the original Carnaby Street days with the suitably-swinging name, "Gear." He had taken over the three-story building with a basement stuffed from floor to ceiling with old merchandise, mostly cheap, stylish homeware and gifts. My first assignment was to organize and inventory that jumble, and that was when the experience of working for my dad at Dalziel Equipment ("Pronounce it D-L," said the promotional stickers) through all those summers and holidays, stocking the parts department and updating the inventory, really paid off.

It seemed to me that what worked for tractor parts and baler twine ought to work for other kinds of merchandise, and I used my dad's parts department as a mental pattern, lining up all the boxes of Union Jack teacups, Carnaby Street-sign ashtrays, East Indian throw-pillows, pink and orange polka-dotted trash cans, and boxes and boxes of a book called

Carnaby Street, written by Gear's previous owner, Tom Salter. After I stacked them in numbered rows, I taped off the floor and ceiling and labeled shelves to make sections of those rows, and wrote them all out in a neat list of descriptions and locations.

Bud seemed impressed with the job I had done, and my next assignment was to clear out the basement of another, smaller building he had bought from Tom Salter, a three-story block of offices with a tiny ground-floor shop and a basement full of similar merchandise, a couple of streets away on Ganton Street. I was given a large wire cart to fill with boxes and push them over to the basement of Gear, and though it was strictly manual labor, I found myself caught up in the challenge of making those boxes diminish at one end and the satisfaction of seeing them pile up at the other.

As I slowly emptied the basement on Ganton Street, the ancient walls of brick and plaster were revealed, and cemented into the wall we discovered bones that dated from the Great Plague in the 17th Century, when a "pesthouse" had stood on the site, "for the entertainment of persons that shall have the plague."

When I was sorting merchandise in the Gear basement, the other shop managers would stop by to pick up some posters or other stock, and someone would fill a little pipe or roll a joint with hash and tobacco, and pass it around. Despite a few experimental puffs of "dirt weed" back in Canada, and one or two LSD experiences, London was where I really discovered the marijuana high, the warm, fuzzy cloud in the brain, the giggly camaraderie, the flights of imagination and fancy, and the way the music playing in the shop sounded when I walked upstairs, richly textured and powerfully dimensional. My mind seemed attenuated, right brain up, left brain down.

One day a thrill of excitement rippled along Carnaby Street, and someone came in to announce, "Yul Brynner's on the street!" The famous actor walked into Gear, looking expensively dressed, with radiant bald head and air of celebrity, and an expensively-dressed blonde glowing on his arm. Standing in front of the counter which contained our "head shop" paraphernalia, he pointed at some pipes of hand-blown glass, and asked me if they were any good. I smiled and said, "Well, they passed quality control," and he smiled and bought one.

In the main stockroom below Gear, I adapted my storage system to stock and keep track of the usual wares of the S. Morgan Jones Group, all of it souvenir tourist-trash with a 100 percent markup ("at least," stressed Bud), like Beefeater dolls, toy London taxis, double-decker buses, Union Jack carrier bags, Carnaby Street teaspoons, and dozens and dozens of posters of pop stars, stills from *Easy Rider* (unbelievably popular with Europeans), and the ever-popular jokey ones, like two of our best sellers: a photograph of a pair of hands emerging from a toilet, and a black-and-white photo montage making up a field of female breasts (Americans liked those ones).

Then there was the one called "Women's Lib," which showed a woman in a suede miniskirt standing beside two men at a urinal. Sign of the times. (Around that time I saw some graffiti on the side of an old brick building, "Women's Lib Means Not Having To Sleep on the Damp Bit.")

Posters were such a big part of the S. Morgan Jones Group business that Stan had invented a poster-rolling machine: a sewing-machine motor rotating a long aluminum tube with a slit along its length. You inserted one edge of the flat poster into the slit, pressed the treadle to turn the tube, and put the rolled poster into a plastic sleeve. Tape a number over the end, and it was ready to stock in the gridwork of the huge custom-made shop fixtures, with each poster displayed in big plexiglas frames that hung at eye level and swung on hinges, like pages in a book.

Brad soon came to work for Bud too, putting aside his dirty boiler suit and ill-paid job as a fitter's mate. We only made about £20 ($50) a week, and our rent, even for a single room at the far end of the Northern underground line, was £5 each per week, so to make a little more money we often worked day and night shifts at the souvenir shops in Carnaby Street and Piccadilly Circus (hand-printing endless bogus newspapers with "Your Name in Headlines," "So-and-so dines at Buckingham Palace," Wanted posters, bullfight posters, that sort of thing).

Bud employed about twenty young people, from a wide variety of nationalities (his only prejudice was against *English* workers; he thought they were lazy), including several other Canadians, Spanish Paco, Dutch Carla, Indian Dhillon, African-American Leonard, Jewish-American Rebecca, New Zealanders (Kiwis) Pat, Gavan, and Dave, Irish Mary, German Angela, South African Paul, and Ahmed and a couple of other Persians (from Iran, it was called by then, but they always called themselves Persians). We also had two English kids, Ellis and Mary, but they were both gay, which perhaps made them more "acceptable" to Bud than *ordinary* English people. In any case, Ellis and Mary soon became two of my closest friends — the first (openly) gay people I'd ever known, and a pattern of not just tolerance, but *appreciation*, was thereby set for life.

Other enduring cultural exposures were Stan taking me around the corner to Bloom's deli and introducing me to corned beef sandwiches and *latkes*, and Dhillon inviting me home to dinner, and mischievously telling his Indian mother that I liked *really* hot curry. As a Canadian kid who had grown up on such exotic delicacies as macaroni and cheese and pork chops with apple sauce, the spiciest thing I had ever tasted was canned spaghetti. I nearly died.

Stan also introduced me to Robin, from Carlisle in the north of England, telling me he was in a band that needed a drummer. English Rose, they were called, and an earlier version of the band had appeared in a movie called *Groupie Girl*. Robin was the guitarist, and they had a singer, keyboard player, and bass player, an "equipment manager" with a van, and a manager, who was promising to get them a recording contract. It was a *band*, in *London* — of *course* I would join.

We practiced a few evenings at the singer's flat in West Hampstead, with acoustic guitars and me drumming on my thighs. The original material was cowritten by the singer, Jimmy, and keyboard player, Lynton, and consisted of more-or-less classic British pop songs, with background harmonies and simple arrangements ("The postman delivered a letter, to the house up on the hill, ooh, ooh, ooh"). So, at least they were not hard to learn, especially compared with J.R. Flood's quirky, complicated, extended arrangements.

One rainy night in August we piled into the van and drove to the Docklands area of East London, winding through the vast grids of warehouses to pick up my crate of drums and records. Now we could practice properly, moving into the basement of Pop Shop (another S. Morgan Jones Group outlet on Carnaby Street, which Robin managed at the time). The band's manager came to see us in the cramped little room, and when he thought we were ready, he arranged for us to record a demo. He also arranged some small, "showcase" gigs at pubs around London, and was full of promises about all the great things he was going to do for us.

Meanwhile, I began to learn a little more about my bandmates.

Robin, for example, lived way in the East End of London, in a rough area called Plaistow, with a pretty young psycho named Irene. She was insanely jealous, even of Robin's devotion to music, and one morning Robin came to work nearly in tears — Irene had taken a saw and cut his beautiful Rickenbacker guitar in half.

Though the guitar was probably stolen anyway. In *The Masked Rider*, I wrote a little about those years in London, and told of joining the band whose van and amplifiers were all stolen, and whose "road manager" made his living by burgling petrol stations. That was English Rose.

In October of 1971, after about two months with them, the other members convinced me to "give up my day job," and go full-time. When I told Bud, he gave me a smile that, in memory, seems to have been "knowing." He said if it didn't work out, I could come back to work for him, and that was good to know — though I couldn't imagine any circumstances under which it wouldn't work out. I was on my way!

We loaded up our gear and piled into the stolen Ford Transit van, and headed up the M-1, pausing for the wedding of the bass player, Paul, and Carol in Leicester. Then we headed farther north, to play a few small clubs in northern towns. I remember Keswick, and Whitehaven, and being struck by the beauty of the Lake District, then staying in Carlisle for a few days with Robin's parents, five of us "dossing" on floors and sofas, and his sweet Mum bringing us cups of tea in the morning.

On the way back to London, I was riding in the passenger seat of the van around Marble Arch in the middle of the night, heading to Maida Vale to drop off the keyboard player, Lynton. The larcenous road manager, Peter, was driving, and I was telling him my whole tale of packing up and coming to England. He said, "That will make a good story for the music papers one day!"

It did, six or seven years later, but at the time it wasn't a happy story.

English Rose's manager had failed to find a record company that was interested in the demo tape, and he was also failing to come up with any gigs, so in effect the band ceased to exist because of a total lack of interest. But we kept hoping, or at least I did.

The manager did get me one session job, hiring me to "sub" in the studio for another band he managed, and I played on a two-song demo for a '50s-style "Rocker" outfit called Jet Black, playing the other drummer's drums, in his band, while he sat in a chair in the corner looking glum.

The £10 session fee was welcome, but given my limited experience in a recording studio, and nonexistent experience at being a session musician, I don't think I was too impressive. In some musicians' stories I've read, such an opportunity would have been a springboard to more session work, but not for me.

With November coming on, I had no job, no band, and no money. I was falling behind on my shared rent with Brad, but I was sure the music thing was going to pick up soon, and I just needed a little money to get by until then. I asked Peter if he might be able to help me get some "work," and I never forgot how he refused to let me get involved in his shady activities, but slipped me a five-pound note from his ill-gotten gains a couple of times.

Winter settled in, cold and damp, and sometimes the streets of New Barnet were obscured by the legendary pea-soup fogs. I'd be walking along the pavement (sidewalk) through a solid gray cloud, unable even to see the cars whispering by on the street beside me. And it was so *cold* everywhere, chilly to the bone indoors and out, and Brad and I would come home to a damp room and feed two-shilling coins into the electric meter so we could turn on the "electric fire" (even sounds primitive) and huddle around it.

To fill the time, I was somehow inspired to start creating a patchwork suit, and I began painstakingly sewing one little two-inch square at a time onto an old pair of my velvet pants and a denim jacket of Brad's. Our record player was a cast-off turntable wired through a tiny guitar amp, but we did have a pair of headphones, and I would sit and listen to music, while I folded and stitched all those tiny patches, like a miniature version of one of my grandmother's quilts. Eventually I got Brad interested in the project as well, and he later described it as "one of the coolest uncool things I ever did!" We finished all of the pants and most of the jacket before I lost interest — and I never did wear them. But, it had been a cheap and harmless pastime.

Too often Brad and I lived on Fray Bentos canned steak and kidney pudding, as it was cheap and filling, and we could heat it up in boiling water on our hot plate. But just like when I ate too many pears off the trees in our yard as a child, from then on (and to this day) the very thought of Fray Bentos steak and kidney pudding made me nauseous.

That was also the winter of the coal strikes, with rotating three-hour power cuts, and some nights we'd be unable to read, listen to music, warm ourselves at the electric fire, or heat up anything to eat.

Through some connection, in late November I got a job filling in for one night with a band called Heaven, but the gig turned out to be hell. Heaven were a moderately-successful white R&B band, with six or seven members and a decent singer, and they picked me up in a large Mercedes van with aircraft seats (serious status for the times). I loaded my drums in the back, and we drove north to Salford University, just outside Manchester. This time, the other members of the band were nice enough, but the keyboard player was an unpleasant, arrogant autocrat. (And another word that starts with "a.")

He never spoke a word to me, just sat in the front passenger seat, radiating an aggressive, superior attitude. When the driver put on a Pink Floyd tape, he growled, "Not those out-of-tune cunts," and we rode in silence again.

The challenge was insurmountable: Heaven played all their own material, I'd never heard any of it before, and even now it's hard to imagine they thought we could do the show without a single rehearsal. Typically, there was no written music, and even if there had been, my sight reading was nowhere good enough for that — it was like a language I had learned and never used.

Backstage at Salford University, the bass player and I set up our equipment and tried to work through some of the rhythmic feels of the different songs, but there was certainly no time to learn the *arrangements*, and I was supposed to just "follow him." I thought I survived the show pretty well, considering, but it was hopeless.

And then they ripped me off. When they dropped me back at New Barnet in the wee small hours, the road manager gave me £10, and I had been promised £20. When I protested, he said, "That's what I was told." Bastards. (Ah, but where are they now . . .)

That Christmas of 1971, my grandma put up the money to fly me home for the holidays, and I went back to St. Catharines all "anglicized" (after a whole six months), with my new corduroy suit from Lord John on Carnaby Street, patterned sweater-vest, and affected accent. In January I flew back to England, only to be held for several hours by Immigration. The problem was that I only had about £2 in my pocket, barely train fare to New Barnet. However, I told the officers I was going straight back to work for Bud, and I did.

I was much wiser about the harsh realities of the London music scene, and the harsh realities of life, and I had tasted poverty. I could see that making a living in music was going to be tough, but, I had also learned that working at a "normal" job could offer certain rewards of security, self-sufficiency, and even satisfaction.

Soon after returning to work for Bud, he made me manager of the Pop Shop (though I was only the "manager" of myself; there was just me and Ahmed, who worked the print-your-name-in-headlines press in the corner). My drums were still in the basement of the shop, so I could continue practicing during lunch breaks or after work, and during the quiet winter days when few tourists wandered into our little shop, I fixed it up a little, arranging the posters and souvenirs nicely on walls and shelves, painting wooden tea chests to make poster storage, and drawing neat little price signs for everything.

As with my warehouse organizing, Bud seemed impressed, and when Leonard, the tall black American, quit his job managing Gear, that job was offered to me: manager of the flagship store of the S. Morgan Jones Group, even the boss of a small sales staff. I was still only nineteen years old, and definitely daunted by the responsibility, but as I said to Bud's managing director, the New Zealander Dave, "I guess it's the next logical step."

In truth, I was a lousy boss — at least from a management point of view. I hated to tell people what to do, and simply expected them to do what they were supposed to. If they didn't, sometimes I would stay after and do it myself, like a couple of times when Brad and I spent the whole night listening to records and cleaning the shelves and poster displays (kind of fun, really, and an experience to be in the middle of London as it slept and came to life again, and still to be in the shop when everybody arrived for work again).

When the street wasn't busy, I couldn't bear to maroon somebody at the lonely back counter, with no one to talk to. All of us were friends, Ellis, Mary, Rebecca, and I, and if there were only a few people in the store, we tended to gather by the center counter and talk. Bud's office was upstairs from Gear, and as he walked in and out (with what Rebecca called his "phalanx" of friends and yes-men), he would send Dave down to tell me to put someone on the back counter. (Once the whole staff signed a copy of Tom Salter's *Carnaby Street* for me, and Bud's inscription read, "As you go through life, don't forget to keep an eye on the back counter." I never did learn that lesson, metaphorically speaking.)

One of my most important jobs (to me, anyway) was choosing the music to be played over the store's sound system, and apart from my own favorites-of-the day like Yes (*Time and a Word*, particularly, which I recently listened to and was freshly impressed by its energy and imagination), Todd Rundgren (especially *The Ballad of Todd Rundgren*, though I was a big fan of all his work for many years), and *Who's Next* (pounding out the drum breaks on those great-sounding Sweda cash registers), I tried to accommodate everyone's taste — even the lesbian who liked Melanie, the gay guy who liked 1920's megaphone singers, and the unwashed hippie girl who only wanted to hear the Rolling Stones' *Sticky Fingers* — every day. 1971 was a big year for singer-songwriters, and I remember hearing a lot of Rod Stewart, Elton John, James Taylor, Cat Stevens, Neil Young's *After the Gold Rush* and *Harvest* (still great), and Carole King's *Tapestry* (about a *thousand* times).

Our music blasted out into the street full of tourists, and could definitely attract them inside; among the classic people-magnets were the soundtrack from the movie of *Woodstock*, especially the side with Sly and the Family Stone's "I Want To Take You Higher," and a live album by Rare Earth, with a sidelong version of "Get Ready."

With the long Tube ride to work every day, forty-five minutes each way, some new lifetime-habits were forged: I started buying a morning paper on the way in and an afternoon paper on the way home, and doing the crossword puzzles. I was also continuing to read books, following recommendations from some of the other kids I worked with, becoming entranced with the *Lord of the Rings* trilogy and reading it through twice. Rebecca decided to quit working at Gear and go back to America, and she brought in a box of books to divide among Ellis (the "hero" I wrote about in "Nobody's Hero," in 1993, who died of AIDS in the late '80s), the Dutch girl Carla, and me. I ended up with a good selection of English Lit from writers like Cyril Connolly, Kingsley Amis, William Trevor, Graham Greene, and Somerset Maugham, and a few great exotics, like Gabriel García Márquez and Jorge Luis Borges, introducing me to the powerful Latin-American style of "magic realism." Another Canadian I worked with, Tom, gave me a copy of *Portrait of the Artist as a Young Man*. So at least my "liberal arts" education was continuing.

On my way home from work one day, I stopped at the small tobacconist by the Oxford Circus tube station for the *Evening Standard*, and noticed a book I remembered from high school, *The Fountainhead*. It was one of the volumes the "Junior Intellectuals" at Lakeport High used to carry around (on "display," I realize now), along with *The Lord of the Rings* and James Joyce's *Ulysses*.

To a 20-year-old struggling musician, *The Fountainhead* was a revelation, an affirmation, an inspiration. Although I would eventually grow into and, largely, out of Ayn Rand's orbit, her writing was still a significant stepping-stone, or way-station, for me, a black-and-white starting point along the journey to a more nuanced philosophy and politics. Most of all, it was the notion of *individualism* that I needed — the idea that what I felt, believed, liked, and wanted was important and valid.

As Nietzsche said, "Self interest is worth as much as the person who has it. It can be worth a great deal, and it can be unworthy and contemptible."

Young musicians have to make philosophical choices early, whether they realize it or not. Like joining the union, for example, at age fifteen — though that wasn't really a *choice*, because you couldn't play in any of the union halls, even the Knights of Columbus or Legion buildings, without a union card.

But from the very beginning of playing in bands, we faced choices about what music we would play: the music we loved, or the music others wanted us to play. Thinking back to Mumblin' Sumpthin' and that bizarre lecture about the prostitute from Jack Johnson in the back room of the roller rink, that had been the kind of resistance that set me on a lifelong course as a "contrarian," determined to find a way to play music I *loved*, even if I had to make my living by other means.

During my second year in London, I was still pursuing my hoped-for music career, at least part time, and I met a bass player from Newcastle named Ian. He was putting together a band with guitarist Tony, and singer Bobby, and we started rehearsing together in the evenings. Their harder-edged, riff-driven music was more to my taste than English Rose's sugary pop had been, and their original material was interesting and challenging — and rather more imaginative than the band name they decided on: Music.

The singer had recruited a manager from somewhere (in every band I was in, from Mumblin' Sumpthin' onward, there always seemed to be a slick young man who wanted to get into the music business by being a manager). Through that summer of '72, we played a few clubs and pubs around London, including the legendary Marquee, where The Who got their start, and at Brighton University, but once again, it all fizzled into nothing. Apparently the manager had been trying to entice industry types to come and see the band, but hadn't been getting any interest. Late one night, after what looked like it would be our last gig, the hired van dropped me and my drums at Pop Shop, and I remember the bass player, Ian, smiling at me, grabbing my shoulders and saying, "You're going to be great, man. You just need *discipline*."

I puzzled over that for a long time, but in retrospect, I guess he meant that I played too much, and too imprecisely. So I learned to be precise.

A couple of weeks later, the guitarist from Music, Tony, asked me if I wanted to join him and an electric-piano player playing "soft jazz" in a London businessmen's club. The extra money would be welcome, and I said I would give it a try. We set up in a corner, me with a couple of drums and a pair of brushes, and plinked out soft standards amid a crowd of portly, stuffy, loudly-drinking "managing directors," all wearing what a friend of mine called "twelve-piece suits."

It was unbearable — I felt cheap and humiliated, squirming at having to play mindless music for heedless boors, and after two sets, I apologized to the other guys, packed up my drums, and left. It was the only job I ever walked out on, and I'm not proud of it, but I just couldn't stand it.

That was the course I would follow, refusing to compromise music for anything, and it could be said that, in a way, I devoted myself to *musical* integrity at the expense of *personal* integrity, in an ideal sense of doing what I wanted. For other young musicians I grew up with, the principle was reversed; the point of honor for them was to make their living as a *musician*, no matter what they had to play, and they would more-or-less happily work in polka bands, or country groups — whatever they had to do. Nearly all of those musicians I grew up with moved into other, more practical professions, but some of them continued to pursue their own ideal of musical pragmatism, playing wherever and whatever they could, and I have to respect that.

In music and in life, I think the concept of "enlightened self-interest" made a good foundation to build upon, and even as I grew and changed over thirty years of life experiences, it pleased me to think that my ideas and behavior still rested upon that premise. The self-interest just continued to grow more enlightened.

But even more important than the books and the life-lessons I encountered in London was the *music* I was exposed to by living there in the early '70s, especially *live* music. Sunday afternoons Brad and I could go to concerts at the Roundhouse in Chalk Farm and see four or five bands for 50 pence (just over a dollar). Sometimes they were good, sometimes not, but it was *always* interesting. Among many forgotten bands (though somehow I remember names like Marsupilami, whose guitar player I once talked to between sets, looking for "tips" on finding a band), we saw Sha-Na-Na there, and Al Kooper backed by a band called Hookfoot, containing many of Elton John's studio musicians. A free concert in Hyde Park with Grand Funk Railroad (okay) and Humble Pie (great), Pink Floyd at the Rainbow (magic), and in September of '71 we saw The Who at the Oval Cricket Grounds, playing all the stuff from *Who's Next*, with Rod Stewart and the Faces. I also talked Brad into seeing Tony Bennett at the London Palladium, which we both enjoyed as a "classy" event. (Tony Bennett always worked in London with a wonderful English drummer, Kenny Clare, and there was a funny moment on his live *Get Happy* recording when Tony introduced him after a drum break as "Kenny Clarke," a black American jazz drummer, then quickly corrected himself.)

In the spring of my second year in London, Brad and I moved to a larger, three-room flat, though it was just as far from Central London — at the extreme *southern* end of the Northern underground line, in Collier's Wood, near Wimbledon. Still, being so far out of town, the rent was reasonable, and we were especially proud of our tiny back garden overlooking the southbound railroad tracks.

Now that we had a proper front room, we even rented a television, so we could watch "Monty Python's Flying Circus" every week. I borrowed a couple hundred pounds from Bud (paying him back £5 a week) to buy my first decent stereo: Denon turntable, Sansui amp, and Celestion speakers (something else I learned about in England, buying and maintaining the sound systems in our various shops). It took me two days to carry the boxes home on the Tube, but I was so proud of that system I wouldn't even let Brad touch it. That seems petty and selfish now, but along with my drums (which I also didn't like anyone else playing), that stereo was like an *altar* to me, sacred and precious.

Music was still the only real indulgence in my life, and now that I had a steady income, every couple of weeks I could afford to buy a new album. Like the tobacconist in New Barnet which took "trade-ins" on books, the tiny record shop at the end of Carnaby Street would trade two old records for a new one, and I began trading in some of the "older" ones I'd brought from Canada. Along with the rock albums of the day, I also began buying some of "my father's music" — Frank Sinatra, Tony Bennett, Duke Ellington, and Count Basie. (One day I tried putting on a Sinatra record in the shop, but the other kids didn't "get it." The girls teased me, "You must be in *love*.")

And just as I was introduced to pot-smoking in London, I also discovered the social side of alcohol, gathering in the pub with friends or bandmates. Something had happened to me in childhood regarding beer, for I would never develop a taste for it (I remember my Dad giving me a sip of his beer when I was six or seven, and it *always* tasted that bad to me), and in those days I drank (I blush to admit) Scotch and Coke (ah, was I ever so young?). My taste soon progressed to Scotch and ginger ale, then Scotch and water, and finally, the proper glass of straight single malt with three ice cubes.

Before then, I might have been really drunk exactly *once* in my whole life, a woozy, numb-lipped, ultimately nauseous teenage experience, but in London, as I crossed into my twenties, I discovered that drinking, like smoking marijuana, could be a civilized, grown-up ritual that did not *have* to be the path to addiction and ruin.

Cole Porter's "I Get a Kick Out of You" was written in 1934 for the Broadway musical "On the Sunny Side of the Street," and featured this second verse: "Some get their kicks from cocaine/ I'm sure that if, I took even one sniff, 'twould bore me terrifically too." Acceptably witty and sophisticated in the 1930s, but not when Sinatra recorded it, in the 1950s, in that hyper-conservative climate of fear and ignorance. The verse was amended to "Some like the perfume of Spain," then again later to "Some like a bebop refrain/ I'm sure that if, I heard even one riff, 'twould bore me terrifically too."

In the London of the early 1970s, we didn't know anything about cocaine yet, and apart from hashish, the only other drug commonly available was LSD. Back in Canada, I had experienced a couple of enjoyable "acid trips," featuring all the tourist attractions of heightened senses and visual special effects (never any hallucinations, in the sense of seeing something that wasn't there, but vivid colors and patterns, and intellectual insights that were entertaining and, sometimes, truly transcendent). For me, at least (certainly not for everybody), the LSD experience could give unique perspectives on life and everything in it, sometimes absurd, sometimes sublime. As with my near-drowning experience, an acid trip seemed to take me through a panorama of my whole life up to that time, turning my whole young brain inside out and allowing me to sift through everything in it. For some people, perhaps already fragile or unstable, that experience could be too much to endure, but it could also offer spectacular sensory experiences and mental adventures.

In the fall of 1972, in our Collier's Wood flat, Brad and I took a well-planned, carefully-orchestrated LSD trip. We locked ourselves into our flat on a Saturday night, filled the electric meter with coins, and settled back to listen to Moody Blues records, smoke cigarettes, and discuss the meaning of life.

Sometime during that timeless night, we came up with a phrase that made us smile, a phrase we continued to circle back to all that night, and we decided it was the ultimate Meaning of Life.

"You get up in the morning and you go to work."

It seems to me that phrase still goes a long way toward defining an existential *modus operandi*, and pretty much sums up the way I have lived my life, whether selling souvenirs on Carnaby Street, stocking farm equipment parts, playing drums on a relentless concert tour, writing lyrics, writing a book, grieving the loss of my family, or setting out on a long drive across the American Southwest. You get up in the morning and you go to work.

But by the end of 1972, I was becoming disillusioned. Having grown up a lot in those eighteen months, supporting myself, working for a living, knocking around the small-time London music world without success (or notice!), I had learned a little more about how the world worked. Even if I "got good," it didn't mean I was going to be successful, and the choice seemed to lie between playing good music and starving, or making a poor living playing bad music. Once again, life seemed to be *standing still*, and I was feeling that itch again. Now what?

A "dear John" letter from my girlfriend back home helped make up my mind, and by Christmas I was back in St. Catharines with my drums and records. I worked with my friends Keith and Steve (who would later "set me up" with their younger sister, Jackie, with whom I would share 22 years of married life and the joys and sorrows of Selena) at Sam the Record Man through the busy holiday season, then went to work for my dad at Dalziel Equipment, starting as assistant parts manager to a quiet older man, Bruce.

Mom went with me to look at apartments, and we settled on one that was dirty and neglected, but cheap, and Mom agreed it had "possibilities." She and Dad and sister Judy helped me paint and carpet the place, and for the first time I had my *own* home. In the summer of 1973, I was suddenly promoted to parts manager, when Bruce quit to take another job, and by then I had bought my beloved MG convertible, had it painted purple, and was roaring around in it on nights and weekends (and spending many evenings trying to repair it in the service shop at work, learning how to replace exhaust systems, do valve jobs, and troubleshoot English electrical systems). I had a nicely-decorated "bachelor pad," complete with waterbed, the stereo I had bought in England, and even a room for my drums, though they were covered with circles of carpet over the drums and cymbals, so I could play them without disturbing the neighbors.

But it was not enough. I was disillusioned about the music *business*, but not about *music*, and I missed playing in a band.

My former bandmates from J.R. Flood, guitarist Paul and organist Bob, had a new band called Bullrush, and they were still the local favorites, but they already had the best drummer around, Glen Gratto. (That summer I saw posters around the area for a concert featuring Bullrush and, by some agent's inspiration, two similarly-named bands, Mahogany Rush and . . . Rush. But I didn't see that show.)

I started talking with a local manager, Arnie Dyker, about helping me put together a band of my own, and maybe he could find us jobs for evenings and weekends. I mentioned a young guitarist whose playing had impressed me, and although he was in another band, he was far too good for them. When I suggested to Arnie that we ask him to join my new band, he said I was "Machiavellian," but I didn't see the harm — I'd have a better guitar player, and the guitar player would have a better band.

Arnie and I also recruited another guitarist I respected, Brian Collins, and used the name of his previous band, Hush, once we had a singer and a bass player. In Brian's parents' basement, we started learning cover songs we liked, ranging from Genesis to Frank Zappa to part of The Who's *Quadrophenia*, then hit the bars. While I was away, the drinking age in Ontario had been lowered from twenty-one to eighteen, and now the bars were the places to play, often for three- or four-night stands. This was tough on me, playing until 2 o'clock in the morning, then getting up at 7 a.m. to go to work, but at least I was playing again, and playing music I liked. I started urging Arnie to get us more jobs, so we could make a living at it. Maybe we should move to Toronto, get a record deal — I was getting all ambitious again.

One hot July morning in the summer of 1974, a white Corvette pulled up in front of Dalziel Equipment. Another drummer from the area, John Trojan, climbed out of the passenger seat, and introduced me to the driver, Vic Wilson, one of the managers of a band from Toronto called Rush. All I knew about them was seeing those Bullrush, Mahogany Rush, Rush posters from the previous summer, but apparently they had been playing bluesy hard rock around the Toronto-area bars for a few years, and had recently released an independent Canadian album financed by the management company. The manager said the album had been picked up by an American record company, Mercury, and an American tour was being planned for later that summer. It sounded very exciting (though by that time I had learned to be skeptical of a manager's promises).

Because of health and interpersonal issues, the band was parting company with their current drummer and looking for a new one, so John Trojan had told them I might be suitable. And, they were offering a salary of $125 a week — a decent living, playing rock music!

When my dad got wind of this, he knew just what to say, "Maybe you'd better go talk to your mother." Mom agreed that I should give it a shot, and a few days later, I borrowed her Pinto, packed my drums into it (they wouldn't fit in my Lotus Europa), and drove to a warehouse in the eastern suburbs of Toronto. As Geddy and Alex and I played together, we seemed to respond to each other's "energies" right away, and even after, when we sat around on the floor talking about "Monty Python's Flying Circus," *The Lord of the Rings*, and bands we liked.

They said they'd let me know, and over the next few days, I had an attack of insecurity — I didn't think I had played well enough at the audition, and realized I really *wanted* that gig. I started pestering the manager on the phone for another chance, but he just kept saying, "It's up to the guys."

Finally, a few days later, I got the word, and the sudden excitement and activity were overwhelming. We were going to be going on *tour*, in the *United States*, and with the record company advance, we went to a music store in downtown Toronto and bought all new equipment, including a double set of chrome Slingerland drums. This, for sure, was going to be the high road.

The first show, opening for Manfred Mann and Uriah Heep at the Civic Center arena in Pittsburgh, in front of 11,000 people, was only two weeks away, so we had a lot of work to do. But first, I had to tell the guys in Hush. Calling a meeting at Arnie's house, I explained that I was leaving the group because of this big opportunity, and Brian Collins wasn't very happy about it. He gave me a disgusted look and said, "I guess everybody has their price."

Fifteen years later, when Brian became an editor at *The St. Catharines Standard*, he contacted our office about the possibility of me writing a story for my hometown paper. He published my two-part "Memories of a Port Boy," and when I mentioned to Brian how ironic his parting shot seemed in retrospect, he didn't remember saying that.

Through Brian, I was also reacquainted with Arnie, and he didn't remember calling me "Machiavellian" either. Just as Margaret Ashukian didn't remember being "surprised" to learn I had principles, and Ian Murray probably wouldn't remember saying, "You just need *discipline*." People "tattoo" you for life like that, then don't even remember.

In any case, on August 14, 1974, Geddy and Alex and I flew from Toronto to Pittsburgh for that first show together, and so began *all that*. Like a verse from "I've Been Everywhere," our lives would be spelled out in itineraries: "Reno, Chicago, Fargo, Minnesota, Buffalo, Toronto, Winslow, Sarasota, Wichita, Tulsa, Ottawa, Oklahoma, Tampa, Panama, Mattawa, La Paloma . . ."

You get up in the morning and you go to work.

Middle Eight

"Filling my spirit with the wildest wish to fly"

America's national parks are said to be its crown jewels, a string of temples to natural beauty strung across the nation, from Haleakala in Hawaii to Denali in Alaska to the Everglades in Florida. Outside of Alaska, the largest national parks are set in the frame of the American West, and their names alone are a poetic roll call of Americana: Glacier, Crater Lake, Redwood, Yosemite, Sequoia, Joshua Tree, Zion, Canyonlands, Arches, Organ Pipe Cactus, Grand Canyon, Yellowstone — visions of soft-focus fantasy if you haven't experienced them, sharp images of sublime memory if you have.

Living in Southern California gave me easy proximity to all that sanctified natural beauty, and because I used the national parks regularly on my overnight motorcycle trips, I valued them highly — they *mattered* to me. I had been fortunate enough to have visited nearly all the major Canadian and American parks in the West, many of them several times, and I sympathized with those who tried to save the parks, whether from a philistine government threatening to drill for oil in Alaska's Gates of the Arctic, or simply from the ravages of their fatal *popularity*.

Denali National Park in Alaska, home of the nation's highest peak, Mount Denali (formerly Mount McKinley), had closed its roads to public traffic, providing shuttles for hikers, campers, and sightseers. Other over-crowded parks, like Yellowstone, Yosemite, and Grand Canyon, were considering that remedy as well. In a way, it was a positive sign that Americans crowded to their wilderness areas in such numbers, taking advantage of and appreciating the natural beauty in its pristine state, but of course that very pristineness was threatened by too many vehicles, too many humans. One park ranger told me that fewer than ten per cent of those visitors ventured more than a hundred yards from their cars.

Another remedy for overcrowded parks might be adding more of them, like a business whose demand outgrows its supply, or making them bigger — expanding operations due to public demand. Perhaps they ought to amalgamate some of the public lands around them, whose signs described them as "Land of Many Uses," which, as Edward Abbey pointed out, too often meant "Land of Many Abuses." Under that designation, the Bureau of Land Management had little power to protect those public lands from the destructive invasions of logging, mining, and overgrazing, and hardly any rangers to enforce what few restrictions they had.

Big Bend National Park, with 1,252 square miles, protected a vast area of the American side of the Chihuahuan Desert, and described itself, in the park newspaper, as "one of the largest and least visited of America's national parks." It certainly felt both large and empty to me, as I drove across its width at sunrise on Sunday morning, aiming for Rio Grande Village, on the eastern side of the park. Checking the list of park activities at the visitors center the day before, I had noted a guided birdwalk at 8:30 the next morning, and decided that experience might be worth getting up early for.

My love of birds went back to earliest childhood, to a set of little books my grandmother had, with shiny red, yellow, blue, and green covers. Grandma showed me how to trace the illustrations of the American robin, the ruby-crowned kinglet, the scarlet tanager, and so on, with pencil and tracing paper. I have those books now, the outlines still visibly imprinted by my childhood tracings, among an ever-growing collection of field guides to the birds of North America, Europe, East Africa, West Africa, Mexico, Brazil, Hawaii, Tahiti, and the West Indies. (I also remember, at four or five, sitting on the head of my bed pretending to be a perching bird, like the deranged character in the movie *Birdy*, or like a child's expression of a title by Rupert Hine's excellent lyricist, Jeanette Obstoj, "The Wildest Wish To Fly.")

Grandma also had a collection of little bird cards that came inside boxes of Red Rose tea. Mrs. Pirie next door used to save those cards for me, but she didn't seem to drink enough tea to keep my collection growing. I asked my mother to buy Red Rose tea so I could collect more of the cards, and was mystified when she protested that she and Dad didn't *like* tea. Whatever did that have to do with it?

The cards were photographed and written by Roger Tory Peterson, the most famous bird-watcher of the day, and he was a hero to me the way hockey players were to other boys. My ambition was to be a professional bird-watcher, and at the age of seven I decided to start a bird-watching club, and asked all my friends in the second grade to meet at my house after school. They all said they would, but I stood in the driveway for over an hour, and no one showed up. Disappointed and quietly disillusioned, I learned an important lesson about what people would say, and what they would do.

Once I was standing in the driveway watching my dad wash and wax the red-and-white 1955 Buick Century "convertible hardtop," and just as he finished, with a final proud swipe of the chamois across the gleaming fender, a robin flew over and dropped a white package on the hood. Dad turned to me and grumbled, "See, that's what your birds do!"

But I carried on loving birds, all my life, with binoculars and field guides and backyard bird feeders. In fact, I never understood how others could *not* be fascinated by birds; how for other people those darting flashes of color and motion could seem like just another part of the world's *backdrop*. But then, so many things just seemed interesting to me, as my curiosity later spread to wanting to know the names of tropical fishes on the reef, the kinds of coral, or clouds, the names of trees in the forest, shrubs in the desert, and lately, even the nature of the rocks and dirt from which it all sprang.

I had only been on one guided birdwalk before, in East Africa, but it had been a good experience, seeing much that I would have missed on my own, and sharing it with like-minded enthusiasts, so I was mildly excited about this opportunity, and determined not to be late and possibly miss it. Rangers, gas station attendants, and hotel clerks gave me varying estimates of the time necessary to drive from Lajitas to Rio Grande Village, a distance of 65 or 70 curvaceous miles.

Thinking about it that night over dinner, at the Candelilla Restaurant beside the hotel, I decided to allow plenty of time, and set off shortly after 6:30 a.m., nourished only by a cup of in-room coffee. The park map showed symbols for a visitors center, campground, gas station and store, and maybe I would find some breakfast-like sustenance there, even a muffin or donut.

Given a bright, clear Sunday morning, with not a single other vehicle, or stirring of wildlife, I immersed myself in the drive and the scenery, and the soundtrack from *Frida* once again. Atmospherically, it was good "morning music," and its combination of traditional Mexican songs and modern interpretations seemed right for a day in which I would range from a few miles to a few feet from Mexico.

I reached the end of the road in Rio Grande Village almost an hour early (journal note: "illegally, but very enjoyably!"), to find everything closed up tight. The meeting point for the birdwalk was described as the "amphitheater parking lot," so I found that, parked, and had a look around in the early morning stillness. The amphitheater was a half-circle of wooden benches facing a white-painted plywood screen, where rangers gave night programs and slide shows for the campers, and I followed a meandering path from there along the grassy picnic grounds by the river. A flock of turkey vultures roosted in a large dead tree (probably killed by their noxious droppings), and as yet only a few doves were stirring, strutting under the broad cottonwoods. I walked down a dirt lane to the river, narrow and placid between thick reeds, and thought again of the unreality of this being the border between Mexico and the United States. I didn't know yet that this was also a *dangerous* place.

Back at the small parking area, a few other vehicles pulled in right around 8:30. Two couples in late middle age were carrying large binoculars and field guides, so I knew they were there for the same reason I was. We exchanged smiles and greetings, though no names, strangely, but that was fine with me; it seemed enough that we shared this common interest.

An older man stepped out of a big pickup and introduced himself as Bernie, our guide, and explained that his wife usually joined him on these birdwalks, but she had slipped on the truck's running board and hurt her leg. Bernie wore a brown uniform with Volunteer Ranger patches, and seemed to be about eighty, though strong and active, with white hair, glasses, hearing aid, and mottled, leathery skin on his face and neck. He asked each of us about our birding experience, and I described myself as "a bird-lover since childhood, though never a 'life-list' keeper." One of the other couples was from the east coast, wearing designer outdoor wear and binoculars, and during the morning they mentioned several journeys taken along the eastern seaboard just to look at birds, so they were more serious. The other couple, from the extreme southeast corner of Texas, seemed to be retirees seeking interesting diversions.

Bernie explained that this Sunday morning excursion was directed more toward beginners, and that he would be leading us on a leisurely walk around the surrounding area, and showing us how to find and identify different species. Somebody asked about the banks of the river, and he shook his head and said we wouldn't be going that way this morning. There was something strange in his voice, and the eastern lady asked why not. Reluctantly, Bernie explained that a few days previously someone had been *shot* at from across the river, and although the shooter had missed, they were avoiding the area until he was caught. The lady asked if the target had been a Border Patrol officer, or a park ranger in uniform, and Bernie said no, then showed his subtle sense of humor by describing the target as wearing an orange vest, blue sweater, dark pants — until we laughed to realize he was describing *her*.

 Bernie explained how recent events had affected the area, closing two former border crossings within the park because of "Homeland Security" concerns, in the wake of September 11th, 2001. At the time of the park's establishment, in the 1930s, residents who couldn't prove they had been born there were deported, and there had been people whose ancestors had settled there for hundreds of years who found themselves unable to document that history, and ejected from their ancestral homes. People in the nearby village of San Vicente, on the Mexican side of the river, were even more bitter now, Bernie told us, as they were unable even to visit their family graves on the American side, without traveling 100 miles in either direction to cross the border at Presidio or Del Rio.

We moved slowly across the tree-shaded lawn of the picnic area, scanning the trees and bushes, and Bernie pointed to a pair of doves on the grass, and asked if anyone could identify them. They looked like mourning doves to me, a familiar companion to my life everywhere from California to Quebec, and even West Africa, with their sad *boo-hoo-hoo-hoo* call, but Bernie pointed out the white along the edges of their folded wings, the clue for one of us to name them as white-winged doves, found only in the desert Southwest, and down into Mexico.

A pair of strikingly black-and-white-checked woodpeckers flitted between the trees and ground, making a raspy, whirring call, and Bernie asked if anyone knew what kind they were. All of us raised our binoculars for a closer look, then leafed through our field guides. They reminded me of the gila woodpeckers I'd seen in Organ Pipe Cactus National Monument, in Arizona, but Bernie shook his head, "We don't get gilas here," and indicated his National Geographic field guide, "That's what's better about this one, it shows the territory map right beside the illustration, instead of in a different part of the book." Then he pointed at the woodpeckers: "Notice the gold color at the back of their heads, the male's red cap, and maybe you can pick out a tinge of gold on their bellies?"

When none of us came up with it, he said, "Golden-fronted woodpecker."

A flash of unbelievably brilliant red flitted to a perch on a nearby treetop, a beacon glowing in the early sun, luring our binoculars. Black eyepatch, wings, and back, slender insect-eater's bill, the rest of it fluorescent scarlet. "Vermilion flycatcher," said Bernie, "and you can see why. Scarlet wouldn't do, or crimson, or ruby, it had to be vermilion!" I breathed a soft "Wow" as I stared through the binoculars; it was one of the most beautiful birds I had ever seen.

In *Small Wonder*, Barbara Kingsolver wrote, "The sight of a vermilion flycatcher leaves us breathless every time — he's not just a bird, he's a punctuation mark on the air, printed in red ink, read out loud as a gasp."

Bernie continued to lead us slowly among the trees and underbrush, and showed us another dozen or so species, including the more widespread ones, like the graceful mockingbird with its white wing patches, the stocky western meadowlark with its bright yellow front, the house finch with its dull red bib, the cardinal (whose red plumage now seemed drab compared with the vermilion flycatcher), and its grayer cousin, the pyrrhuloxia, both with their natty crests, and those species unique to the region — a smaller dove called the Inca, another less colorful flycatcher, the ash-throated, and a cute little yellow-headed bird, the verdin. We watched a roadrunner zip up and down a slanted tree trunk, and someone asked if roadrunners could actually fly. Bernie said, "Yes, they can fly if they want to, but they generally prefer to run. You've seen how fast a lizard can move? Well, a roadrunner can catch them."

Looking at Bernie's *National Geographic* field guide, I was surprised to read that the roadrunner is a member of the cuckoo family, though twice as big as the others, at nearly two feet long. I also noticed a one-page index he had taped inside the cover, a quick reference prepared by the Tucson Audubon Society, and when he offered a copy to one of the others, I asked for one too — I had already decided to buy that field guide, because Bernie said it was better, and he was my new birding hero, my new Roger Tory Peterson.

In the course of walking and talking, I learned that Bernie and his wife were from New York originally, and had retired to this area and become volunteers at the national park. He knew so much about the region, both human and natural history, and when I asked him about the masses of green, feathery trees I had seen over by the Santa Elena Canyon, at the other end of the park, he told me they were indeed tamarisk, and that something was going to have to be done about them. As an introduced Asian species, fast growing and drought resistant, they had originally been planted as windbreaks, then quickly spread across the whole desert Southwest, choking out the native plants. Bernie also told us what the local settlers had grown, the cotton, grains, and food crops that had sustained several settlements in the Big Bend area, where only a few ruins remained.

Bernie obviously possessed a wide range of interests and a lifetime of collected information, and his calm, good-humored manner suited him perfectly to imparting it to others so easily, a natural teacher. Later, I made a journal note inspired by the idea of people like Bernie:

> Thinking with regard to Bernie and all his knowledge of birds and nature and local history — you just start to learn a few things, and you get old and *die*, and all that dies with you. Aging is just *wrong!* For me, and all other "good people."
>
> Knowledge, experience, wisdom all *valuable*, more than youth and ignorance.
>
> But then there's lots of ignorant old age too . . .

Bernie just seemed like one of the good ones, regardless of age, and the ongoing loss of people like him seemed a terrible loss to the world. I remember when I heard that Frank Zappa had died, for example, I shook my head and thought, "The world *needs* Frank Zappa." I felt the same way when other people who had made a positive mark on the world were taken away, no matter how long they lived: Duke Ellington, Frank Sinatra, Edward Abbey, Georgia O'Keeffe, Walt Disney, Martin Luther King, my grandma, my daughter, my wife, several good friends, and on and on forever. Not just that it was a shame these people had to *die*, but that the rest of us had to do without them.

In the early '60s, while Duke Ellington was still alive, Ralph Ellison wrote a "birthday message" for him, a moving tribute to his enduring greatness, and a testament to what would be lost with his passing:

During a period when groups of young English entertainers who based their creations upon the Negro American musical tradition have effected a questionable revolution of manners among American youths, perhaps it is time to pay our respects to a man who has spent his life reducing the violence and chaos of American life to artistic order. I have no idea where we shall all be a hundred years from now, but if there is a classical music in which the American experience has finally discovered the voice of its own complexity, it will owe much of its direction to the achievements of Edward Kennedy Ellington. For many years he has been telling us how marvelous, mad, violent, hopeful, nostalgic, and (perhaps) decent we are. He is one of the musical fathers of our country, and throughout all these years he has, as he tells us so mockingly, loved us madly. We are privileged to have lived during his time and to have known so great a man, so great a musician.

As we walked back toward the parking area, Bernie added up the species we had seen, and apologized that there were only thirteen. "Usually we see more than that." I told him I certainly didn't feel cheated, and that the vermilion flycatcher alone had been worth getting up early for. The park was home to more than 450 species of birds, more than anywhere else in the United States, and two species were found only there, the Colima warbler and the Lucifer hummingbird, so it would obviously be a rewarding site for some more birding, especially for a serious "collector," or life-list keeper.

Saying goodbye to Bernie and my birdwatching companions about 10:30, I drove back toward the Chisos Basin, in the middle of the park. I had been up and active for four hours by then, and still hadn't had any breakfast, so that was my first mission. The park's only restaurant was at the lodge, and I turned off at the Chisos Mountains Basin Junction. The "Green Gulch" road was open again, after the previous day's snowfall had been cleared, but streaks of white remained on the monumental formations of gray rock and in the sheltered areas of woodland. The road wound its way up to the 5,400-foot Chisos Basin, an oasis of green surrounded by high, rugged mountains of gray rock, all of it set high above the surrounding desert like an island in a dry sea, a bowl held aloft in hands of stone.

I parked at the lodge, but the restaurant, alas, was closed, and would not reopen for another hour. Walking down to the visitors center in the cool air and strong sunshine, I asked a ranger about hiking possibilities, concerned that lingering snow or ice might affect my choices. The previous day I had spent a dollar on a small booklet, *Hiker's Guide to Trails of Big Bend National Park*, and had settled on a trail to the highest point in the park, Emory Peak, at 7,825 feet. It was described as a "Strenuous Day Hike, for experienced, conditioned hikers only. Rough trails and longer distances. Sturdy hiking boots are a necessity." I had been doing quite a bit of hiking in California lately, over in Temescal Canyon and Will Rogers State Park, as well as in Big Sur a few weeks previously, so I felt "conditioned," and I had my old hiking boots with me, originally bought for the climb up Mount Kilimanjaro back in 1987, in which I had hiked sixty miles in five days, to 19,340 feet and back, without a single blister.

But considering the previous day's weather, and the possibility of snow and cold temperatures higher up, I wondered if one of the lower elevation trails would be wiser, to The Window, or Chimneys. The ranger thought the snow would melt pretty quickly on the trails up to Emory Peak, and that I shouldn't have any trouble, so I went into the small general store and picked up a couple of sandwiches, a square of chocolate cake, some water and fruit juice. I packed them in my little daypack with my camera and binoculars and set off to the trailhead, eating one of the sandwiches as my so-called breakfast.

At the beginning of the trail I stopped to read a sign, "Lion Warning."

"A lion has been frequenting this area, and could be aggressive toward humans."

It said that if I saw a lion, I should appear large, wave my arms, shout aggressively, and throw stones or sticks. I should not show fear, crouch down, or run away. "If attacked, fight back" — that was a difficult scenario even to picture. Elsewhere I had read that three people had been attacked by mountain lions in the park in recent years, though all of them "recovered," and I was a little spooked by the image of a powerful lion prowling through the rocks and trees, leaping upon me from above and sinking its powerful fangs into my neck. I tried to keep my eyes wide open as I hiked, to "appear large," and I picked up a pointed, fist-sized rock and carried it with me, determined not to go down without a fight (the same defensive strategy I had adopted against the grizzly warnings on a hike in Glacier National Park in Montana, and I noted the same wry comment, "Yeah right!").

There were black bears to worry about as well, for they had moved back into the park in recent years, spreading north from Mexico after having disappeared during the pre-park settlement era. Farther up the trail I saw another sign, "Bear country, do not leave backpacks unattended." I knew bears would be more interested in my food than in me, but I did have that ham and cheese sandwich in my pack, and no doubt a bear would be willing to fight for my chocolate cake. I held on tighter to my pointed rock, and marched on.

Catching a glimpse of brownish-gray fur among the trees, I tensed for an instant, but saw it was only a deer, one of several browsing among the live-oak trees, seeming unconcerned by my passing. They were a rare species called the Carmen Mountains white-tailed deer, and in the United States, they were found only in the Chisos Mountains. Similarly, several plant and tree species survived only in the higher elevations, isolated remnants from the cooler, wetter ice age.

The Pinnacles Trail led me up steeply for three and a half miles, much of it in a series of switchbacks. Breathing was labored in the thinning air as I climbed through 5,000, 6,000, 7,000 feet. Most of the time I was shaded by pinyon pines, junipers, and occasional deciduous trees, but the sun was strong in open areas, and had already melted most of the snow and dried the trail. At the turnoff for the Emory Peak trail, the final mile to the summit, a couple of bear-proof lockers were provided for backpackers wishing to leave their packs, but my little daypack was not that heavy, and in any case, I wanted to bring my lunch to enjoy at the summit.

The last 25 feet were a scramble up a wall of tumbled boulders, using

hands and feet on a sharply vertical climb, then I finally stood on Emory
Peak, at 7,825 feet, joining two other climbers who were eating their
lunches and talking quietly in what sounded like South African accents.
They asked me to take their picture and passed me their camera, and I
took advantage of the opportunity to have them take mine. Then I settled
back with my sandwich and cake, and enjoyed the hard-won view. A pair
of antennas and some weather instruments were a jarring technological
note, and were apparently part of Big Bend's two-way radio system, pow-
ered by solar cells. Beyond them, a limitless view stretched in every
direction, thin green sheets of vegetation draped over rugged, furrowed
mountains and canyon walls. Everything to the south was part of Mexico,
and to the north rose the towers and battlements of gray rock around the
walls of the Basin, its floor speckled with green and the tiny dots of the
lodge buildings.

After a half hour's rest, I climbed carefully down the boulder wall (as
always, more difficult to find hand- and footholds going down than up),
and hiked back down to the lodge, starting to feel a little tired and footsore.
My mind wandered in a million directions as I walked, and I thought back
to the outdoor adventures of my childhood, spending Saturdays hiking out
to Paradise Valley, or going on "bike hikes" out to Rockway or Balls Falls.

One summer when I was ten or eleven, I used to hike with a boy named
Brian Unger. He shared my taste for word games, and as we walked along
the rural two-lanes we used to make up long alliterative sentences (one I
still remember: "My mother Mary maybe might make me marvelous
Martian muscular monkey mcat"). A couple of years later, when I was taking drum lessons, Brian's older brother, Danny, played guitar in a local band,
and we watched them practice in the Unger basement. Brian bragged that I
could play "Wipeout," and their drummer passed me his sticks. Too nervous
even to take off my winter coat, which was heavy and restrictive, I sat down
and gave it my best, and the older guys seemed moderately impressed —
maybe just that this punk kid could play "Wipeout" in a winter coat.

Around that same time I was at a band practice with my Uncle
Richard's band, The Outcasts, and somehow I asked, or was asked (or

challenged) to play "Wipeout" on my Uncle Richard's drums, in front of his bandmates. They made a big fuss over how fast I played it, and at first I felt proud. Then I noticed Richard was kind of subdued on our way home, and I felt strange, though I didn't know why.

As nearly all boyhood friends seem to do, Brian Unger and I drifted apart, but nine or ten years later, I ran into him again, still in St. Catharines. It was the day after Rush played at Toronto's Massey Hall for the first time, in late 1974 (opening for Nazareth), and I was driving my old Mercedes 230SL across town, all excited, when I was stopped for speeding. The cop was Brian Unger, and to his credit, he let me off. (If he hadn't, I'm sure I could have changed his mind with a chorus of, "My mother Mary maybe might make me marvelous Martian muscular monkey meat.")

In the ceaseless train of thought propelled by walking, I fell into thinking about the music of the early '60s, and how the big change in the British Invasion had actually been less a progression forward than a reversion to the *roots* of rock 'n' roll: *black* music.

After Elvis popularized what had formerly been called "race music" in the mid-'50s, the rock 'n' roll edginess of wilder performers like Jerry Lee Lewis, Bo Diddley, and Little Richard degenerated into the sugary white pop style of singers like Frankie Avalon, Fabian, Gene Pitney, Lesley Gore, Lou Christie, and Phil Spector's various girl groups. All that music was fine as far as it went, which usually wasn't very far (though I confess I liked a lot of those songs), and it was the *real* gift of the Beatles and the Rolling Stones to bring back the original R&B influence that had started it all, emulating, or even simply *reproducing*, hits by black artists — just as Elvis had done.

In this connection, I thought of a guy I had traveled with on a bicycle tour across the Canadian Rockies in the late '80s. Bruce was an American in his forties, a devout Christian, and perhaps one of the most proudly *ignorant* people I had ever been obliged to spend time with. Once he and I were pedaling along a mountain road together, and the subject of music came up. Bruce told me he had stopped listening to music when he gave up drugs and found religion (I missed the connection — still do), but that he kind of liked "that Swedish group." He could only have meant ABBA, and I just nodded silently. I had never met an actual ABBA fan (though there were obviously millions of them *somewhere*), but I figured that if he liked them, then fine for him.

He said he liked the Beatles, too, and when I mentioned in the course of conversation that they and the Rolling Stones had started out imitating black American music, he giggled and shook his head, saying in an admonishing tone, "No they *didn't!*" You would have thought I had made an off-color joke, or an outrageous statement, like his mother was his sister, or Jesus was a Jew.

One day Bruce overheard my brother, Danny, and me talking about books, and observed, "Gee, you guys are real book freaks, aren't you?" Danny and I laughed, a little, and guessed we were "book freaks," in Bruce's eyes. Bruce went on, "I was in a bookstore once, and a guy was there signing his books, so I bought one. I can't remember who it was. My wife read some of it and said it was awful."

He also bragged about buying a fake Rolex watch for his wife, and how much money that had "saved" him, though he didn't mention if she knew it was fake. Perhaps she did, and thought he was every bit as clever as he did.

One evening over dinner, the subject of homosexuality came up, with a couple of us referring to gay friends and expressing our dismay over the growing AIDS epidemic (this was in the late '80s). No one asked for Bruce's opinion, but he shook his head and said, "It's just *wrong.*"

Somebody asked, "Do you mean AIDS, or being homosexual?"

He giggled and said, "homosexual," then frowned and shook his head with obvious disapproval.

When asked why, he giggled again, and said, "The parts don't fit." Hee hee hee.

Another time he mentioned having taken his kids to an art museum, and when they looked at some modern art, one of his kids said, "*I* could do that," and Bruce, giggling again, said he probably could have. No doubt, if the kid was a smug genius like his father.

There had been nine of us on that bicycle trip across the Rockies, some older and some younger than me, and it was interesting to note that the older people were tolerantly amused by this ignorant bigot, while the younger ones, including me, were driven to anger and disgust by his incessant giggling, inane remarks, and poisonous opinions.

Companions like that were another reason it was often nicer to be traveling alone. Company could be pleasant, if it was *good* company, like my friend Brutus, where we could ride together through the day and compare impressions over a good meal. But most of the time, I was happy to be riding, driving, or hiking alone, as I was that Sunday afternoon, coming down from Emory Peak in the bright sunshine.

By the time I made it back to the car in the lodge parking lot, I was thoroughly fatigued. It felt good to change back into lighter shoes, and let the car carry me back down the Green Gulch road, most of the snow gone by then, listening to more Mexican music, a "progressive mariachi" group called Mariachi Cobre.

It was with Brutus that I first discovered real mariachi music. We were traveling by motorcycle in Mexico in March of 1995, the first time there for both of us, and had arrived in Oaxaca after a long, scary ride from Cuernavaca. If a traveler could visit only one place in Mexico, there would be a strong argument for suggesting Oaxaca. At an elevation of 5,000 feet, with clear, dry air, the city was set in a wide valley circled by mountains, a multi-faceted jewel in an elegant setting. The pre-Hispanic and colonial cultures remained alive in the blend of Spanish architecture, the vast and crowded indoor market of neatly-displayed produce and colorful textiles, and in the lively street life. Even our hotel contributed to the atmosphere of romantic timelessness, built into an old Spanish convent with massive walls and arched colonnades overlooking quiet green courtyards.

Brutus and I had only been in Oaxaca a couple of hours, and had barely begun our travels in Mexico, but I was already so struck by the charms of this city that I said to Brutus, "I get the feeling this place is going to be tough to beat." I was right.

Just after dark, we sat on the balcony of the El Asador Vasco restaurant, overlooking the tree-filled zócalo, the main square, with its ornate bandstand. The older part of town and the zócalo area were closed to traffic, and among the sidewalk vendors and shoe-shine stands, couples and families strolled around the square, the stone-paved streets, or sat at the cafés. Sipping margaritas, Brutus and I tucked into a soup of green corn with poblano chiles, while a trio of sad-faced guitarists began to strum from the back of the restaurant. However, they were soon overwhelmed by exuberant trumpets from the street below, where six or seven mariachi groups moved around the square, alternating from one café to the next. Each outfit had its uniform, mostly in the flashy style popularized by Mexican cinema and inspired by the *charros*, or gentleman cowboys: the tight pants and short jackets with rows of silver buttons, and the familiar wide sombreros.

Our "first row balcony" seats beside the wrought-iron railing were perfect for this concert, and as we ate, drank, watched, and listened, the sad-faced trio behind us were forgotten and unheard. Perhaps they gave up and went away.

At the end of two or three songs, the members of each group took up a collection, in baskets or in the sound-hole of the big *guitarrón* (acoustic bass guitar), and from my balcony seat I noticed that the people seemed to contribute willingly, appreciatively. Every city in Mexico had a tradition of street music, and it was one of the country's greatest charms, from the mariachis of Guadalajara to the marimba bands of Veracruz. And everywhere, the Mexican audiences were happy to pay for their entertainment, while the musicians retained the dignity of professional *performers*, not beggars.

This was my first exposure to *real* mariachi music, in its natural setting, as opposed to that offered for "atmosphere" in hotels of the American Southwest, where it would be either second-rate or an out-of-context parody. I had no idea of the rich heritage conveyed in mariachi music, or its impressive, passionate musicality, but in Oaxaca's beautiful zócalo, as so often happens when a time-honored style of music is played live, by good musicians and in its proper element, I suddenly understood it. Or, more accurately, I *felt* it.

Mariachi's roots grew in the state of Jalisco, out of local folk dances and song forms, originally played by a trio of harp, guitar, and violin. One story holds that during the French occupation of Mexico, in the 1860s, local musicians were hired to play at French weddings, or *mariages*, which gave the style its name. Another theory says the name came from the now-extinct Coca Indian people in the state of Jalisco, the word *mariachi* referring to the wooden platform on which the musicians and dancers performed.

Over the years a fixed repertoire of songs was established — simple melodies with sentimental lyrics of love and heartache, or the beauty of one's hometown — but, depending upon the skill of the musicians, the rhythms and harmonies could be inventive and complex. Mariachi's alloy was forged from the rich ore of gypsy music, flamenco, opera, Spanish folk music and its Moorish undertones, and purely Mexican exuberance. As the groups began to travel, the harp was replaced with more portable guitars, and trumpets were introduced in radio broadcasts of mariachi music in Mexico City. By the late 20th century, when Brutus and I were in Oaxaca, a mariachi group typically consisted of three guitarists — tenor, *vihuela*, guitar, *guitarra*, and six-string bass, *guitarrón* — two trumpet players, and a violinist or two. A few ensembles leaned toward the mariachi avant-garde, incorporating a saxophone, an upright bass, or even an accordion.

Taking it all in, smiling to each other in appreciation, Brutus and I were delighted with Oaxaca's blend of Old World elegance and Latin American gusto, and equally delighted with our second margaritas and main course of *pollo mole*. (A signature dish of southern Mexico, pronounced *"molay,"* it is a rich and complex dark sauce blended from a combination of spices, often including chocolate, and different every place it was served.)

At first the whole Oaxacan zócalo scene was merely *entertaining*, a novel and picturesque mise-en-scène, but before long I found myself responding to the music, beginning to feel it like an electric tingling in my veins. When performed by the better groups, the simple melodies could elevate to a sublime elegance, the instrumentation into a driving force, and the singing could rise above sentiment, and soar into deeply felt emotion.

The musicians who took their turns in the street were all competent players, and some of them were even excellent; especially impressive considering they would no doubt have had day-jobs as well. One group, resplendent in dark brown suits and wide sombreros bedecked with silver, had a particularly showy pair of trumpeters; their close-harmony answering phrases were intricate and impressive, and during one slow passage they moved wide apart on the street, like gunfighters, then played an alternating duet of sweet melodies in this "wide stereo," as if dueling.

So often it has been a single player who brought an unfamiliar style of music alive for me. A blistering guitarist in a gypsy quartet playing a Paris bistro, a bass player in a Caribbean reggae band, a dashing violinist in St. Mark's Square in Venice, or a West African playing a piece of brass with his fingers and a stick; even that subtle, expressive flow of rhythm behind the village choir was undeniably the voice of an artist. These gifted and totally committed musicians were able to pour their whole lives into their music, and because of that complete existential passion that went *into* the performance, so much life and passion radiated *out* of it.

Among all the mariachi musicians in Oaxaca's zócalo, there was one who shone that way for me, a singer and guitarist with a fire in his performance that was unmistakably deep and sincere. In his silver-buttoned brown suit and sombrero, his features were knotted with intensity and naked vulnerability, his eyes closed as he sang, and his talent was equal to the challenge of expressing that intensity and vulnerability through his singing and playing. His wide brown face was completely rapt in his singing, while his fingers sped over the fretboard and his strumming hand flew, igniting and elevating the music from sidewalk entertainment to compelling art.

He was one of the rare ones, the precious ones; indeed, perhaps the *only* ones who can communicate an unfamiliar style to the listener. History has shown that it is difficult for such a burning spirit to balance the rest of life on that level of intensity and vulnerability, not only for musicians but for all kinds of artists, but what a gift it is to the *art*.

In music, any competent player can evoke the listener's response to a familiar piece. Even the bare notes of the melody carry a resonance of association, and the song itself has already been communicated, and rests somewhere in memory. Any half-decent combo can crank out jazz standards or rock covers and please an audience. Even if the performances are shallow or inept, melody sparks memory and some warmth is felt.

This would be true of familiar *styles* as well, for even a banal composition in a given style can serve to evoke a pattern, a dance, that is already intuitive, and can spark feelings the listener has already experienced. There is an African saying that "wood that has burned once is easier to set alight." Popular music is full of hackers and panderers who know how to rekindle an automatic response, who know which buttons to push to *simulate* emotion or excitement, but only a real master can spark a *new* response. That passionate, talented, and skilled mariachi master in the streets of Oaxaca had lit the fire of his music inside me.

The pièce de résistance of the performance was the "mariachi Woodstock," when three of the groups joined together on the street to form an impromptu orchestra of nine guitars, three violins, and six trumpets. Again, the trumpet players stood well back, dividing the first and second parts among themselves in dynamic counterpoint, while all those guitars strummed out a driving rhythm, the violins soared, and the voices rose up with power and passion.

And what a great song it was! Even after just one hearing, fragments of the melody continued to play back on my inner radio for the rest of the trip, and when Brutus played me the mariachi CDs he'd bought for the soundtrack to his video, I knew it as soon as I heard it again. It was called "Guadalajara," the capital of the state where mariachi was born.

The album I heard "Guadalajara" on was by Mariachi Cobre, and I bought some of their CDs for myself. They were a uniquely progressive mariachi group, who took liberties with the traditional songs and arrangements, and introduced flamboyant musical and vocal embellishments — something akin to what a hot-blooded jazz group might do with an old standard.

The bilingual liner notes from one of their CDs gave an insightful statement of the mariachi aesthetic:

> Mariachi contains a pride, boisterousness, and spirit that exist only in the best forms of folk music. Using the contemporary

instrumentation of guitars, vihuelas, violins, guitarrons, and trumpets, mariachi musicians employ impeccable technique and audience-pleasing showmanship rivaling the finest classical ensembles. For mariachi musicians, the music is a legacy of love, as the music is passed without notation from musician to musician.

The liner notes also gave me a surprise by explaining that the group's name, Cobre, or "copper," came from the motto of the state of Arizona, "The Copper State" — because ten of the twelve members (an exceptionally large mariachi lineup, with six violins) were from *Tucson!* Apparently Tucson had long been the American heartland of mariachi, home to the annual International Mariachi Conference, and Mariachi Cobre began there. Their big break seemed to have been playing in the Mexican Pavilion at Disney World, in Florida, for more than ten years, five days a week, seven shows a day:

> It is that intense performance schedule that has honed the skills of these musicians to world-class level. The guitars strum boldly, the violins resonate with emotion, and the trumpets, while precise, are never piercing. The voices are strong and pure, and sing of loves won and lost, of family and friends, and the beauty of their homeland.

Mariachi Cobre was obviously grown from the seed of true mariachi, but perhaps the soil of the American Southwest made them freer, more adventurous. Rather than simply repeating the traditional arrangement of a mariachi anthem like "Guadalajara," they played it instrumentally, stating the main trumpet melody and the familiar tempo, but reworking the vocal melody through acoustic guitar and syncopated phrasing. I also recognized an old Mexican song that appeared on the *Frida* soundtrack I had just been playing, "La Paloma Negra," said (by *its* liner notes) to have been Diego Rivera's favorite song, performed by a woman who had been Frida Kahlo's lover.

Mariachi Cobre also recorded the old Spanish song, "Granada," which I knew from childhood and my dad's hi-fi — though quite a different version, with English lyrics by Dorothy Dodd added to Agustin Lara's melody, a sizzling swing-band arrangement by Billy May, and a soaring vocal by Frank Sinatra. In later years, I first heard the Spanish version of "Granada" performed by the Gipsy Kings, and coincidentally, they would be the next music I heard that day, at dinner, as one of their live CDs played in the Candelilla restaurant. (I still remember first hearing the Gipsy Kings, too, at a friend's house on Île des Soeurs in Montreal sometime in the early '80s, and I loved them immediately.)

Candelilla was the name of a desert plant with slender, round, segmented stems that produced a waxy substance to protect it from drought, and the wax had once been used to make candles, polishing waxes, gum, and even phonograph records. It was an attractive plant, and a pretty name for a restaurant, but unfortunately it was in the Candelilla restaurant that the resort's pretentions to being "The Ultimate Hideout" were most betrayed. As difficult as I imagined it would be to attract *guests* to Lajitas, being several hours from even the nearest city, El Paso, and many hours (even by private jet) from larger, richer centers like Houston and Dallas, I had to wonder how they would ever find *staff* way out there, or convince good people to move to Lajitas and work at the golf course, spa, conference center, front desk, or . . . Candelilla restaurant. (Foreign students had often been recruited, I noticed, in national parks and outlying resorts.)

The décor of the Candelilla was pleasant, with upscale table settings, furniture, and lighting, and a view out over the golf course toward the cottonwoods lining the unseen river, and the mountains of Mexico beyond. The menu was sensibly limited, and mainly meat, so the food was acceptable, but the problem was the *service*. Slow, inattentive, forgetful, careless — though I guess I have to say they were at least *polite*, apologizing when they forgot the bread, or the soup, or the glass of wine, or just disappeared for long periods of time. Judging by two dinners there, with two different waiters, and by what I observed happening — or *not* happening — at the tables around me (older couples and golfers, by the look of them), the

Candelilla had a serious bottom-of-the-barrel waitstaff problem.

To make matters worse, when the Gipsy Kings CD finished on Sunday night, the music changed to what I described in my journal as "generic soft jazz — yuk!"

On my first visit to the Candelilla, the night before, there had been live entertainment, though I had been a little doubtful when I walked in and saw a guy on a stool wearing light-colored cowboy shirt, tight jeans, cowboy boots, and furled straw hat, playing acoustic guitar in front of a microphone — in fact, I can't think of a more unpromising sight — but he proved to be that *rara avis*, a *genuine* "cowboy singer."

When I first sat down, I was looking at hiking trail maps and making journal notes while I waited for the waiter to notice me waiting and wait on me, and the music was unobtrusive, but when I heard the opening notes of Hank Williams' "I'm So Lonesome I Could Cry," I put my pen down and listened. And to my surprise, the guy really *sang* that song, from the inside out, immersed in the lilting waltz-time guitar strumming and the doleful lament of the vocal: "The midnight train is whining low, and I'm so lonesome I could cry."

Hank Williams was another of the totemic artists in a genre, like Duke Ellington or Miles Davis or Frank Sinatra, who seemed so obviously set apart from all the lesser lights, imitators, and fakers, and I guess he was the first artist to show me that country music could simply be *good* music, haunting, sincere, and well crafted.

(Once when Buddy Rich was on the road in Michigan, he suffered a heart attack and was rushed to the hospital. As he was wheeled in on the gurney, the nurse ran alongside and asked him if he had any allergies, and Buddy growled, "Yeah — country music.")

Country-and-western music, it used to be called, with roots in bluegrass, folk music, gospel, work songs, string-band "hoedowns," and cowboy songs. Nashville had become the official capital of country music, or at least the *industry*, and because of the entertainment machinery centered there, it was sometimes referred to as "Nash Vegas," or "Nash Angeles." Certainly that industry no longer had much to do with the music's *roots* anymore — the technically-demanding instrumental playing of bluegrass, or even how real cowboy songs had at least reflected a true-to-life "home on the range," a rough, simple music to reflect a rough, simple life. No more the old-time Nashville of "the higher the hair, the closer to God," or even, "the higher the *hat*, the closer to God."

The liner notes in the soundtrack for the movie *O Brother, Where Art Thou?* offered some similar observations:

> There is another Nashville, with a kind of music so distant from what the city's commercial center cranks out as to be from a different planet. It thrives in the community's nooks and crannies like a cluster of quietly smiling mountain wildflowers in the shadow of those cultivated hothouse blooms that flaunt their colors on radio stations from coast to coast.
>
> Terms such as "roots" and "Southern vernacular" are bandied about to describe it. But what this seemingly ethnic sound is, is "country music." Or at least it was before the infidels of Music Row expropriated that term to describe watered-down pop/rock with greeting card lyrics.

The music industry referred to their country performers as "hat acts," and too often that old showbiz term of "acts" was appropriate — playing a role, portraying an image for the audience, and investing nothing of *themselves* in the music. Sweat, maybe, but little heart or soul. They could play and sing what they wanted, of course, and listeners could like it or not, as they chose, and in any case, I certainly knew that being a performer of any kind was a hard life, grinding it out onstage night after night and suffering the inevitable dislocations and stresses. So, I'll . . . take off my lyric-writing cowboy hat to them.

For me, learning the difference between like and dislike and good and bad was an important lesson, and I had learned it early, as a teenager. But it had *mattered* to me — and it didn't seem like a personal threat to admit that even if I liked Blue Cheer, it didn't mean they were great, and if Eric

Clapton was supposed to be great, it didn't mean I had to like his music.

Along the way, a musician also learns all the *tricks*, the clichés, the "hooks," that can be a shortcut to pleasing an audience. Certain chord changes trigger feelings, certain tempos encourage dancing (disco was carefully measured in BPMS, beats-per-minute), and certain word combinations (hopeless love, broken heart, cruel world) touch the audience's *own* emotions in ways that are *already familiar*.

By learning how these effects were created, or imitated, and seeing all the ways such tricks were used, after many years a musician learned to have a built-in sense of what was real and what was fake — when the music came from the calculating brain and not the desperate heart.

In Nick Hornby's *Songbook*, he wrote about his own feelings for that quality of sincerity, and what he too wished other listeners would value the way he did:

> "I don't care who you listen to, or how good they are," you want
> to say to kids who are about to embark on a lifetime of listening.
> "Just make sure that whoever it is *means* it, that they're burning
> up in their desperation to communicate whatever it is they want
> to say."

In later years, I would come to love reggae music (from a chance hearing of Bob Marley's "Natural Mystic" in a limo drive home from Toronto airport), and traditional African music, but it didn't mean I thought it was all especially *great*, in terms of artistic achievement, or that other people should like it, too. Similarly, I eventually got over the semi-guilty feeling that classical music and jazz were *intended* to be higher forms of music, and therefore music I should aspire to learn to appreciate. With a few notable exceptions, I just didn't enjoy listening to that music very much.

Did musical integrity have to be an either/or proposition? Perhaps not; sometimes I can hear where an artist has put together a collection of sincere, personal songs, without compromise to commercial considerations, then very obviously added at least one formulaic "single" — a shallow, repetitive candidate for mass appeal and radio play — what the business people called the "money track." Maybe it was just my imagination that even that artist's genuine music seemed a little tainted by that calculation.

Realistically, maybe it was just good business for an artist to think about such practicalities, but it corrupted the entire fabric of the *intention.* Again, I come back to that same "note," which, like one voice in a harmony, seems to color everything around it. The keystone of any artistic construction is contained in that simple question, what is the *intention?*

Perhaps the most important lesson I carried with me after a year's immersion in yoga in 2000 was that concept of "intention." A yoga class often began with a few minutes of peaceful "centering," sitting cross-legged while the instructor spoke calming words, or a Hindu chant. Sometimes the more philosophical instructors evoked yoga's meaning of "union," of body and energy, mind and spirit, and on a few occasions, a particularly eloquent teacher would elevate those concepts into philosophy.

"Make it your intention to enjoy your practice." It meant more than semantics that a yoga class was not a "workout," or a "session," but a *practice,* but the key word for me was *intention.* Not "goal," or "ambition," but intention. Still focused and directed, but gentle — forgiving and undemanding. Not the harsh demand of "I *will* do it," but "I *intend* to do it."

I *intend* to do better work today; I *intend* to be a better man.

The yoga instructor might say, "Let your intention be to push yourself gently, to exert yourself with care."

These are good words, and a good philosophy.

And it was by that soft criterion of "intention" that I tried to judge the music I heard, and if there was no genuine commitment there, *if they didn't mean a word they sang,* then there was not much intention, and I could only get out of it what the artist put into it.

Of course there were exceptions, brilliant ones, like Hank Williams, Patsy Cline, Willie Nelson, and many others. In their very different ways, each of those artists took the American folk music that country music was *intended* to be, and gave it a voice that was full of emotion instead of sentiment, images instead of clichés, and soul instead of style.

As I walked out of the Candelilla restaurant in Lajitas, Texas, the Ultimate Hideout, I saw the cowboy singer standing outside in front of a blazing fire, talking to a couple of guests. The perfume of mesquite smoke lured me over, and as the other guests wandered off, he and I talked a little about the weather, the snow, and the Big Bend area. As I wished him a good evening and turned to leave, I said over my shoulder, "You sing very well." He couldn't know what it meant for me to say that to a cowboy singer, but he thanked me all the same.

Verse Four

"Driving down the razor's edge between past and future"

So I got up in the morning and I went to work. Or in this case, I got up in the morning and I . . . drove all day. I was headed for home now, with 1,250 miles to cover in two days, and plenty of hours to listen to music — and *think* about it. My unknowing inspiration from that first evening in Lajitas — "A story could be written just around the music I've listened to on this trip" — would continue to grow roots and branches in my unconscious garden.

Patsy Cline sang me out of Lajitas before the sun was up, the *Heartaches* collection opening with her beautiful version of "Crazy" ("Crazy for feeling . . . so lonely"), written by one of the other members of my small country pantheon, Willie Nelson. It was sung so, so beautifully by Patsy, with the catches in her voice perfectly placed, and the way she held onto the long vowels with heart-wrenching sustain. The ache was real; she felt it, and I did too.

Owen Bradley's production was perfect as well, with Floyd Cramer's unique piano touch, a kind of "honky tonk minimalism," over the spare, haunting orchestration, and the chorus of male backing vocals setting the mood for Patsy's voice, and for my drive across Southwest Texas. The narrow, winding two-lane followed the Rio Grande and the rugged terrain, a roller-coaster ride of blind crests and off-camber corners, so I just took it easy, cruising along as the sun rose in my mirrors.

The cover shot of Patsy on *Heartaches* was a '50s treat, with her sitting on a red background wearing bright red stretch pants, scarf, and lipstick, with a pink blouse, and tiny gold lamé boots. No other female country singer has ever compared to Patsy Cline, I don't think, in her style or her music, and once again, as with Sinatra, it wasn't just the allure of her voice as an *instrument*, but the inimitable quality of *sincerity* that made her singing so compelling; she meant every word she sang.

I often think of a phrase used by the legendary literary editor, Maxwell Perkins, who worked with great writers like F. Scott Fitzgerald, Ernest Hemingway, and Thomas Wolfe. When asked if he thought Thomas Wolfe was "a great writer," Perkins — who had spent countless days and nights sifting through boxes of manuscript trying to assemble Wolfe's writing into coherent books — reportedly replied, "Hell, no. He's a divine wind chime."

A divine wind chime. So many entertainers, especially singers, could be defined that way, able to make a pretty sound if someone else "breathed" on them, gave them words and music, direction and control.

Even a true artist like Patsy Cline had to be persuaded by Owen Bradley to record the songs that would become her first hits, "Walkin' After Midnight" and the irresistible "I Fall To Pieces" (written by the prolific songwriter Harlan Howard, whose definition of country music was "three chords and the truth" — among his many other compositions was "You're a Hard Dog To Keep Under the Porch"). Similarly, Tina Turner was against recording her "comeback" triumph, "What's Love Got To Do With It?", claiming it wasn't "right" for her. One begins to understand the phrase, "shut up and sing." (You divine wind chime, you.)

And oh, how Patsy could sing, and what great songs were on that collection: "Crazy," "I Fall To Pieces," "She's Got You," "Sweet Dreams of You," and another great old traveling song, "You Belong to Me." "See the pyramids along the Nile/ Watch the sunset on a tropic isle/ Just remember, darling, all the while/ You belong to me." I remember hearing that song on the radio as a boy, though by one of those male singing groups, the Duprees. "See the marketplace in old Algiers/ Send me photographs and souvenirs/ Just remember when a dream appears/ You belong to me." Those images of the far-off, exotic world seemed so romantic and mysterious to a young boy in the suburbs of a Canadian town. "Fly the ocean in a silver plane/ See the jungle when it's wet with rain/ Just remember 'til you're home again/ You belong to me."

All those aching "going away" songs from the late '50s: Bobby Vinton's "Sealed With a Kiss" ("I don't wanna say goodbye, for the summer/ But darling, I promise you this/ I'll send you all my dreams, every day in a letter/ Sealed with a kiss"), or another early "guy group," the Tempos, doing "See You in September" ("Have a good time, but remember/ There is danger, in the summer moon above") — perhaps another template for Lennon/McCartney, in the Beatles' early hit, "All My Loving." I even remember that old Burl Ives waltz-time song playing on the radio of my Dad's Buick, "Mary Anne regrets she's unable to see you again/ She's leaving for Europe next week, she'll be busy 'til then" (also written by Harlan Howard, and another one of those "death songs" of the era).

Patsy's *Heartaches* collection ended with yet another traveling song, "The Wayward Wind," as she sang so plaintively about a lost love who was "born to wander": "I guess the sound of the outward bound/ Made him a slave to his wandering ways." And what a sound *that* is, too, the distant blare of a train's air horn dopplering away in the night, and it echoing right back to my own childhood and all the way forward. Like a complete song, words and music, that somber chord always evoked a whole set of emotional responses, from a lonely siren-call to come away and roam, to a poignant tug of memory.

When I was a boy, our family sometimes stayed overnight with some farming friends, the Emslies, who had five children. The twins, Dale and Diane, were the same age as I was, and at ten and eleven we would play in the hayloft all day, building forts out of hay bales and playing "house." At night I'd lie tucked into my cowboy sleeping bag on their living-room floor, hearing the occasional long, mournful chords of the passing trains, and the more frequent whine of the truck tires on the highway, all interspersed with the transistor pressed up to my ear. All those chords and voices together seemed to make a song that resonated in me forever, a song of the road that might someday carry me to the wide and wonderful world I already yearned for.

What a romantic myth hangs over the old "hobo songs," at least the best of them, like "Big Rock Candy Mountain," "I've Been Everywhere," "Four Strong Winds," "Gentle on My Mind," or Rod McKuen's "Love's Been Good to Me." All those paeans to American restlessness and the American road carried a tinge of wistfulness, an acknowledgment of the hardships of the vagrant life, the notion that wanderlust could be involuntary, *exile* as much as freedom, and indeed, the understanding that freedom wasn't free. (In the mid-'70s, the band was driving to a show in downtown Los Angeles, at the Shrine Auditorium, and I noticed some graffiti splattered across a wall: "Freedom isn't free," and I adapted that for a song on *2112*, "Something for Nothing.")

Those nuanced and resonant hobo ballads stood in vivid contrast to what I suppose was the shallow *parody* of the genre, Roger Miller's "King of the Road." How I *hated* that song when I was a kid, the way it seemed to play on the radio every few minutes, and the way it would get stuck in my head all day long. In T. C. Boyle's novel *Drop City*, set in the '60s, one character ranted about how much he hated that song, and I felt a certain vindication, or at least affirmation — it's always good to know you're not the *only* one.

In "The Wayward Wind," the narrator meets her wandering lover "in a border town," and as that song ended the Patsy Cline CD, I drove into the small border town of Presidio, just waking up on this Monday morning. Though tempted by a tiny line on the map continuing along the river to Ruidosa and the end of the road at Candelaria, I had a long way to go that day, and turned north on a wider, smoother two-lane highway, through grassy rangeland. On the long, straight stretches, I picked up the pace, noticing once more than on that sort of road, the "proper" speed, safe and mile-eating, seemed to be 110 mph. Not 120, and not 100, but 110 (workin' them angels). Certainly I was endangering no one but myself, and that marginally, and I considered it my version of "acceptable risk."

The road had been gradually climbing since leaving the river at Presidio, and as I approached Marfa the elevation was more than 4,000 feet. The treeless plains reached to the horizon under a vast blue sky, the bleak and eerie landscape that was such a powerful presence in the mid-'50s movie *Giant*, starring Rock Hudson, Elizabeth Taylor, and a couple of young unknowns: Dennis Hopper and James Dean.

In the late '70s, I was on tour somewhere in Texas, and switched on the television one afternoon in the hotel room, just for "company." A movie I had never heard of was playing, *Giant*, and I watched it until I had to leave for soundcheck. I never saw the ending, but I do remember a surprising amount of what I did see. Elizabeth Taylor's character arrived from her Virginia home to a bleak-looking Gothic mansion in the treeless plains of West Texas. She was newly married to the Rock Hudson character, who was heir to the family ranching and oil kingdom. In one scene, Taylor was being driven around by a young ranch hand, and though he only seemed to mumble and slouch and look evasive, there was *something* about that character, and I was riveted by his presence — "Who *is* this guy?" Of course, it was James Dean.

And it was during the making of *Giant* that James Dean was killed, in September of 1955, as he drove with a friend in his Porsche Spyder 550 to a sports-car rally (he was a keen racer and motorcyclist) in Salinas, California. Apparently he stopped for an apple and a Coke at Blackwells Corner, a store and gas station in the middle of nowhere (which still bills itself as "James Dean's Last Stop"), then continued west into the glare of the sun along Highway 46. It is not known how hard he was "workin' his angels," but near a spot on the map called Cholame, a young man named Donald Turnupseed pulled onto the highway in a '54 Ford Tudor, and, claiming he never saw the low, silver Porsche, hit Dean's car head-on. Turnupseed and Dean's friend survived, but James Dean was killed instantly, at the age of 24. (On the *Test for Echo* tour, Brutus and I made an unintended James Dean odyssey, as we chanced to ride through his birthplace of Fairmount, Indiana; Marfa, Texas; his "last stop" at Blackwells Corner, California; and that intersection of Highways 46 and 41 where he died.)

Back in 1955, little attention was paid to the death of a young, relatively unknown actor, for of the three films in which he appeared, only *Rebel without a Cause* had been released. *East of Eden* and *Giant* would come later (apparently some of his dialog in *Giant* remained so unintelligible that it had to be dubbed in later by another actor), and start to build the larger-than-life legend of James Dean, the consummate frustrated American youth.

And speaking of frustrated American youth, Patsy Cline was followed by the only "teenage music" in my collection, and the only so-called "boy band" I willingly listened to: 98°. These four young guys from Cincinnati were different from their predecessors among the teenage white-boy singing groups, from the Osmond Brothers to New Kids on the Block, the Backstreet Boys, and N'sync. The difference was best exemplified by the label 98° recorded for, Motown Records, or the subtext of Stevie Wonder recording a duet with 98° on their second album. They were old school R&B of the first water, and a real *singing* group, just like the ones who so impressed me on *The T.A.M.I. Show* when I was twelve.

The guys in 98° didn't look like the other boy groups, and they obviously hadn't been "put together" the way the others had been, hand-picked and assembled to create a "look," an image. The guys in 98° weren't especially good looking (no offence), or exceptionally good dancers, but they all had excellent voices, and their singing, and their choice of material, showed an obvious understanding of the roots of R&B music.

It was the first, self-titled 98° CD I was listening to as I sped up Highway 67 from Presidio to Marfa, and it had been an enduring favorite of mine for almost four years. For a pop record, that was an unbelievable "shelf life," but it had all the ingredients: great songs, great arrangements, great performances, and great sound. Rich layers of keyboards and rhythm tracks (in the modern fashion, drum machines were used, but they were artfully programmed, and as in Massive Attack, they suited the music); the background vocal harmonies were rich and carefully arranged, and the lead vocals were soaring, soulful flights. Those boys could *sing*, and it especially showed in the slow ballad-type songs, like "Take My Breath Away" and "Heaven's Missing an Angel." I've always been a sucker for that kind of thing, the kind of song you lost yourself in, and wanted to listen to over and over again.

Nick Hornby wrote about his own love for pop music in ways that I understood:

> Oh, of course I can understand people dismissing pop music. I know that a lot of it, nearly all of it, is trashy, unimaginative, poorly written, slickly produced, inane, repetitive and juvenile (although at least four of these adjectives could be used to describe the incessant attacks on pop that you can still find in posh magazines and newspapers); I know too, believe me, that Cole Porter was "better" than Madonna or Travis, that most pop songs are aimed cynically at a target audience three decades younger than I am, that in any case the golden age was thirty-five years ago and there has been very little of value since. It's just that there's this song I heard on the radio, and I bought the CD, and now I have to hear it ten or fifteen times a day . . .

The lyrics to 98° songs were unabashed teen anthems, yearning and hormonal, dressing up a teenage boy's lust as boundless, obsessive love, aimed at the fairy-tale images of a teenage girl's romantic fantasies. Idealistic love songs in "Invisible Man," "Hand in Hand," and "Was It Something I Didn't Say?", with less-subtle expressions in songs like "Completely" ("Let yourself go/ We'll take it slow/ And let's go all the wa-ay-ay tonight"), and "Don't Stop the Love" (in which it's not exactly the *love* he doesn't want her to stop).

But again, it was *supposed* to be pop music, aimed mainly at young girls (and sappy old men). That's what 98° were trying to do, and they did it very, very well. It was telling to hear how good they were in concert, too. Carrie and I went to see them perform in 2001, at an arena in Hamilton, Ontario (with several thousand teenage girls). Through our friend Andrew, who was doing a photo shoot with the group before their show, we met them backstage. They were all polite and friendly, and seemed pleased by an old rock drummer's appreciation of their music, especially when I told them Carrie and I had used "Heaven's Missing an Angel" as the first dance at our wedding. During the show, they dedicated that song to us, which was awfully nice of them, and I was only a *little* embarrassed.

And they made perfect cruising music, as I drove rapidly through the wide-open grasslands toward Marfa, looking forward to finding some breakfast there, and having another look at a curious little town. Although Marfa stood out prominently on the map, standing at the crossroads of highways running north-south and east-west, its prominence seemed mainly due to there being so little *else* to put on the map of Southwest Texas. Marfa was founded in 1881 as a railroad water stop, like so many western towns, and named, the story goes, after a character from Dostoyevsky's *The Brothers Karamazov*, which the founder's wife was reading as they passed through town in their private rail car.

As far as I knew, the filming of *Giant* almost fifty years previously was Marfa's main claim to fame, but apparently there was also something called the Marfa Mystery Lights. A State of Texas roadside marker told about the "ghost lights."

> The Marfa Lights, mysterious and unexplained lights that have been reported in the area for over one hundred years, have been the subject of many theories. The first recorded sighting of the lights was by rancher Robert Ellison in 1883. Variously described as campfires, phosphorescent minerals, swamp gas, static electricity, St. Elmo's Fire, and "ghost lights," the lights reportedly change colors, move around, and change in intensity. Scholars have reported over seventy-five local folktales dealing with the unknown phenomenon.

Marfa's population was listed in the road atlas as barely 2,000, and the main part of town had a spacious, half-vacant look. However, the residents were obviously resisting their town's decline, and many of the storefronts along the wide main street, Highland Avenue, seemed to have been restored, or at least spruced up with a fresh coat of paint. As the seat of Presidio County, Marfa had a huge 19th-Century courthouse dominating the top of the street, with a Gothic, Victorian style (called "Second Empire") of imposing architecture and a central dome topped by a white statue.

I turned in and parked facing the curb, then walked across to a neat-looking café called Mike's Place. Western streets were supposed to have been made wide enough to turn a stagecoach around, and this one was wide enough for cars to park nose-in on both sides, and still leave more than two lanes in each direction.

Mike's Place was a typical small-town diner, with a picture window in front, a row of stools at a counter across the back in front of the kitchen, booths along one wall, and an array of square tables in the middle. I loved it already. As I sat at one of the tables, I heard "The Star-Spangled Banner" playing on the radio in the kitchen, and someone whistling along with it (even harder than singing it, I imagine). Hearing the national anthem on the radio at 8:45 in the morning had to be a sign of the times, reflecting the recent swell of patriotism over the war in Iraq. Around that time, those same patriotic radio stations started a boycott of the Dixie Chicks, encouraging people to burn their CDs, because one of them, onstage in Europe, had dared to criticize President Bush, by saying they were *ashamed* he was from Texas.

Bumper stickers are often a good indicator of the popular mood, and as I bicycled around Santa Monica in early 2003, I noticed a proliferation of cars wearing messages like "Give Peace a Chance," "War Is Not the Answer" (both from *songs*, and with true irony, by singers who had been *murdered* with guns: John Lennon and Marvin Gaye), and "Peace Is Patriotic." (Another one that made me laugh: "When the Rapture comes, can I have your car?")

But away from that liberal enclave, as I drove toward the heartland of America, I saw countless American flags on cars, trucks, buildings, and lawns, and stickers reading, "We Support Our Troops," and "These Colors Don't Run." Even the tired and moronic "Love It or Leave It" ultimatum had been resurrected from the Vietnam era.

In Mike's Place, Marfa, Texas, "The Star-Spangled Banner" reached its histrionic climax, and I glanced back to the kitchen and recognized (from a caricature on their business card) Mike himself whistling along so impressively. When the next song came on the radio, it was tempting to believe the DJ had a fine sense of irony, for it was Sonny and Cher's hit from the '60s, "The Beat Goes On," with social commentary along the lines of *Plus ça change, plus c'est la même chose.*

"Men keep marching off to war, uh huh."

Yes they did.

And "drums keep pounding a rhythm to the brain."

Yes they do. (Hal Blaine again.)

"La de da de de, La de da de da."

That's about the size of it.

After a fine breakfast of pancakes and eggs-over-easy, I turned west on Highway 90, driving through flat, empty grasslands and ranches, occasionally punctuated by rocky outcroppings (not volcanic, but upthrust ancient seabed, the Junior Geologist decided). It was time for some more Big Frank — one of his hottest records, *Swing Along with Me*, from 1961, arranged and conducted by Billy May. This was another one I remember hearing on my dad's hi-fi player, when I was nine years old, and the arrangements, the musicianship, Frank's singing (in his absolute prime), and even the recording quality just *sizzled*. Crisp, driving, swinging, and richly orchestrated, especially the exotic numbers like "Granada" and "Moonlight on the Ganges," spiced with ethnic percussion, it was one of Frank's finest.

As the snappy liner notes blurbed, "A bold, buoyant Frank Sinatra, breaking it up on twelve of the most uninhibited things ever recorded!" On the front cover Old Blue Eyes pushed open a saloon door (a *swinging* door, of course), wearing a dark suit, white shirt and narrow tie, and a snap-brim fedora with a wide, silver-gray band. On the back cover photograph he was swinging a golf club, wearing a cardigan and ball cap, beside the caption "Sinatra Swings." He definitely did on that record, from the driving bitterness of "The Curse of an Aching Heart" to the subtle discovery of new love in "Have You Met Miss Jones?" Another one of my all-time Sinatra favorites.

An hour and 100 miles later, I was back in Van Horn, then back on Interstate 10 again, as I would be for well into the next day, and 1,000 miles. Staccato punches of guitars and drums burst out of the speakers, something more modern this time, *A Rush of Blood to the Head*, by the British band Coldplay. A couple of days before, on the third day of my drive to Big Bend, I had been listening to their first album, *Parachutes*, which remained among my favorite records since its release in late 2000, and a very successful debut for them, but I had yet to make up my mind about this one. Sometimes music hit me the first time I heard it, other times it took a few listens, and this one was remaining a bit opaque to me through my first few auditions. Simply put, I wasn't yet sure what they were trying to achieve, or how well they had achieved it, and it seemed to me that an artist's second album might be the most crucial of anything they would ever do. The sophomore blues, it was sometimes called.

Sometimes the toughest act to follow can be *yourself*, and a wise musician once pointed out, "You have your whole life to prepare for your first record, and six months to prepare for your second." Rush had been more fortunate than some bands, not only in gaining popularity at all, but because ours had grown slowly, and there had been no sudden focus of attention and expectation on us. But still, for our first few records together, we would come straight off the road with a handful of songs sketched out on acoustic guitar and scraps of paper, go into a recording studio, and try to stitch together a new album with limited time and budget. Then go straight back on the road.

If a young band was fortunate enough to have a successful first release, like those we've already "listened to," Linkin Park, Coldplay, or Vertical

Horizon (their first major-label release, anyway), they would be swept up in a whirlwind of touring and sudden, overwhelming attention — for which *no one* can be prepared — and it could all be too . . . unbalancing.

When they finally took a breath and started to work on their next record, they had some serious decisions to make: should they try to emulate what they *think* made their first album successful? Or worse, try to answer their critics by changing to suit them, or maybe just shaking things up to try to demonstrate some growth? Worst of all, should they bend to the inevitable pressure and meddling that are going to come down from their record company's A&R people?

In the early days of the record business, a record company's A&R, or "artists and repertoire" department, was, as the name suggests, the middlemen between performers and songwriters. Facing obsolescence in the '60s, when artists started to write their own material, these people naturally sought to survive those changes and justify their existences. They gradually mutated in two directions: the relatively benign "talent scouts" searching out new artists for the label to sign, and the darker design of those who actually presumed to meddle with the *music,* taking it upon themselves to tell the writers how to write, and the performers how to perform, holding over them the power and purse strings of the record company, and thus their apparent destiny.

Some people's careers had been helped by such "guidance," especially if they had no particular direction of their own anyway (divine wind chimes), but I have personally known a few bands and artists whose careers have been truly destroyed by this arrogant interference. Sometimes they are "encouraged" (not to say "forced") to keep writing and submitting "demos" to the company until their songs, and their music, become completely diluted by trying to aim them at the lowest common denominator of public taste. Or, that soul-destroying process simply *takes so long* that their potential audience forgets about them, or the ever-changing styles of popular music leave them behind. As I had written to Matt from Vertical Horizon, "It seems to me that if *anyone* is going to ruin your career, it ought to be *you.*"

In the case of Coldplay's sophomore release, they seemed to have resisted that sort of interference, though off the top they had consciously tried to make their first impression more aggressive than *Parachutes*, coming in with a roar, as it were, with those loud, staccato sections of the opening song, "Politik." However, that defiant statement soon gave way, reverted, to a gentler, prettier combination of texture, melody, and rhythm, and stayed there right the way through.

Along the way, some songs started to work their way into my blood, it felt like, during "In My Place," "The Scientist," and the lovely "Warning Sign," I was feeling that familiar tingle, in my brain and under my skin, and even as I drove along that flat, featureless Interstate, my body began its automatic response, feeling the melodies and harmonies in my brain, shoulders moving with the beat, head nodding, and fingers drumming on the steering wheel.

Looking over the CD package (later, when I wasn't driving), I saw the booklet contained a kind of political manifesto, under the title "Politik," against "ridiculous international trade laws." They gave a list of Web sites for political and environmental organizations (followed by a phrase that took a clever metaphorical step back: "Thanks for Listening"). I admired the band's wish to use their platform to advertise causes they believed in, though I was disappointed the printed lyrics were not included, not only professionally, but as a listener, for occasions when the words were indistinguishable. No doubt they were available on the band's Web site, for those who were interested, but this listener would have preferred it the other way around: the politics on the Web site, and the lyrics in the package. Priorities.

Around 1973, I went with some friends to a concert by the American duo Seals and Crofts, who had a few soft-rock hits in the late '6os and early '7os: "Summer Breeze," and one that I always liked, musically and lyrically, "We May Never Pass This Way Again." During the show they talked about their devotion to the Baha'i faith, and at the end, invited people to stay behind and discuss it with them. Proselytizing at a concert seemed strange, and made me feel uncomfortable at the time, and from then on it somehow tarnished my response to their music. Like many songs I liked in years past, "We May Never Pass This Way Again" still comes up once in a while on my mental transistor radio, but I notice it carries a whiff of propaganda now, and remains tinted in the soft-focus tones of, say, a television commercial by the Church of Latter-Day Saints.

A very fine line meandered grayly between the sincerity and integrity of imbuing your art with your convictions, and preaching from an inappropriate pulpit, like movie stars using their celebrity to spread their jejune political opinions — though at least there you knew what you were getting. Perhaps I would define propaganda as a political or religious message *hidden* in something that purports to be art for its own sake, a painting, a book, a movie, a song. (It is telling that the word "propaganda" actually derived from a committee of cardinals in the Catholic church, *congregatio de propaganda fide*, or congregation for propagating the faith.)

I find myself on a stimulating kind of thin ice here, or at least in a glass house, when I contemplate songs I've written, like "Free Will," "The Big Wheel," and many more, that contained a kind of religious message, even though it was patently *anti*-religion.

Years ago there was a brief flurry of accusations of "backward masking," when paranoid, finger-pointing zealots were "finding" satanic messages in rock songs played backward, and assuring the gullible that these demonic practitioners of evil were spreading subconscious malevolence through the nation's youth. Metal bands with names like Judas Priest and Black Sabbath were natural targets for such accusations, but subliminal messages were also "found" in Beatles records, and even purely commercial bands like Kiss were said to be "Knights in Satan's Service." (Having toured as an opening act with Kiss for months on end in '74 and '75, I knew the dominant members, Gene and Paul, had a "master plan" — I saw Gene's high-school sketches for their costumes and makeup — but its main goal was only to achieve popular success. And they were good to us, back then.)

Our own band was not immune to that idiocy, and the five-pointed star on our *2112* cover from 1976 (the same innocent geometric figure used in the American flag) was mistaken by the ignorant for a pentagram, and so we too were tarred by the black magic brush. A fan sent me an article from a Texas university newspaper which accused dozens of bands of practicing this insidious propaganda, and even said that a Rush song played backward "revealed" the message, "Oh Satan you are the one I worship" or something. Outraged, I wrote a letter to the paper's editor stating that I didn't even *believe* in these "spirits," good or evil, and pointing out that I happened to know many of the other bands named, and that they were far more concerned about their chart numbers and ticket sales than about spreading *any* kind of message.

Ironically, that statement, not the accusation of devil worship, annoyed some readers, who didn't like me saying their "heroes" might be more committed to mass popularity and commerce than to the rock ethos of "rock 'n' roll all night and party every day," so of course they reacted by criticizing *me*. However, in the face of evil and untruth, I had done my best to spread a little sanity, and closed my letter by assuring the reader that I, for one, was not an evil Antichrist, and called upon the witness of a Higher Authority: "If you don't believe me, you can ask my mom!"

The Coldplay CD carried me most of the way to El Paso, and when it faded off with the slow build of "Amsterdam," I saw "CD-5" come up on the screen. The car filled with an ethereal wash of sparkly keyboard sounds, then a soft female voice, "I traded fame for love, without a second thought." It was Madonna's *Ray of Light*, another pop classic, and, for this listener, her enduring masterpiece. As a pop artist, in the truest sense of both those words, Madonna had produced a string of great pop and dance songs over her long, sensational career, especially beginning with her *True Blue* album, where she began to mature vocally and musically with gems like "Papa Don't Preach," "La Isla Bonita," and "Live To Tell." I remember watching her sing that last song live on the televised Academy Awards show, and noticing she was visibly nervous, and obviously concentrating very hard on singing well. It may have been then I decided she was "for real." She obviously *cared*.

One of Madonna's secrets was that she had always been smart enough to hire the very best people to work with: cowriters, producers, musicians, drum programmers, photographers, all the best that money could buy, and combined with her strong, daring vision, the result was *quality*. On *Ray of Light*, the main collaborators were William Orbit, who gave her a fresh, modern soundscape of electronic effects, electric guitars, and effective percussion accents, and Patrick Leonard, who brought his classic sense of song construction and orchestration to some of the more passionate songs, like "Skin" and "Sky Fits Heaven." Then there was the "big ballad," "The Power of Goodbye," that I always had to turn up louder, even when it was already loud. Another part of the appeal of *Ray of Light*, as with all Madonna's recordings, was the sound quality; music that was crafted so well, both in its design and the way it was recorded and mixed, was simply a sensual pleasure to listen to, especially on a good sound system.

In the way music often evokes a time and place, usually of its first hearing, or when it was first heard in a certain way — in love, broken-hearted, happy, or sad — *Ray of Light* always seemed to echo the summer of 1999, which I spent at the house by the lake in Quebec, with occasional guests, but mostly alone, and in a state of constant turmoil. I think of that music wafting through the whole house on a warm summer day, up through the hallway and staircase to my desk on the top floor, where I sat writing letters full of desolation and tenuous hope. Or the music drifted out through the screen doors and windows to the wicker chair, where I sat drinking, full of desolation and tenuous hope. That summer was a sad and confusing time for me, and music became part of the sadness, and part of the cure.

Music, if it's any good, will always transcend those associations of memory, and in any case, I had continued to listen to *Ray of Light* since 1999, so it had come to be embraced by all of that time. When you listen to music a *lot*, in different times, places, and moods, it eventually becomes less a trigger than a bullet, and instead of reminding you of anything else, it reminds you only of itself.

A house, though, grows to contain all that has transpired in and around its walls, and that house by the lake always had a supernatural luminescence in my memories, a green-and-yellow summer mood and a blue-and-white winter mood, and darker shades from that time of sadness in the summer of '99. I still held onto the stronger frame that surrounded that richly-painted image, other, happier summers: swimming in the cool, clean water that always felt like silk against the skin, rowing in the hot sun across the mirror-smooth surface leaving a wake of parallel ripples, sitting on the dock until the sun disappeared and the mosquitoes came out, and sleeping with the windows wide open to the fragrant night air through the screen, the bright stars, the loons' calls echoing in the darkness.

The memories of other times were something to hold onto, but there was also a time to let go of them. I had come to believe the house on the lake would never be a "happy" place again, and adding in the realities that I hardly ever got there, and what it cost to keep it perfect, I almost had myself talked into putting it up for sale in time for the coming summer, when it would look its best.

During my last visit to Canada, in early February, I had driven the six hours from Toronto to the Laurentians, and as always, a long drive was a good opportunity to think. Rather than dwell on the past and the wrench of parting with the old, I was trying to think about the future, and imagine what I would do if I sold that property. Even though I found myself living in California, I had been a Canadian all my life, with winter a fundamental part of its cycles. When I discovered cross-country skiing and snowshoeing in my late twenties, I became a real *lover* of winter, and I knew I would always want "A Place in the Snow." It was important psychologically, too, just to keep a toehold in Canada, and not lose at least some connection to whatever roots I had there. I had thought of selling the main house and its lot in Quebec, and keeping the island and eighty acres of "back land," then building a smaller cabin over there. However, then I would be overlooking the old house, and the old life, and the more I thought about that, it seemed like a bad idea.

As I drove across Southern Ontario on the long, boring slab of Highway 401, a black ribbon between snowfields, under a gray sky, I was bouncing around radio stations as I passed in and out of their ranges. For awhile I was listening to the CBC station from Ottawa, and this started me thinking about that area, and especially an out-of-the-way region around there that Brutus and I had explored by motorcycle a couple of times. Hillier than most of Southern Ontario, it had some curvier roads, and it seemed far enough away from Toronto to avoid the congestion and high prices of so-called "cottage country." Maybe I should consider moving out of Quebec entirely, and starting fresh somewhere like that.

Later that week, Brutus came to visit, and I told him I had been feeling maybe it was time for me to get out of that house, away from the memories and high upkeep. Though he too had long been in love with the Laurentians, and especially that lake — which he had found for both of us, and had once owned a piece of land there himself — he understood my feelings. When I mentioned the area I was thinking about, he was immediately enthusiastic about the idea, and no sooner had he left and driven back to Toronto than he started sending me internet listings of pieces of land that were for sale between Ottawa and Algonquin Park. In March I sent him some expense money to go up there and do some preliminary looking around for me, and he sent me a well-organized set of packages on four different properties, with digital photographs and humorously-written descriptions of the land and his adventures in viewing it, by snowmobile, snowshoes, and even snowplow.

As I drove west through El Paso and into New Mexico, *Ray of Light* made a good musical backdrop for the careful mental dance I was doing through that minefield — avoiding the sentimentality of thinking about the house and all it represented by concentrating on the practicalities of the present and the possibilities for the future. A good plan would be to travel to Quebec before the summer and make the necessary arrangements to put the place up for sale, then maybe drive or ride over to Ontario and meet Brutus to look at some land in that area. So there — it was decided. Like Madonna was singing, it was time to "learn to say goodbye." Again.

Carrie and I went to see Madonna's "Drowned World" tour at the Staples Center in Los Angeles in September of 2001, and it was a spectacular show, on every level. Madonna's concert productions aimed for the same high standard of artistry and quality as her records, and again, succeeded so well by the strategy of hiring the best people to design, choreograph, direct, costume, light, perform, and present what was essentially a theatrical event.

Although the staging, costumes, and choreography were spectacular, the focus did seem to remain on the music, in contrast to footage I had seen of the earlier "Blonde Ambition" tour. Right from the opening song, "Substitute for Love," where she just stood and *sang*, to her use of electric and acoustic guitar as both prop and accompaniment, it seemed she was determined to make that show as much about music as about spectacle.

The show we attended was just a few days after September 11, 2001, when so many events were being canceled for fear of more terrorist attacks, and I had to admire Madonna's stubbornness, resolve, and professionalism for simply carrying on regardless. When Carrie and I debated whether or not we should go to the concert, I decided that if Madonna was brave enough to show up, we should too.

It had been a strange time to live in the United States, then and since, with undercurrents of dread, defiance, and desperate patriotism swirling around me. The state of unease reminded me of the fall of 1962, the Cuban Missile Crisis, when, to my ten-year-old mind, the whole world seemed to have gone crazy, and it is equally certain that children felt the resonance in the aftermath of September 11, 2001, in a profound way. While trying to understand what they were *seeing*, those airplanes exploding, those buildings crumbling, and how it was different from the explosions and death they saw on TV and in movies every day, they also absorbed the panic and agitation of the grown-up world. They overheard the fearful conversations and television commentary about what might happen next, the possible spread of germs of killer diseases and something called "weapons of mass destruction." Children in 1962 and in 2001 understood that the world they might have felt was safe and enduring, was suddenly dangerous and unsettled, verging on panic and collapse. And as usual, a bunch of old men were to blame for frightening the children, warping their innocence with uncomprehending fear.

In the spring of 2003, the children of the western world also had another war to try to understand, just as my generation had grown up with the television specter of the escalating Vietnam War, and the increasing unrest and violence south of the border, in the United States. The race riots of the mid-'60s, then the antiwar demonstrations on the college campuses, the Students for a Democratic Society, the Black Panthers, the Weathermen, Patty Hearst and the Symbionese Liberation Army, Charles Manson, tear gas and murder in Ohio, Lyndon Johnson on television delivering his mournful speech, "My fellow Americans, I come before you with a heavy heart." It all seemed out of control.

In late-'60s St. Catharines, we had our very own draft-dodger, Norbert, a cool, peaceful young man with sandy hair, beard, glasses, and a "mellow vibe." He was a favored guide for people taking their first acid trips, and a photographer who took pictures off the TV screen of the Beatles' final live appearance, playing "Revolution" and "Hey Jude" (another Lennon/ McCartney juxtaposition, the edgy Lennon and the smile-and-sing-along McCartney).

Again, remembering all that, good and bad — what Wallace Stegner called "the very richness of that past" — I think about Ben, Andrew's young photo assistant who was born in 1976. He truly did miss so much. As Albert Camus wrote, "You cannot create experience. You must undergo it."

On Interstate 10, the car stereo was rocking again, with a digital technology that might have been unknown twenty or thirty years before, but with guitars, drums, and vocals that were clearly part of the rock 'n' roll continuum.

It was Canada's own The Tragically Hip again, and their *Phantom Power* album, from '98. It came out during my own grief-imposed exile from pop culture, but I remember during the summer of '99 I was in Toronto on my motorcycle, taking care of some business and staying overnight at the Four Seasons hotel. I turned on the television to check the weather, as usual, and flicked past a music video channel. For some reason I paused, and heard a country-flavored song, and saw an image of the singer driving a big old American car through a bleak, early-winter landscape. Even though I thought I'd landed on the country music channel, which I would not normally visit willingly, there was something immediately appealing about the song, and I paid closer attention.

As the song wove its spell, eventually I recognized the singer, Gord Downie, and the band was gradually revealed, appearing to set up their equipment, then join in playing the song. It was the Hip, of course, and the song was "Bobcaygeon," named after a small town in Ontario's "cottage country," north of Toronto. As usual, Downie's lyrics were cryptic, but beautifully poetic: "It was in Bobcaygeon, I saw the constellations/ reveal themselves one star at a time." Then later in the song he used a lovely parallel construction, "the sky was dull, and hypothetical/ and falling one cloud at a time."

Lyrically, vocally, and musically, "Bobcaygeon" was a little masterpiece, I thought, and it became one of those favorite songs I had to listen to every day for weeks and months. There was no obvious emotion in the song's lyrics, and yet a certain *implied* pathos, married to the seductive music, plucked my heartstrings, teased them, every time I heard that song.

Gord Downie may eventually be recognized as one of the finest lyricists of our time. He could combine literary allusions — like a song called "Cordelia," referring to King Lear's youngest daughter, the loyal one, and "Courage (for Hugh MacLennan)," after the Canadian novelist — with quirky little stories and great clincher lines, like "no one's interested in something that you didn't do" (one of those lines I hear and think the highest compliment, "Wish I'd written that").

Downie also made the most of his voice, using it as an instrument for characterization rather than range and technicality, delivering the vocal part as an *actor* portraying a role as much as a singer vocalizing a melody. When I first heard the whole *Phantom Power* album, I was convinced the first two songs had been sung by other members of the band, so different was the timbre and phrasing. When I mentioned this to Gord one night in 2000, backstage after their show at the House of Blues on Sunset Boulevard, he seemed pleased to have "fooled" me, and said, "I guess I was doing my job, then."

And they were so *good* live, as Carrie and I and our friend Andrew watched them from the balcony at the House of Blues. Andrew and I were fellow Canadian expats and longtime fans of the band, and turned to each other often as a song began, nodding and smiling with recognition and delight. And although I wrote earlier about how The Tragically Hip seemed to have been somehow cheated out of American popularity, the audience they *did* have was fiercely engaged, singing along as one with every song. Later, when I was telling Gord how much I loved "Bobcaygeon," he remarked how their crowds seemed to love singing along with the lines, "'Til the men they couldn't hang/ stepped to the mic and sang/ and their voices rang with that Aryan twang."

As *Phantom Power* played on, some of its songs continuing to grow on me with every listen, I continued working my way westward on Interstate 10. I picked up a sandwich at a gas stop near Las Cruces, and ate it while I drove into the afternoon sunshine and bright blue desert sky, piling up the miles across Southern New Mexico and back into Arizona.

Another Sinatra CD came on, his post-retirement album from 1973, *Ol' Blue Eyes is Back*. Style-wise, it picked up where he had left off in 1971, with *Sinatra & Company*, also produced by Don Costa. That one came out when I was living in London, at age nineteen, first rediscovering that music for myself, and I used to play "I Will Drink the Wine" ("You can drink the water, but I will drink the wine") on the jukebox at the Red Lion pub, my "local," on the little lane between Carnaby Street and Regent Street.

The first side of *Sinatra & Company* harkened back to Frank's '60s collaborations with Brazilian composer Antonio Carlos Jobim, while the second side led into a more mainstream, pop direction, with songs by John Denver and Burt Bacharach. *Sinatra & Company* was also notable for a beautiful rendition of Joe Raposo's "Bein' Green," written for Kermit the frog on "Sesame Street," as a metaphor for self-acceptance (and again, Frank sang so movingly, even as a *frog!*). Something must have clicked there, for *Ol' Blue Eyes Is Back* featured four songs by Joe Raposo. Also notable was Kris Kristofferson's "Nobody Wins" (which might be the longest Sinatra track ever, at more than five minutes) and perhaps the definitive version of Stephen Sondheim's "Send in the

Clowns" (no "perhaps" about that, for anyone who appreciates Sinatra).

The arrangements by Don Costa and Gordon Jenkins were lush and dynamic, the musicianship superlative, and the recording quality excellent. In those ways, and in the rhythm and style, it was a thoroughly "modern" record, with no trace of the swing beat, driving rhythm section, and blaring horns that would have been a Sinatra trademark through the '40s, '50s, and '60s. In material and treatment, it all grew out of a '60s pop sensibility, but the music was still undeniably Big Frank's, and as always, he made every song his own. His longtime arranger and conductor, Nelson Riddle, offered some insights on how he accomplished that:

> Frank accentuated my awareness of dynamics by exhibiting his own sensitivity in that direction. It is one thing to indicate by dynamic markings how you want to have the orchestra play your music. It is quite another to induce a group of blasé, battle-scarred musicians to observe these markings and to play accordingly. I would try, by word or gesture, to get them to *play correctly*, but if after a couple of times through, the orchestra *still* had not effectively observed the dynamics, Frank would suddenly turn and draw from them the most exquisite shadings, using the most effective means yet discovered, sheer intimidation.

(Like the sign outside Sinatra's home in Rancho Mirage: "Never Mind the Dog. Beware the Owner.") Still, it was mostly about the Voice. As Stan Cornyn wrote in the liner notes, "Ol' blue eyes is back as the singer who'll still close his eyes when he's getting into it."

Recently I saw the television special made to accompany the release of *Ol' Blue Eyes Is Back*, and when Frank walked through a series of sets representing dimly-lit saloons, and sang a medley of "Violets for Your Furs," "Angel Eyes," and "One for My Baby," I could only shake my head at the *perfection* of it — on that day, in that studio, in front of those cameras, he gave that performance. Wonderful.

And across Arizona we went, Frank and me, then gave way to another couple of modern pop collections, the latest by 98°, *Revelation*, and the first by Matchbox 20, *Yourself or Someone Like You*. By that point in the journey, I had worked (or played) through most of my "current rotation," as the radio station programmers would put it, and was delving into some other CDs that just happened to be still around in my traveling album, to see if they *deserved* to be. These two candidates made decent driving music, passing the time with occasional treats of melody and texture, but they were both examples of musical "fast food," I guess. They pleased momentarily, but didn't satisfy over the long term, and it was time for them to rotate out.

And time to return to my current "must hear" favorite, Linkin Park. Once again, I had been saving this one for late in the day, and as I passed through Tucson, and having put over 600 miles behind me, it was time to perk myself up with some *exciting* music.

It occurred to me that another reason I appreciated Linkin Park was because I had no idea what they looked like, or how they projected themselves visually. I had never seen one of their videos, or even a photo of them. I had no idea where they were from, what age they were, what race they were, what kind of haircuts they had, or even how many of them there were. It was just about the music.

And this music was about the power of *real* rock music, the way no other style, no matter how much I might *enjoy* it, could affect me like loud electric guitars and drums surrounding a young man or woman wailing out their frustrations and fantasies. Subtlety and sophistication were all very well, and I loved them too, but if I were to orchestrate the soundtrack of my life, it would not be an Academy-Award winning sweep of symphonic splendor; it would be a noisy bunch of guitars and drums and singing.

Maybe some keyboards, for texture, or better, a singer who also played keyboards (stand-alone keyboard players are not noted for their humility — though neither are stand-alone singers, and I was always glad Rush had neither, but instead an overworked bass player, Geddy, who also sang and played keyboards). One time a keyboard player of my acquaintance was complaining about touring, and he said, "Did *Beethoven* have to ride in a van all night?"

Well, no. Beethoven wasn't pictured in vacuous videos and mealy-mouthed magazines, pressured by record company A&R men to write a single, ambushed by paparazzi, trashed by tabloids, chased by a fan through a shopping mall, or interrogated by a stranger while he struggled through his sit-ups at the YMCA (as happened to me yesterday afternoon).

Of course, I didn't put Linkin Park, or myself, in the same "van" as Beethoven (hey, I'm not even a keyboard player!), and I have certainly felt the pious, ardent celebration in "Song of Joy," the restrained, insistent yearning in "Moonlight Sonata," the exquisite, delicate loveliness of "Für Elise," not to mention similar responses to Mozart, Tchaikovsky, Debussy, and — especially — Puccini's operas. However, no classical music could feed, or touch, my everyday need for affirmation, for catharsis, for the vicarious expression and release of vein-tingling excitement and anger and love and outrage at the world's injustice.

No symphony or jazz trio could reach the heights, or depths, I had attained in the thrall of electric guitars and drums framing a young man or woman who sang out the very lifeblood of their youth. For me, that was the music, the soundtrack, for the lifeblood of *my* youth, the very richness of that past.

✪

Not far to go now, as I drove away from the Holiday Inn in Casa Grande, Arizona, just after sunrise. I had covered almost 700 miles the previous day, so I had "only" about 500 to go. It felt like the homestretch now, heading west on I-8 to Gila Bend, then north to pick up I-10 again.

The day began with perhaps my all-time favorite Sinatra record, if I had to choose. Usually I avoided those "all-time great" kinds of lists, if only because my taste seemed always to be changing with my constant hunger for new music, but at this point in the writing, and in my life, I was toying with the idea of finally trying to decide on my top ten "desert-island discs." It seemed impossible, but if I ever did manage to make that list, Sinatra's *Watertown* was sure to be on it.

Watertown was released in 1970, and was fated to be one of Frank Sinatra's least successful recordings, and yet one of his most *loved*, among those who were fortunate enough to discover it. *Watertown* was what used to be called a "concept album," a song-cycle narrating the first-person story of an Everyman character who lived in a generic sort of small town, Watertown, with his two sons, after his wife had left them to move to the big city.

The story is carried forward in a sequence of beautifully crafted lyrics shaped in soliloquies and love letters, and set to classic pop melodies and structures. Frank committed himself, as always, to *living* those songs, to conveying from his own heart an aching portrait of the character's range of emotions: heartbreak, resignation, confusion, tender reverie, and, of course, loneliness (his "vein of gold"). The music was composed by Bob Gaudio (an original member of the Four Seasons, ironically, and thus sang on the first record I ever owned — or half-owned), and Jake Holmes wrote the lyrics, crafted with a perfect economy of telling detail, evoking subtle nuances of character, weather, and setting. Like all good writing, there was also a great deal that was only *implied*, stated between the lines, about the character's life, family, job ("All those years I worked for Santa Fe/ Never missed a single day/ Just one more without a raise in pay/ And I'm leaving"), neighbors, and small-town American life.

Interviewed for the liner notes in the CD reissue of *Watertown*, Jake Holmes commented, "There is a lot going on beneath the surface."

Apparently the composers chose the town's name from a map of New York State, as a "typical" small town name. In a Rush song called "Middletown Dreams," from 1985, I chose the fictional town's name in a similar way — because there seemed to be a Middletown in every state (and I seemed to have bicycled through half of them). The other two guys wanted me to change the town's name at first, because it reminded them of a freaky teacher they'd had in high school, named Mr. Middleton — I was glad they got over it.

Also, now that I think about it, the third verse of "Middletown Dreams" was modeled after my imagining of the departed wife and mother in *Watertown*, "Middle-aged Madonna, calls her neighbor on the phone/ Day by day the seasons pass, and leave her life alone/ But she'll go walking out that door, on some bright afternoon/ To go and paint big cities, from a lonely attic room."

The first verse of that song was inspired by the true-life stories of writer Sherwood Anderson and painter Paul Gauguin (as well as Somerset Maugham's fictionalization of Gauguin's life in *The Moon and Sixpence*). These artists found their vocations late in life, and abandoned their jobs, and even their families, to pursue their dreams. "But he's still walking down those tracks, any day now for sure/ Another day as drab as today, is more than a man can endure." (I believe Sherwood Anderson actually *did* walk down the tracks, leaving his small Ohio town for Chicago, to become a writer.)

Unexpectedly, "Middletown Dreams" became a kind of litmus test for listeners. Although I had obviously modeled it after characters who *did* realize their dreams, or at least continued to be nourished by them, some listeners heard it as a cynical portrait of the defeated, of losers who were trapped in a dull existence and would never dare to escape, or pursue their dreams.

The second verse was certainly about my youth, and that of every musician I knew, "The boy walks with his best friend, through the fields of early May/ They walk awhile in silence, one close; one far away/ He'd be climbing on that bus, just him and his guitar/ To blaze across the heavens, like a brilliant shooting star." My friend Matt from Vertical Horizon mentioned that song to me one day, saying how he felt it was about him and his friend James — one who had left and one who had stayed — and it made me feel good that after eighteen years, that song still touched the reality of his life, a generation after mine.

In the same way, *Watertown* had continued to resonate throughout my life, reflecting on different facets of grown-up experience as I traversed them: marriage, fatherhood, love and loss, and the songs grew ever deeper and more relevant to me through the past thirty years.

Even as CDs took over my music collection through the '80s, and most of my LPs were sold off to used-record dealers, I hung onto maybe 100 of them as treasures I couldn't part with. During my time living in England, where record stores in those days displayed the empty LP covers in clear plastic sleeves and stored the actual discs behind the counter in plastic-lined paper, I bought hundreds of those protective covers and liners for my collection. I always handled the delicate vinyl discs with fingertip care, and used dust cleaners and static removers, so even after thirty years and more, my records still looked like new.

Recently I pulled out my double-LP copy of *Tommy*, perhaps the most-played record I ever owned, and held one of the discs (Side One backed with Side Four, so you could stack the first two sides on an automatic record changer). I felt the long-playing record settle into the familiar cradle against a corner of my thumb and two fingers in the center. Its surface was pristine and unmarked, like the beautiful cover and enclosed booklet (the graphic arts are the real loss in changing formats: that old 12" gatefold sleeve).

I also looked at my original copy of *Watertown*, a gatefold cover on heavy stock, embossed inside and out, and printed with a special silver ink. The package was obviously intended to be a major release by an important artist. However, my copy told another story: a ¼" hole was drilled through the cover to indicate, in the retail code of the times, that it was a "sale" record, wholesaled off at a reduced price to clear out the over-stock of unsold copies.

According to producer Bob Gaudio, the original plan had been to launch the album with a TV special, with Frank portraying the character in a small-town setting. But Sinatra wasn't happy with his singing at the time, and didn't want to do any live performing or television (this was shortly before his first retirement). Frank was also unwilling to hold back the album's release, and thus, according to Gaudio, it didn't get the "launching pad" it needed.

In an essay which accompanied the CD, Ed O'Brien wrote, "Though its commercial success has been elusive, over the years it has garnered a seri-ous cult following among dedicated connoisseurs of popular American music. *Watertown* might appear to be a simple story of love gone awry, but a careful listening reveals it is much more than it seems to be on the surface." He quoted a friend who told him it was impossible for her to listen to the album without getting all teary-eyed, because "It rings so true. It's what happens to you in life."

Opening the LP cover, the front and back were spanned by a pen-and-ink drawing, sepia on silver-gray, of a quintessential small-town train station and Main Street, shiny with rain. One solitary figure faced two smaller ones: the abandoned husband and his two young sons, Michael and Peter ("Michael is you/ he has your face/ he still has your eyes/ remember?"). Inside the foldout sleeve, the lyrics and credits were decorated by an artful scattering of photographs, letters, and greeting cards, as if on top of a dresser, which also had a sharp resonance to the story's resolution, when we realize that all the letters the character has been writing were never sent ("the letters still are lying in my drawer"), all those feelings never expressed to his wife, and she's never coming back.

Sinatra's subtle, sincere expression of that character's life carried all the emotional subtext Jake Holmes had woven into the lyrics so skillfully, reinforced by Bob Gaudio's poignant melodies and the spare, yet emotive arrangements by Gaudio, Charles Callelo, and Joe Scott. For this listener, *Watertown* had more than stood the test of time; it had grown *stronger*, and remained not only a personal classic (the whole album perfect for in-helmet singing on a long bicycle or motorcycle ride), but also a great American work of art.

In an online review of *Watertown*, I was struck by one admirer's comment that he thought it was the East Coast version of *Pet Sounds*. The comparison hadn't occurred to me, but I felt a thrill of recognition. Like Brian Wilson's enduring masterpiece, released in 1966, *Watertown* was a work of high ambition, originality, painstaking attention to every detail of its creation, unique orchestrations and sound combinations, heartfelt lyrics and vocals, and as a total musical experience, it fostered the same *intimacy* between music and listener.

The care taken with the CD re-release, with added elements like O'Brien's deeply felt essay and the in-depth interviews with the composers, was all obviously a labor of love, coming 30 years after a relatively unsuccessful record. That showed the regard in which the album was held by an appreciative (perhaps discriminating) minority. Typical of many such CD reissues, *Watertown* included a "previously unavailable track," a song called "Lady Day," and according to the liner notes, this had been designed to be the story's closing statement. Instead, they decided (wisely, I think) to end the story with "The Train," to leave the conclusion a little more uncertain, open to the listener's interpretation.

A different version of "Lady Day" was released on Frank's next record, *Sinatra & Company*, in 1971, slightly reworked with a slower tempo and more dramatic arrangement, as a tribute to Billie Holiday. For me, that song had always held the title of "the saddest song I know," and there had been times in my life when I indulged my own misery by playing "Lady Day" over and over.

Happy or sad, there have been relatively few songs I have ever wanted to listen to repeatedly like that — or more precisely, songs I *had* to hear again and again. There were many albums I fell in love with and listened to a lot, but that's not the same as becoming addicted to one song. In my teens, I would lie in bed with my little radio and stay awake until I heard "Just Another Face in the Crowd," by local group the Veltones, or later, the Hollies' "He Ain't Heavy, He's My Brother." My friend Tuck and I used to sit in his basement and play the LP version of Simon and Garfunkel's "America" over and over. In later years, I had similar infatuations with songs I had to hear every day, like "Only Human," by the Human League, "No Promises," by an Australian group called Icehouse, "Seven Seconds," the duet between Youssou Ndour and Neneh Cherry, and lately, the Beach Boys' "Don't Worry Baby" and (speaking of *Pet Sounds*) the heart-swelling "I Just Wasn't Made for These Times."

And if *Watertown* was my favorite Sinatra album as a whole, then my favorite compilation was next up, on a Sinatra double-header to accompany this early morning in western Arizona. A couple of years before Frank's death in 1998, when he was nearing eighty, his daughter Tina worked with him to compile a set of *his* personal favorites from his recordings on the Reprise label — all 450 of them. The nineteen songs he ended up choosing had been recorded over a 21-year span, from 1960 to 1981, and reflected the personal choice of an artist for a particular song, and a particular performance, from a career that spanned six decades at the forefront of American music. The title, *Everything Happens to Me*, worked beautifully with a cover painting of Frank in his later years that the artist, Paul Clemens, described as "a man withdrawn into himself, thinking private thoughts."

The songs he chose reflected that same withdrawn, private man, but this man had the gift of expressing his inner soulscape through the medium of some of the 20th century's finest songwriters, from Rodgers and Hart to Antonio Carlos Jobim to Jimmy Webb, and as always, making those songs his own. Tina Sinatra wrote in the liner notes, "I was relieved each time Dad passed over the more obvious choice for the more obscure. After all, this was to be more than another greatest hits album . . . and it is. *Everything Happens to Me* reveals the soul of Frank Sinatra like a musical looking glass, a man reflecting upon a rich and wonderful life."

I first heard this compilation at the home of my brother, Danny, and his wife Janette, during my tormented wanderings as the Ghost Rider, and right away it felt different from all other such collections. It had a kind of unity, an integrity, and even the running order of the songs seemed carefully considered, like a performance. The songs on *Everything Happens to Me* were so obviously personal, nothing like a greatest-hits package (no "My Way," no "Strangers in the Night," no "New York, New York"), and while there were a few familiar classics, like "Summer Wind," "The Second Time Around," and Jimmy Webb's sublime "Didn't We," there were many more unfamiliar treasures.

The song "Everything Happens to Me" was the one that grabbed me hardest, especially at that period of my life, when I was reeling from tragedy and wandering aimlessly in search of redemption. I sat down and wrote out the lyrics to memorize them, so I could sing that song in my helmet on those long, lonely rides across the American West. (As much as I loved to sing Sinatra songs on my own, I noticed that I rarely sang along with his records — a kind of sacrilege, I guess.)

Later, my dad played me an older version of the song, recorded by Frank in 1940 with the Tommy Dorsey band, and Dad and I agreed the Voice had certainly changed over the years, growing in both size and emotional range, but even back then, the phrasing was unmistakably Sinatra. That older version was more jaunty and tongue-in-cheek, with the hapless hero merely *unlucky* ("I make a date for golf, and you can bet your life it rains/ I try to give a party, and the guy upstairs complains/ I guess I'll go through life just catching colds and missing trains/ Everything happens to me"), and that version was later recorded by other singers like Billie Holiday, Chet Baker, Rosemary Clooney, and . . . Neil Sedaka.

This title track on Frank's personal collection was recorded in 1981, and the first two verses of the lyrics had been rewritten. The words carried a more mature depth of bittersweet irony, an irresistible sadness-with-a-smile philosophy. The same lyricist was credited, Tom Adair, and in trying to find out if he had done the rewrite himself, I was led through some interesting stories along an internet trail, which is often the beginning of a fascinating ride through arcane history and free-association trivia (oh, the places you'll go!).

Composer Matt Dennis worked with Tom Adair for the Tommy Dorsey band in the early '40s, and together wrote such great standards as "Angel Eyes," "Violets for Your Furs," and "The Night We Called It a Day." Tom Adair went on to write for films (like Disney's *Sleeping Beauty*, in 1956), and Broadway shows, and lived until 1988, so it's possible he did do that rewrite of "Everything Happens to Me," more than 40 years later.

The modern version was imbued with an air of genuine heartbreak, however lightly borne by a long-suffering heart, but it still retained the irony and dark humor ("Telegraphs and phones, I sent an airmail special too/ Your answer was goodbye, and there was even postage due/ I fell in love just once, and then it had to be with you/ Everything happens to me"). Frank's updated delivery was less blithe, more reflective, more regretful, with a catch in his voice on verses like, "Now in the school of life, well I was lucky just to pass/ Now I'm chasing rainbows with the losers in the class/

But pal, you don't find rainbows in the bottom of a glass/ Everything happens to me." As always, Sinatra made you *feel* that despair, that loneliness, and the combination of singer and song is as good as it gets.

And the miles passed rapidly under my wheels, I-10 leading west through Arizona. Mid-morning, bright and sunny, fuel up at the Rip Griffin Truck Stop (Merv Griffin's brother, I think I read somewhere), and back on the highway.

The next musical selection was a whole different thing: *No Angel*, by the English singer, Dido (the single nickname replaced her birth name of Florian Cloud de Bounevialle Armstrong). Released in late 1999, the opening song, "Here with Me," grabbed me the first time I heard it, on 98.7 in Los Angeles, during my first few months of living there. I bought the CD, and gradually the whole thing grew on me, mostly on the strength of its songs and Dido's delicately passionate voice, though the production was attractively lush too, with its roots solidly in the '80s heritage of rich keyboards, electronic drums and percussion, and a potpourri of producers, mixing engineers, and programmers (more credits for programmers than musicians, in fact — so '80s!). Along with the Celtic girl-singer influence, the ghosts of Enigma, Tears for Fears, and Propaganda were alive in Dido's music.

In early 2000, just after I bought *No Angel*, but before I knew it well, I was driving on a Los Angeles freeway, caught in slow-moving traffic (yes, really!) and bouncing around radio stations. My normal staples were 98.7 for "active rock," 95.5 for "classic rock," and 101.1 for "oldies," switching among them to find something decent. Sometimes all of them were playing songs I couldn't bear (or worse, no songs at all, just commercials), and I would search further afield. That day I happened to land on something that wouldn't normally hold my attention, a rap song, but I sensed something about it right away, and turned it up. (What quality it was that grabbed me so quickly like that, in a matter of seconds, I can only call a kind of radar, or "professional intuition," a sense that this was *for real*.)

The verses were spoken by a strong male voice, full of hip-hop "attitude," recounting the story of a fan writing to his hero about how his life had been touched by the hero's music. Gradually the fan's letters moved into the area of delusion about their "relationship," and finally resentment and bitterness. He and his hero were "meant to be together," and how could the hero ignore him this way? (Obviously this resonated strongly with my own experiences with such fans, as in the World Health Organization's definition of schizophrenia: "The most intimate thoughts, feelings, and acts are often felt to be known to or shared by others, and explanatory delusions may develop.")

The rap verses alternated with choruses sung by a gentle-voiced female, a soft Celtic lilt over processed guitar and drum machine. I knew I recognized that tune, but couldn't think from where. The story went on with the narrator's anger growing into a psychotic rage, until the chilling climax when he drives off a bridge with his pregnant wife locked in the trunk. Then, in the final verse, the "hero" is writing back, apologizing for taking so long to answer, and urging the fan to get help.

I was galvanized by this performance, amazed by it, but I was left with no idea who the performer was; the station went straight into another song, and I had to park the car and go to my appointment. I figured I would never know. Many times in life I've been haunted by pieces of music I heard in passing but didn't know by name — "Für Elise" in a Mercedes-Benz commercial, a Puccini aria in a Honda ad, Debussy's "Arabesque" by a cocktail pianist, many, many pop songs over the years — and it would become a quest to identify them, usually successful eventually.

A short time after hearing that gripping rap performance, I was visiting the Rich family in Palm Springs, and when I described that piece of music to Buddy's teenaged grandson, Nick, he said, "That's Eminem!" He played it for me, and sure enough, once we got through the torrents of profanity that began the album, it was the song called "Stan," a huge hit for Eminem. From then on, through all the controversy and pulpit-pounding about Eminem, it was clear to me that any artist who was capable of producing that piece of work, whatever his other "issues," had my respect.

The female voice on the choruses was, of course, Dido, from her song "Thank You." She had already sold a million records before that, but with the added boost of Eminem's massive popularity, she ended up with the best-selling album of 2001, something like twenty million copies sold.

"And the hits just keep on comin'," as they used to say on AM radio. Next up was another relatively modern album, both in time (1997) and in style, Radiohead's OK *Computer*. Radiohead were as different as possible from Dido's warm, melodic, richly-textured music, being angular, abrasive, noisy, bizarre, fascinating, and utterly unique, but despite all that, they had also managed to be popular. Therefore, they qualified as "pop artists." I was never sure if I really *loved* Radiohead's music, or not all of it, anyway, but I sure loved the *idea* of it. There were some artists whose records I would buy whether I liked a particular piece of work or not (David Sylvian and Joe Jackson come to mind), just to support their very *existence*.

Defiantly nonformulaic, uncompromising, inventive, full of swirling guitars, edgy drums, electronic frippery wafting in and out — song titles like "paranoid android," "subterranean homesick alien" — their work was artful, in the true sense of the word, right down to the package design, all the text in ever-stylish lower case, *à la* e.e. cummings and k.d. lang. The credits included such attributions as, "artistic freedom in the marketplace maintained by," and "lyrics used by kind permission even though we wrote them." Radiohead even had a sense of humor.

Despite their quirkiness, Radiohead had clearly achieved popularity and success, and on their own terms. OK *Computer* was particularly revered, winning a Grammy for Best Alternative Record in 1998, and even being voted Best Album of All Time by the readers of *Mojo* magazine. I don't know if I'd go that far, about *any* record, but they might have chosen worse.

In digging up background information on some of these artists as I wrote about them, I found some contemporary reviews that were so wrongheaded as to be laughable. One example was the *Rolling Stone* review of Jeff Buckley's *Grace*, following its release in 1996. In a three-star (out of five) review, the writer grudgingly praised Buckley's *intentions*, though with many reservations about how he went about it, and remarked that Buckley wasn't "battered and desperate enough" to deliver "Hallelujah" properly — the beauty of which attracted so many, including this reviewer, to his music.

Later that year, the magazine awarded him Best New Artist honors, and after Buckley was dead and so many others had recognized his greatness, *Rolling Stone* included *Grace* among the "Essential Albums of the '90s."

Another *Rolling Stone* reviewer, writing for a discography of The Who in a collection of interviews published in 1975, gave his mid-'70s perspective on *Who's Next*, then only a few years old, by damning it with faint praise as a self-confessed "fan," apparently never guessing the place that album would occupy in the all-time rock pantheon:

> Amid much speculation — most of it on Townshend's part — about whether or not they could ever transcend it *[Tommy]*, they released their first new studio album in two years, *Who's Next*. As cerebral heavy metal it was absolutely untoppable: As The Who it was another substantial bring-down when it wasn't exuding self-importance and profundity, it suffered from an only-slightly-less-annoying self-consciousness.
>
> [Some punctuation problems there, I'm presuming.]
>
> Superbly performed and awesomely produced, it might well be used as a primer for Seventies heavy (in all senses of that term) rock. Which, not to be coy, is the crux of the problem for those of us who were weaned on their early stuff and to whose ears this tends to sound slick, contrived, and self-conscious.

If only music criticism came close to the quality of literary criticism. I can read a review of nearly any book in the *New York Times Book Review*, and feel as though I'm not only learning about the most important recent books, but also learning from the high standard of writing and reflection from the reviewers themselves.

One book review editor, Laura Miller, wrote an article for the *Book*

Review called "The Hunting of the Snark," in which she described a Web site called Snarkwatch as "bluntly put, a place to complain about book reviews." (One humorous entry was "the author of a volume of poems inspired by the rock band Queen, who maintains that his book was not given a fair shake by this publication.") Her personal definition of "snarkiness" is contained in a telling observation:

> I learned that you had to be careful in assigning books by young, celebrated authors to young, uncelebrated reviewers; the results could be either starry-eyed hero worship or (in the case of the more talented writers) a snide fury out of all proportion to the subject at hand: snarkiness.

Rolling Stone's editorial tone as arbiters of hipness — starry-eyed for the chosen, snide fury for the rest — was set from the beginning by founder Jann Wenner, who, back in 1967, wrote a worshipful article about the Beatles, but along the way felt compelled to attack the Beach Boys and Brian Wilson, saying that the label "genius" was "essentially a promotional shuck" Brian himself believed.

Around that same time Wilson himself stated, "I'm not a genius, I'm just a hard-working guy," and what a *price* he paid for that reputation — the weight of those expectations on every piece of music he tried to create after *Pet Sounds*, of feeling that everything he did had to spell "genius." Certainly that pressure on an already fragile mind contributed to his breakdown, and to the drug abuse that accompanied it.

Under the weight of his own reputation, Stewart Copeland told me that after the Police broke up, he stopped playing drums for a few years because of what he called the "Eric Clapton Syndrome" — he got tired of feeling that every time he touched the instrument, he had to be *brilliant*, and dazzle everyone around.

Wenner also sniffed that "Good Vibrations" (still an all-time masterpiece) was "not really rock 'n' roll," in an article praising the Beatles and *Sergeant Pepper*, about which, surely, the same could be said. George

Martin again: "If there is one person that I have to select as a living genius of pop music, I would choose Brian Wilson."

Whose opinion is worth more, Sir George Martin's or Jann Wenner's?

Everyone's personal opinion is worth the same, in religion, music, and politics, but some *expert* opinions are definitely more informed, more reflective, and more *valuable.*

These reflections bring us smoothly to the next and final selection on this five-day, 2,500-mile musical extravaganza: *Vapor Trails*, the latest release by a certain Canadian rock trio. Continuing my twelve years of ignoring the few reviews our albums usually received, a smart, protective practice inspired by the decision Tom Robbins had made and described to me in a letter, I assumed that any reviews of *Vapor Trails* would be the usual knee-jerk excoriations. No value there.

Back in 1996, Geddy told me he was talking to a writer from *Rolling Stone* who let slip that Rush was their readers' most requested subject for a feature story. The writer admitted it would never happen, though, because we weren't "cool" enough for them. According to a quote I read on the Rush Thirtieth Anniversary calendar, at the time I said they weren't cool enough for us, either.

Throughout this journey I had been careful to keep my playlist "natural," and the binder of CDs I carried with me necessarily represented my general playlist at that point in time, March 2003. Even after I began to consider the notion that my musical odyssey formed a kind of story, I still didn't listen to anything just to be able to *write* about it. However, even just considered as an arc of musical selections, something seemed ineffably right about concluding the program with our own latest work. A summing-up, an objective reassessment of where I'd been musically, and maybe even where I wanted to go.

After listening to each song dozens of times during the recording and mixing, and then again through various running orders and final masters, I had often had about enough of it. Once the final product was manufactured and I held it in my hands (always a great moment), I might listen to it once more, to hear it as others would (somehow that reality made it sound completely different), and then put it away. Of course, I might play those songs dozens of times in concert in subsequent years, but that was not a *listening* experience.

Every time we released a new album, it always seemed to take at least six months to get enough distance on that piece of work (piece of *life*) to see it whole; to see it in context of yourself as a music fan, not just the "author" of the work. With time, you gained perspective on the music as an *entity*, and began to see it, in a way, as a certain "color," an assigned mood and character it had come to embody for you.

Especially after playing many of the songs on tour, they became familiar in every detail, worn into grooves in the brain by sheer repetition. There were also recordings of the live shows to listen to along the way, to review my performance, examine the technical aspects of execution and time control. But all of that was entirely different from the experience of simply *listening*, of trying to step back and experience the music as just one more music lover.

What would I think of this if it wasn't me? That was always the question I tried to answer, though it was difficult, perhaps impossible, to really see it that clearly.

If a piece of work was an honest expression of its maker, it was also a milestone of his progress, and a benchmark to build upon in the future. As much as the notion of "progressive" music has been mocked, used to denigrate a particular style of experimental, ambitious arranging and musicianship, it was really the only possible kind of honest music.

Not to say that the simple passage of time meant that one's work necessarily got *better*; it didn't have to be *qualitative* progress, but it was certainly a chronological progress. Life cannot be seen any other way than as a progression — forward, if not necessarily upward — and thus it followed that one's work had to be looked at that way too. For me, each milestone, each benchmark was necessarily progressive, reflecting what I had learned musically, as a drummer, and what I had learned existentially, as a lyricist. As my friend Mendelson Joe said, "Art doesn't lie," and that was especially true in cases where it *tried* to lie — pretending to be something it wasn't to attract an audience it didn't deserve. That's what it *really* meant to be "pretentious."

In an unfortunate contradiction, progressive music was described by ignorant, biased critics as "pretentious," but what a confused value system that terminology represented. Seldom was there a more *honest* style of music, based on solid principles of musicianship, exploration, and fascination. It did not "pretend" youth, or adolescent passion, like so much pop music written by aging men and women with cynical formulas, and it did not "pretend" rebellion, like so much pop music written by leering mercenaries in motorcycle jackets and careful hairdos. (From "The Sound of Muzak," by Porcupine Tree, a modern-day "progressive" band: "The music of rebellion makes you wanna rage/ But it's made by millionaires who are nearly twice your age").

At its worst, progressive rock may have become bloated and top-heavy, but inevitably it had to collapse on itself anyway, in the cycle of self-correcting mechanisms common in popular music: the previously-described "garage band" principle. As soon as popular music outgrew the ability of beginners to emulate it, a revolution would follow. How few of the '50s pioneers survived commercially into the early '60s, and how few of the early '60s bands survived into the late '60s, and so on. It is unfortunate, in a way, that many good artists become undeservedly marginalized by an imagined line drawn in the sand, between old and uncool, and new and hip, and there's nothing they can do about it.

When punk and new wave styles exploded in the late '70s, some established artists were nimble enough to respond to the changes around them. Some grumbled, "What am I supposed to do, forget how to play?", and continued to ride their dinosaurs into extinction, but others willingly adapted to the streamlining and back-to-basics urges of the times, without giving up all they had learned. Former Genesis singer Peter Gabriel, for example, or former Yes keyboardist Trevor Horn, continued to produce vital, influential music through the '80s and '90s. Ian Anderson has continued to lead Jethro Tull out of the '60s and '70s and quietly through the decades, making high quality music and finding a large enough audience to continue recording and touring worldwide.

Rush happened to be working in England a lot during the late '70s, touring and recording for months on end, and thus we were right in the middle of that ferment. Seeing the Sex Pistols thrashing out "God Save the Queen" on the BBC's "Top of the Pops" was unforgettable, galvanizing, and though the lightning-rod charisma of Johnny Rotten in his strait-jacket and safety pins was short-lived, it prepared me, it seems now, for things like the first Talking Heads album, Elvis Costello and Joe Jackson, or Television's hypnotic "Marquee Moon" — reintroducing me to simplicity and repetition as musical tools.

Loving that music, I couldn't help but be influenced by it, and the whole band gradually moved from full-blown "progressive" epics like *Hemispheres* in 1978, through the slightly more concise architecture of *Permanent Waves* (the title sniffing at that "new wave" discrimination) in 1979, and finally what still remains our most popular album, *Moving Pictures*, in 1980. We seemed to capture the right balance of our traditional values of musicianship and challenging construction with a contemporary sense of conciseness, relatively streamlined and direct, and struck our nexus with radio and rock fans. For that one year, our audience suddenly doubled (even if temporarily), and on that *Moving Pictures* tour, as we played two nights in cities where we had always played one, we noticed a lot of people in the audience who had no *idea* about our music or our songs; we just happened to be the concert to be at that year. ("Are you going to Rush?" "Oh yeah man, for sure.") Briefly, and uncomfortably (for us and our *real* fans), we were "in."

By that time punk and new wave had themselves, inevitably, progressed, as they were bound to do (even if a band started out genuinely inept, they were likely to improve and grow). By 1980, the leading edge of pop music had metamorphosed into ambitious, creative bands like Ultravox and the Police, and all that flux crept into Rush's music. "You are what you eat," or what you *hear*, and for me, the same motivation applied that had moved me at the beginning: I loved to listen to music, so I wanted to play it.

The same drives and values had been at work in the creation of *Vapor Trails*, all those many years later. As I drove back into the constellation of suburbs in the orbit of Los Angeles, after that long journey and all the music that had accompanied it, I listened to that "time capsule" from 2001, the lyrics spanning the odyssey of the previous few years, all I had endured, all I had learned, and the music recounting the parallel odyssey that had brought the three of us, together, through the decades of our apprenticeship; all the experiments, all the influences, all the struggles, labors, changes, and adaptations.

> Celebrate the moment, as it turns into one more
> Winding like an ancient river, the time is now again
> All this time we're burning like bonfires in the dark
> Here we come out of the cradle, endlessly rocking

The moment, the river, bonfires in the dark, endlessly rocking. The moment that was *Vapor Trails* became another drop in the river, another drop in the ceaseless flow of modern music. All those streams and tributaries, the very lifeblood of that youth, the very richness of that past. Not one of those veins flowed from a music reviewer, or from a multinational corporation. Every note of real music surged up from the human heart, driven by the passion and ambition of a million voices, and *that* traveling music flowed on and on, through a million more hearts, endlessly rocking.

It sounded pretty good, but I thought we could do better.

I turned up the music and smiled, eyes on the road ahead.

Chorus Four

"Drumming at the heart of an African village"

My escape from St. Catharines to the wider world had carried me far, first to London, then, with my bandmates from Rush, on a 30-year creative odyssey of songwriting, recording, and touring throughout the world, but even then, I continued to seek new adventures, new challenges, and new escapes.

The life of a touring musician could also seem stifling, seeing only the inside of the tour bus, hotels, and arenas for weeks and months on end. In my first years on tour with Rush, I filled the empty hours with books, but by the early '80s, I was carrying a bicycle with me on the tour bus, and getting away on my own when I could — riding from city to city on days off, or even just around Indianapolis, Seattle, or Richmond for a few hours on the day of the show, visiting the local art museums and continuing my liberal arts education.

It is not too much to say that traveling became a kind of *home* for me, and also a kind of music. Adventure travels moved from inspiration to perspiration on a quest for new horizons, with daily challenges of problem-solving and adaptation, each journey taking on a shape and structure from beginning to end, and resonating in my life forever after.

In 1985, I took my first extended bicycle journey, to China, just after its doors, closed since the revolution in 1948, were reopened to Westerners. I signed up for a two-week tour with a company called China Passage, joining about 20 cyclists from Canada, the U.S., and Australia. That difficult, but fascinating, adventure inspired a song, "Tai Shan," which appeared on our *Hold Your Fire* album in 1987, and I also became friends with some keen cyclists from New Jersey — Bob, Rosie, and Gay — who liked to design their own tours. In subsequent years I joined them to bicycle from Munich to Venice over the Swiss Alps, Barcelona to Bordeaux over the Pyrenees, Calgary to Vancouver over the Rockies, and from Munich to Istanbul over the Austrian Alps, and through the Greek Islands by ferry to Turkey.

Each year through the late '80s and early '90s, between touring and recording obligations with Rush, and spending time at home with my family, I tried to find a few weeks to escape — to get away on my own, with strangers or like-minded friends, and get as far away as I could from my comfortable, yet demanding life. Sometimes these journeys also became a kind of traveling music, in more ways than one.

Without a doubt, the DNA of American music — *my* music — traces back to Africa, and I have retraced those roots on a series of return journeys to that continent where both life and art began. A camping safari to Kenya and Tanzania, bicycle trips to Cameroon, Chad, Togo, Ghana, the Ivory Coast, Mali, Senegal, and the Gambia, and by motorcycle through Tunisia. Eleven African countries altogether, and all of those adventurous travels included experiences of African music and drumming. Most of the time I just watched and listened, sometimes I took part, and other times it just seeped into me, the way Youssou Ndour's music was so omnipresent in Senegal, in every bar, restaurant, bus, or market stall, that I was ultimately seduced by its rhythmic lyricism.

One hot night in a village in Togo called Assohoum, in November 1989, I laid out my sleeping bag on an adobe rooftop and lay looking up at the bright stars in the perfect silence of an African night — no traffic, no television, no radio, just scattered conversations or distant dogs. As I was dozing off, a drum rhythm echoed from across the valley, two hand-drummers playing an interlocking pattern, and it stuck in my head, only to emerge months later as the basis for a rhythm I used in a Rush song called "Heresy" (*Roll the Bones*, 1991). (True cultural cross-pollination, an African rhythm played by a Canadian drummer with Japanese drumsticks on American drums with one Chinese cymbal in a song produced by an Englishman about the fall of communism in Eastern Europe and the Soviet Union.) Later, the same rhythm became the foundation of a solo piece I created in the early '90s to serve as a backing track while I practiced my marimba playing, called "Momo's Dance Party." A version of that little *étude* appears at the end of my instructional video, *A Work in Progress* (1996).

"Momo's Dance Party" was also inspired by a real-life experience on that same African journey, a trip with guide David Mozer and his Bicycle Africa tour group through Togo and Ghana, which ended with me cycling on alone to meet my family in the Ivory Coast, at (of all places) a Club Med. I had traveled with David the previous year in Cameroon (*The Masked Rider*, 1996), on my first bicycle tour of West Africa, and had joined this group at the last minute when I heard about it from David and found I could make the time.

We were a group of about ten cyclists, and one night we stopped in another small, remote village in Togo called Agbo Kope. Again, no electricity, no machines, no running water, just houses of mud brick and woven grass, and streets of rutted dirt. David had visited Agbo Kope once before, when he reconnoitered this tour, and had met Momo, an ambitious young man who had received some education away from the village. Momo seemed to be the only villager who spoke the colonial language of French, and he seemed to be trying to put his village on the tourist map.

Since David's previous visit, and a letter he'd sent Momo to let him know he planned to bring a group of cyclists to Momo's village, an open pavilion had been constructed of branches and palms, and we moved our bicycles and bedrolls under its shelter. The women of the village cooked nearby on clay firepits, preparing us the usual dinner of rice and "mystery meat" stew (which I had dubbed in Cameroon as "rice with junk on it"), and in the evening, the entire village gathered to put on a show for us. The children sang and danced while the men drummed, then the women (some of them with sleeping babies tied to their backs with colorful cloths that matched their traditional *pagne* dresses) performed graceful, narrative dances. The grand finale was the village choir, the rich voices of men and women harmonizing beautifully, accompanied only by one man playing a shaker, and another playing a metal disc with a stick. This syncopated pattern hypnotized me at the time, and remains in my memory as one of the most *musical* performances I have ever heard. Even fourteen years later, I can still conjure the aural image of those blended voices and that simple percussion accompaniment.

After the choir finished, the drummers struck up again, and the American girls from our group jumped in and danced with the African women. They were greeted by whoops of delighted laughter as they imitated what we had described among ourselves as the "funky chicken." I crept around behind the crowd to where the drummers were, and managed to overcome my shyness enough to get them to "assign" me a drum. They gave me a drum made from a hollow log with skin over one end and a bent twig to play it with, and the drummer beside me showed me the rhythm to play. The drum was flat sounding, with little tone or resonance, and the rhythm was a simple one-two-three, rest, one-two-three (a common pattern in traditional music, I had noticed it in prayer chants in Chinese temples, and adapted it for the song "Tai Shan," and also while cycling past Ghanaian churches on a Sunday morning, whence I brought it home to use as another rhythmic element of "Momo's Dance Party," played on claves).

Whenever I tried to get more out of my part, or more *into* it, by using both my bare hands, for example, to get different sounds with fingers flat or cupped, as you would on a conga drum, the man beside me would shake his head, pick up the stick and push it back into my hand. He insisted I play it that one way only. I realized that for them, there *was* only one way to play that drum, and that part, and it was generally true that as part of an African drum troupe, you had to submit to the ensemble voice, play one small part the way it had *always* been played. This music was not about expression or exploration, but simply the rote performance of a traditional piece, as in

Western classical music. Nothing wrong with that, of course, in that context, but it was such a contrast to the way I was used to thinking of drumming, as a whole ensemble of voices that I could orchestrate, and take where I wanted, in interaction with other musicians.

Next morning, as we packed up our bicycles to leave, Momo was hanging around, expecting something, it appeared, but I didn't know what. Money maybe? David had paid for our food and shelter, but Momo still seemed distraught, nearly in tears, and I surmised that he simply expected *more* from us — he had imagined that we were somehow going to *change* things for him and his village. As we rode away and left Momo and his village the way they had always been, I felt bad for him.

The song "Momo's Dance Party" appeared as an instrumental behind the credits on *A Work in Progress*, but I had written lyrics for it as well (though they were never sung, except in my head), with this chorus:

> Momo is a young man from the village
> Momo left to learn the white man's tongue
> Momo has ambitions for his people
> Momo has the big dreams of the young
> And he wants more . . .

In October of 1992, I joined my third bicycle tour in West Africa (each time saying I was never going to put myself through that again, and each time going back), through Mali, Senegal, and the Gambia. The tour began with two weeks in Mali, then moved on to Senegal for the next two-week leg. In Senegal's capital, Dakar, our tight little group of five "clients" and David met up with four other cyclists arriving from the U.S., and all traveled south through Senegal to the Gambia and back to Dakar.

As well as keeping a written journal, I carried a microcassette recorder in the handlebar bag in front of me, and where the road conditions permitted, I could pick it up and record my observations as I rode along. The following is a series of entries taped during one day's ride between the capital city of the Gambia, Banjul, and the village of Bwiam, about three weeks into the tour. They offer a fair summary of the ups and downs of a day's travel in West Africa.

• Just rolling out of Banjul, or Bakau, the neighborhood where we were staying at Cape St. Mary. Last night's dinner at the Jungle Bar, presided over by Fred, one of those dissolute expatriate Englishmen you run into in Africa, and in the Caribbean too. Fred: glasses, kind of stooped, wispy hair thinning on top. Been knocking around Africa for eighteen years, half a dozen or a dozen different countries, civil engineer, worked with the UN for a long time, development projects, then a lumber company in Liberia until the war there forced him out. Depressing to hear him say that of all the development projects he worked on, he was not sanguine about their hopes because as soon as they'd leave the thing would fall apart. Now he's got about five businesses going here, on a small enough scale not to be bothered, he said. Three little restaurants, including the Jungle Bar and this morning's breakfast stop, where we had fried eggs and chips, a nice treat, plus two oranges and two bananas. Not enough cups, but Herb and I had our portables, folded.

Couple of plantain eaters [birds] rowing overhead there.

• Important to note how Senegal and the Gambia couldn't get along in a federation [Senegambia] for even a couple of years, even though they're made up of the same ethnic groups. Simply the language [Senegal had been a French colony, while the Gambia was British] meant that they didn't think the same — tie that in with how I feel I adopt a different personality in French, become more expressive, more given to exaggeration in gesture, statement, and expression.

• Wonderful to feel refreshed after a day off the bike, or as Murray [another rider] said, "I feel like a fucking human being." I told him not to waste it, meaning don't burn himself out. He was racing ahead with the front pack, on my wheel for awhile until I dropped behind him.

As unpleasant as it was in some ways to be in the white English world of the Cape Point Hotel, I do feel much better able to deal with Africa and Africans today, as a result of it, and springy on the bike legs too.

• Funny talking to Omar [young Gambian] last night, calling himself a Rasta. When we inquired further into exactly what that meant, wondering why he smoked cigarettes and drank beer, and after Haile Selassie [unpopular in West Africa] et cetera, he finally came down to admitting that for him being a Rasta was just about the music, *mon.*

"It's *cool . . .*"

• I haven't made note anywhere I don't think of the perception of mileages, where at home a fifty-mile ride is a nice thing you could do before breakfast, and a hundred-mile ride starts to become an epic. Here a *fifty*-mile ride is an epic, dealing with the terrain sometimes, but more often just the heat, the bad roads, and the general living conditions. Though feeling today as I did on the San to Bla ride — what a difference a day off the bikes can make. So restorative, I feel strong and good-natured, and ready to power through.

• Some reason thinking about Keith Moon this morning — I think the "Bellboy" song from *Quadrophenia* got it going, and that came from sleeping on the beach I guess, that train of thought [from a classic Pete Townshend middle eight: "Some nights I still sleep on the beach, remember when stars were in reach?"]. It might be interesting to do a little tangent about poor old Keith, what he meant to me starting out, and how sadly he ended up. The importance of The Who in my life.

• Herb reminded me the other day of the *Kwasi Obloni* name they called us back in Ghana, Johnny Red-nose I think it meant.

• Little burst of adrenaline there. Collision with a rooster. Idiot bird standing in the middle of the road, then instead of running away, runs straight into me. Gave me a scare, but the instinct for self-preservation took over. Fortunately I was down on the [handlebar] drops, just held it steady, felt the stupid thing bounce off me and head for the side of the road. I thought it would be crushed, cut up in the spokes, but seemed to be unharmed.

• During a wakeful period last night I remember thinking about generalities, and how people dislike them because they always feel themselves to be the exception, whether they are gender generalities, or racial ones, or whatever. So, to counter that we can use "all generalities are false, including this one," and also "if you accept my generality, I'll accept your exception from it."

• Well, really motoring out today. Heading along this south side of the Gambia "highway," top speed, hitting the shoulder if I have to. A few women back there were safely walking along the road, I was on the left shoulder, and one of them looked back and just panicked. They dove in front of me and then across into the ditch, while if they'd just stayed where they were everything would have been fine.

Anyway, now we're cruising along, the road's smoothed out a bit. Had some nasty laterite [red clay] and very rough paving for awhile, put me on the shoulder. Some big trees and feathery palms here now, very green.

• An old man there saying "welcome." Beautiful thing. Just saw an interesting poster, saying "Islam is not against family planning." One thing I certainly wondered. [Some African cultures believe the promotion of birth control by Western aid organizations is a racist plot.]

• Lots of palm trees out here, green fields, everything pleasant, and nice to see big trees overhanging, and just acres of palms off to the side there.

• Crowd of boys there yelling out "give me things, give me things." So much for the hope that people would be more polite away from the cities. Good forty miles outside of Banjul now, just as bad, maybe worse. Just had to wave my [tire] pump at a bunch of boys to get them off me, running and grabbing at my bike. Just ignorance. Incredible rudeness. An old man just called me *toubab* [white man], and I asked him if that's how he greets visitors.

• I am out of here — let's get to Dakar. Today, tomorrow. This place sucks.

• Just have to think of what a good mood I started out in, and how these people have worn me down. Somadougou [Mali] is always the point of comparison, where I was in a bad mood and the people so nice they charmed me out of it.

• Stopped there for an hour and a half, read a little Nietzsche. [Midday rest under a tree, avoiding the African noon. Just as during the Cameroon trip I had read Aristotle's *Ethics* in the daytime and van Gogh's letters at night, this time I carried *The Portable Nietzsche* and *The Cerebral Symphony: Seashore Reflections on the Structure of Consciousness*, by William H. Calvin. Calvin offered a poetic frame for many profound statements by himself and others on the subject of human consciousness, but I was most grateful for the Three Primal Questions: 1/ "Where are we going?" 2/ "When do we get there?" and 3/ "Why do I have to sit in the middle?"]

• Schopenhauer quote in Nietzsche: "Every great pain, whether physical or spiritual, declares what we deserve; for it could not come to us if we did not deserve it." (What an asshole!)

• Thinking about Nietzsche and *The Antichrist* today, and his idea of the Christian despising of the body. How true that is in every sense, particularly sexually, or additionally sexually, and his little joke about if thine eye offend thee, pluck it out — and they don't mean your *eye!*

Interesting that he, along with Voltaire, are the only philosophers who had a sense of humor. The idea too of the hypocrisy of this body-hatred, and vows of chastity, priestly pederasts, and the joke about how beside every nunnery there's an orphanage.

Was it maybe Nietzsche's anti-Christianity that led to his discrediting — first under guise of "madness," then under the stain of fascism, after the Nazis warped his thoughts to their ends?

Nietzsche's last words [perhaps his last-known coherent statement]: "I am just having all anti-Semites shot."

• Now back on the road again, like a force of nature. Inexorable. Still a "Four Rs" kind of day: Rested, rehydrated, refueled, and ready. Covered something over 90 k, maybe 93 k, something like that by now, still storming down the road. Nobody knows how far to go, but I'm sure we're going to get there.

That night we stayed in a village called Bwiam, in a forested area along the Gambia River, another rustic (not to say primitive) Bicycle Africa destination. We leaned our bikes against a shade tree in the chief's compound, set up our little mosquito tents on the sandy earth, then bathed out of buckets and filtered drinking water with our little hand-pumps.

In the late afternoon stillness I took a walk around the few tree-shaded streets of rutted earth, and heard tentative bursts of drumming from one of the compounds. Irresistibly attracted, I peeked my head over a wall of woven palms and saw a woman in the courtyard working over an open fire. She looked up at me, I gestured toward the hut of mud and grass from which the drumming seemed to be emanating, and she motioned me to go inside.

The weathered wooden door was ajar, and I slowly pushed my head into the dimness of the hut. An older African man, gray and sinewy, sat in front of a tall wooden drum, and beside him sat a young white man — *boy*, really — with a smaller drum. As formal, leisurely greetings were exchanged, in the African manner, the boy told me he was an Irish missionary, recently assigned to the area, and the old man was trying to teach him how to drum. As they carried on with the lesson, the African man tried to get the young Irishman to repeat even the simplest pattern, but he couldn't seem to grasp it. The older man became frustrated, and took hold of the boy's hand and tried to *show* him how to move it, but it was no good.

With a questioning look, I asked if I could try the boy's drum, and I began to listen to what the master played, then repeat it for him. With a grunt of approval, he made the patterns more intricate, and I replayed them as best I could. Eventually we were playing together, first in unison, then breaking off into complementary patterns, and both of us began to sweat, and to smile at each other as we played.

I felt the shadow of the woman looking in the window-opening, then a commotion in the courtyard as children began to crowd into the little room, staring and chattering. A row of women's faces gathered at the window, and they pointed and laughed in whoops of apparent disbelief at seeing a white man play a drum. The children started dancing, and soon the women joined in too, crowding into the bursting hut as the master and I pounded away, smiling and sweating.

Finally we wound up with a long, triple-forte roll and a decisive flam, and the room erupted into happy laughter. The young Irishman looked at me with his mouth open, and stuttered out, "How . . . how can you *do* that?"

With an aw-shucks manner and a shrug, I said, "Oh . . . I'm in the business."

✪

Three weeks before, our original group of five cyclists had begun the trip in the dusty, busy city of Bamako, in Mali, and followed David to Koulikoro, where we loaded our bicycles onto a crowded riverboat, the *Kankou Moussa* (named for a king of the ancient kingdom of Mali, around the 12th century, who had led a *hadj* to Mecca of 72,000 people and distributed so much gold along the way that local economies were undermined for years). We traveled by riverboat down the Niger for two days, surrounded by the colorful pageant of African life along its banks. Late on the second day, we disembarked at the town of Mopti, then bicycled through the brief African twilight and into darkness, guided by a full moon, to the village of Songo.

The next day we rode to Djiguibombo, where we left the bikes the following morning and hiked down the Bandiagara Escarpment into the heart of Dogon country, with a local guide, Nouhoum. The scattering of thatched-roof villages sheltered by the escarpment, or *falaise*, had remained isolated, and thus unchanged, since ancient times, and the Dogon people were celebrated for their wood carving, and for the colorful rituals which surrounded their rich cosmogony. Even in the 1990s, their isolation remained so complete that each Dogon village still had a completely separate language (87 of them, Nouhoum told us), most of them unintelligible to the others, and in one village Nouhoum was asked if a teenage boy could join us to walk to the next village, two miles away — because he didn't know the way.

After the hike, we returned to the bicycles and set out to ride to the village of Bandiagara. I left a little quicker than the others, and trailed our guide, Nouhoum, on his moped, following the route he navigated through the ruts, and when darkness descended so swiftly, I used Nouhoum's headlight to see what was coming. In the smoother, faster sections, sometimes I even rode in his draft, so for me, that ride was exciting and daring ("workin' them angels"), and by the time I arrived at the bridge just outside Bandiagara, where we had agreed to meet, I was feeling good.

The full moon floated over the river as I watched the village boys swimming, laughing, splashing, and jumping naked from the bridge. I had to wait about an hour for the others, but it was a nice place to wait, and eventually Herb rode up to lead me to our lodgings, where the others had arrived. Herb was a San Francisco firefighter, about 40, an avid cyclist and explorer of exotic parts of the world, and he and I had traveled together back in '89, on the Togo-Ghana Bicycle Africa tour. He proved to be a good companion on both journeys, keenly interested in the local cultures, and always ready to help if anyone needed it, or to stop and wait while you fixed a flat tire.

We left our bikes at the Auberge Kansaye, and followed our flashlight beams through the dark, unpaved streets in search of some dinner. After that long hike under the sun and the scary bike ride under the moon, we were ravenous. Near the bus-park we found an outdoor food stall, and sat at a table around a kerosene lantern and devoured big bowls of rice and sauce.

It was evident that my high spirits were not shared by the others, and it didn't seem as if anyone else had found this second night ride quite such a "spiritual" experience, so I kept it to myself. Everybody seemed tired and lethargic, but beneath the fatigue, the good humor remained. There was no complaining, and even a few jokes emerged: David, usually the Stoic, said that if he ever suggested another night ride, someone should hit him. Theresa mentioned that she thought cycling at night was "against the rules" of Bicycle Africa. "In fact," she said, "isn't there something in your book about it?" David had to laugh and nod agreement: in his book *Bicycling In Africa*, he had written: "Every effort should be made to stay off the roads at night."

"Well," he said, "from now on, that's the rule!"

The Auberge was a low concrete building with no charm whatsoever, one of those overpriced African hotels which must be profitable no matter how few guests they receive — because they have absolutely no overhead: no electricity, no plumbing (except for the dribble of a shower fed by gravity from an oil drum), the rooms tiny cells with foam slab beds, no paint or even water having been applied anywhere since colonial times. But as we had found before in such places, these rooms were perfectly adequate — as garages — and we squeezed our bikes into them and hauled the foam slabs outside to the terrace and set up our mosquito tents *en plein air*.

The moon was still near-enough full to deceive Bandiagara's multitude of roosters into cheering for an all-night dawn, and all through the night we were serenaded by that rich chorus, with the occasional counterpoint of braying donkeys and barking dogs. Just before dawn the *muezzins* joined in, singing the call to prayer from different quarters of the town. I lay awake in my tent, truly amazed by all that racket, and looked down the field toward the river. A big tree on the bank was studded with white blotches, which the increasing light revealed to be cattle egrets, hundreds of them gathered to roost in the one tree. Gradually each bird stretched its wings and joined the flock lazily circling the tree, warming their wings. As the sun's crown appeared, they all took flight, making a humming noise like swarming bees.

My good feelings of the previous night lasted into the morning, and I rode out of Bandiagara feeling strong, happy, and at peace with myself, my companions, my bike, and the world. After a good breakfast at our friendly neighborhood chop-house — omelette, *baguette*, Nescafé *noir*, and a nice pineapple soda, *ananas*, for dessert — we started north, spreading out along the road as we each found our morning cadence. Some cyclists liked to start out slow and build up the exertion as the day went on, while others, like myself, came out of the chute pumping, feeling strongest in the morning. David tended to be the same, and he and I shared the lead, sometimes talking and sometimes drifting ahead or behind. Behind were the two sisters from Seattle, Theresa and Patty, the Italian psychiatrist, Silvia, keeping her slow but steady pace, and Herb at the back, feeling weak and unwell that day.

We met a few donkey carts on their way into Bandiagara, often loaded up with large family groups who greeted us as we rolled by. One little girl perched right under the cart, riding precariously on the axle, while sometimes dogs ran along beneath them, keeping to the moving patch of shade. We passed a large billboard reading *"Lutte contre la désertification"* (fight against desertification), with an illustration showing a strange spherical object on three legs. This mysterious totem represented a cooking-stove design which the government and international aid agencies were encouraging people to use, as it made more efficient use of limited firewood. On the other side of the billboard was a warning against starting fires, and both signs were a reminder of the perilous environment these people inhabited. If not for the barrier of the Niger River, this northern edge of the Sahel, "the border," would long ago have been swallowed up by the Sahara.

The first part of our route was the same good road we had traveled a few days before, coming out of Songo, but after a few kilometers David stopped and waited for everyone to catch up, then led us off on a side road — if "road" was the right word to describe a vague route through the bush, something between a cart track and a goat path. No four-wheeled traffic used this local short cut, for there were better roads to the same destinations, though not so direct. The only wheel marks were from mopeds and donkey carts, and although it was always nice to be cycling without traffic to worry about, sometimes we were just *walking* without traffic to worry about, pushing those heavy bikes through stretches of deep sand, or over a rocky streambed. And even though we had no trucks or speeding minibuses to fear, the road itself provided plenty of excitement from the saddle. When I could spare a hand from steering, I grabbed my little recorder out of the handlebar bag and recorded these comments:

> While the road is not so horrible for a minute, I want to talk about how horrible the road is! Thinking that it's not such a torment early in the morning — not so tired, not so hot, not so grumpy — but terrible rocks and sand, and some scary-looking big thornbushes too, which I hope not to encounter . . . pneumatically.
>
> Unbelievably hard to see the road sometimes, never mind follow it. Surface here is what I think is described as hardpan, with some bits of soft sand, but usually not too deep, fortunately. Some larger rocks embedded in it, dry grass all around, which, probably in the next month or two as things dry out even more, will largely

disappear or turn brown. And the aforementioned thornbushes, a few other scrubby bushes, and not much else to call a tree really; once every great while you see a decent-sized tree, meaning thirty feet tall or so.

Theresa called it "just your average Bicycle Africa road!", and a new catch-phrase was born, giving irony to Bicycle Africa meals, Bicycle Africa hotels, and "just your average Bicycle Africa day." There was never anything average about a Bicycle Africa day, of course, and that one was no exception; it was an epic trek, a mega-endurance event, a boot-camp survival course, and a test of will, strength, stamina, and good humor. Herb was having a difficult time, saying he still felt drained from the previous day's hike, and he wondered if he'd caught some bug that was making him feel so weak.

Several times we lost the route completely, and had to stop and regroup while we scouted around, or tried to find someone to ask. Few people inhabited this barren landscape, though; we passed two or three tiny villages, but hardly saw a soul. At one point a wide mesa dominated the landscape to our right, surrounded by dry millet fields. The geometric outline of an adobe village was silhouetted across its top, an attractive skyline of houses and granaries, with one taller turret of mud: the mosque. Nearing midday by then, and with that high-effort kind of cycling (and pushing), we were drinking a lot of water and looking for more, but that village seemed to be accessible only by climbing the side of the mesa on foot, so we pressed on.

After another hour of that, the sun was high, we were tired, sweaty, and dirty, and the water situation was growing critical. When we came upon another millet field, crisscrossed by footpaths, we decided those paths must lead to a village, and to water, so we followed one of them. At a sandy clearing overhung by trees and surrounded by millet stalks, dry but still green, we spotted an open well. It was framed at ground level by logs, which were deeply scored by the rope used to haul up the bucket. The circular interior was walled in stones, with bits of greenery between them, and the surface of the water, just a few feet down, was opaque and greenish-brown. As we looked down at this well a little doubtfully, Herb pointed at a couple of resident frogs resting between the stones. This would have to be our oasis.

We leaned our bikes against the trees and stripped off gloves and helmets, while David went off to find the village itself, and to borrow their bucket. We were all infested with another pest of the Sahel: tiny burrs called *kram-krams*, which had hooked themselves to every piece of cloth we owned, from socks to shorts to panniers, and then hung on with barbed spines. Those sea-urchin-like clusters of thorns were too sharp and too enmeshed to be removed by hand, so we developed various methods of plucking them out — with Herb's tweezers, or by scraping them off with the sharp edge of a shard of pottery I found in the sand (sure that I'd discovered an ancient tool made just for that purpose, and we joked about marketing the "Kram-Kram Whiz").

David returned with a bucket on a rope, trailed by a few women and children. They gathered around to watch silently as we squatted in the dirt with our water filters, and began to fill all our bottles. This was slow work, since we emptied our bottles as fast as we could fill them, finally able to drink all we wanted without the constant worry of running out. And the big surprise was, it really *was* delicious water. Any water would have been welcome in that time and place, but it was more than that. Once the greenish liquid had passed through our filters, it emerged clear and delicious, and I was to remember it as the best water on the tour, better than any of the deep-bore wells, or even the store-bought spring water we were sometimes able to buy. Herb said he thought it was the frog piss that made it so special.

For the villagers, however, lacking our excellent filters, that water was not so salubrious. Although most of these remote people spoke no French at all, a passing farmer wandered by with his crude hook-shaped hoe over his shoulder, stood awhile to stare at us and listen to the women, then mustered enough French to translate their wish: *"médicaments pour les enfants."* They wanted medicine for the children. One of the older women, certainly a grandmother, mimed a baby in her arms, then stroked her own eyelid imploringly, and I understood the problem: eye infections, river blindness, *onchocersiasis* — one of the many effects of using and drinking unsafe water. I shook my head regretfully, feeling bad that those people not only lacked clean water, but a few cents worth of medicine to save a child from blindness.

Later that day in Somadougou, another woman brought her baby out and placed him tenderly on a blanket beside me, caressing away the flies which were drawn to his milky, running eyes. Once again she mimed the question, her finger gently rubbing an imaginary salve over the baby's eyelids, and again I could only shake my head sadly. Inside I made the decision that I had to try to do something about this when I returned home. Some of Africa's tragedies seemed so huge and hopeless: political corruption, droughts, civil wars, AIDS and other infectious diseases, conflicting cultures, exploding populations. But this one seemed approachable: a little *médicaments pour les enfants.*

The basic issue was clean water, of course, and that was the main focus of most of the secular aid organizations, and of my own charitable contributions. But, as David pointed out, that only contributed to Africa's other big problem: overpopulation. More wells providing safe water allowed many more children to survive infancy, and yet the birthrate still reflected the traditional wish to produce as many children as possible, both as a matter of pride, and a pragmatic facing of the odds. In Mali, even in the 1990s, nearly one in five babies would not survive infancy — but not long ago that ratio would have been two or even three out of five, so in an ironically tragic way, the blessing of clean water only exacerbated the curse of overpopulation.

The only corrective would be birth control, not just as an altruistic wish for Africa's future, but as the greatest problem facing the world. China's methods of enforcing its "one couple, one child" program had been questioned, but the Chinese had achieved it, and in the process they had saved their descendants from being even more overcrowded and underfed than their suffering ancestors were.

Again, birth control was a politically-charged issue in Africa, because of the paranoid delusion that its promotion by the West was a racist plot to wipe out the Africans. And the Pope, with shockingly *blind* faith, had recently shared this wisdom with the African people, as I quoted it in *The Masked Rider*:

> Birth control programs carry a powerful antilife mentality. They suppress the African people's healthy love of children. You must beware of the streak of crass Western materialism in development.

Family planning was "antilife?" The "healthy love of children" was incompatible with a love of healthy children? But when the aid organizations faced that kind of political and religious resistance to reproductive issues, they backed away and concentrated on less-controversial programs. Following my own experiences in Africa, I contributed to these organizations and wrote letters to them, urging them to devote more resources to this worthy cause, but they claimed they had to leave such a delicate matter in the hands of the national governments.

All afternoon we scrabbled across that plain, pounding over the hard mud or skidding in the sand. Several times we lost the road again, and had to regroup and scout for it, but eventually we emerged at a real road, with only a few miles to go now to our destination, the town of Somadougou. While we waited at the junction to regroup before making the turn north, a battered old truck went roaring by in a cloud of dust and diesel, which enveloped and choked us for a long minute. Then just as that subsided, a minibus went racing by in the other direction, trailing another shroud of dust. At least, with all we'd been through on that back route, we'd had no fear of traffic and no choking dust.

Before we set off I tied my bandana over my face, bandit-style, then followed David and Patty up the road, the rest trailing behind. After almost forty miles of such arduous cycling, Herb was completely exhausted. He told us he would be taking it slow the rest of the way, and probably stopping often to rest. No problem, we would wait for him at the crossroads in Somadougou.

As I rode along the gravel road, a secondary route leading down to Burkina Faso, I found it offered its own challenges — deep trenches and washboard corrugations left from the rainy season — and I had to steer to either side of the road to avoid them, and sometimes onto the smoother footpath above the roadside. Bright clusters of people were traveling toward us, returning home from the market in Somadougou, and we were greeted with a smile and wave by every one of them. People riding in donkey carts, or women walking in rows with headloads, all of them were smiling and gracious. Although I felt tired and a little disheartened by the day's hardships, their genuine smiles of welcome soon charmed me into my own genuine smiles of appreciation.

The only extra difficulty this entailed was the right-handedness syndrome. In most parts of Africa, the right hand had to be used for every action of etiquette, from eating to pointing out which oranges you wished to purchase, and that dexter-bias included waving. Thus I spent most of that ride with my right hand in the air greeting the steady stream of passing people, and my left arm had to support my weight on the handlebars as well as control the bike. My body was already tired and aching, and it would have been nice to alternate the waving hand at least, but one doesn't want to offend when only wishing to be neighborly. (This custom would become so ingrained during our travels that for weeks after I returned home I found myself avoiding the use of my left hand, always careful even to put down my drink and pick up a potato chip with my right hand.)

The road ended at the crossroads of Somadougou, where it met the main road — a *paved* road, I was pleased to note, the first one we'd seen since riding from Bamako to meet the riverboat at Koulikoro, almost a week before. In late afternoon, the town was still bustling with the end of market day, and the main road brought a steady stream of minibuses and trucks through the milling crowds. While David went off to reconnoiter, Patty and I parked our bikes against a stone wall and settled in to wait for the others. With Herb feeling as he had been, we expected a bit of a wait, but at the end of a long ride, sitting down to rest for awhile was no hardship. I leaned back against the wall, and even though it was made of jagged rocks and was about as comfortable as leaning against a porcupine, I sighed with pleasure and stretched my legs out in the dirt and stones.

"I don't know how this can possibly feel good, but it does," I said to Patty, and she agreed that at the end of a long struggle, anything felt good as long as it was over. She had just finished training for a marathon back home in Seattle, so she knew about suffering and relief. While we waited, I told her about some of the bike rides I had done in the U.S. during our concert tours. Talking about it with her, in that environment, it occurred to me that apart from the feeling of independence and escaping from the machinery of the tour for a day, one of the great joys for me on those rides was *arriving* — after spending eight or ten hours on the bike, laboring through whatever the day's obstacles had been: heat and dust, cold and rain, winds and traffic, rolling Carolina hills or unpaved Utah mountain passes, I would check into a good hotel, drink some whisky, take a long hot shower, then order a room-service dinner and just lie around feeling drained, yet so *vital*.

During our *Power Windows* tour, in 1986, I rode from Savannah, Georgia, to Atlanta, a distance of about 175 miles, the most I'd ever ridden in one day. I had left in the dark, before dawn, and was still riding fourteen hours later, navigating the suburbs of Atlanta, when it got dark again.

I arrived at the Ritz-Carlton and wheeled my bicycle into the lobby, asking for my key. A hotel security man came up and started to tell me I had to leave my bicycle outside, but he had picked the wrong time, the wrong place, and the wrong man. For once I wasn't afflicted with what Saul Bellow called *trepfverten*, the words you think of on the stairs when you're leaving, and I turned around and said through gritted teeth: "I am paying for 40 rooms in this hotel, and I have just ridden 175 miles. Leave me alone."

He did.

I was telling Patty about the joy of rolling my bike into a room at the Ritz-Carlton in Houston, say, or the Four Seasons in Newport Beach, and pampering myself with every luxury and a room-service feast after a day of dirt, exhaust fumes, sweat, exertion, and inevitable fear caused by road hazards and traffic —

Then, all at once I stopped talking about all that luxury, realizing it was an unprofitable fantasy at present. I leaned back against the sharp stones, legs splayed in the dirt, wiped my grimy face with a dirty bandana, and took another sip of the warm, frog-tinctured water from the nameless village. As Patty and I agreed on the surprising excellence of that water, and the surprising comfort of leaning against a wall of pointy stones, a new theme for our journey was born: "The Decline of Western Values." Of course it wasn't really a *decline*, more a realignment to reduced expectations, but it became a running joke throughout the tour as our standards of necessity and luxury were . . . rebalanced.

Back home, you might be accustomed to a comfortable bed, but you learn to be grateful for a foam slab between your mosquito tent and the ground. You can learn to live on fried-egg sandwiches every morning, and rice with sauce every night; you can survive filtering water out of clay pots or green wells; you can get through a day with dirty fingernails and gray socks. After a week of hole-in-the-ground toilets and bucket baths, a stained toilet with no seat and a cold shower looked like luxury. Maybe you would seldom drink soda pop at home, but riding a bike in Africa might make you so hot and dehydrated that you only pedal onward inspired by the hope of a warm Fanta in the next village, maybe even two. Some people won't drink water if it's warm — on a bicycle in Africa, you like it hot. And frog-flavored.

The Decline of Western Values. Sometimes I had referred to it as "The Cleansing" — leaving my comfortable life and comforting vices to go off to Africa for a month of physical exertion and privation, with tropical heat and bugs, no chocolate bars, infrequent plumbing and electricity, bucket baths, too much rice, and no single malt whisky.

The reasons for taking those Bicycle Africa trips were hard to justify to some people. Like your wife, or husband; it was illustrative that five of our six cyclists in Mali had spouses at home who wouldn't *think* of joining their partners on such a masochistic enterprise. And when I told my friends that I was going back to Africa, after the stories they had heard from last time, they usually just asked, "Um — why?"

I struggled for an easy answer, but it was too complicated. I could never explain the ineffable reward, why it was worth a bit of hardship to experience Africa in that way. The only response I could think of was, "It's good for my values." Not the whole story, but in truth a large part of it. At home I led a happy, rewarding life, lacking nothing I really wanted, so once in a while it was healthy for me to Get Basic, to reduce life to elementary concerns: Will I have enough water to drink? Will this leaking tube hold air for another 40 kilometers or should I stop and fix it? Can I buy a warm Fanta in the next village? Will we find a place to stay tonight? Some rice? Some water?

Perhaps my two themes belonged together: "The *Cleansing* of Western Values." Maybe that answered the "Why do it?" question.

But it was still more complicated than that. In the short term, those African journeys refreshed me by the contrast with my own way of life, but in the long view, I felt a permanent sense of growth. Although I remained willingly attached to my own culture, I had experienced the positive aspects of African ways, and I embraced them — added them to my world-view, and thus it expanded. While I remained ambitious, punctual, and hedonistic at home, I had learned to better appreciate the timeless beauties and blessings of nature, to value sincerity as a cardinal virtue and reject the Western reverence for affectation and hypocrisy, and to make my frantic life pause for sunrises, sunsets, and full moons.

And of course, when I returned to my frantic life after a month in Africa, I *really* appreciated it. The simple things were special again, and often remained that way for a long time. Hot showers, flush toilets, cool sheets, clean dishes, good food, unlimited drinking water — the basic Western amenities which too many of us took for granted, and too many others did without.

Also in the "Why do it?" department, I was always reminded of the old joke about the man who was asked why he kept banging his head against the wall, to which he replied: "It feels so good when I stop!" In America, that was the sense of blissful relief that made checking into a luxurious hotel after a hard bike ride a heavenly reward, instead of the usual routine of stumbling off the bus in the predawn hours and complaining because the luggage was slow to arrive, or there was no twenty-four-hour room service. After an African trip I loved my home and my life in such a wholehearted way for the same reason: simple relief. It was good to feel that I had suffered to achieve a goal, but it was even better to know that the suffering was over.

So I told people: "I like Bicycle Africa because it's good for my values . . . and . . . It feels so good when I stop!"

Herb, though, wasn't feeling so good that day. When he finally came riding up with Theresa and Silvia, who had stayed with him during his slow progress, he straddled his bike like a broken man and slumped over the handlebars. The last part of the ride had been hell for Herb, and he looked it. He had felt increasingly weak and light-headed, and had to stop and rest every few minutes toward the end. Runners called that "hitting the wall"; cyclists called it "bonking" — being completely drained of all energy and reserves — and Herb said he'd never had it so bad. He felt like he could lie down at the side of the road and just pass out, but he didn't want to stop until he could *stop*, so we pedaled on into the town together, looking for a place to buy drinks and let Herb rest.

Although Somadougou was a busy market town and minibus terminal, its amenities were limited. We pedaled down the main drag looking for a store or a *buvette* (a drink stand), but we found no signs, and after a half mile the town abruptly ended. We turned around, realizing we were going to have to look harder. David and I started asking people, and finally we were directed to a doorway in a mud wall. Inside was a tiny courtyard with a couple of benches to one side, where Herb immediately collapsed. A hand-lettered sign advertised all kinds of soft drinks, but in reality, all those sodas and juices existed only on the *sign* — the shop had only three bottles of the pineapple soda, *ananas*, and a couple of bottles of tonic water. I passed the first bottle of *ananas* back to Herb, who drank it down gratefully, and the rest of us made our choice between the last two bottles of *ananas*, or tonic water. Fortunately David said he didn't want any, so there was one for everyone — though most of us would have poured down two or three bottles if there had been more.

Over many years of traveling in Africa, David had learned what a costly addiction soft drinks could become, and being something of a Stoic, as well as on a tight budget, he seldom indulged. Because you were constantly hot and thirsty, bored with drinking endless liters of water, and also because there were no other luxuries available, many people who wouldn't ordinarily include Coca-Cola or Fanta in their diets were shocked to find themselves drinking six or eight bottles a day, and it could get expensive. Some days your thirst seemed unquenchable, and there were no fruit juices, no electrolyte-replenishing sports drinks, no California Coolers — just plain, warm water, and even that was seldom as deliciously frog-enhanced as the supply that was currently dwindling in our water bottles. So even if you allowed yourself one soda each time you stopped for a rest at a *buvette*, and maybe had one or two Fantas with your rice and sauce (a natural combination, I think, like Sauterne with *foie gras*, frozen vodka with caviar, chocolate with cognac), they soon added up. The sugar in those drinks was probably also a welcome stimulant, and sometimes the caffeine in Coca-Cola could be a much-needed lift (though it would probably be better if it still had a little coca in the formula). One morning in Senegal, when we'd been unable to find any breakfast, Herb rode up beside me and laughed to admit that he'd reached new depths in the Decline of Western Values. With a mixture of pride and shame, he announced: "Two Cokes before breakfast today!"

Asking among the locals, David learned that Somadougou's *case de passage* (hostel) was across the street, and he left us with Herb, who was as immobile on the bench as Lenin in his tomb, and went over to see about our accommodations. Soon we were pushing our bikes across the street into a larger courtyard, full of goats, chickens, children, and cooking fires, and the usual row of airless guest-cells which made such fine garages. Warned against coming within range of one of the goats, which was *méchant* — vicious — we pushed our bikes into the cells, where Herb immediately found another narrow wooden bench and assumed the Lenin pose.

Now that we had actually arrived somewhere, my own body decided it was pretty tired, and I felt a sudden wave of fatigue. Feeling overheated and overworked, light-headed and unsteady, I found an inviting pile of dirt in the corner of the courtyard and lay down on it, watching as the children carried heavy buckets of water from the well outside to a small enclosure behind a corrugated metal door — the bathroom. A slender little girl struggled from the well with a full bucket that probably weighed more than she did; I wanted to get up and help her, but . . . I couldn't. Soon Patty, Theresa, and Silvia were taking turns in the mud closet, enjoying their luxurious bucket baths, and once my turn came, I could wash the sweat and dirt away and pour some cool water over my head. I began to feel a little better.

A steep mud stairway, sculpted into the adobe wall, led to the roof of the quadrangle, where peanuts and stringy-looking beans were spread to dry in the last rays of the sun. As we erected our mosquito tents in a row once again, I stood for a moment and looked over the rooftops of the town, cubes and rectangles of adobe among the trees, and heard the busy din of a crowd, shouts, laughter, blaring radios, and the roar of trucks and buses on the street beside us. This did not bode well for a restful night in Somadougou, but in fact it proved to be quieter than the smaller villages had been during the rooster-fest of the full moon. In any case, when you're that exhausted, there isn't much you can't sleep through, and I stretched out gratefully to rest until dinner was ready.

We gathered around a rough wooden table in the courtyard, where a kerosene lantern illuminated the inevitable rice and sauce. Maybe exhaustion had sapped my appetite, as it can sometimes do, but I had no interest in the lumpy rice and thin, unsavory sauce. The heat in the courtyard seemed unbearable, yet I had to spread my *pagne* over my legs to keep the flies off — the dilemma of a buggy place: you either try to put up with them, or cover yourself in repellent, which felt nasty, smelled worse, and even if you washed it off your hands, they soon picked it up again from scratching at other parts of your body, and it seemed to taint everything you ate and drank.

So I only stayed at the table long enough to eat a few bites of rice and filter some water (sadly, from the bucket which held the water our rice had been cooked in, so it was warm and had an acrid taste and smell I would have to live with all the next day). Then, although it was only 7:30, I retreated to the sanctuary of my tent, glad to stretch out in a bug-free zone and try to catch up on my notes. We had been on the move so much in the past few days, and had experienced so much input — the sights of Dogon country, the information imparted by our local guides — that we all agreed we felt a little dizzy from it all, that it would have been nice to have had an extra day to take it all in.

David understood that this wasn't complaining — if anything, we'd had too *much* of a good thing — and we certainly knew that in putting together an itinerary for a tour like this, which had never been done before (David liked to keep *himself* interested, and offered two or three different tours every year), he had so much to balance: the riverboat schedule, allowing as much time as possible in Dogon country, hitting the market days in towns like Bandiagara, or the next day's destination of Djenné, all while keeping the daily mileages reasonable.

On previous tours with David, I had seen the conflicting demands he could be faced with by unthinking clients: one complaining about having to leave so early every day, someone else going on about having to ride in the hot midday hours, another one not wanting to be riding late in the day; or one grumbling that the bike rides were too long, while another wanted the tour to cover more ground. Some people were less specific, and simply complained about everything. So David first had to put a lot of work into designing his itineraries, and then exercise a lot of diplomacy, cajolery, and pure will to get people to stick to them.

Fortunately our little group was an uncomplaining bunch, and the individuals were down-to-earth enough to face the realities of cycling in Africa with resilience and good humor. After ten days of traveling together, I had come to appreciate that, particularly after the punishing day we'd just endured, and I realized that this was the best Bicycle Africa group I had ever joined. Signing yourself up to spend a month living with a group of strangers under difficult conditions was definitely a risk, but even though I was feeling low that night in Somadougou, I was glad that at least I was suffering with people I liked.

The darkness had only just begun to fade, and the stars were still visible when I heard the beeping of David's watch alarm. We had agreed to get moving at 5:30, and try to be on the road by first light, around six. Everyone seemed to be awake already, and to rise almost in unison, folding their tents and bedding and carrying it down the steep steps to pack the bikes. By quarter to six it was twilight, and we were gathered around the rough wooden table in the courtyard filling our water bottles.

The morning was starting out badly for me, in the most basic ways — my water had that nasty rice flavor, and the mosquitoes had been so voracious during the night that if one of my feet or an elbow touched the tent wall it was attacked through the screen. The mosquitoes were still a torment, circling my face as I folded the tent; but promptly at ten to six they were gone, and the flies took over. Shift change. Now dozens of flies were crawling on my arms and legs while I tried to pump some more water — *sans riz* this time.

And more, both my tires were soft, with slow leaks, probably victims of all the thorns we'd ridden over the previous day. I hoped I could get through the day's ride by pumping them up as I went, and I would fix them properly, along with my punctured spare tube, somewhere more . . . comfortable.

And of all things, there were no *oranges*: one commodity that was almost always available in West Africa, and the one morning ritual I liked to count on. Quartering an orange with my Swiss Army knife, then squeezing out the juice between my teeth — no big deal, but a nice way to start the day, and I usually kept a few in my packs, but I hadn't been able to buy any for a few days. All I had in my packs was a sour, unripe tangerine, which was awful.

And no breakfast: the omelette man down the road had told David he would be there all night, but of course he was gone when David showed up. I had to settle for a hunk of bread and a Nescafé at a roadside stall, while constantly twitching under the hordes of flies. Even through my mood of silent frustration, I spared a thought for the people who had to *live* there, glad that at least I could leave — the sooner the better. Before the others had even wheeled their bikes outside I was gone, David pointing me in the right direction.

What a relief it was to be moving through the cool morning air on a paved road, with no traffic yet, and to be riding away from Somadougou, to be leaving all that behind me — except for the bad stuff I carried with me: evil-tasting water, soft tires, empty stomach, and ugly mood. I found myself having mental arguments about meaningless things with people who were thousands of miles away.

At least the paved road was a blessing that morning, and a layer of cloud was another welcome relief. Only once did I see my shadow stretch out long beside me as the sun peeked briefly through the overcast, and this helped to attenuate the morning heat, already bearing down on me heavily by 7:30. The landscape was desolate in that gray light, gravelly soil with a few scrubby bushes and thorn trees, and only a few low formations of layered rock to punctuate the flatness.

Even the glossy starlings looked dull with no sun to ignite their iridescence. A few hawk-like kites circled in the sky, hornbills flitted among the sparse trees, and gangs of pied crows scattered ahead of me, lifting heavily off the road as I interrupted their picking and scavenging — the odd crushed frog, but mostly donkey dung. A few small villages of adobe cubes and rectangles dotted the bush, huddled around some source of water which allowed ragged grass, millet fields, and a few greener trees, but the only real flashes of color were the Abyssinian rollers, vivid blue with purple wings and long black outer tail feathers, the jewels of the Sahel.

A slight headwind was just enough to make me feel I was laboring uphill all the time, and, after an hour and a half of steady pedaling, I had to pull off the road and pump up my front tire, still hoping I could keep my last spare tube in reserve in case I had a real flat. But an hour later the tire had gone dangerously soft again, so I decided I'd better resign myself to changing it, and started looking for a place to stop — preferably where I could get something to eat, or even a warm Fanta. I recorded this entry in the Captain's Log:

• Well, coming up to 9:00 now, three hours on the road. Just passed through a succession of tiny villages, but no towns big enough to have a *buvette*, or any drinks. Could use something now, feeling pretty hungry, and . . . well, hungry in the broader sense — I just *want* something. Land gone dry and gravelly again, but still overcast.

Spotting a baobab tree, I coasted off the road and leaned my bike against its wide trunk, pulled off the front wheel, and sat down to perform the familiar operation. Patty and David caught up with me while I worked, and informed me that the omelette man had arrived just after I'd left, and they'd all had breakfast. Great. David went ahead to the crossroads a few miles on, where we'd be turning north to Djenné, and as soon as I had reassembled my bike, Patty and I followed. Once again, there was nothing in the way of food or drink available at the crossroads, so I left David and Patty there waiting for the others, and started on the last stretch — thirty kilometers of unpaved road, which, David warned me, might be a little sandy.

Indeed it was. The road was heaved and rutted from the rainy season, and mined with patches of loose gravel and sandpits. The overcast had begun to break into shreds of blue sky, and the midday sun shone through to intensify the heat. Eventually the road became a dike running through a floodplain of low bush, rice fields, and stagnant waterholes left by the rains, and the terrible road and the featureless landscape just seemed to go on and on. I came to a settlement built of sculpted mud with an ornate mosque in the middle, and that fit the description of Djenné as far as I knew, so I stopped an old farmer to ask if it was. *Non.* He pointed up the road.

One long hour later I came to another settlement of sculpted mud, a bigger one this time, and with a larger and more ornate mud mosque. This must be it, I thought, and pedaled down off the dike and along one of the dirt paths into town, through the narrow mud-walled streets, and up to the mosque. Two boys were chasing me, so I asked them: "Djenné?," as I pointed around me. *"Non,"* they answered, and pointed up the road.

Man, I thought, with all these miniature Djennés, the people around here must be the masters-of-the-universe when it came to mudpies and sandcastles. But, where *was* this place?

Or, as I recorded my feelings at the time, with more feeling:

• Well, it's noon now and I still haven't got to this fucking place.

After six hours on the bike, changing a flat, no food, nothing left to drink but the acrid rice water, and an ever-worsening road, I was not having a good time. Although, if I'd known what an awful day Herb was having, way back there behind me, I wouldn't have felt so bad. He was perishing — weak and shaky as he struggled along without joy or hope, having to stop every twenty minutes just to collapse on his back at the roadside. The best cure for overexertion was definitely not more exertion, and since the day of the hike to Teli and the moonlight ride to Bandiagara, Herb had never regained his strength.

Early in the previous day's ride, Herb and I had been talking about the Decline of Western Values in terms of possessions: what were the most important things to us right now? "Well," he said, "my bike of course, but maybe the water filter most of all. I wouldn't want to try to get along without that."

"Agreed," I said, "the mosquito tent too, that's pretty precious to me."

Our priorities: water pump, bicycle, tent. Clean water, transportation, and shelter from insects.

Djenné never did appear, but the river did, a wide tributary of the Niger called the Bani. The road came to an abrupt end at the water's edge, as if there had once been a bridge there, perhaps in French colonial times, but now it ended bluntly at the river. There was nothing on the far shore but bush, so I was a little worried. I had asked every person I'd seen along that terrible road — both of them — if this was the right way to Djenné, and they had assured me it was. But maybe they had only been answering me in the literal African way: maybe it *used* to be the road to Djenné, until the bridge washed away, but now, "You can't get there from here."

A rutted track led off the dike and down to the riverside, so I followed it, hot, tired, disgusted with everything, and grimly hoping for a pleasant surprise — any pleasant surprise. And sure enough, they started coming at me.

At the river's edge stood a couple of crude buildings, and a gathering of people under a tree. As I straddled my bike, two youths came up immediately and welcomed me, and answered enough questions to put my mind at rest. Djenné was a few kilometers away on the other side of the river, and there was a ferry to carry us across. One of the young men introduced himself as Ibrahim, and told me that the owner of the hotel in Djenné had told him we were coming, and he had come to meet us. That was unlikely, but quick thinking on his part, as he began his "sales pitch," offering his services as our guide and telling me all the sights of Djenné he could show us. I held up my hand to stop him, and pointed to my water bottle — "*D'abord, de l'eau.*" First, some water. He nodded and smiled, and returned with a bowl of water while I unpacked my filter and started pumping, although once again I was drinking it down as fast as I could filter it.

As usual, the pump itself aroused much curiosity among the Africans, and all eyes were on me as I operated that mysterious device. A dozen women and children sat on the ground beneath a spreading tree, amid an assortment of produce and bracelets of beadwork or brass, but they made no attempt to sell me anything, just watched. Ibrahim seemed to be a sophisticated young man, though; when I explained that the pump made the water "*plus sain,*" healthier, he nodded sagely, "*Oui.*"

Once I had poured down enough water to satisfy my thirst for the moment, I committed a terrible faux pas — I took the bandana from around my neck and went to dip it in the last of the water. Ibrahim grabbed my hand. "*Non, non, pas comme ça!*" Not like that! Instead, he poured a little water onto the bandana, so the clean water would not be soiled. A thoughtless mistake — you never wasted clean water by plunging dirty hands or a sweaty bandana into it.

While I washed my face with the wet bandana, relishing the coolness and the relief of wiping away the dirt and sweat, I was eyeing the river. The wide sweep of glittering brown water seemed so tempting — dare I go for a swim? I asked Ibrahim if it was safe to swim in the river, and he assured me it was. I said that sometimes the rivers carried *les maladies*, and once again he nodded sagely, but he assured me this river was *"pas malade."*

Against my better judgment, I couldn't resist it. Pulling off my socks and shoes, I waded in — up to my knees, then to my waist, then to my neck. The water was warm, but at least a few degrees cooler than the early afternoon air, and cooler than my overheated body. With a sigh of glorious relief, I pulled up my legs and began to float, just keeping my head above water.

When I waded back to shore, Ibrahim asked, *"C'est bien?"* and I smiled and nodded, *"C'est fantastique!"*

Ibrahim and his friend Bambui had a low shelter of straw mats on the other side of the track, and I followed them over to it, ducked into the shade, and took a seat on the small stool they offered me. Ibrahim began to talk again about being our guide, and told me that Bambui had a pirogue which could take us across the river instead of the ferry, or if we wished we could hire a motorized pirogue to take us on a river trip. I explained to Ibrahim that he would have to talk to *le patron* — David — when he arrived, and he turned off the sales pitch.

Bambui seemed to be in the souvenir business, and I was soon surrounded by trays of bracelets, earrings, bronze figures, and carvings, though they were just placed around me, not shoved in my face. Ibrahim and Bambui were charming and friendly young men; they had business to conduct, but it was to be done with politeness and dignity. The three of us began to converse about all manner of things, stretching my French to its limit and beyond. Ibrahim told me he thought I spoke well, but he said my accent sounded *"comme les hollandaises."* I sounded like Dutch people speaking French? Ibrahim nodded and said, *"Oui."*

After almost two weeks of traveling in a French culture, speaking the language constantly and rehearsing it in my head all the time as well, I did feel it starting to flow a little. My original intent in learning French had been to converse with my neighbors in Quebec, and during a couple of our concert tours, the three of us in the band had arranged for the local Berlitz schools to send a French teacher to the arena for a lesson before the show. We had enjoyed that, and developed some facility with the language, but we were learning *Parisian* French. The slangy *Québécois* accent, *le joual*, continued to elude my ear: I could usually say what I needed to say, but I couldn't understand the *answers*.

After the 1989 Bicycle Africa tour, in Togo and Ghana, I had arranged to meet my wife and daughter at a resort in the Ivory Coast, for a more *civilized* family holiday. During our stay, I asked the archery instructor if he could teach me in English, and he replied, "I can *speak* English, but I don't *understand* it." That seemed an absurd statement, but I had come to know exactly what he meant, for that's how I felt in Quebec: I had learned to *speak* French fairly well, but I didn't understand their *answers*.

Other places I got along better, like in West Africa, or on the francophone Caribbean islands of Martinique or Guadeloupe. Those people naturally spoke slower and more distinctly, and consequently I had a much easier time understanding them. And there on the banks of the Bani River, talking with Ibrahim and Bambui under the straw-mat shelter, I found myself not just *speaking* French, but *being* French, no longer translating every phrase into the English language (and attitude), but listening and responding as a francophone version of myself, gesturing and "dramatizing."

Sometimes, groping for a word I couldn't find in French or English, I found myself caught between the two languages, in an autistic stutter. But when I got going and the phrases began to flow, I became drunk on words — feeling a little dizzy from the mental effort, but thoroughly enjoying myself.

Ibrahim asked if I would like to try a cup of their tea, which he called *da*, and I gladly accepted. Bambui stoked up a small charcoal brazier and filled the teapot with red flowers, the kind we'd seen growing in gardens around Dogon country and wondered what they were cultivated for (with water so scarce, nothing was grown just to *look* nice). After the flowers had boiled for a few minutes, Bambui poured the red liquid into a tiny teacup and passed it around, each of us taking small sips of the hot, sweet syrup, and it was delicious. They laughed when I kept asking for more. Ibrahim told me Europeans always liked *da* tea, and compared it to sweet wine or grenadine.

I asked if there was any food I could buy — I'd still eaten nothing but a crust of dry bread all day — and Ibrahim stooped out from under the shelter and walked over to the women and children under the tree, returning with a big green watermelon. That might not have been my first choice from a menu, but under the circumstances, a juicy watermelon seemed like a pretty good idea, and I bought it. When Ibrahim saw me pull out my little Swiss Army knife to try to slice it up, he went off again and borrowed a proper knife — a machete-sized cutlass — and I began to hack out slices and devour them, spitting the shiny black seeds out into the sunlight.

David and Patty arrived, having waited over an hour back at the crossroads for Theresa and Silvia, though Herb still hadn't shown up by the time they left. They joined me under the low pavilion of straw mats, and I offered them a slice of watermelon while Bambui stoked up the fire again, making more *da* tea. Ibrahim asked David if he could be our guide, but David was noncommittal, and when a family of whites in a Nissan 4x4 pulled up beside us, Ibrahim decided to try his chances with them, and left us. A short time later, Theresa and Silvia arrived, hot and tired, and when I invited them into the shady pavilion and offered them slices of melon, Theresa laughed and said, "You look like the *king* sitting there on your little throne, surrounded by your courtiers and dispensing favors."

"I *feel* like the king," I told her, and it was true; by that time I felt recovered and pampered and truly happy, and it hadn't taken much. The ingredients of happiness: some water to drink, a swim, a rest, some *da* tea, and a couple slices of watermelon.

It had been two hours now and Herb still hadn't appeared, and we were getting worried. As the small ferry made one of its infrequent appearances on the shore, I asked David if he wanted to go on to Djenné with the girls and I would wait for Herb, who had always been so good about waiting for me if I had a flat or something. But David thought the rest of us should see the market in Djenné before it got too late, gave me directions on how to find the *campement* where we were staying, and sent us off on the ferry. I had been guarding the last slice of watermelon for Herb, and David promised to save it for him.

Bambui and I had been casually bargaining over a pair of ebony earrings with copper *cloisonné* work for my daughter Selena, and an artificially-aged carving of two linked figures which I liked (Bambui had won my trust by willingly describing how it had "aged," buried underground for a few weeks). He and I hadn't been able to agree on a price yet, and in our sudden departure I forgot about it. A young boy appeared on the ferry as it was loading the 4x4 and a Land Rover from some development agency, and I saw that he was holding the earrings and the carving up to me. I offered the last price I'd mentioned, which Bambui had rejected, and the boy nodded and handed them over, carrying the few dollars back to Bambui.

The road on the other side of the Bani was even worse, almost unbelievably turbulent, like the double-black-diamond mogul run at a ski hill. The main track continued to run on top of a French-built dike, but the surface was so degraded that once again drivers had pioneered routes down to either side, and these too had become heaved and rutted during the rains. After a few kilometers, an adobe arch appeared, and as we rode nearer it came to dominate the view like an immense tower, its opening big enough for a bus to pass through, and the squared-off top artfully decorated with turrets and loopholes. This, we would soon see, was a fitting gateway to the medieval city of Djenné.

Djenné was set on an island formed by the inland delta of the Niger and its tributaries, and was one of the oldest towns in West Africa, dating at least from the 9th century. During medieval times it grew on the profits of trans-Sahara trade, like Timbuktu, and a European visitor in the early 18th century reported that the citizens were literate, busy, well-dressed, and enjoyed a good standard of living. It had remained remarkably unchanged, and the Lonely Planet guidebook called it "unquestionably one of the most interesting towns in West Africa."

Over a bridge and into the narrow dirt streets of the walled town, winding through the uniform brown of adobe walls and buildings, sometimes studded by beam-ends and decorated with ornately-carved wooden shutters. Passing a wall under repair, I could see how they were made: bricks of mud and straw over a frame of wood, then plastered over with wet mud, sometimes in ornamental relief. The interior layout of the houses also testified to the history of slavery in Djenné, going back long before the arrival of Europeans — traditionally, the top part of the house was for the masters, the middle for the slaves, and the bottom floor for storage and selling.

In the center of town we emerged into the wide marketplace, filled with the color and noise of market day, and one side of it dominated by a monumental mosque, a splendid palace of mud towers and minarets capped by ostrich eggs. Considered the best extant example of Sudanese-style mud architecture , Djenné's *Grande Mosquée* dated from 1905, though it replaced a similar one which had stood for nine centuries, until it was destroyed in a religious disagreement. The other constant enemy of the mosque was rain; every year large areas of the mud had to be resurfaced, and for this purpose the exposed beam-ends were used as scaffolding.

We paused only briefly for an open-mouthed look at the *Grande Mosquée*, then kept riding, looking for the *campement* so we could dump our bikes and walk around freely. The walled compound of the *campement* was built around a circular driveway, the main building with an outdoor dining terrace, and a row of round, thatched guest cabins. Once again, we would only use those cabins as garages, for cooler and more scenic sleeping was available on the adobe roof of the main building.

As soon as I had checked us in and wheeled my bike into the "garage," I headed back to the market for a longer look at that incredible mosque, and to wander among the stalls. Djenné's would-be guides, merchants, and mendicants were all extremely persistent, and if Ibrahim and Bambui had represented the "soft sell," the courtyard of the *campement* was definitely the hard sell. It began as soon as we pulled up on our bikes. Tables under the trees were spread with masks, carvings, jewelry, and bronze figures, and the young men behind them were constantly trying to cajole us into looking at their wares. A crowd of lounging youths on the terrace represented the "guide guild," and they also began their overtures, until I used the same excuse I'd used with Ibrahim — they must wait for *le patron* and talk to him. A platoon of small boys made up the beggar squads, some of them crippled, but many just following the Islamic custom: young boys studying with the *marabout*, or holy man, were expected to survive by begging on the streets, to teach them humility.

David was to call Djenné the "in-your-face" town — especially when he arrived and everyone I had told to wait for *le patron* jumped on him — but it was true for all of us. We started calling them the "*kram-kram* people," after those pesky burrs that attached themselves to us and were so hard to remove. The Lonely Planet book recommended hiring a guide even if you didn't need one, just to keep the other ones away, but I got along by following the usual rules: move fast; don't make eye contact; just say "*Non.*" Herb came up with a good line for the pests: "I said *no* — which word didn't you understand?" Even delivered in English, the message seemed to get across.

On my way through the courtyard, I managed to shrug off most of the guides, pedlars, and beggars, but one young mendicant wouldn't give up. He wore a homemade leg-brace and a single crutch, but he was amazingly agile, and ought to have been tearing up the Special Olympics. His irregular clumping followed me out into the street, *da-clomp, da-clomp,* though I refused to look around, just picked up my pace to lose him. But he would not be lost so easily; he was still right there behind me, speeding up his own rhythmic *da-clomp, da-clomp.* It was becoming a little creepy, and I strode into the crowds around the market, thinking I would surely lose him as I wove through the people around the stalls.

But no — there it was behind me again, *da-clomp da-clomp.* I whirled around to confront him, waving my hand and hissing: "*Allez, allez — laissez-moi de la paix!*" Go away — leave me in peace!

He just looked up at me with a twisted, defiant smile and held out his hand, palm up. I turned and sped off again, weaving between the people and hurrying along the rows of produce. I slowed for a moment to look for some oranges, and there he was again, *da-clomp da-clomp*. Exasperated both by this morbid shadow and the lack of oranges in the Niger Delta, I stepped over some baskets of yams, squeezed between two stalls and into the next lane, then almost *ran* down to the end of the market square and in the open door of a shop. Feeling hidden in the shadowy interior, I looked around for a few minutes, inspecting the selection of wares in this typical West African store: blocks of coarse soap, dusty boxes of biscuits, sugar, and salt, old bottles reused as containers for kerosene, cheap flash-lights and batteries from China, battered tins of cooking oil, tomato sauce, and condensed milk, burlap bags of rice, and a stack of exercise books, a baby outfit on a hanger, and a used tire for a moped.

And when I went outside, there he was: standing across the street, lean-ing against one of Djenné's few trees with that cold, challenging smile — and his leg-brace in his hand. With an expressive little nod, almost a bow, he turned and walked away, perfectly sound. I shook my head, and went to look at the mosque for a while, then headed back to the *campement*, to find that Herb and David had finally arrived.

It had taken Herb two hours longer than the rest of us, but he had made it. Now he slouched in a chair on the terrace, shattered, but able to smile at least, as he sipped a beer and thanked me for saving him a slice of watermelon. He said that during the last eighteen miles, while riding along that terrible road atop the dike, he'd been setting the alarm on his watch for twenty minutes at a time, and forcing himself to keep pedaling until it beeped. Then he would stop, drop his bike at the roadside, and lay down, whether or not there was even any shade available.

It was then that a quote I'd found in Nietzsche joined our growing list of Bicycle Africa mottoes: "What does not kill me makes me stronger."

We would all be considerably stronger before that trip was over.

✪

And for me, even after it.

Two weeks after I arrived home, I was stricken with a vicious fever of

104°, alternately sweating and freezing, and feeling what I could only describe as "pain in every molecule." My doctor sent me to the Tropical and Infectious Diseases department at the Toronto General Hospital, and my wife Jackie dropped me off there, to spend four hours in their waiting area, delirious most of the time, shivering in my winter coat. I occasionally dozed off into hallucinatory, febrile dreams, between staggering off into the vast labyrinth of the hospital to submit bodily fluids to hidden laboratories. By that time, late in 1992, AIDS had long been a full-blown epidemic, and its victims were also treated in the Infectious Diseases department (though sadly, there *was* no real treatment then), and I sat in my feverish nightmare state watching cadaverous, doomed shadows come and go.

I had first suggested to the nurse that I might have caught malaria, and she agreed that seemed likely. The chief specialist of the department must have overheard her, for sometime during that phantasmagoric day, I heard a stern voice scolding her for daring to hand out a diagnosis. When I finally saw the specialist myself, he said I should come back the following day for the malaria test results.

The fever continued through that night, with bed-soaking sweats alternating with uncontrollable shivering, and I was back the next morning, sitting in the hard plastic chairs in my winter clothes, still delirious, hardly aware of time or place. The malaria test was negative, and I was sent to various labs around the hospital to have my bodily fluids analyzed some more, this time for the various strains of hepatitis. On the third day of my delirium, the chief specialist called me into his office and said they had tested me for the usual tropical diseases of malaria, yellow fever, hepatitis, typhoid, and cholera, but I didn't have any of those. When I asked what I *did* have, he said that people sometimes returned from Africa with mysterious fevers that were *never* identified. They either went away on their own, or, he smiled, "you die."

And with those uncomforting words, he sent me home.

That night the fever broke, I felt it clearly. Although my symptoms remained the same, I just *knew* it was over. I was soon feeling fine again, and forgot all about the "Oogabooga Fever," as I had christened it (with great cultural insensitivity).

Several months later, I was at a residential studio, an old farmhouse in a rural area just outside Toronto, working with the band on what would become our *Counterparts* album. I began having some strange new symptoms: large, itchy red welts appearing on my arms and legs, sometimes in prominent egg-sized bumps, and I felt constantly tired, unwell, and generally allergic, with irregularities of color and frequency in the "plumbing" as well. Also, I seemed to have developed asthma for the first time in my life, and my doctor prescribed one of those ventilators. That alleviated the symptoms, but not the condition, and one cold winter day I was out in the park with our dog, Nicky, and suddenly I couldn't breathe. Trying not to panic, drawing in slow, steady breaths, I walked slowly and carefully back home, back to the ventilator, and from then on I never went anywhere without it.

As the symptoms piled up and gradually worsened, I began to worry a little, but tended to put it down to the stress of working on the new record. I had suffered from strange stress-related symptoms before, from heart arrythmia to toothaches to anxiety attacks, so I knew how insidious stress could be.

Along with working on lyrics and drum parts for the Rush album, I was also transcribing my notes and tapes from the Mali-Senegal-Gambia trip, and I paused when I encountered the quote from Schopenhauer I had recorded in the Gambia, "Every great pain, whether physical or spiritual, declares what we deserve; for it could not come to us if we did not deserve it" — not to forget my automatic editorial comment at the time ("What an asshole!"). Wanting to know more about a so-called philosopher who could write such an evil thought, I walked out to the bookshelf in the living room of the old farmhouse, to an old set of encyclopedias. I pulled out the appropriate volume, and as I paged through looking for Schopenhauer, I came across an entry for "schistosomiasis," and thought, "Hmm, I've heard of that."

I read the description of the disease, and its symptoms: "skin rashes, asthmatic episodes, malaise, urinary infection," and suddenly the thunder rolled, the lightning flashed, and the penny dropped: "Ohmygod! — I *have* this!"

Other phrases leaped off the page and into my brain, "severe morbidity and mortality," "chronic ill health," "ultimately fatal," and I immediately called the Tropical and Infectious Diseases department at the Toronto hospital, asking to speak to the big-shot doctor.

"Did you test me for schisto?"

"Hmm, let me check your file . . . Well, no, but I don't think you have *that.*"

I don't know why he felt so sure, as the World Health Organization listed schistosomiasis as the "second most prevalent tropical disease after malaria," but I told him, "I am coming in tomorrow, and you are going to test me for it."

Sure enough, that's what I had picked up in my ill-advised float in the Bani River, a water-borne parasite that passed through the skin and into the bloodstream, spreading its infectious eggs through the internal organs, especially the liver (I flashed back to the doctor looking at my test results and remarking that my liver function was reduced, then giving me an accusatory look ("Any idea why *that* should be?,") as if it were somehow my fault. He knew I was a musician, and perhaps presumed I was by definition a raging alcoholic).

Fortunately, though the disease was considered "ultimately fatal," there was a cure, but it didn't sound pleasant. Until the '70s, the remedy had been a dose of *arsenic*, described as "nearly as dangerous as the disease." The trick was to prescribe a dose strong enough to kill the schisto flukes, but not the host. The modern remedy was still a poison, but apparently more controllable, and consisted of about eight large capsules to be taken at once. And the doctor warned me, "Don't plan anything for the day you take them — you won't be feeling very well."

And I was deathly ill for a couple of days, a rerun of the "Oogabooga Fever," then the symptoms seemed to fade away. A few weeks later, I returned to the Tropical and Infectious Diseases department to be tested.

The doctor pronounced me cured, and when I remarked what a strange ordeal it had all been, he looked at me with his usual self-satisfied expression and said something I could hardly believe: "Well, at least we were able to catch it."

We?

I just looked at him for a beat, then said, "*We? We* didn't 'catch' anything! Remember, you told me I would either get better or *die*, then sent me *home*. It was pure luck that, four months later, *I* happened to look up Schopenhauer in the encyclopedia!"

He just gave me a withering look, and I shook my head, turned and walked out of his office, carrying away a newly diminished respect for him and his profession.

However, I had learned that even a bad philosopher could save your life.

Verse Five

"Riding through the Range of Light to the wounded city"

A few days after I got home from the Big Bend trip, with that one journal entry gathering strength and size in my head — "a story could be written just around the music I've listened to on this trip" — I started writing. Setting a modest goal of a page or two a day, I kept the project from taking over my whole life (for awhile). As I listed all the CDs I had listened to and thought of the story they added up to, I considered all the other stories I might want to weave into it, digging through the past, like an auto-archaeologist.

The etymology of "nostalgia" derives from root words meaning "return home" and "pain," though its common usage seems to signify more of a sigh of longing — not for home, but for the *past*, a sense that "then" was better than "now." Or at least, the nostalgic person *remembered* it that way.

Not me. I have no desire to relive any of those times. I was just passing through — "just looking." And taking notes. And names.

The longing for "home" is a common theme in art and life, but that attachment to a *place* is surely overrated, or misstated. "Home" is a feeling about yourself, not the place around you, and you *can* take it with you.

The longer I stayed in my "hometown" of St. Catharines, the less at home I felt there. London felt like home, as it still does, but the more I traveled, the more the *world* became a comfortable place to be. Africa, America, Toronto, Quebec, and a thousand hotel rooms in between.

As I discovered when I first moved to Santa Monica, all I *really* needed was a small suitcase, a portable stereo, and a bicycle. And love. Now Los Angeles was home too.

The title *Traveling Music* seemed obvious and right (with a nod to Jackie Gleason), and I began thinking about everything those two words meant to me, and what I might want to put into a book with that title. A larger shape began to materialize, almost of its own accord.

In the two perspectives I wanted to explore, present day and distant past, I saw a pattern that reminded me of songwriting. Those alternating moods, or frames, could be cast as verses and choruses, maybe even with a middle section set apart somehow, to be a "middle eight." I could see the possibilities, and started trying different ways of imposing that architecture (or "archi-texture," as my editor, Paul McCarthy, and I came to call it during the revisions). I would begin each section with a lyrical line, and maybe try to tie them all together into an actual song at the end.

My ambition for the work was growing, but most of all it felt good to be writing again, watching the pages mount up, even one or two at a time. I didn't worry about imposing form yet, but just worked at the difficult, but satisfying task of translating experience into words. As the great editor Max Perkins counseled, "Don't get it right, get it *down*." Or a more urgent version that occurred to me recently, "Get it down before it gets away."

Despite my early addiction to reading, and years of writing lyrics, prose writing had not really begun to interest me until my 20s — perhaps once there was *room* for it alongside the obsession with music. However, the connection was the same: I had first wanted to play music because I loved to listen to it so much, and likewise with books: I loved to read, so I wanted to write.

In my mid-20s, while on the road with Rush, I went to a pawnshop in Arkansas and bought a used typewriter. I carried it with me on tour, and made an attempt at the inevitable first novel, first trying a science fiction story built around the songs from *2112*, then a Hemingwayesque evocation of a "fictional" musician, who just happened to live and work in the same world I did.

However, I found I couldn't sustain my *own* interest, never mind a reader's, and in the way Ralph Ellison described his first apprenticeship writings, I set those early efforts aside. I also worked on several short stories that were "promising" (as they remain), and toward the end of the '70s, I began to turn out an ongoing series of background stories as press releases and "bios" to accompany Rush tour books and album packages. In that forum, what I wrote was more important than how I wrote it, so I challenged myself by experimenting with form and "voice." Around 1977, the Toronto *Star* asked me to write a story about beginning a tour, and although it was a disaster (badly written, and even more badly edited), perhaps all of those early essays (in the sense of the French word *essayer*, "to try") helped steer me toward wanting to learn how to write about real people and real places. No doubt doing hundreds of interviews about myself and the band over the years taught me to verbalize my thoughts and feelings, and I also began the habit of writing letters to distant friends, which was not just good therapy, but also good writing practice.

For twenty years I also answered every fan letter that passed into my hands, whether through the office, *Modern Drummer* magazine, or just thrown onstage. As a young musician who had so recently been a young fan myself, it seemed the Right Thing To Do. During the first two or three years with Rush, the fan letters were few, but I answered them elaborately, with little drawings and decorations, and as our popularity grew and the letters began to multiply, I had postcards made with a photo of me and my drums on the front, and, using a template on my computer, composed a little answer for each one, personalized and offering appreciation and encouragement, as appropriate. Every few months, I would set aside a whole day and plow through as many as I could, often fifty at a time, adding up to hundreds, if not thousands, from the '70s to the '90s.

By about 1996, though, with the rise of the internet and its "fan sites," too many people began to know about my little postcards, and suddenly the flood of mail multiplied, and became impossible for me to deal with. Feeling guilty, and not knowing what else to do, I asked *Modern Drummer* to run a little announcement that I would no longer be answering my fan mail, and explaining why ("because of the World Wide Gossip Net"). To my shock and hurt, the subsequent letters section was filled with attacks on me, for apparently criticizing the internet (a kind of religion in those early days), and for implying that people had given away some kind of "secret."

However, recently I did an interview with a writer from *Drum* magazine, and the young writer showed me a framed postcard I had sent him in 1992, encouraging him in his drumming and writing ambitions, and I felt a kind of vindication of my karma.

In September of 1985, I joined that bicycle tour in China, and carried a journal and microcassette recorder with me, but deliberately no camera, experimenting with the idea of seeing the journey entirely through my own lenses, and trying to put it down in words. After that experience, I was moved to spend some time refining the narrative to a modest degree, and printed up a small private edition of fifty copies for fellow travelers and friends. *Riding the Golden Lion* led to other bicycle journeys, from Munich to Istanbul, from Barcelona to Bordeaux, from Calgary to Vancouver, and other little books: *The Orient Express, Pedals over the Pyrenees, Raindance over the Rockies*. Knowing these writings weren't for public consumption, I experimented freely with modes of description and narrative, from stream-of-consciousness to incorporating myths and tribal wisdom. Then came Africa, with an initial camping safari and Kilimanjaro climb that became *the african drum* (fashionably lower case, that one), followed by a bicycle tour in West Africa which would finally produce a book I was ready to publish, *The Masked Rider*.

In prose writing, as a "second career," I wasn't obliged to do my "growing up" in public, as I had in music, and personally, I would not mind if my first five years of drumming and lyric-writing with Rush could be consigned to oblivion, or limited to "private printings." But there it is, one's early, groping efforts remain on display forever, like a child's drawings on the refrigerator.

After writing a few magazine stories on bicycling and motorcycle touring, gaining more experience and confidence, the circumstances of my life dictated the next book, *Ghost Rider*, a story I pretty much *had* to write, as it became part of the very "healing road" described by the subtitle, "Travels on the Healing Road." *Ghost Rider* had been remarkably well received, considering the dark theme, and had driven me to explore new aspects of "travel writing." More experiments were developed and refined in essays written to accompany our *Vapor Trails* album, and the *Rush in Rio* DVD, and now I wanted to cast my net a little wider, covering more than just a single voyage, but rather the *big* voyage.

Sifting through those decades and those memories, I realized I wasn't interested in recounting the facts of my life in purely autobiographical terms, but rather I became inspired by the notion of trying to unweave the fabric of my life and *times*. As one who was never much interested in looking back, if only because I was always too busy moving forward, I found that once I opened those doors to the past, I became fascinated with the times and their effect on me.

The songs and the stories I had taken for granted suddenly had a resonance that clearly echoed down the corridors of my entire life, and I felt a thrill of sudden interest, the sense of a kind of *adventure*. A travel story, but not so much about *places*, as about music and memories. And a journey that was still unfolding.

In May, I traveled up to Quebec with a list of questions for the book I wanted to look up in my library and archives at the house on the lake. Later in the week, I drove over to Ontario with my property manager, Keith, to meet with Brutus and look at some *new* properties. After Brutus's initial reconnaissance of the area in March, he had chosen three pieces of land that he thought were most interesting, and we went scouting.

At the second one, I had a "Brigham Young moment" (after Young led the Mormons on their cross-country trek in 1847, as they stood above the valley of the Great Salt Lake, he is reported to have said, "This is the place"). It was a 400-acre farm with a combination of rolling pastures and woods, a vast wetlands of reeds and meandering watercourses alive with birds, and a long stretch of shoreline on a large lake. Pastoral splendor of every kind. On the inland side, the original farm had been centered on a 150-year-old square-log farmhouse (abandoned, but restorable), with a couple of equally ancient, tumbledown barns. I knew I would want a house overlooking the lake, though, and along the property's mile of shoreline, at the end of a long wooded point, was the perfect site for a cabin.

The important thing was to find something to distract me from the wrench of giving up the Quebec house and its woods and lake, and as Keith, Brutus, and I explored the 400 acres and the shoreline, I began to get excited. The price was reasonable, and right then I decided to make an offer on the land. If I got it, I could wait until the Quebec place sold, then eventually build myself a little cabin on the end of that point.

Soon after I returned to Santa Monica, my offer on the land was accepted, and I became the owner of a farm in Ontario. My new neighbor up there wanted to continue renting the pastureland for his beef cattle and draft horses, and that would cover the land's expenses until I found a buyer for the Quebec property. I knew that might take a while, as it was both expensive and remote, but I could wait — the all-important "now what?" question had been answered.

Other questions continued to be answered too, as I continued my research in books, movies, music, and memories, and carried on writing, all the while enjoying home life, cycling to the Y three times a week, and my regular rounds of grocery shopping and cooking for my bride (of nearly three years now). Then one morning in the last week of June, I received a phone call from Rush's manager, Ray. He said he just wanted to "make me aware" of a situation that was developing, and a difficult decision we might have to make.

In the wake of the SARS epidemic in China, and its spread to Toronto, the city had been placed under a travel advisory by the World Health Organization, which amounted to a virtual quarantine on the whole city. Conventions, concerts, and sports events had been canceled, visitors were avoiding the city, and Toronto's restaurants and hotels, and their employees, were suffering — operating for months at a fraction of their capacity. The victims of the actual disease were relatively few, but the victims of the bad publicity were many.

Ray told me about a giant concert that had been proposed to help in revitalizing the city, and apparently the Rolling Stones were signed up to headline. They would be flying over for the one show, in the middle of their European tour, accompanied by their opening act, AC/DC. A vast park in North Toronto, a former airfield, was the planned venue, the date was July 30th, and the hype machine was working overtime — there was talk of hundreds of thousands of people attending, the biggest audience ever (or at least the biggest *paying* audience), and Ray told me it was already becoming a huge media event, with Canadian corporations getting on board as sponsors, promising to buy hundreds of thousands of tickets to give away in contests, and more and more different acts were being added to the show every day. It was a big story, and getting bigger.

Inevitably, as the most successful band ever to come out of Toronto, or Canada, our name had been mentioned. Geddy and Alex had grown up in the suburbs of Toronto, and still lived right downtown, and I had grown up just on the other side of Lake Ontario, and had lived in Toronto for fifteen years, so we were definitely a "hometown" band. Just that morning I had seen an article on America Online about a benefit concert that had been held the previous week in Toronto, in which several Canadian bands and performers had appeared, and even in that article the parenthetical question was raised: "Where's Rush?"

Already I could see it was going to be difficult to say no, yet it seemed impossible to say *yes*. We had been off the road for six months, out of practice for live performance; our equipment was packed away in its cases in the Toronto warehouse; most of our crew were out on other tours — including our main man, tour manager Liam, and my drum tech, Lorne. Apart from everything else, how could we do a show without them?

Geddy was vacationing in France with his family; Alex was working twelve-hour days in the studio on the tapes for our *Rush in Rio* DVD, and

I was leaving the next morning to spend a few days getting lost in the mountains, riding my motorcycle up into the Sierra Nevada. Ray said he thought the other two would agree to do it if I did, but he would need an answer soon.

"*How* soon?"

"Oh . . . tomorrow?"

Despite my misgivings, the issue seemed important enough not to dismiss out of hand, and I told Ray, "I doubt it, but I'll think about it." All night the question rattled around in my unconscious, and early the next morning it was right there, front and center, when I awoke and stole out of bed at 5:30, trying not to wake the light-sleeping Carrie. I had a quick breakfast, loaded up the bike, and rode into the cool morning twilight of the deserted streets of Santa Monica to the Pacific Coast Highway, then up along the misty shoreline through Malibu and Ventura, and inland to Ojai.

From then on I was free of traffic, buildings, or police, on one of my favorite roads, lonely, winding Highway 33, running north through the chaparral mountains and arid woodlands of Los Padres National Forest. Whether my getaway excursions were planned or improvised, they were always loops in and out of the metropolis, so as not to repeat the same roads, but they always seemed to include *this* road, in one direction or the other. The endless variety of corners, bends, switchbacks, and short straightaways, the rounded mudstone boulders in Adobe Canyon, the climb up to 6,000 feet, looking down into green, folded valleys, or out to the rugged badlands to the north — it was a perfect ride.

In early summer the road was lined with waist-high shrubs blooming with fragrant yellow flowers, filling my helmet with a strong, pungent, almost sickly-sweet perfume. Ground squirrels darted across the road ahead of me, scrub jays and mockingbirds flitted in the underbrush, and hawks and occasional vultures soared on high.

And all this time, as the front of my mind rode the motorcycle, choosing speed, lean angle, gear, and lane position, watching the pavement ahead of me for spilled gravel or other surprises, in the back of my mind I was mulling over the Concert for Toronto, weighing the pros and cons.

Difficult to say yes, impossible to say no.

The only actual con I could think of, other than all the *work* it would demand, was, "I don't want to do it," but that didn't seem sufficient against my usual criteria, trying to determine the Right Thing To Do.

At Maricopa I stopped for gas, then called Ray in Toronto. It was three hours ahead there, late morning, and I knew the decision needed to be made that day. I told him I was going to be out of reach for the next couple of days, but that I'd been thinking about that show. "I think we have to do it," I told him.

And with that, my mind switched over to work mode. I continued north through the bleak, dusty landscape and nodding oil derricks around Taft and McKittrick, thinking over every aspect of what I was in for, just one month away. The organizers only wanted us to play a half hour or so, but I knew that would take nearly as much preparation as a whole tour, because, after all, it had to be *good*.

So how much rehearsal would we need? My usual program in preparing for a tour was to have two weeks on my own, before the other guys came in, to smooth out my drumming technique and build up the calluses on my fingers by playing along with the CD versions of songs we were likely to play in concert. That would cement the definitive performances as a benchmark in my head, the arrangements, the parts, and especially the tempos, and also forced me to rise to the level of performance I had attained on the recordings. So, this time I would want a few days on my own, at least, then probably a few days with all three of us running through the songs together.

It was so hard to know how to approach this challenge. It was going to be different from anything we had ever done, in every way. Not just for its size, though that was part of it — we were hardly a "festival" type band. We were going to be an opening act, going on before AC/DC and the Stones, without the usual control over the technology, monitors, and such, and many of our songs depended on us being able to hear specific parts played or triggered by each other. We wouldn't be able to *count* on that at such an event, so it would be wise to minimize the complexity, the technology, and thus the risk of disaster. I thought about paring away some of my drumset, eliminating the electronics as much as possible (with old-fashioned drums and cymbals, at least you knew they were going to *work* when you hit them). Also, if Lorne wasn't going to be there (he was out on tour with Steely Dan's excellent drummer, Keith Carlock), I had to make the setup and the show as simple as possible for his replacement, so he wouldn't have to be worried about triggers, cables, hard drives, and programming changes.

Over all of that, there was the notion of playing in front of a huge crowd that wasn't necessarily there to see *us*. For the first time in maybe twenty-five years, we wouldn't be playing to "our" audience, preaching to the choir, and it seemed to me that, like the Chinese definition of "crisis," it was both danger and opportunity. If we chose a few songs from our thirty-year repertoire that were strong and accessible, we might be able to win over people who just *assumed* they didn't like us.

So what songs should we play?

As I rode through the dusty tan landscape and the unpretty, metal-trussed derricks of the oilfields along the western fringe of the San Joaquin Valley, I considered the possibilities. Mentally, I played through various Rush songs and considered their relative "accessibility" (as much as *I* could tell, anyway).

Strangely, though, it was Rolling Stones songs that kept ringing in my brain. Although I hadn't thought about it that way consciously, my unconscious seemed to be aware that we would be sharing the stage with that legendary band — whose resonance in my life, after all, went right back to *The T.A.M.I. Show*, almost 40 years ago, before I'd ever even touched a drumstick. (When I was asked for a press statement about the show, I remarked that after thirty years together, it was nice for us to be among the *younger* bands on that stage — considering the ages of the Guess Who, on before us, and AC/DC and the Stones after.) However superannuated Mick and the boys might be, and whether or not they lived up to their frequent billing as "the world's greatest rock 'n' roll band," they were certainly the most *successful* over the long run. And even though I had never been a huge Stones fan, had never owned any of their records (other than the album of standards released by Charlie Watts and friends, *Warm and Tender*), I could hardly escape *hearing* them over the decades (perhaps, as with the Beatles, I heard them so much it wasn't *necessary* to own their records!). My mental transistor radio started replaying some of their songs I did like: "Time Is on My Side," "Under My Thumb," "Paint It Black," "Playing with Fire," "Sympathy for the Devil," "Gimme Shelter," "You Can't Always Get What You Want."

As I turned eastward across the irrigated farmlands of the low-lying San Joaquin Valley toward the mountains, the morning grew ever hotter, baking up from the asphalt under a clear blue sky. I wore my summer, per-forated leathers, but the air seemed to be about 100°, and did little to cool me, however fast I rode. ("But officer, I was just trying to cool off!")

A quarter of America's food was grown in that long Central Valley, stretching up north to include the Sacramento Valley, and some of those humble, sleepy-looking towns, like Arvin, Weed Patch, or Corcoran, had surprisingly dramatic histories — the labor struggles of the *Grapes of Wrath* days, violent strikes, riots, vigilante attacks, shanty-town torchings (of "Okies," Chinese, Japanese, and Mexicans in turn), killings, and even lynchings. In the 21st century, such violence was still there, but confined in the state and federal prison complexes that many small California towns, like Corcoran, had welcomed as employment-generators. Passing the hundreds of field-workers bent over under that blazing sun, once again I could only feel like a fortunate man.

East of Bakersfield I finally began to climb into the lion-colored foothills, the rounded mounds of golden grass punctuated with dark green live-oak trees, then into the southernmost tip of the Sierras. Up through the ghost towns of Caliente and Bodfish toward Lake Isabella, and the little town of Kernville, where I had stayed a few times in my Sierra wanderings.

I stopped for lunch at a perfect little diner, Cheryl's, where I had stopped a couple of other times for breakfast or lunch, and enjoyed a fine cheese-burger and a refreshing strawberry milkshake. When I got up to pay my bill, one of the waitresses, a plump, fortyish woman, intercepted me with a strange look on her face, "Are you the famous drummer from Rush?"

I nodded, mind and body suddenly on edge with that familiar feeling of . . . what? A strange mix of embarrassment, apprehension, unreality. Then the woman said, "I didn't recognize you, but Cathy did," and suddenly there was another plump, fortyish woman beside her, both of them standing too close to me, their friendly faces fixed intently on mine.

The one called Cathy said, "I waited on you once before, and I didn't recognize you, but this guy that was here that morning, he went *apeshit!*"

I smiled at that quaint expression, and remembered one morning a couple of years before when I'd stopped at Cheryl's for breakfast and, just as I was leaving, paused outside to call Carrie and let her know I was on my way home. A thirtyish man in work clothes came bursting out of the restaurant and interrupted my phone call to ask if I was me. I admitted I was, and he just went "goofy" for a minute (as Robert Pirsig, in *Lila*, recounted Robert Redford's apt description of how people behaved when they recognized him).

This time, the first waitress said, apologetically, "I didn't recognize you, but I *love* the music." Both of their faces were so close, and staring at me so intently. But I reassured her, quietly saying, "Thank you, and don't worry — I never mind *not* being recognized."

"No," she said, with a sympathetic nod, "I'm sure you don't."

Friends often think that after almost thirty years of minor celebrity, I ought to be used to such encounters, but perhaps because they *were* relatively rare, between such "recognitions" I tended to settle into a comfortable anonymity. I never got used to it, never began to *expect* it, and thus when I said "goodbye and thank you" to the two waitresses and put on my helmet, jacket, and gloves, threw my leg over the bike, and rode away from Cheryl's, I felt kind of "rattled."

My friend Michael, the private detective (and *Vapor Trails* riding partner) who looked after my security issues and kept things anonymous around our house, our mail, our phone lines, utility bills, and such mundane details of life, kept telling me I should just *deny* my identity. He told me he used to work with Drew Barrymore, and when people approached her and said "aren't you . . . ," she would just laugh and say, "Oh no, I get that all the time," and even joke, "She's so much *fatter* than I am!"

Her coolness was admirable, but the idea of it felt too weird to me — to lie like that, for one thing, and to deny being who I was. I kept saying I was going to try it, but then a stranger would catch me by surprise, and before I had time to think, I would tell the truth. "Yes, I am me."

Oh well, "deal with it," is all anybody can say, and what I always said to myself. Every time.

Looking over the map at lunch, I had decided to run north along the Kern River, then pick up a series of small, winding back roads that would carry me into some higher, cooler elevations, twisting through the forested mountains to the two national parks, Kings Canyon and Sequoia.

Late in the afternoon I stopped at the Grant's Grove visitors center to get the "passport stamp" for my journal, and it happened again, in almost the same words. Behind the counter, a young man with red hair and a dark green shirt (not a ranger, maybe an intern) came up and said, "Say, aren't you the world-famous drummer from Rush?" This time I finally tried it, almost accidentally, shaking my head and saying, "Oh, I get that all the time" (not really *lying*). To my surprise, it actually *worked*. Whenever I had imagined that scene in the past, the questioner would always point a trembling finger at me and scream "*LIAR!*" But this guy just said, "Oh."

Then he pointed to my motorcycle outside, and said, "And you're traveling by motorcycle, too — *he* travels all around by motorcycle." I just nodded, feeling increasingly uncomfortable, guilty, and *wrong*.

He moved back from the counter, and I heard him say to another staff member, "It must be tough to look like somebody famous, and be hassled all the time."

Oh, the irony. Oh, the weirdness. Oh, the guilt. For the whole rest of my stay in Grant Grove Village, I wanted to return to the visitors center and confess my duplicity.

As I wrote in my journal: "Phooey — now *I* feel weird."

I looked over the shelves of books in the visitors center, volumes about the national parks and different topics of natural science, and noticed the usual selection of books about John Muir, the legendary naturalist, tireless campaigner for wilderness, champion of the earliest national parks, and father of the Sierra Club. I had read much about him, but never any of his own writings, and when I saw a slim volume called *John Muir, In His Own Words: A Book of Quotations*, I bought it.

That night, by coincidence, I happened to stay at the John Muir Lodge in Kings Canyon National Park, and as I looked through the book of quotations, I found they spoke to my own rapturous love of nature, and echoed exactly the way I felt when I got into the mountains: "These beautiful days must enrich all my life."

> "Nature is always lovely, invincible, glad, whatever is done and suffered by her creatures. All scars she heals, whether in rocks or water or sky or hearts."

(It's true.)

> "Few are altogether deaf to the preaching of pine trees. Their sermons on the mountains go to our hearts; and if people in general could be got into the woods, even for once, to hear the trees speak for themselves, all difficulties in the way of forest preservation would vanish."

(Like the great Beach Boys song, "Wouldn't It Be Nice?")

> "Then it seemed to me the Sierra should be called, not the Nevada, or Snowy Range, but the Range of Light."

(Amen.)

In my wide-ranging reading of California history, I had learned that these very parks, Kings Canyon and Sequoia, had ended up being preserved as the result of a political power-play in the late 19th century, between the farming interests of the San Joaquin Valley and the lumber companies of the Sierras — not to preserve the forests for their natural beauty, but to preserve their effect on holding the snowpack, and thus releasing the water to the valley below when it was needed for agriculture.

Whatever the motive, of course, the outcome was admirable (the means justified the end), but as the present-day debates about oil drilling in the national parks of the fragile Arctic illustrated, these preserves were never safely *permanent*. Back in 1895, just after Yosemite National Park was established, a bill was placed before Congress to cut the park in half, and open up the land again to lumbering and grazing. In attacking that plan, Muir drew a clever parable:

> The very first reservation that ever was made in this world had the same fate. That reservation was very moderate in its dimensions and the boundaries were run by the Lord himself. Yet, no sooner was it made than it was attacked by everybody in the world — the devil, one woman and one man. This has been the history of every reservation that has been made since that time; that is, as soon as a reservation is once created then the thieves and the devil and his relations come forward to attack it.

Muir knew the struggle to save any part of nature from short-sighted greed would never end, and he also wrote, "The battle we have fought, and are still fighting, is a part of the eternal conflict between right and wrong, and we cannot expect to see the end of it."

The next day I toured around the parks, riding the Scenic Byway along the Kings River (agreeing with Muir that Kings Canyon rivaled Yosemite), hiked down to visit the Crystal Cave, and later that afternoon, I finally made it to a remote part of Sequoia National Park I had been wanting to visit for years.

The Mineral King Valley, at 9,000 feet, lay like a vast amphitheater of meadows surrounded by high peaks of barren granite above the tree line, still dotted with a few small patches of snow, even in July. The Mineral King Valley was another area of great natural beauty that had been saved from developers only narrowly, amid great controversy. Originally a mining center, when the marginally-profitable mines began to close, Walt Disney and his brother, Roy, conceived a plan in the 1960s to build a ski resort at Mineral King. After Walt's death, the Disney Corporation continued to pursue the development, against resistance from environmentalists, and finally the valley was preserved by making it part of Sequoia National Park.

When I reached the end of the long, narrow, winding little road of rough pavement and occasional stretches of dirt, gravel, and sand (like many High Sierra roads, closed in winter because of the volume of snow) and arrived at Mineral King and the cabins at Silver City, I had another Brigham Young moment, feeling that I had finally found the Sierra hideaway I had been seeking — "This is the place."

Many of the cars, pickups, and SUVs parked at the trailheads had their front ends strangely swathed in heavy plastic tarpaulins, and I learned that this protected them from marmots, groundhog-like mammals which had a taste for the rubber hoses and insulation of engine wiring. It was a long way to any parts or service facilities, and no one wanted to return from a long hike in the Sierras to find their vehicles disabled by gnawing rodents. Presumably they had the same taste for *motorcycle* parts, but fortunately I was parking well away from the meadow, beside the tiny, rustic cabin I had rented, in a grove of giant sequoias.

In the early evening, I sat outside on the wooden deck with a glass of The Macallan, looking through the shadowy trees to a bright mountainside of barren rock catching the last rays of the sun. I was struck by the way the sharp-edged, pale gray granite seemed to radiate the light, a luminous brightness like what the Swiss called alpenglow, as if the living rock gathered heat from the sun all day, then radiated it back as light in the evening.

I was reminded of a quote by John Muir I had copied down on my second visit to Grand Canyon, in 2002, when he described the canyon at sunset, "as if the life and light of centuries of sunshine stored up in the rocks was now being poured forth as from one glorious fountain, flooding both earth and sky."

By that time I had put aside all worries about the *other* kind of living rock, and, waxing all mystical, I was moved to compose a Sierra rhapsody dedicated to this "Range of Light," and to John Muir, who, if not exactly a "prophet without honor in his own country," was certainly never listened to as much as he *should* have been.

> *Above the lion-colored hills*
> *Above the ancient, tall sequoias*
> *Shining peaks of silver granite*
> *High Sierra, Range of Light*
>
> *Wingtips brush the perfect sky*
> *Solitary golden eagle*
> *Soaring high above the forests*
> *High above the Range of Light*
>
> *A circle of pines around a sky-blue lake*
> *A draft of light in every breath I take*
> *Darkness closes in, and the stars descend*
> *Wilderness begins where the pavement ends*
> *In the Range of Light*
>
> *Drifting through the Range of Light*
> *A prophet without honor*
> *Champion of right, in a lifelong fight*
> *Urging us to choose*
> *Honor without profit*
> *Taking the high road — into the Range of Light*

Three weeks later, Sunday, July 20th, I flew to Toronto to start rehearsing for the Concert for Toronto, or "SARS-fest" and "SARS-stock" as it became

known (rather insensitively, I thought). Beginning the following day, I
would have four days on my own to get-up-in-the-morning-and-go-to-
work, then four days with the other two guys, a day to move the gear and
hopefully have a sound check, and I hoped that would be enough to prepare
for the show. There had been no convenient way for me to start earlier; our
little townhouse in Santa Monica was not drum-friendly (or at least, drums
were *never* "neighbor-friendly"), and there hadn't been time to organize a
rehearsal room and a borrowed set of drums and cymbals. However, we had
all been doing this for a long time; we should be able to put together a half-
hour set and play it decently after eight days of rehearsal.

Friends in Toronto had been telling me about the effects of the SARS
scare on the city, how the hotels and restaurants had been operating at less
than a tenth of their capacity, and now I saw the effects of six months of
that kind of attrition. My hotel was nearly empty and wretchedly under-
staffed, room service had been cut from twenty-four hours to a few hours
in the morning and evening, and since the hotel had only a private garage,
I had to wait for the one bellman to bring my car up, and it could take up
to an hour. I could only adjust to these "siege" conditions, but I did start
tipping the staff about twice what I usually would, just out of sympathy
for their undeserved plight.

During a break in the Steely Dan tour, Lorne had flown into Toronto
and set up my drums at the rehearsal hall, and shown George the basic
operations to cover for him. George had worked many Rush tours as a carpenter, looking after stage sets, props, cases, and building the drum boards
(custom platforms where the drums and stands were mounted). So after
Lorne, he knew the setup best, and seemed the most likely candidate for a
one-off show. We had figured out a way to leave the drums set up while
they were transported to the show and moved onstage, so hopefully there
would be a minimum chance for error or catastrophe.

I had thought I was coming in strong and fit, for lately I had been able
to maintain a regular routine of bicycling to the Santa Monica YMCA and
working out three times a week, moving among the aerobic machines,
yoga and stretching, weight machines and free weights, an hour of solo

racquetball, then finally a quarter mile in the lap pool. I was probably as fit as I had ever been, but I was soon reminded that being fit was not the same as being conditioned to start playing drums as hard as I could for hours on end.

After playing the instrument more-or-less constantly for 38 years, I had developed the ability to set it aside for a few months and pick up where I left off, with no apparent loss of technique or fluidity. When I was first starting, at age thirteen, I practiced every day, as I did thirty years later, while working with my teacher, Freddie, back in '94 and '95, but usually when I finished a long period of work, I didn't mind stepping away from the drums for awhile. Indeed, I often came back to drumming with fresh energy and new ideas. In the recording studio, there was a natural process of building up to full power over days and weeks of casual experimentation with new songs and new parts, and before a tour, I gradually worked my way up to full-out performance mode, a process I always enjoyed.

However, in this situation, there was no time for a gradual buildup. On Day One I started out at ten-tenths, from a brief, free-form warmup to playing along with the original recordings of the songs the three of us had agreed were candidates to be played in the show: "Tom Sawyer," "Limelight," "YYZ," "Dreamline," "Free Will," "New World Man," "Closer to the Heart," and "The Spirit of Radio." I attacked all of the songs at performance level, hitting the drums and cymbals as hard as I could with hands and feet to get the proper sound and feel, digging my sticks deep into the snare drum, and pounding the pedal deep into the bass drum. Then I took a break, then played them all again. And again. And again.

By the end of that first day I was sore in every muscle and every joint, soothing my pain with single-malt whisky and Extra Strength Tylenol, and I realized that the difficult thing about playing drums wasn't so much the exertion, but the *impact*. It wasn't the motion, but the stopping. Like a piston engine, I had to come to a dead stop at the top and bottom of each stroke, and that was the part that hurt — the proverbial irresistible force meeting the immovable object.

It was nice to be back in Toronto, though, able to hang around with my best buddy Brutus again, for we hadn't seen much of each other in the past year. He and I had dinner a few times that week, talking about our lives and jobs, and he laughed at my physical complaints.

"I guess it's bound to get tougher, at *your* age!"

Thanks, friend. (I didn't need to add, "friend-who-is-*older*-than-me.")

During the week, the other crew guys started to gather at the rehearsal hall and assemble their gear, and some of our regulars from the *Vapor Trails* tour, and in some cases many other tours, had been able to make it for this show: Rick on guitars, Russ on basses, Tony on keyboards, and Peter, our go-everywhere, do-everything personal assistant. One of the key guys missing, apart from drum-tech Lorne and Liam — the boss of everything, who was supervising the whole operation from a distance, while he worked as tour accountant with the Ringling Brothers madness of the Metallica/Linkin Park/Limp Bizkit summer tour — was monitor engineer Brent, who controlled the complex mix of what we heard of ourselves and each other in every song. We had to hope there would be time to work it out with the new recruit, Tim.

That Friday, Day Five, I showed up at the rehearsal room a little later, to give the other two guys a chance to sort through their gear. Thus we began our working day, appropriately, with *lunch* — joking that it was our favorite part of work, anyway (no joke, really). It was great to see each other again, for although we had been in touch fairly often by e-mail, we hadn't been together since the Rio de Janeiro show, back in November, and we talked and joked and laughed and fooled around, until we couldn't put it off any longer, and went to work.

We had narrowed the set down to seven songs, eliminating "New World Man" (with its risky sequencer beginning that might go awry in such a chaotic setting), and reviving the old warhorse, "Working Man," as a possible encore song. As I had done, we played through the set, took a break, played it through again, and so on, four or five times a day. On Day Six and Seven, we also worked up an instrumental version of the Stones' "Paint It Black," which we thought would be fun to go into during our set. It was starting to go pretty smoothly, but I was still taking nothing for granted.

And I was still *hurting*. At day's end, I would drive back to the hotel, slouch to my room and just *collapse*, thinking that I had never felt so tired, never felt so sore. In years past, I had made friends on bicycle trips and such who knew nothing about the music world, and when they came to see me play for the first time, they would often say something like, "I never knew drumming was such *hard work*."

At first I would be taken aback by that observation, then I would think of them seeing other drummers on television, often faking it or playing less physically demanding music, and understood why they had that impression. I guess drumming wasn't hard work for every drummer, but it certainly was for me, the way I liked to play — as hard as I could, as fast as I could, as long as I could, and as *well* as I could. Playing a Rush concert was the hardest job I knew, and took everything I had, mentally and physically. I once compared it to running a marathon while solving equations, and that was a good enough analogy.

Carrie flew in on Sunday, and when I picked her up at the airport after Day Seven rehearsals, she took one look at my slumping body and drawn, baggy face, and said, "What's the matter with *you?*" She had seen me play many times during the *Vapor Trails* tour, right down to the final show in Rio de Janeiro (with the extra ordeal of recording and filming), but she had never seen me like that. I hadn't either.

The day before the show, Day Nine, the equipment was moved to the concert site, and we were scheduled to do a sound check, so we drove out to Downsview Park in the afternoon. All week the media had been full of talk about the concert, the front pages of the newspapers showing photographs of the Rolling Stones arriving in town, the construction of the stage, and running stories about every detail of the preparations for the show. In this beleaguered city, the Concert for Toronto was big news.

And it was a big event, in every way. The stage was massive, the backstage area was vast, and the dressing rooms were in an old aircraft hangar, a large area sectioned off for the Stones with temporary partitions, and the rest divided into small cubicles for all the opening acts. Among the rows of little rooms with the performers' names outside, we were sandwiched between signs for the Guess Who and AC/DC, with Justin Timberlake at the end of the row. Those signs alone were a surreal marker of what an experience we were about to face.

On Day Ten, show day, I was tense from the moment of waking. On any "work day," I always feel a certain mental and physical awareness of that difference, a focus of energies and inner sense of resolve toward that climax in the day, but this time it was much more than that. Somehow this felt like the most important show I had ever played in my life, and there was so much that could go wrong. In the global sense, there could be a storm, a riot, some terrible catastrophe, and in the personal sense, my drums could fall apart, the monitors could fail and leave me stranded in a musical vacuum, or — worst of all by far — I could play badly.

My mantra for the day, in the slang of the day, became something like, "Just don't suck." (In reading about wild animals and their instinctive behaviors, I was intrigued to learn that the only instinct humans are thought to possess at birth is the urge to *suck*. That is a disturbing metaphor.)

We were scheduled to play around 7:00 in the evening, but had to leave for the venue in the early afternoon. At least the weather was perfect, a sunny, windless day under a clear blue sky. That was one sigh of relief, one prayer answered. We were driven to a commuter train station in Mimico, in the southwestern part of the city, where special trains were being run to the site with all the performers, their guests, media people, and various VIPs. The train moved slowly northward through the sun-washed city, until there was a sudden chorus of amazed voices ("Look at that!" "Ohmygod!"), then silence. We all turned to look over an endless sea of people stretching to the horizon, broken only by islands of towers for speakers and video screens. Buses carried us from the train to the hangar, through a series of security gates and a backstage crowd that must have numbered in the hundreds, maybe thousands. Out front, there were 450,000 people — a good-sized city.

Already overwhelmed by just the backstage scene, I took refuge in one of our cubicles and hid inside a book, and thus inside myself, as I would for most of the day. (The book was Nick Hornby's memoir of his life as a soccer fan, *Fever Pitch*, about people and situations I knew nothing about, but his "friendly" writing style made it diverting and undemanding.)

The other two guys, always more sociable than I was, visited a little with some of the other performers, but I just stayed in my cubicle. In retrospect, I can see that in the middle of such chaos, I was trying to preserve my *focus*, to keep my energy from being scattered in all directions. I had burrowed down deep inside myself, mentally coaching my mind and body with the mantra, "Just don't suck," and tried to think of nothing else but the upcoming performance. Brutus and Carrie tried to keep me company, but soon realized I was not really "there," and they left me alone too. (Later Brutus remarked, "I've never *seen* you like that" — and he'd been with me for the whole *Test for Echo* tour of 76 shows. I could only repeat, "I haven't either.")

To simplify matters, I had told Lorne and George not to bother with the small practice drumset I usually had backstage, where I could warm up before the show — and smooth out the jitters, I realized that afternoon. It was another upset to the preshow ritual, and another way in which everything was just too *weird*. When Alex came in with his guitar, turned on his little amplifier, and started to play, I tried pounding on a practice pad and stamping my feet along with him, but it just wasn't the same.

Finally, it was showtime. We walked across the vast area backstage and up the high steps to the massive stage, and stood at the back corner, waiting. Apparently there was some technical problem, and it would be a few minutes. Our production manager from the last two tours, C.B., happened to be in town, working with the band Chicago at a nearby casino, and he had his headset on, waiting for the word to go. The Who's "Baba O'Riley" played over the P.A. system, and in my ear-monitors, and I played along with my drumsticks against my legs — just as I used to play that song on the Sweda cash register in Gear on Carnaby Street, back in '71 and '72, and a coincidental reminder of my earliest influences, The Who and Keith Moon.

A couple of people came up and said hello, some of them old friends (like the show's promoter, Michael Cohl, who had promoted many Rush shows since the '70s), some of them strangers, and there seemed to be about a thousand cameras pointed at us the whole time. Normally that would have driven me mental, but under the circumstances, I hardly noticed.

A short, older man stepped up to me, sticking out his hand and saying something I couldn't hear. Thinking, "Now who's *this?*" I took out one of my ear monitors and said, "Sorry, I couldn't hear you."

He spoke again, smiling, "Hello, I'm Charlie Watts."

"Oh!" I said, taken aback, "Hello." And I shook his hand.

He asked if we were going on soon, and I said yes, any minute, and he said, with a twinkle, "I'm going to *watch* you!"

I suppose if I could have felt more pressured, that might have done it, but I was already at maximum intensity — there was no time to think of Charlie Watts and the Rolling Stones, watching them on *The T.A.M.I. Show* or "Ed Sullivan" when I was twelve-and-a-half, hearing "Satisfaction" snarling down the midway at Lakeside Park, *Gimme Shelter* at the cinema in London, listening to Charlie's beautiful solo album, *Warm and Tender*, so many times late at night in Quebec, or any of the other million times Charlie Watts and his band had been part of my life.

Geddy e-mailed me later and mentioned that scene:

> BTW, I will never forget that moment before we went onstage when Charlie Watts came over to shake your hand (at the worst possible moment!) and watching your face go through all the motions of . . . a. who is this old guy? b. what does he want ? c. oh for god's sakes it's *Charlie Watts!*

Finally, we were running out onto the stage. I settled myself behind the drums, waited to see that Geddy and Alex were ready, then counted in "Tom Sawyer." I tried to ignore that sea of people, the ranks of cameras, that short, gray-haired Englishman at stage left, and stayed in a place deep inside myself, concentrating on playing the song, the right parts at the right tempo (one of the hardest challenges for a drummer, when your heart and adrenaline are racing, is to keep your *playing* from racing too).

George crouched behind the line of dryers to my left (a prop from the *Vapor Trails* tour, three Maytag dryers devised by Geddy as a humorous visual "balance" to Alex's massive stacks of amplifiers on stage right), and I'm sure he was as desperately hopeful as I was that nothing would go wrong. Early on I realized I wasn't hearing much guitar, which would be a problem in later songs that Alex started, like "Limelight" and "The Spirit of Radio." I decided I had better risk upsetting my concentration, and tried to mouth the words "more guitar" to George. He didn't read me at first, but eventually somebody else did, and it was fixed.

When I did glance out over the humanscape, it seemed completely surreal. The horizon on every side was a blur of distant faces. The stage was so high, and the security barricade so far from it, that even the *closest* people seemed remote. One of the unfortunate flaws of the in-ear monitors is that you can never hear the audience very well, so I wasn't even sure if they were *liking* us or not. We kept the pace pretty rapid in any case, playing a series of up-tempo songs with the briefest of breaks between them.

We blazed through our short instrumental arrangement of "Paint It Black," making me think of Charlie Watts again, but he seemed to have left by then — having seen and heard enough, no doubt, whatever his impression was. Then, just as we paused for the acoustic intro to "Closer to the Heart," a calm interlude of guitar, glockenspiel, and vocals, suddenly the monitors and speakers were full of congas and bongos — some careless technician had started the Stones' tape-loop of percussion for "Sympathy for the Devil," perhaps just testing it and not knowing it was going to the "house," and it was playing *everywhere*. We tried to ignore it and keep playing the song (at a completely different tempo from the loud tape), and eventually someone turned it off. Once we were "grounded" again, we looked at each other and made twisted faces of mock panic.

Toward the end of the set, I noticed one of my crash cymbals had a good-sized crack in it, and its sound was dull and lifeless, but I decided to put up with it rather than disrupt everything by telling George about it. He would have to figure out what I meant, run back to the cases and find a spare 18" cymbal, then climb up there and switch them — better just to keep my head down and worry about playing right. ("Just don't suck.")

At the end of "The Spirit of Radio," we ran offstage, waiting to see if we should play an encore or not. Everyone was supposed to know about that plan, but somebody obviously didn't. Taped music started playing over the P.A., as if our set was over, and stagehands began walking onstage to strike the gear. We were still standing at the side of the stage, tensed for action but not knowing what to do, when Alex turned to go, saying, "Forget it. It would be embarrassing to go back on now." He was right. It was over.

On the long walk back to the dressing rooms, a police officer stepped in front of me and said he was a big fan, and asked if I would pose for a photograph with him. Wearily, I acquiesced, knowing it was always a good idea to be friendly with a cop who was a "big fan," and I stood beside him while his brother officer snapped a picture.

I was feeling drained and exhausted, though not from the exertion; a normal Rush show was almost three hours long, and we had played barely half an hour, not even long enough to loosen up, or build a decent sweat. Nevertheless, it had been an overwhelming experience, the most difficult performance I had ever given, and I was *beat*.

Given the complexities of the shuttle buses and trains, we had to leave while AC/DC was just taking the stage. We had played shows with them in the U.S. a few times back in the '70s, and even then I had been delighted — it seems the only word — to watch Angus Young in his weird and wonderful state of "possession," prowling the stage with his schoolboy uniform like a force of nature, jamming his whole little body into grinding out riffs on his Gibson SG.

We never saw the Stones at all, except on the television back at the hotel. Two of the local networks had been broadcasting from the concert site all day, showing selections from each performance, and the strangest thing was watching *ourselves* on TV like that, just hours after we had played. The camera that had been in my face throughout the performance showed someone who looked a lot different than I had *felt* — the stranger playing those drums looked calm, intense, confident. I was relieved to hear that despite my inner sense of *acceleration* (pulse, adrenaline, awareness), somehow I had managed to keep the tempos nailed down. The sound quality was not great, but I was relieved to hear that we had played pretty well. A triumph of preparation and determination over environment, biology (or chemistry), and lack of *time*.

At least I could say, with all humility, we didn't suck. That alone answered the prayers I had sent out all day to anyone who might be listening and could help, but it occurs to me now it was really a prayer to *myself*: "Please don't suck."

Amen.

Rideout

Repeat to fade . . .

On December 8th, 2003, I took *Traveling Music* on one last roadtrip, driving the Z-8 to Grand Canyon National Park, where I had rented a cabin for a few days. As the writing had piled up through those eight months, I set myself a "soft goal" of completing the first draft by the end of the year. Now that the book had grown so long, complicated, and unwieldy, I knew that if I was going to pull it all together, I needed to get away and really *concentrate.*

Slipping through Los Angeles at dawn, I headed east through the Mojave Desert on I-40, across the width of California and into Arizona. Just over the state line I picked up old Route 66, following that tightly wound, crumbling piece of history through the quaintly revived "gold-rush town" of Oatman. Wild burros wandered the street, begging food from the tourists (few, early that December morning). The town's other historic highlight was the Oatman Hotel, where Clark Gable and Carole Lombard spent their wedding night in 1939, after being married in Kingman, Arizona.

On through Kingman, I stayed with the long loop of 66 through Hackberry Springs and Seligman, then a short stretch of I-40 to Williams,

the turnoff for Grand Canyon. All through Arizona I was gaining elevation, driving into winter, and I watched the outside temperature fall from
the 60s to the 30s. As I drove north on Highway 64 through the ponderosa
pine forests, approaching 7,000 feet now, flakes of snow began to fill the
air. When I parked at the national park visitors center for the inevitable
"passport stamp," I got out and stood for a moment in the cold wind.
"Smells like snow," I said to myself, with a big smile. I had been missing
my winter soulscape.

Although Grand Canyon was one of the busiest national parks in
America, with five million visitors annually, I had picked the right time of
year. That Monday in early December, I was able to get a cabin right on
the canyon's rim, with a little table looking out the window to that stu-
pendous view. As I set down my overnight bag and my box of papers and
books, a phrase came to mind, "I grinned out loud."

Every day and night, I watched the light change on the multi-colored
strata, the sculptured rock walls descending a mile down, and a mile
across to the North Rim. Over that ever-changing, monumental vista,
the light effects were infinite, and as I had known it would be, it was a
wonderful place to work. And while I worked, I seemed to view that
canyon in nearly every possible aspect, from bright winter sunshine to
lowering clouds, rain, fog, gentle snowfall, and even a couple of full-blown
blizzards. The moon was full, and the night-time view was equally spectacular, the canyon's depths silvered with ledges of snow in a fantastic play
of blue light and shadow.

Straight in front of me was Bright Angel Point, named after the Bright
Angel Creek, far below on the canyon's floor. The creek had been named
by Major John Wesley Powell (a one-armed Civil War veteran leading an
1868 expedition on the first-ever descent of the Colorado River, he had
certainly been "workin' *his* angels"), and the choice of name was intended
to be a kind of "atonement" for a creek previously named after a member
of the expedition not given to bathing — the Dirty Devil.

When I think of great hotel room views I have experienced, they are
many, from the Chateau at Lake Louise, in the Canadian Rockies, my win-

dow open to the glacier-fed, turquoise waters surrounded by conifers and high snowy peaks, the Wickanninish Inn in Tofino, British Columbia, over the stormy Pacific, the Princeville Resort on Kauai, above sublime Hanalei Bay, or the St. Regis in Manhattan, overlooking Central Park in September. However, none has been more powerful and affecting than looking out at the Grand Canyon through the days and nights of work, even as I sorted through the multi-colored strata of my _own_ "geology."

On the first morning, I awoke before dawn, curtains wide (wanting to be open to that view even when I was _sleeping_), and dressed up warm to walk into the cold twilight, down the icy path along the rim to the lodge. While I ate breakfast, I paged through the written journal I had kept during my various travels that year, wanting to make sure I hadn't missed anything worthwhile, then returned to my little cabin and sat down to work. Opening the two three-ring binders, the 300-page typescript that represented eight months of steady work — and fifty-one years of my life — I started at the beginning, reading with red pen in hand. From the outset I had followed Max Perkins' advice, "Don't get it right, get it down," and by that point I had a lot of it _down_, and now I wanted to try to get it _right_.

Immersing myself in those pages, I retraced the highways of the Southwest, the music I had listened to, my memories of St. Catharines, London, Mexico, the American Southwest, and Africa, and I was soon lost in the timeless _absorption_ that I always found in creative work, with music or with words. At one point I paused and looked out the window, taking in the splendor in front of my worktable. Fully appreciating the _moment_, I chuckled to myself and said, "Just kill me now."

Another quote from Fred Nietzsche came to mind:

> Whoever cannot settle on the threshold of the moment forgetful of the whole past, whoever is incapable of standing on a point like a goddess of victory without vertigo or fear, will never know what happiness is, and worse, will never do anything to make others happy.

I knew what happiness was, just at that moment, to be working in that inspiring setting, closing in on the first draft of the biggest challenge I had ever set myself in prose writing — my life and times, my music and memories, my songs and stories. The trick, though, and the *real* challenge, were trying to "make others happy," to attempt to make this story unfold in a way that might be interesting for a reader, to describe the places and the feelings, the events and the connections, and make the past come *alive*.

Pausing only to walk to the nearby lodge for meals, sometimes just bringing a sandwich back to the cabin with me, I carried on correcting, adding passages, cutting others, and rearranging the pieces. Without haste or distraction, I worked my way steadily through the manuscript, for one day, then another, and then another. Just as I developed drum parts by playing a song again and again, gradually refining my experiments into a smooth flow of structure, rhythm, and detail, or assembled song lyrics by tinkering with each word and each line for days on end, every time I went through the Verses and Choruses of the book, a host of little refinements gradually built an overall *elevation* that sent me back to the beginning, to "play" it again.

Once or twice a day a busload of Japanese tourists unloaded at the lodge, and for an hour or so my solitude would be interrupted, but mostly it felt like I had the place almost to myself. One evening I was talking to Carrie on the telephone, and I looked out the window into the blue twilight and saw a mule deer tiptoeing lightly through the snow, followed by a yearling fawn, and then another. Asking Carrie to hold on for a moment, I put down the phone and grabbed my camera. When I pushed open the creaking screen door and stepped outside, they didn't even flinch, and hardly even looked at me when the flash went off. With five million visitors a year, they must be used to it.

And of course, I had brought music with me for the journey, much of it more "purposeful" this time, considered as research, as so much of my reading and movie-watching had been lately. (The internet had been very useful for some questions, like "what year would Ricky Nelson have sung 'Travelin' Man' on 'Ozzie and Harriet?'") On the drive to Grand Canyon,

I had listened to CDs like The Who's *My Generation* and *The Who Sell Out*, refreshing my memory of those early favorites, as well as a CD of selected modern songs made for me by my friend Matt. With a mix of "sample" tracks of artists he thought I might like, Matt introduced me to some great new bands, like Dredg, the Mars Volta, and Porcupine Tree, younger musicians who were still pursuing excellence and honesty in rock music. (Porcupine Tree's song, "The Sound of Muzak," had a chorus bewailing the cheapening of modern music, "One of the wonders of the world is going down, it's going down, I know/ It's one of the blunders of the world, that no one cares, no one cares enough"). As Count Basie once said, after listening to a playback of Sinatra and Duke Ellington's *Francis A. and Edward K.* album, "Always glad to hear about that kind of carrying on!"

Over the passing months, Matt and I had become close friends, hiking together in the Santa Monica Mountains nearly every week, and talking about our lives and work. During those hikes, Matt had been hearing a lot about my struggles with the book, and I had been hearing a lot about his struggles with the record company. Vertical Horizon's latest album, *Go*, had run into a wall of record-company apathy and mismanagement, and hadn't sold very well — after their previous release, *Everything You Want*, had topped the charts and sold over four million copies. Something was wrong there, and it *wasn't* the music. So Matt was considering his options, thinking it was time to free himself from that record company, and perhaps even his band, and try it on his own, maybe be a "songwriter-for-hire" for awhile, and eventually, make his own record.

All unexpectedly, by that time I had become mildly obsessed with the Beach Boys and Brian Wilson, and on the drive there I had been playing his acknowledged masterpiece, *Pet Sounds*, finally beginning to understand what all the "fuss" was about — thirty-seven years after its release, in 1966. However, I'd only been thirteen then, and in any case, hardly *anybody* understood his achievement when that album first came out. I was just glad to have that rich vein of music in my life *now*, with unexpected depth and resonance, for it had been reintroduced to me by a thread of coincidence and happenstance.

Back in 2002, when I was first talking with the publishing company ECW about *Ghost Rider*, they sent me a box of books as "samples." One of them was a biography of Dennis Wilson, *The Real Beach Boy*, and I started reading his story. As previously described, it was sadly reminiscent of Keith Moon's biography, a tragic story of an apparently loveable young man driven to extremes of self-indulgence, destroyed by his own demons and lacking the will to resist them.

After I finally found a copy of *The T.A.M.I. Show*, in the spring of 2003, and watched Dennis Wilson, the radiant young surf-god, pounding his drums and shaking his blond hair while the girls screamed, I was browsing in Barnes and Noble one day, and was drawn to buy *Heroes and Villains*, the biography of the whole band written by Steven Gaines. Then I found another biography of Dennis Wilson, *Dumb Angel*, becoming fascinated by those cautionary tales, captivated by all the harrowing *stories* about the Beach Boys. I still hadn't gone back to their *music*, but the more I read about it, the more curious I became. Apparently there had been much more than "Fun, Fun, Fun" going on there.

I started buying the CDs, and appreciating them in a way I never had before: with my own deepened experience, maturity, and understanding. The beautifully crafted early material, and the ultimate expression of a naked spirit confronting life and love, *Pet Sounds*, all of it was a joyous revelation to me, pure listening pleasure. I was powerfully intrigued by Brian Wilson as a true artist, at his best certainly the "genius" he had often been called, and by Dennis Wilson as a *character*.

I even felt compelled to seek out a rare copy of Dennis Wilson's solo album, *Pacific Ocean Blue*, from 1977, just to hear his own, personal music. It was described lovingly in the words of his friends and biographers, but I suspected that might have been partly because people seem to have loved *him* so much. Dennis Wilson was often described as the "soulful" member of the Beach Boys, and true enough, that was the essence of what he tried to achieve in his own music, and often succeeded pretty well.

But why was it the flamboyant, exhibitionist, extrovert, self-destructive drummers like Keith Moon and Dennis Wilson, who descended into helpless addictions and died at thirty-two and thirty-nine, who seemed so intriguing to me, more *romantic* — or at least more *tragic* — than the higher musical inspirations of Buddy Rich's tempestuous career ended by a brain tumor at age seventy, or Gene Krupa changing the world's perception of drummers forever, and dying of leukemia at age sixty-four?

Perhaps it was because Keith Moon and Dennis Wilson had embodied a quality I recognized a small part of in myself, a dark side, a secret fascination with the "anti-hero," in friendships, in life, and in art. I considered the most important gift a person could receive genetically to be strength of *will*, and apart from any talent or sensitivity to words and music, that was certainly the quality to which I attributed much of my own success (or at least *survival*). I was grateful for other genetic gifts, once reflecting that I had inherited "my father's sense and my mother's sensibility," but none of that was any good without will — and it was surely the *lack* of that will that had been the fatal flaw that brought down others before me, like Keith Moon and Dennis Wilson. As someone wise once said, "There are no failures of talent, only failures of character."

By late in 2003, when I was driving along the Pacific Coast Highway, to the appropriate soundtrack of the Beach Boys (once glancing out toward the ocean and seeing a pair of porpoises pacing me in graceful arcs just offshore), I sometimes imagined the events of a day in 1968. Dennis Wilson was driving his Ferrari down the Pacific Coast Highway, and he picked up a couple of young hitchhikers, "hippie chicks." He brought them back to his sprawling estate on Sunset Boulevard to share some "free love," made a night of it, and thought no more about it. But the next night, arriving home from a recording session, Dennis saw an old school bus parked in his driveway — the Manson "family" had moved in.

Like so many others had been, Dennis was captivated by Manson's snake-charmer charisma, and with Dennis's apparent innocence, generosity, and lack of will, he was soon drawn into a vortex of drugs, sex, and violence. Manson once held a knife to his throat, and Dennis, ever fearless, said, "Do it, man." Charlie laughed and put down the knife. Dennis's prized Ferrari, his AC Cobra, and his Rolls-Royce were wrecked, the rented estate was trashed, his clothes and money were stolen, and the whole situation was out of his control. Dennis, no longer fearless, eventually abandoned the house and took shelter in a friend's basement apartment.

In my Santa Monica life, I often drove or rode my motorcycle past that estate at 14400 Sunset Boulevard, a low ranch house in perpetual shade under a spreading canopy of trees, just across from Will Rogers State Park. Knowing what had transpired there, and what it had led to in the horrifying Tate-LaBianca murders, the place always gave me a chill. I could never tell if the dark ambience of the property was imaginary or real.

On my last afternoon at Grand Canyon, Thursday, I drove down a scenic road along the rim to Hermit's Rest (another advantage to being out-of-season, as that road was closed to cars in the busy summer months, when shuttle buses handled the crowds). As I slowly cruised along, stopping at the overlooks to view different aspects of the canyon, I was listening to *Surfer Girl* and *Shut Down: Volume II*, and when I returned to the lodge for lunch, I noted in my journal, "Wonderful, to put it mildly. So experimental, so original, so vulnerable, so *beautiful*. Perhaps unparalleled. 'In My Room,' 'Don't Worry Baby,' 'The Warmth of the Sun' — Brian Wilson was doing all *that* in, like, 1964!"

Amid the rugged landscape, the wintry air, and the white quilt of snow under the ponderosa pines, that sunny California music made me think of Carrie, and home, and driving back there the following day. My drives along Sunset Boulevard, past Dennis Wilson's former estate, had been more frequent lately, because Carrie and I had finally bought a bigger house over that way, partway up the Santa Monica Mountains. It had a view over the city and along the coast, even a slice of the blue Pacific, and that had been enough to sell me, along with the wonderful kitchen, spacious garage, and — especially — my very own office, with a door I could close on the world when I was writing.

I was excited about moving into that house in the new year; however, I was also fully (and sadly) aware that I would be *leaving* barely a month after that, flying up to Toronto to rehearse and maybe do some recording with my bandmates. In a sweet parallel with my own wanderings through my musical past, a seed I had planted during the *Vapor Trails* rehearsals in 2002, about us learning some old cover songs to play live, grew into a suggestion from Geddy that we commemorate our 30th anniversary by *recording* some of the songs we grew up on — coincidentally creating a soundtrack to my "soundtrack," as it were. We began searching our memories and digging through old records from the mid-'60s, by The Who, the Yardbirds, Buffalo Springfield, Blue Cheer, Cream, and the like — the bands from our teenage years, the ones whose songs we learned chords, lyrics, and drum parts for, and even played in our own early bands — and trading suggestions by e-mail.

If we decided to go ahead with the idea (our answer to that eternal "Now what?" question) and were pleased by the results, we might release five or six "cover tunes" on a little EP ("Extended Play," a suitably old-fashioned term for a record that was longer than a single, but shorter than an album), call it *Feedback* (Geddy and Alex had already decided that, in the mid-'60s spirit, there should be lots of feedback and backward guitar on every track), and maybe play some of them on the upcoming 30th anniversary tour.

Yes, that four-letter word, tour, was again looming on my horizon.

As much as you ever can, by the time I drove to Grand Canyon in early December, I *knew* what was coming at me for most of the next year. The bustle of Christmas (still a difficult season for me, with too many Ghosts of Christmas Past), then try to get the book finished and sent to Paul for editing before the end of the year, and hopefully get to work on the revision and finish that before I had to travel to Toronto for the possible recording and the certain six weeks of rehearsing for the six-month, fifty-seven show 30th Anniversary Tour, which would start in May. I didn't want to go, but I knew it was the Right Thing To Do.

Pride had prevailed, I suppose. Rush was probably the first band ever to survive thirty years together with the same members, and it seemed we ought to celebrate that achievement. In early discussions with Ray, I had "opened the bidding" at forty shows, but just as with the *Vapor Trails* tour, I was soon outbid. By the time Europe entered the discussions (after more than ten years, we felt we pretty much *had* to go and play for our fans there), the total had risen to fifty-seven. And counting . . .

For me, after thirty years of touring, the constant upheaval and intrusion of that life, as well as the sheer difficulty of the job, had long ago stopped being glamorous and exciting. It still meant everything in the world for me to *play* well, and I would give everything I had to prepare for and deliver the best show I could — but it wasn't exactly *fun*. Like Mark Twain's definition of work, "anything you'd rather not do," touring was work. But it was my job.

Once again, I planned to travel by bus and motorcycle, and control my environment and my destiny as much as I could. During the *Vapor Trails* tour, I once tried gamely to define the things I *liked* about going on tour. I came up with two: one, after burning so many calories onstage, you can eat anything you want, and two, there's lots of motorcycling. (Ray, thinking as a manager should, likes to point out that I can also "pick up a little gas money" along the way.)

At least I had a solution for the conspicuous lack of stories in this book concerning those thirty years with Rush. Also, a solution for the ten pages of notes that had been collecting at the back of *Traveling Music*, all the stories and facts I hadn't found a place for. After that drive to Hermit's Rest, I sat in the lodge restaurant with my journal, writing down more thoughts and memories I still wanted to get into the book, and ended with a tongue-in-cheek challenge to myself, "Work all that into the book and I'll . . . buy you a drink!"

Wanting to earn that drink, I thought about it awhile, then began flagging those notes "next book." Remembering the project I had abandoned halfway through in 1997, *American Echoes: Landscape with Drums*, I thought I might try to document the upcoming tour the same way, and turn it into a narrative that could also contain more of Rush's history, *our* lives and times. Beginning with my earliest experiments in prose writing, in the mid-'70s, I had wanted to try to capture and convey the *real* "archi-texture" of a modern concert tour, and maybe I was ready to tackle that mighty challenge. I might call it something like *Roadshow: Landscape with Drums*.

But for now, I already had one book to finish, and I drove back from Grand Canyon the next morning with the pages of my two black binders filled with notes in red ink, then started revising and typing in the changes. Along with getting through Christmas, shopping, wrapping, boxing, and shipping gifts to my family and friends in Canada, cooking the Christmas turkey dinner for Carrie's family (with help from her mother, Marian), I managed to squeeze in enough work on the book to be able to send off the first draft on December 30th — my goal of finishing it by the end of the year achieved, if only narrowly.

In January, the editorial responses to *Traveling Music* started coming back at me, first from my brother Danny, always a trusted reader, and he had some good suggestions that I immediately adopted, then from my editor and agent, Paul. After the rewarding experience of working with Paul on *Ghost Rider*, I knew that his editing style focused less on criticizing what was *there* than on enthusing about what *could* be there. To describe Paul's approach to my work, I coined the phrase "critical enthusiasm." As Freddie had done with my drumming, Paul paid less attention to *what* I was playing than to how I *thought about* what I was playing. The conception, the "dance," the "archi-texture."

And at first the challenge was equally daunting — reinventing my drumming with Freddie, and now reinventing my writing with Paul. He urged me to elevate the book conceptually, to aim for a kind of nobility ("take the high road"), a higher "Emory Peak" of creative ambition, and I realized that along with trying to recount my life and times, my own evolution and its inspirations, the book should be a "celebration of excellence," rather than lamenting its lack. At that lofty elevation, negative commentary on music and specific performers had no place.

Paul also had grand ambitions for how I might shape my material more effectively, expand my canvas from the six days of the Big Bend journey to the entire year of my creative life, and he inspired me with his vision of the highest-level-memoir Ideal that I — *we* — were going to pursue.

Almost from the beginning, I had imagined I might try to compose an actual song from the lyrical lines that began each Verse and Chorus, but as the book itself kept growing and demanding more and more attention, that idea was set aside. One day in February, I decided to see if the notion had a chance of working, or, with my writing time growing short, if I should forget about it and concentrate on the stories, and let the song lines stand alone. I made a list of the lyrics on a page, and at first they seemed like a column of disparate scraps, with no connection to each other. I felt a little doubtful about the idea's future.

However, once again the missing element proved to be *will* (and time, and a *little* imagination), as I worked over the lines again and again, smoothing in some "connective tissue," and finding the distillation of words and rhythm that seemed most resonant, in the poetic sense of being *suggestive* of meaning, but allowing the reader's *own* music to create the soundtrack.

Sometimes the song was set aside for a day or two, as I worked on another part of the book with Paul, but eventually, line by line, stanza by stanza, the song came together to a point where I was satisfied with it (or at least content to "abandon" it). Like many song lyrics I had written over the years, "Traveling Music" was woven from pieces that had often been conceived separately — in this case, even scavenged from another lyrical project I had been toying with throughout the year, *The California Quartet*, vignettes set in locales like Big Sur and the Sierra Nevada and interwoven with different interior moods.

Finally, looking at the "Traveling Music" song in the context of the book of which it was to become a part — a beginning and an ending — it occurred to me that the process of the song's building was a microcosm of the *book's* building.

I was reminded of my Grandma Peart's sewing basket, where she kept all her multicolored bits of material for patches, shining polychrome spools of thread, fluffy pastel yarns, knitting, sewing, and darning needles, the little wooden "egg" for darning socks, the C-clamps for her quilting frames, and other implements of rural self-sufficiency. To me, that resembled the collection of material and tools I had jammed into the first draft of the song, and the book.

Ideally, I wanted both of them to be more like one of the beautiful quilts my grandmother produced throughout her life, many of them from recycled, and thus memory-rich, pieces of cloth. The scraps had sometimes come from family members' castoff clothing, or old curtains and such, and thus the individual pieces were imbued with a certain intimacy, and even narrative. The geometry with which they were patterned together in the final quilt was intricate, colorful, attractive, and, perhaps most of all, a *comfortable* place in which to wrap yourself.

I wrote to Paul that day and described the metaphor, saying, "From now on *that's* the highest-level-memoir form, the quality we want: Grandma's Quilt." He agreed (with "critical enthusiasm"), and a new template joined our highest-level-memoir ideals of "archi-texture."

Day after day, week after week, the edit notes kept coming, as Paul devoted his own life and creative being to this book, without compromise, living up to his company's motto, "Striving for the Ideal." Chapter by chapter, word by word, we worked through it again and again, for four months, distracted from our poor neglected wives and everything else in "real life," even as I traveled to Toronto at the beginning of April to start rehearsing for the tour and recording the songs for *Feedback*.

Paul stayed with me the whole way through, setting all else aside, working through the night and e-mailing me edited chapters that were ready for me when I got up at 6:00 a.m., to be able to spend a few hours on the book, until I had to leave for my "real job" at the studio or rehearsal hall.

Even with all of Paul's help, encouragement, and dedication, it was still up to me to "make it so," and as with Freddie, I would have to start all over. "Take this thing a little further." "Put the pieces *together*." "Get out of the way — *let* it happen!"

There was only one way to "let" all that happen: get up in the morning and go to work.

The first show of the tour is tomorrow.

Where are we going?
Halfway across the world.

When do we get there?
Oh, fifty-seven times over the next six months.

Why do I have to sit in the middle?
Because that's where the drums are, stupid.